THE
WINNING
HORSEPLAYER

THE WINNING HORSEPLAYER

A Revolutionary Approach to Thoroughbred Handicapping and Betting

Andrew Beyer

HOUGHTON MIFFLIN COMPANY
Boston   New York

For information about permission to reproduce selections
from this book, write to Permissions, Houghton Mifflin Company,
215 Park Avenue South, New York, New York 10003.

Library of Congress Cataloging in Publication Data

Beyer, Andrew.
The winning horseplayer.
1. Horse race betting — United States. 2. Beyer,
Andrew. 3. Horseplayers — United States — Biography.
I. Title.
SF332.B494   1982   798.4′01′0973   83-142
ISBN 0-395-37761-7 (pbk.)
Printed in the United States of America

AGM 19 18 17 16 15

Contents

Foreword

When I wrote *The Winning Horseplayer* in 1983, I was keenly conscious of the changing nature of parimutuel competition: the betting public was becoming more knowledgeable and a handicapper had to develop new skills to stay ahead of the crowd. But I couldn't have imagined then how important this precept was going to be in the 1990s.

I had always relied on speed figures as the principal basis for my betting decisions. So, too, had a generation of horseplayers, many of whom had been influenced by my book *Picking Winners,* which was published in 1975. Because a handicapper had to have either the time to calculate his own figures or the money to buy them from commercial sources, those players constituted a small enough group that they possessed an edge over the majority of bettors who didn't use figures. But the nature of parimutuel betting changed permanently after the *Daily Racing Form* asked me to provide speed figures for inclusion in its past performances. Beginning in April 1992, my associates and I began to produce figures for every race at every track in North America. Overnight, a mass audience had access to the most

potent of all handicapping tools. When readers saw the effectiveness of these figures, a sizable percentage of the racing public became speed handicappers.

Because of the parimutuel system, the effect of speed figures'
popularity was inevitable. For most of my life as a horseplayer,
I could have reaped a profit by betting blindly on the horse in
each race who had earned the highest figure in his last start.
Now this was no longer true. When I wrote *Beyer on Speed* in
1993, I asked the *Daily Racing Form* to analyze the performance
of the Beyer Speed Figures over thousands of races, and this
study confirmed what had happened to payoffs on pure speed-
handicapping plays. The horse with the top figure won about 30
percent of the time, but payoffs had been lowered so sharply
that wagers on these horses produced a net loss of 5 to 7.5
percent. Even the strongest speed-figure standouts barely produced a profit. Figures were still a potent tool — they were able
to overcome much of the 17 percent takeout to which bettors
are typically subjected — but handicappers obviously needed
additional knowledge and skills to make money at the track.
Where could they get that extra edge?

The answer lies in this book. By watching races carefully and
employing the skills that fall under the heading of trip handicapping — the subject of *The Winning Horseplayer* — bettors can
substantially improve their chances of making a profit. In fact,
because of the wide availability of speed figures, I believe the
methods of analysis discussed in this book are even more important than they were in 1983.

These methods are, for the most part, subjective in nature.
One astute race watcher may see a horse encounter some type
of adversity — bad racing luck, an ill-judged ride — that another observer overlooks or dismisses as unimportant. One
handicapper may come to the conclusion that a track bias exists
on a particular day, while a fellow handicapper thinks the racing
surface is uniform. By its very nature, trip handicapping doesn't
lend itself to the bandwagon effect that killed prices of speed-
figure standouts.

Moreover, many American horseplayers have been reluctant
to embrace the principles of trip handicapping, perhaps because

they don't like the subjectivity and the seeming imprecision of making visual judgments. They are instead enchanted by numbers, by mathematical approaches to the game that purport to turn the art of handicapping into an exact science. This preference is reflected in popular methods of dealing with pace. Disciples of the California pace-handicapping guru Howard Sartin employ numbingly complicated, computer-generated ratings based on horses' velocity, in feet per second, during each quarter-mile component of a race. Yet the practitioners of the method are unlikely to watch races and make any qualitative judgments about the way horses perform. They are too busy looking at their numbers to note that a horse showed guts and tenacity while engaging in a four-horse battle for the lead, parked four-wide around the turn. The speed-figure "Sheets" sold by Len Ragozin and by the firm Thoro-Graph also are based on systems of mathematical rigidity. They take into account one aspect of horses' trips — how much ground they lose on the turns — but they do so according to an inflexible formula. A horse will be upgraded for racing four-wide on the turn even if, on a given day, a bias existed and racing four-wide was the optimal position on the track.

Although horseplayers are better informed and more sophisticated than ever before, so much of their wagering is based on mathematical and statistical methods that a skillful race watcher can find edges with which to beat the game. The profitability of the methods in *The Winning Horseplayer* have not diminished with time (as did the speed-figure methods in *Picking Winners*). Some of the most lucrative events in my own gambling life have been trip-handicapping plays since the original publication of this book. Swale and Pine Circle both were hindered by a powerful rail-favoring bias in the 1984 Preakness, while the victorious Gate Dancer benefited from that bias. When the horses faced each other again in the Belmont Stakes, Swale and Pine Circle ran one-two and produced a $125.80 exacta. And in the 1988 Kentucky Derby, Winning Colors and Forty Niner were the beneficiaries of a slow pace as they finished one-two, while Risen Star and Brian's Time were hindered both by the pace and by wide trips. Risen Star had clearly run the best race at Churchill Downs while finishing third. Vindication came in the Preakness, when he paid $15.60 to win, and the exacta with Brian's Time returned $93.80. Even in the competitive modern racing game, highly profitable betting situations can still be found — as long as a horseplayer is willing to expend the necessary energy to look for them.

ONE

The Nature of the Game

W HEN I STARTED playing the horses and trying to comprehend the mysteries of the game, I thought I was searching for great, immutable truths. I thought there must be a set of principles that governed the outcome of races and was waiting to be discovered, just as the laws of physics had always existed and were waiting for Newton to find them. By the middle of the 1970s I had realized that there were no such timeless verities — but I wished there were.

After struggling for years to understand the sport, I had finally isolated the most important handicapping factors, marshaled them into a coherent approach, and written a book, *Picking Winners,* that explained it. This was no academic theorizing; my method was working with spectacular success. In 1977, after gambling intensely at Gulfstream Park, Pimlico, and Saratoga, I finished the year with a profit of $50,000 that represented the fulfillment of a lifelong dream.

Once I might have thought such an accomplishment would signify that I had irrevocably mastered the art of handicapping. But at the end of that year I had the uneasy sense that the game was starting to change just as I had begun to understand it. I had scaled a mountain, but as I admired the view the ground was crumbling beneath my feet.

Since I had begun to play the horses seriously as a Harvard undergraduate in the early 1960s, I had seen the sport undergo many significant changes: the advent of year-round racing, the proliferation of legal and illegal drugs, the increase in turf racing, all of which had affected the handicapping process in subtle ways. But the most important changes were the ones built into the very nature of the parimutuel system. There are no immutable truths, no absolute rights and wrongs, because the only meaningful measure of any handicapping method is its profitability. Certain systems may produce profits for a while, but as the betting public catches on to them the odds drop and the systems eventually cease to work.

At the turn of the century, the famous gambler known as Pittsburgh Phil went to a track in the West and found himself losing because the races were teeming with larceny. So he formulated a novel plan: He bribed a jockey to be honest. He offered to pay a rider named Tod Sloan $400 for every race he won, giving him ample incentive to try to win all the time. The gambler knew he could bet confidently on Sloan's mounts when they figured, and knew he would also cash some bets he didn't deserve when Sloan's rivals weren't trying. Pittsburgh Phil won more than $80,000 before the bettors and the bookmakers realized how well the jockey was doing. After a few weeks, however, the public started to bet enthusiastically on Sloan's mounts, and the bookies accordingly lowered the odds on them. Horses who had been paying 3 to 1 were now going off at 6 to 5. Pittsburgh Phil promptly terminated his arrangement with Sloan, knowing that his system had been rendered unprofitable, and looked for new ways to continue amassing his fortune.* His experience was a microcosm of what happens in the sport over the long run. As the betting public becomes more knowledgeable, winning players have to adapt their own methods to stay ahead of the crowd.

At one time the crowd knew very little. Its lack of sophistication was reflected by the low quality of the published literature on handicapping. Even Robert Saunders Dowst, the best-known writer on the subject in the 1930s and 1940s, acknowledged that he was liv-

* *Racing Maxims and Methods of Pittsburgh Phil,* by Edward W. Cole, is published and sold by the Gambler's Book Club, Box 4115, Las Vegas, Nevada 89106.

ing in a benighted era and addressing himself to a benighted audience. "The reason for a real lack of turf literature in this country is quite obvious," he wrote. "The man most apt to become interested in betting is exactly the sort that one never sees within two miles of a bookstore. The kind I have in mind already has a book — a paper-covered dream book or a pamphlet on astrology he found in a race-train. Since very few race-players are of a studious nature, very few analytical works ever get published."

Probably the most successful bettor of this era was Al (the Brain) Windeman, a former cab driver from Coney Island, who perceived that he could beat the game simply by compiling enough handicapping information, and assembled a crew of assistants to help him do it. They timed every race with stopwatches calibrated to hundredths of a second. They took photographs of every race at several different stages. They used anemometers to measure the wind velocity. All this data gave the Brain enough of an edge over the crowd to become a wealthy man. He would not have that edge today.

Electric timing devices, closed-circuit television replays, and the computer-generated past performances in the *Daily Racing Form* give the modern-day bettor extensive and accurate information that his predecessors lacked. But it was a free-lance writer named Richard Carter who raised the sophistication of the American horseplayer to a new level. Writing under the pseudonym Tom Ainslie — a name he picked from a brand of Scotch — his books educated a whole generation of racing fans in the 1960s and 1970s. He taught them how to read the *Racing Form*'s past performances intelligently and critically. And he wrote so literately about the handicapping process that he appealed to a smart, educated breed of horseplayer. But while Ainslie was elevating the sophistication of the betting public, racetracks were still relentlessly taking 17 cents or so from every dollar bet, which meant that no greater percentage of the players could be winners. What Ainslie did was to make the game much more competitive. It became virtually impossible for a horseplayer to win in the long run simply by analyzing the *Racing Form* past performances, because that information was common currency. If I hear a bettor talking in textbook Ainslie terms, saying, "I like this horse because he ran well for $8500 and he's dropping to

$6500, and coming back after seven days with a switch to a better jockey," I may not be able to quarrel with his analysis. But I know he is not a winning horseplayer; he can't be. To overcome that 17 percent takeout, a handicapper needs insights and information not shared by the masses.

In the 1970s, I had them. After wandering down a hundred blind alleys in my early years as a horseplayer, I had learned that it was possible to beat the game by analyzing the final times of previous races and identifying the fastest horse in a field. A college classmate taught me how to measure the inherent speed of a racetrack each day so that I could compare the times of horses who had run on different days. He showed me how to evaluate the times of horses who had raced at various distances. Then I devised a way to compare the performance of horses who had run at different tracks, even in different parts of the country. It was exciting to calculate speed figures and exhilarating to use them, for they solved the perennial riddles of handicapping. How do you evaluate the sharp $5000 horse stepping into $10,000 company? I didn't have to guess anymore. My figures told me when he was good enough to win, because the race went to the swift.

This may sound like a truism now, but at the time I started to work with speed figures the notion was somewhat heterodox. While small numbers of horseplayers had been using speed-handicapping techniques profitably for decades, the majority believed that the final times of races were misleading and that the proper way to evaluate horses was to judge that elusive quality called class. Ainslie inclined toward this view; so had Dowst. Most handicappers maintained that if a $5000 horse had run three quarters of a mile in 1:11 and now was meeting a $10,000 animal who had run in 1:11⅖, the slower horse's superior class would somehow enable him to win. Because of this mass delusion, I was able to collect remarkable prices on horses I knew were clearly superior.

Of course, this was too good to last. More and more horseplayers were discovering independently the effectiveness of speed handicapping. Many more were willing to learn. When I explained my method of calculating figures in 42 dense pages of *Picking Winners,* I thought it would appeal only to a handful of zealots. But just as Ainslie must have been surprised to find out how many intelligent readers were waiting for a literate book on handicapping, I was stunned to discover how many people were willing to deal with all these mathematical complexities. Speed handicapping was becoming intellectually respectable. Soon it even became fashionable. Almost every new handicapping book now included an obligatory chapter on the subject. William Quirin, a mathematics professor at Adelphi University, wrote a book called *Par Times* that performed one of the most tedious calculations in the figure-making process. Len Ragozin, a New York speed handicapper, sold a highly sophisticated set of figures to a small clientele of big bettors, and when the "Raggies" liked a horse they could cut his odds in half. Even that old skeptic, Tom Ainslie, was selling figures by mail.

The result was inevitable. In the fall of 1982 I went to Belmont Park to bet a filly named On the Bench, who had earned a big figure winning a maiden-claiming race and was now stepping into allowance company. Just a few years earlier, class-oriented handicappers would have shunned her and I would have expected to get odds of 4 to 1. Now On the Bench paid $5.20. Speed figures were still enthralling and illuminating; they were still the best predictive tool in the game; but they had become much less profitable.

Certainly, I did not see many people beating the races with figures. The new wave of speed handicappers were smart people, mathematicians, computer whizzes, converted chess players or bridge players, but many of them were looking for mathematical certainties in a game where they didn't exist. They brought to the racetrack a rigidity of mind that virtually insured their defeat. Instead, most of the successful bettors I saw in the late 1970s were members of a school of handicapping that, for a long time, didn't even have a name. For want of a better term, their methods came to be called "trip handicapping."

These handicappers were subjective, not objective; visual, not analytical. What they did was to watch races carefully and form judgments of horses based on what they actually did on the track. They believed that the way a race developed — the fact that some horses would have "easy trips" and others "tough trips" — would largely determine who won or lost. They paid special attention to the position of horses on the turn, noting who raced wide and who saved ground along the rail. They observed the actions and tactics of jockeys. They watched the performance of horses in relation to any track biases — the tendency of racing strips to favor certain post positions or running styles. They believed strongly in the importance of pace, a handicapping factor that I had always thought was grossly overrated. I was amazed that the practitioners of this new art could use these imprecise observations and achieve greater success than most speed handicappers. The explanation was that the trip handicappers now occupied the position relative to me and my brethren that we had once occupied relative to the class handicappers. Possessing knowledge and insights shared by the few, they were collecting big prices on their horses, while I was using methods that had become commonplace. I recognized these trends at the end of 1977, and even as I was savoring the glory of winning $50,000 I knew I was going to have to alter the methods that had won it. I was going to have to learn what the trip handicappers were doing and probably adopt some of their methods.

While handicapping techniques and philosophy were undergoing this subtle evolution, a full-scale revolution was also in progress. In the early 1960s, American tracks had started to introduce new forms of wagering to supplement the traditional win, place, show, and daily double. Some tracks attempted to resist the change, but by the end of the 1970s so-called exotic bets were almost everywhere, from the East Coast tracks where triples could produce $10,000 payoffs to the California tracks where the Pick Six could pay more than $300,000. There were few races left that did not offer exactas, quinellas, daily doubles, or some other form of exotic wagering.

Some purists ignored the exotics and continued to bet win, place, and show. Many horseplayers decried them as an evil temptation — especially after the experience of picking a winner, playing him in the exotics, and losing everything. Most people, even those who liked these new wagers, viewed them as gimmickry. They were all wrong. The exotics were truly revolutionary; they had greatly expanded and forever altered the definition of a good bet. Ever since men had started wagering on thoroughbreds in the middle of the eighteenth century, there had been only one way to play the game: to try to identify the superior horse in a field and bet him (usually to win) if his odds were favorable. If Al the Brain concluded that a

4-to-5 shot had no chance and considered a race a tossup among three 5-to-1 shots, there was no way he could capitalize on his opinion. But now there was. If a modern-day horseplayer encountered the same circumstances, he could combine those three contenders in the exacta and get a sizable return on his investment.

While good bets were taking countless new forms, very few horseplayers were making an effort to understand them. I knew only one bettor, a New Yorker named Doc, who was dealing intelligently with these important changes in the game. Doc handicapped races in the most perfunctory fashion, but he tried to recognize and exploit all the promising situations that the exotics had created — and he made money doing it. I wanted to do the same. Even while I was making substantial profits at the track, I felt that my betting techniques were as erratic and error-prone as anybody else's. I had no coherent philosophy or strategy of money management. But at least I perceived that exotics were not an invention of the devil, and I was determined to take advantage of the new opportunities they were offering.

At the end of 1977 I promised myself that I was not going to be caught in a trap I had seen ensnare other winning horseplayers. Having achieved a measure of success, they become so wedded to their methods that they fail to adapt to changes in the game. So I set out to understand exotic wagering better and to learn at least the rudiments of trip handicapping.

I paid a year's tuition for my self-education. Learning to watch races perceptively was not easy for me. And when I tried to reconcile my visual observations with my speed figures, I was often hopelessly confused. I lost the clear, simple vision of the game that the figures gave me, and without it my profits dropped precipitously in 1978. I wondered if I had made a terrible mistake by trying to depart from a winning formula.

But eventually I became more comfortable with these new techniques. I was beginning to see how an understanding of trips explained some of the inconsistencies in horses' figures. I saw situations where trips rendered the figures almost irrelevant. I was learning to watch races well enough to make money from some of my observations. By 1979 I had restored my profits to a healthy level, and felt that I was on the brink of a great breakthrough.

In 1981 I made it. Everything fell into place. No longer was I thinking that a horse had such-and-such a figure and such-and-such a trip, and wondering how to relate the two. Now I was using all this information to form in my mind a single appraisal of a horse's ability. And I was able to translate my judgments into the proper action at the betting windows. I was wagering boldly, mostly on exactas and triples, and sometimes so creatively that I was able to make money from seemingly indecipherable races. At the four-week Saratoga meeting that summer I made a profit of more than $50,000 — more, in fact, than I had ever won in an entire year — and knew for certain that I had advanced to a new plateau as a horseplayer.

The approach I formulated is not one that every reader will be able to adopt, or that any reader will be able to master in a day or a week. Trip handicapping demands that a horseplayer have the freedom to get to the track with some frequency — at least a couple of times a week, or almost every day if possible — and concentrate intensely when he is there. Speed handicapping demands that he make a further commitment of time and energy. And to employ a proper betting strategy, he must have an adequate bankroll as well as the temperament to cope with the pressures that inevitably accompany aggressive gambling. I don't expect legions of horseplayers to follow my path. But I didn't expect more than a few readers to adopt the methods in *Picking Winners,* either. Modern horseplayers have demonstrated that they are willing to come to grips with all the demands and complexities of the game in order to beat it. The techniques of trip handicapping, used in conjunction with speed figures and a sound betting strategy, will beat it.

I know I still have a lot to learn about the game, especially about the physical appearance of horses. I know that future changes in the sport may necessitate changes in the way I handicap. Nevertheless, I feel very secure with my present methods; the ground is not crumbling beneath my feet this time. Because trip handicapping is so subjective — different people can watch the same race and draw very different conclusions from it — the payoffs it produces are not going to fall the way prices on speed-figure standouts did. The approach doesn't lend itself to being packaged, marketed, and sold as speed figures were. And because it is so flexible, it can be easily adapted to fit changing conditions in the sport. Having reached this new plateau, I expect to remain here for a long time.

Trip Handicapping: The Art of Watching Races

IN 1908, Pittsburgh Phil granted an interview to a journalist and explained the methods that had made him America's most successful horseplayer. He said that he paid close attention to the animals' physical condition. He believed strongly in the importance of class. He calculated figures that took into account time and weight, but recognized that the early pace of a race could influence horses' final times. He was closely attuned to the larcenous intentions of jockeys, trainers, and owners.

Seven decades later the sport of thoroughbred racing had changed so much that Pittsburgh Phil would have barely recognized it, but handicapping methods had not changed much at all. In his *Complete Guide to Thoroughbred Racing,* the book that helped educate a whole generation of horseplayers, Tom Ainslie devoted a chapter to each of the factors he considered most important: condition, class, weight, speed, pace, stables, and jockeys. Modern-day bettors were presumably more sophisticated than their counterparts at the turn of the century, but they were still working with the same old tools.

So it was genuinely revolutionary when horseplayers started talking in a new language, in terms that did not fall under any of Ainslie's chapter headings. The most successful bettor I knew, a New Yorker named Charlie, might say, "I don't like the favorite. Last time he sat on the fence behind two dueling speed horses and went past them when they fell apart. Today he's breaking from the outside and he figures to get hung out wide in a speed duel." My friend Paul Cornman might say, "This horse made a premature move on the backstretch into the hottest part of the pace in his last start. With a different kind of trip today he should beat the same horses." I might ask another of my racetrack compatriots, Joe Cardello, what a horse did in his last start and hear him reply, "He was one slow, three on the turn, five entering."

This was the new language of trip handicapping, whose practitioners judged horses by watching them run. In one sense, this was nothing new. Bettors have always recognized the importance of watching races, looking for horses who were blocked or bumped or put under strangleholds by their jockeys. But the new breed of trip handicappers found significance in the way every horse ran his race; they seemed just as interested in the routine as in the dramatic. Quietly they were challenging one of the most fundamental premises in the game.

I grew up with the assumption — shared by most horseplayers of my generation — that the secret of beating the races lay buried within the great mass of data in the *Daily Racing Form*. When I was 13 I was already toying with the numbers in the *Form* and inventing systems to use them. My speed-handicapping method was the ultimate way to take data from the *Form,* analyze it, and use it to pick winners. I hadn't rejected other ways of playing the game. It had never even occurred to me that there might *be* other ways, that a successful horseplayer could say (as Charlie does periodically), "The *Form* just throws you off." The trip handicappers believed that bettors who tried to beat the game solely by analyzing published past performances were looking in the wrong place entirely. Those bettors were looking at numbers that purported to describe what happened in a horse's previous race, while the trip handicappers were looking at the race itself — looking at reality.

Their way of viewing races challenged another assumption that had once seemed basic: that horses are judged according to the results of their previous races. As a speed handicapper I analyze a horse's final time and translate it into a number that expresses his ability. A class handicapper who rejects this approach may instead evaluate animals from the who-can-beat-whom standpoint. He might note that a horse who finished sixth in a field of 12 last week had defeated rivals who were better than any he is meeting today. That is a valid way of handicapping, too. But the trip handicappers would question both approaches. They would argue that speed handicappers and class handicappers err because of their preoccupation with the finish of a race. This can be deceptive or even irrelevant, because the outcome of a race is determined by the way it develops, by the fact that certain horses have easy trips and others have difficult trips. A horse who earned a good speed figure or beat superior rivals may have done so because of favorable circumstances that arose in the running of a race. Every horse's finish must be viewed in the context of his trip.

There were, presumably, some horseplayers who held this philosophy before the trip handicappers began to proliferate in the late 1970s. But there weren't many. "Ten years ago," said Charlie, "there were only two of us in New York who knew anything about trips — and the other guy eventually lost his mind. What a time! You could make more money than the President of the United States if you knew what you were doing." Where did all the trip handicappers come from? They graduated from the harness tracks of America.

Charlie himself had started his racing career by perching atop a billboard, watching the harness races at Yonkers through binoculars, and flashing the results to the bookmaker who employed him. Members of the new generation typically come from a somewhat different background, but they got their education from the same source. Most of them went to college with respectable intentions before they were enticed by the excitement and challenge of the track. Most started going to harness tracks because they operated at night and were thus more convenient. Paul Cornman attended Boston University but got his education from the harness races at Rockingham Park. Joe Cardello developed an interest in both standardbreds and thoroughbreds while he was working on his doctoral dissertation in history at Hofstra University. (When a budget cut eliminated his fellowship, he was forced to earn his living at the track.)

Intelligent people who become interested in harness racing will discover the nature of the game very quickly. It is much different in this respect from thoroughbred racing, which usually leads handicappers down so many blind alleys; there are people who have spent a lifetime in the thoroughbred sport and still think it significant that a horse is carrying three pounds more than he did in his last start. A harness fan has relatively little difficulty perceiving that the results of races are almost always determined by horses' trips.

The most obvious and important factor in harness racing is the ground that horses lose on the turns. A standardbred who is "parked" — forced to race outside another horse — during half of a one-mile race can almost never win. A horse who is parked wide on just one turn can lose as much as four lengths, enough to make the difference between victory and defeat in most races. So the ability of drivers to get a good position and to make their moves with a minimal loss of ground is critical.

Harness handicappers also learn quickly how much the early pace will affect the outcome of a race. A horse who goes the first half mile in 1:02, with minimal pressure, probably will remain strong enough to fight off any challenges in the crucial stages of the race. But if the same horse is forced to pace the first half mile in 1:00, the stretch-runners will be flying past him.

A third crucial factor in harness racing is wind resistance. Some horses will be shielded from the wind — "get cover" — while others must run headlong into it. "Don't ever underestimate the effect of air," a professional harness bettor told me. "A lot of times when people say a horse has no heart they really mean he can't take air."

These are the factors — more than the ability of the animals — that determine the outcome of harness races. Many tracks stage invitational races in which the same group of horses face each other week after week. Rarely will one horse establish his clear superiority. One week a horse will sit second on the rail behind a leader who is giving him cover, then swing past him into the stretch and win decisively — as the beneficiary of a perfect trip. The next week he may be forced to go "first over" (make a move without cover), challenge leaders who have set a slow place and are still strong, wind up parked three-wide around the final turn, and lose badly—because of an insurmountably difficult trip.

Bettors at harness tracks learn that they cannot hope to beat the game by analyzing the sketchy past performances in the program. They must watch races carefully and make note of the horses who have had easy trips and difficult trips. But a significant number of these bettors choose not to apply their lessons at the harness tracks where they learned them. Many may conclude that the sport is too corrupt for an outsider to beat it. Others are lured to thoroughbred racing because its greater complexity makes it the supreme gambling game.

The bettors who made this transition to thoroughbred racing in the 1970s brought with them a keen, probably exaggerated sense of the way trips affect horses' performances, and so they approached the handicapping process in a whole new way. In my first 15 years at the track I don't think I ever once heard a bettor say he liked a horse because he had raced six-wide around the turn in his last start, while his chief rival had sneaked through along the rail. But such perceptions were elementary to the converts from harness racing.

Those who converted in recent years did so at a time when videotape had made trip handicapping feasible in the thoroughbred sport. While it is easy to follow eight harness horses who are traveling single-file most of the time, it is almost impossible to keep track of 12 thoroughbreds sprinting three quarters of a mile. Old-time horseplayers knew they couldn't hope to see every detail of a race through their binoculars, so they trained their eyes to pick up the most dramatic events — horses getting blocked or checked or strangled. But the introduction of videotaped instant replays changed the game. Now a horseplayer can watch the race through his binoculars, view one or two replays, and even (at some tracks) see it in slow motion. He has the opportunity to observe every horse's trip in every race.

When I first saw the trip handicappers staring intently at televised replays, scribbling notes in their programs, and talking their new language, I was skeptical — even contemptuous — of what they were doing. My speed-handicapping techniques enabled me to cut through all the ambiguities in the game and express every horse's ability in a neat, unequivocal figure. Even if two horses had run at different distances on different days at different tracks, I could calculate that one of them was exactly one length superior to the other. In a game where the margin of victory is commonly a fifth of a second or less, a handicapper needs such precision. How could anyone hope to beat the races with the vague observation that one horse had had an easy trip and another a tough trip?

I didn't know. But I soon found that when the trip handicappers held an opinion that flatly contradicted my figures they were right more often than not. Once I flew from Washington to New York to bet on a horse at Aqueduct who appeared several lengths faster than all his rivals, and mentioned my opinion to a trip handicapper. "Well," he said condescendingly, "your horse may have a big figure, but he doesn't have anything else." The remark was inherently contradictory, I thought, because the figures were supposed to express everything about a horse's capabilities. But he was right: My horse didn't have much, as my loss for the day proved irrefutably.

Sometimes the trip handicappers picked winners that made me wonder if they possessed occult powers. Charlie is usually very close-mouthed about his opinions, but once at Saratoga he suggested that I bet a filly named Miss Prism. When I looked at her record, I thought he must be joking. In her previous start, Miss Prism had raced on the grass for the first time and had finished tenth, 15 lengths behind the winner. Now she was running on the turf again against the same class of horses. I would have dismissed her at first glance, but Charlie assured me, "This filly loves the grass." I bet with blind faith in Charlie's opinion, and when Miss Prism led all the way to win at odds of 13 to 1 I was absolutely stunned. "Last time," Charlie explained, "she broke from the outside post position and she was three wide going into the first turn, fighting for the lead. She was wide all the way down the backstretch, and on the stretch turn she was practically on the outside fence. When she straightened out in the stretch she was still in contention, but her jockey knew she wasn't going to get anything and he didn't push her after that. I saw some other things that I can't tell you about. You understand, this is my business."

Charlie had shown me enough. Obviously there was validity in what he was doing. And as I thought more about the concept of trip handicapping, I realized that I had already perceived its importance in some circumstances. As I worked with my speed figures, I had noticed that a horse who was able to take a clear early lead would usually run faster than he otherwise could. If he customarily earned a figure of 80, he might run an 88 after getting in front by himself. I had thought that this was a special type of case. But might not getting loose on the lead be just one of the countless varieties of trips that affected horses' final times, their figures, their performances?

At the 1978 Saratoga meeting I started observing the trip handicappers more closely, asking questions, watching races, and making notes as they did. But still I couldn't bring myself to make a single bet on the basis of this new method. I needed the reassurance that a horse's superior figures gave me; otherwise I felt like a high-wire artist working without a net. And then one day that fall I went to Belmont Park and summoned the courage to bet on a filly named Hildy's Grey despite the absence of obvious merit in her past performances.*

Hildy's Grey **Gr. f. 2, by Pontoise—Charming Hildy, by Sheilas Reward** **St. 1st 2nd 3rd Amt.**
Br.—Stone Maurice (NY) **1978 1 M 0 0 $510**
Own.—Hochman Merry E **Tr.—Pagano Frank X Jr** **119**
16Aug78- 3Sar fst 6f :22⅕ :46⅕ 1:11⅘ ⒻMd 40000 8 12 $9^{8\frac{1}{4}}$ $6^{7\frac{1}{2}}$ $4^{9\frac{1}{2}}$ 4^{10} Samyn J L 115 34.40 71-16 Baby Snooks $119^{8\frac{1}{2}}$ My Dear Tam $115^{\frac{3}{4}}$ Water Baby 115^{1} Slow st. 12
LATEST WORKOUTS Aug 30 Bel 3f fst :37⅕ bg Aug 11 Sar 4f fst :47⅖ h

Having watched Hildy's Grey make her career debut at Saratoga, I knew she was much better than her figure or her unimpressive running line in the *Racing Form* suggested. She had broken last in a 12-horse field and did not get into gear for an eighth of a mile. But when she did, she accelerated powerfully and rushed past half the field in a matter of a few strides. Hildy's Grey was running wide, and on the turn her momentum carried her even wider; she lost so much ground that she dropped behind rivals she had already passed. After turning into the stretch she needed time to get back into full stride again, but she finished well in the late stages of the race. Now she was entered against a weak field of New York-bred maidens, and with any kind of decent trip I thought she would annihilate them. Having congratulated myself for seeing all this, I was surprised when Hildy's Grey went to the post as the 8-to-5 favorite. But I didn't care; more than money was involved here. I bet $800, and when Hildy's Grey won by four lengths, with consummate ease, I knew that it was time to get serious about trip handicapping.

* Appendix I, pp. 175–188, explains how to read the *Daily Racing Form*'s past performances and charts.

What trip handicapping demands, most of all, is discipline. It is difficult to practice because it conflicts with human nature. The running of a race is a time of pure excitement for most horseplayers; having studied the *Form* and placed their bets, they cheer for their selections, exulting if they win and cursing if they lose. Yet a serious handicapper must try to suppress these emotions and observe a race dispassionately. To keep track of 12 horses in an event that may last for only 70 seconds demands disciplined concentration. When he is watching the race through binoculars, the handicapper must resist his natural inclination to follow the horse on whom he bet and concentrate instead on the animals in the back of the pack. This is the only chance to see a horse who might be getting into a lot of trouble while he is in tenth place. The handicapper will have ample opportunity to make note of what the leaders were doing when he watches the closed-circuit television replays.

A trip handicapper does not need to memorize every jockey's silks so he can identify all the horses, but he should make note of the colors worn by horses in whom he is especially interested. If he sees a horse doing something notable but doesn't know who it is, he will usually be able to identify the animal on the televised replays. Sometimes, though, this can be tricky, as in those annoying races where eight jockeys are wearing different shades of red. In such cases, a handicapper ought to note which horses are equipped with blinkers or shadow rolls so he can distinguish them more easily.

As he watches, the trip handicapper attempts to observe all the things in the running of a race that the *Daily Racing Form* charts and past performances won't tell him. He will make notes in his program, save all his programs, and refer to them when he handicaps. When I start to work on a day's card, I fan out my previous programs on my desk, look up the last race of every horse, and transcribe the notes from my program into today's *Form*.

When a trip handicapper makes these hurried notes, he doesn't have time to write lengthy essays about what each horse did: "Gluepot broke about a length behind the field, made his move three-wide around the turn, and was five-wide when the field fanned out into the stretch. After he was obviously beaten, the jockey didn't persevere in whipping him in the late stages of the race." Instead, the handicapper might scribble: "1 slo 3T 5E NPL." While no two horseplayers take notes in exactly the same way, many usages of shorthand have become fairly standard, because they grow naturally out of the observations that trip handicappers attempt to make at each important stage of a race.

AT THE START

Casual horseplayers watching from the grandstand usually do not realize how eventful the first few seconds of a thoroughbred race can be. They would understand if they had the opportunity to watch the head-on films that the stewards use. Horses do not move like trains on a track. When the starting gate opens, some will break more alertly than others; some will swerve instead of maintaining a straight course. There will inevitably be jostling and sometimes serious trouble that can knock a horse out of contention.

When a horse breaks tardily and comes out of the gate behind the rest of the field, I estimate how many lengths he lost and note it in my program: "2 slo" would indicate that he broke two lengths behind the field. The effect of such a slow start can vary. For a natural stretch-runner, who would be expected to drop far behind the leaders anyway, it may not mean much. But for a horse who usually runs on or near the lead, a slow start can be very harmful, forcing him to alter his usual style. The effects can be even worse if his jockey doesn't let him settle into stride and instead rushes him back into contention. I note "Rush" under these circumstances. Some horses, of course, are chronic slow breakers, and I am usually wary of betting them. But if a horse happens to miss his break once, I will upgrade his chances the next time he runs.

Without seeing the head-on films, a handicapper cannot tell precisely what kind of trouble a horse encounters coming out of the gate, but he can see the signs of it through his binoculars or on the regular television pan shot. If the jockey seems frozen, half-standing in the irons, not pushing the horse at all, it is very likely that he has encountered some heavy traffic, with other animals swerving in front of him, and has no place to go. Under those circumstances I will write "Steady G" — steady being the most mild gradation of trouble, G being the abbreviation for gate (which I use to signify anything that happened at the start of a race). If the trouble is more serious, if the jockey has to yank the reins or the horse appears to be knocked back, I will describe that as a "check" along with an estimate of the number of lengths of trouble he encountered: "Check G (4L)." If the jockey forcibly restrains his horse at the start of a race, but seems to be doing so for tactical or larcenous reasons, I will write "NPG" — no push gate — and pay further attention to him as the race develops.

THE FIRST TURN (IN ROUTE RACES)

Trip handicappers all envision and talk about a racetrack as if it were a track for human runners with clearly defined lanes. If a number of horses were fanned out across the track with little space between any two of them, and the innermost horse was next to the rail, the horse just outside him would be said to be in the 2-path. The next horse would be in the 3-path, and so on. The path in which a horse is racing may or may not be important in the backstretch or the homestretch. (If the track has a bias — if, for example, it seems to be harder and faster on the rail — a handicapper will want to know where every horse was at every stage of the race.) But position on the turns is always important, because that is where horses will lose or save ground that can determine the outcome of a race.

Students of harness racing know they must pay careful attention to a loss of ground at any stage of a race. But most thoroughbred handicappers don't notice the ground that a horse loses on the first turn of a route race. I was unconscious of this aspect of racing until Hialeah offered a virtual clinic on its importance. The track is 1⅛ miles in circumference, but for some reason Hialeah started carding some races at 1 1/16 miles, which meant that the gate had to be placed at the start of the clubhouse turn. The horses breaking from outside post positions were invariably hung out wide all the way around the turn, and after racing this way they could not win. After a season or so, jockeys realized that they either had to take back immediately and angle to the rail (as harness drivers do from post position eight) or gun hell-for-leather to get to the lead on the rail. But if a jockey let nature take its course and stayed wide all around the turn, he was doomed.

The effect of ground loss on the turns can be measured mathematically. A horse who races 10 feet from the rail all the way around a one-mile track covers an additional 64 feet. On one turn, this would mean a loss of 32 feet. Assuming that the width of a path (i.e., the width of a horse and rider) is between three and four feet, and that a length equals eight or nine feet, a horse loses a bit more than one length for every path by which he is removed from the rail on a turn. If he races on the rail, he is of course covering the shortest possible distance. If he races in the 2-path all the way around one turn, he loses about a length. If he races in the 3-path, he loses about two lengths. Some horseplayers attempt to calculate this loss of ground with precision. Speed handicapper Len Ragozin adjusts every horse's figure according to his distance from the rail. I think this may be overly refined, and possibly deceptive, because the effect of running 10 feet from the rail may very at different tracks. On Belmont Park's sweeping turns it is not terribly disadvantageous; on a half-mile track like Timonium it is usually fatal. And the effect of running wide may be related to the existence of a track bias. If the inside part of a track is very deep, the optimal place for a horse to be may be 10 feet from the rail.

Instead of making these sophisticated calculations, I simply note a horse's position on each turn and appreciate the fact that going wide hurts. If a horse races in the 2-path most of the way around the first turn, I would write "2 FT." For a horse who was parked wide all the way around the first turn at Hialeah, I might write "7 FT" and know that he was doomed, because horses who travel an extra six lengths at the start of a race don't finish first very often.

Noting the position of horses on the turn is especially important in grass races. Most turf events are contested around two turns, and because those turns are relatively sharp, horses have trouble maintaining their momentum if they are running wide. Losing ground becomes especially costly. Turf racing bears some resemblance to harness racing in this respect, and thus almost all trip handicappers have a special fondness for the grass.

ON THE BACKSTRETCH

Now the nature of a race, and each horse's trip, begins to take shape. The ideal place for almost any horse to be is loose on the lead; if he is not being pressured and not racing in the midst of traffic, not many bad things can happen to him. Probably the second-best type of trip is to sit behind two or more horses who are battling each other for the lead, within easy striking distance of them. If a horse is in this favorable position, it may not be clear from the *Racing Form* past performances, and so I write "Stalk" in my notes to indicate it.

When a horse finds himself in the midst of a strung-out field, with clear sailing and no rivals inside or outside him, I note "GP" — for good position. If he is surrounded by heavy traffic, he may not be able to give his optimal performance even if he encounters no actual interference. Paul Cornman suggests the notation "V" — for vise — to describe such circumstances.

Of course, traffic problems can cause a horse to be steadied or checked on the backstretch and here, as at the start, I try to estimate how many lengths' worth of trouble he suffered. I do this by looking for another horse who was racing abreast of him at approximately the same rate of speed, and then noting how far that rival moved ahead when the trouble occurred. If the other horse gained four lengths, I might note: "Check B (4L)." Serious trouble can usually be spotted easily, when a jockey virtually stands up in the irons and his mount drops back suddenly. A more subtle type of interference can occur when one of the leaders in a race tires suddenly. If a horse who is racing behind him, in the same path, does not have room to get around him, he will be forced to drop back to avoid clipping the heels of the quitter. Even though the jockey may not check his horse in a dramatic fashion, he may be forced to lose many lengths until he can get clear.

Sometimes trouble like this can be deceptive, of course. Just because a horse is blocked does not mean that he would have run well if he had had room. The most meaningful type of trouble is that which occurs after a horse has started to accelerate strongly. Rarely have I seen this happen so memorably as I did in the winter of 1980. Facilitate, a 5-year-old claiming horse, came into a race at Hialeah with a streak of seven straight out-of-the-money finishes. He had lost these races by an average of a dozen lengths. In view of his dismal record, I could hardly believe what I saw him do on the track. In the early stages of the race, Facilitate lay within striking distance of the leaders, and on the backstretch he began to make a powerful move. He looked as if he were going to surge to the lead, until another horse suddenly dropped in front of him. Jockey John Oldham had to yank Facilitate's reins, losing at least five lengths and dropping out of contention. If that had been the end of him — if I had written only "Strong move B, check (5L)" in my notes — that would have been a sufficient basis for a serious future bet. But Facilitate wasn't finished. Oldham now swung him to the outside of the pack for running room, and he lost ground all the way around the turn. But when he straightened out into the stretch and regained his momentum, he accelerated as if he were a stakes horse rather than a $15,000 claimer. He finished fifth, beaten by seven lengths, but I had no doubt that he was the superior horse in the field. When I opened the *Racing Form* the next day and saw that the footnotes for the race made no mention of all the trouble he had encountered, I had a strong feeling that Facilitate and I had a date with destiny. Every day thereafter I looked eagerly in the entries for Facilitate's name, but I never saw it. What was the trainer waiting for? Had the horse been hurt?

I was sitting in the press box, mulling over this question, when Bernie Dickman of the *Miami News* asked me a question that made me wonder if he were endowed with psychic powers. "Do you know anything about a horse named Facilitate?" he inquired.

I wasn't about to tip my hand, especially to a handicapper for a newspaper. "Didn't he run here a couple weeks ago?" I asked.

"Yeah," Dickman said. "I thought I saw him get into a lot of trouble in the race and I've been waiting to bet on him. Well, I do a radio show on Saturday night where I give the race results for all the out-of-town tracks and . . . take a look at this!"

My heart sank as Dickman handed me a page from the United Press International race-result wire, on which he had circled a couple of lines. They read:

NINTH BEULAH
Facilitate $30.80

The horse of my dreams had been shipped to Beulah Park and had beaten the best horses on the grounds at odds of more than 14 to 1. The edition of the *Racing Form* circulated in Florida does not carry the entries for Beulah. And besides, if your ship is going to come in, who would think to look for it in Columbus, Ohio?

ON THE TURN

To a trip handicapper, the final turn is the heart of a race. Here is where horses will most often make decisive winning moves. Here is where they will save or lose the ground that can spell the difference between victory and defeat. Here is where jockeys may give signs that they are not terribly interested in victory.

Because the turn is so important, trip handicappers will try to note horses' paths in two places: as they race around the midpoint of the turn, and as the field fans out entering the stretch. "Rail T 2E" — rail on the turn, 2-path entering the stretch — would indicate that a horse had a very easy trip. A notation of "6T 8E" would suggest that the jockey had been trying to get a better view of the parking lot. Sometimes even the most routine observations can form the basis of future bets — which is what happened when Lady of Promise faced Pretty Does in the Lady of Baltimore Handicap at Pimlico on July 6, 1981.

Lady Of Promise — Ch. f. 4, by Par Excellent—Land Of Promise, by Promise
Own.—Walker W F — Br.—Walker W F (Md) — Tr.—Sheffer J William
111 — Turf Record: St. 1st 2nd 3rd: 1 0 0 0

	St.	1st	2nd	3rd	Amt.
1981	9	2	2	0	$31,660
1980	19	5	1	2	$34,498

13Jun81- 6Pim	fst	1 1/16	:47⅗	1:11⅘	1:44⅖	3↑ⒻAllowance	8	5	4^{2}	1^{hd}	1^{3}	2no	Wright D k	124	*2.30	83-14	PrettyDoes121^{no}LadyOfPromise124$^{2\frac12}$ParisianFool116^{3}	Lugged in	8
4Jun81- 6Pim	fst	1 1/16	:47⅖	1:12	1:44⅖	3↑ⒻAllowance	6	1	1^{2}	$1^{1\frac12}$	2^{hd}	1^{3}	Wright D R	121	3.80	83-18	Lady Of Promise121^{3} Jerry Z. 121$^{1\frac12}$ Mobulee 114$^{2\frac12}$	Driving	6
14May81- 8Pim	fst	1 1/16	:47⅖	1:11⅖	1:43	ⒻAllowance	5	3	$3^{1\frac12}$	3^{2}	2^{4}	2^{5}	Wright D R	115	15.60	85-18	Misty Mala[illegible]LadyOfPromise[illegible]PrettyDoes115$^{1\frac12}$	2nd best	7
24Apr81- 8Pim	fst	1 1/16	:47	1:12⅖	1:45⅘	ⒻAllowance	1	6	3^{3}	$2^{\frac12}$	$1^{1\frac12}$	$1^{1\frac14}$	Gilbert R B	114	6.90	76-25	LdyOfPromise114$^{1\frac14}$SplitFether110^{no}CenterField112^{nk}	Drew clear	8
11Apr81- 8Pim	fst	6f	:23⅖	:46⅖	1:11⅕	ⒻAllowance	8	1	$7^{2\frac14}$	6^{4}	$6^{5\frac12}$	6^{5}	Gilbert R B	114	32.80	85-18	IllustriousLis107^{2}Phoebe'sPhncy115$^{2\frac12}$CntrFild114^{no}	Lost ground	9
12Mar81- 8Bow	fst	6f	:23	:46⅖	1:11⅕	ⒻAllowance	2	5	$4^{1\frac12}$	$3^{1\frac12}$	5^{5}	$6^{6\frac34}$	Passmore W J	113	9.00	77-24	Caught In Amber 115$^{2\frac12}$ Center Field 113^{hd}Rejuvavate112$^{1\frac12}$	Tired	6
14Feb81- 8Bow	fst	1 1/16	:47⅗	1:12⅘	1:47	ⒻAllowance	1	3	$4^{1\frac12}$	4^{3}	$7^{3\frac34}$	$9^{7\frac12}$	Passmore W J	113	15.00	63-24	Crimson April 115½ Devon Pal 119^{nk} Tote Em Up 107$^{1\frac12}$	Tired	9
7Feb81- 8Bow	fst	7f	:23⅕	:47	1:25	3↑ⒻⓈAllowance	4	4	4^{nk}	$4^{\frac34}$	6^{6}	$6^{9\frac12}$	Beitia E	117	23.10	70-22	Contrary Rose 122¾ Caught In Amber 119$^{1\frac12}$ DenimGal117^{hd}	Tired	6
19Jan81- 8Bow	fst	1 1/16	:48⅘	1:14⅕	1:48⅖	ⒻAllowance	1	1	$1^{1\frac12}$	$1^{3\frac12}$	3^{nk}	4^{nk}	Bracciale V Jr	112	8.40	64-30	Fair Hit 115^{nk} Dottie O. 112no Rejuvavate 107no	Weakened	7
31Dec80- 9Lrl	fst	6f	:23⅕	:47⅘	1:12⅘	3↑ⒻAllowance	3	7	$6^{2\frac14}$	$6^{1\frac12}$	$4^{1\frac34}$	$3^{1\frac14}$	Passmore W J	112	7.40	81-18	Pro Supper 119¾ Bill's Fancy 119½ Lady Of Promise 112^{1}	Rallied	8

4FT 3T

Pretty Does — B. f. 4, by Herbager—Amber High, by Ambiopoise
Own.—Retter Mrs R — Br.—Retler Mr-Mrs R H (Md) — Tr.—Kousin Jack
109 — Turf Record: St. 1st 2nd 3rd: 8 1 0 1

	St.	1st	2nd	3rd	Amt.
1981	10	2	0	4	$36,060
1980	19	3	0	4	$36,025

13Jun81- 6Pim	fst	1 1/16	:47⅗	1:11⅘	1:44⅖	3↑ⒻAllowance	1	8	$7^{5\frac12}$	7^{10}	$4^{4\frac12}$	1no	Franklin R J	b	121	9.40	83-14	Pretty Does 121no Lady OfPromise124$^{2\frac12}$ParisianFool116^{3}	Driving	8
4Jun81- 6Pim	fst	1 1/16	:47⅖	1:12	1:44⅖	3↑ⒻAllowance	1	5	$6^{6\frac12}$	6^{9}	$6^{8\frac12}$	5^{7}	Pino M G	b	121	3.10	76-18	Lady Of Promise 121^{3} Jerry Z. 121$^{1\frac12}$ Mobulee 114$^{2\frac12}$	Outrun	6
14May81- 8Pim	fst	1 1/16	:47⅖	1:11⅖	1:43	ⒻAllowance	6	4	$4^{5\frac12}$	4^{5}	$4^{5\frac12}$	$3^{6\frac34}$	Pino M G	b	115	12.10	83-18	Misty Mala[illegible] LadyofPr[illegible]115$^{1\frac12}$	Late bid	7
24Apr81- 8Pim	fst	1 1/16	:47	1:12⅖	1:45⅘	ⒻAllowance	5	8	8^{8}	$6^{4\frac12}$	$5^{3\frac12}$	$4^{1\frac12}$	Wright D R	b	119	8.60	74-25	Lady Of Promise 114$^{1\frac14}$SplitFeather110^{no}CenterField112^{nk}	Rallied	8
10Apr81- 8Pim	fst	1 1/16	:47⅖	1:11⅗	1:45⅕	ⒻAllowance	1	5	7^{7}	$8^{9\frac34}$	$6^{8\frac14}$	$3^{3\frac34}$	Whitacre G^{5}	b	114	7.70	75-22	Livonia 115$^{2\frac34}$ Crimson April 119^{1} Pretty Does 114½	Brushed	9
27Mar81- 8Pim	fst	1 1/16	:47⅗	1:12⅗	1:45⅖	ⒻAllowance	1	7	$8^{6\frac34}$	$7^{7\frac12}$	$5^{4\frac12}$	$4^{2\frac34}$	Whitacre G^{5}	b	114	7.70	75-26	Tote Em Up 112¾ Itsa Bitter Day 112^{1} Noble Chick 119^{1}	Rallied	9
28Feb81- 4Bow	fst	1 1/16	:49⅕	1:14⅘	1:47	ⒻAllowance	5	5	$6^{8\frac12}$	$6^{4\frac12}$	$5^{3\frac12}$	$3^{5\frac14}$	Black A S	b	119	3.00	66-24	Run Em Up 112^{5} Crimson April 119^{nk} Pretty Does 119^{nk}	Rallied	6
12Feb81- 7Aqu	gd	1 1/16 ⊡	:48⅕	1:13⅘	1:45⅘	ⒻAllowance	7	9	$8^{7\frac12}$	6^{7}	$5^{6\frac12}$	3^{6}	Asmussen C B	b	117	9.30	79-18	Skagerrak 117$^{5\frac12}$ Cinto Tora 121½ Pretty Does 117^{1}	Mild rally	9
29Jan81- 8Bow	fst	1 1/16	:50⅕	1:15⅕	1:49	ⒻAllowance	1	2	$4^{1\frac34}$	$4^{2\frac12}$	$1^{\frac12}$	$1^{2\frac12}$	Whitacre G^{5}	b	109	16.30	61-31	Pretty Does 109$^{2\frac12}$ NobleChick112^{2}CrimsonApril115^{hd}	Ridden out	7
19Jan81- 8Bow	fst	1 1/16	:48⅘	1:14⅕	1:48⅖	ⒻAllowance	6	6	7^{15}	$6^{8\frac12}$	$4^{3\frac34}$	$5^{\frac12}$	Whitacre G^{5}	b	108	27.10	63-30	Fair Hit 115^{nk} Dottie O. 112no Rejuvavate 107no	No factor	7

LATEST WORKOUTS Jly 4 Lrl 3f my :38⅗ b (d) ●Jun 25 Lrl 7f fst 1:29⅗ b Jun 11 Lrl 3f my :39⅗ b (d) May 26 Lrl 5f fst 1:02⅕ b

Rail all way

A student of the *Racing Form* would have difficulty choosing between these fillies on the basis of their last race against each other. On June 16, Pretty Does had come from last place and rallied strongly to win by a nose over Lady of Promise, who blew a three-length lead in the stretch. But a trip handicapper would know that their rematch was a mismatch by looking at these notes from their last race:

Pretty Does	**Rail all way**
Lady of Promise	**4FT 3T**

Breaking from the outside post position, Lady of Promise was parked in the 4-path on the first turn, contended for the lead on the backstretch, then accelerated when she was three-wide on the final turn to take command. Meanwhile Pretty Does had been held far behind this battle for the lead. She advanced along the rail on the backstretch and the turn, had clear sailing most of the way, and caught the leader at the wire. Now, in the Lady of Baltimore Handicap, Lady of Promise had post position two and figured to get a clear early lead. Pretty Does was starting from post No. 5 in a six-horse field and figured to have a more difficult trip.

EIGHTH RACE
Pimlico
JULY 6, 1981

$1\frac{1}{16}$ MILES. (1.41) 7th Running THE LADY BALTIMORE HANDICAP. Purse $25,000 Added. Fillies and mares. 3-year-olds and upward. By subscription of $50 each, which should accompany the nomination, $125 to pass the entry box, $125 additional to start, with $25,000 added, of which 65% of all monies to the winner, 20% to second, 10% to third and 5% to fourth. Weights five days before the race. Starters to be named through the entry box by the usual time of closing. Closed Monday, June 15, 1981 with 44 nominations. (Originally carded to be run at 1 1/16 miles turf course.)

Value of race $29,075, value to winner $18,899, second $5,815, third $2,907, fourth $1,454. Mutuel pool $46,741. Exacta Pool $69,441.

Last Raced	Horse	Eqt.	A.	Wt	PP	St	1/4	1/2	3/4	Str	Fin	Jockey	Odds $1
13Jun81 ^{6}Pim^{2}	Lady Of Promise		4	111	3	4	1^{2}	1^{6}	1^{5}	1^{5}	1^{6}	Wright D R	1.20
24Jun81 ^{7}Mth^{1}	Nasty Jay	b	6	110	6	3	6	4^{hd}	$3^{3\frac{1}{2}}$	$2^{1\frac{1}{2}}$	$2^{\frac{3}{4}}$	Attanasio R	22.30
31May81 ^{8}Key^{3}	Averell		4	108	1	1	2^{hd}	6	6	4^{6}	3^{1}	Miller D A Jr	4.90
24Jun81 ^{8}Pim^{1}	Crimson April	b	4	113	2	6	4^{1}	$3^{1\frac{1}{2}}$	2^{1}	3^{2}	4^{6}	Black K	2.90
11May81 ^{8}Pim^{5}	Jamila Kadir	b	7	111	4	5	$3^{1\frac{1}{2}}$	2^{hd}	$4^{\frac{1}{2}}$	$5^{1\frac{1}{2}}$	5^{5}	Pino M G	6.20
13Jun81 ^{6}Pim^{1}	Pretty Does	b	4	109	5	2	$5^{1\frac{1}{2}}$	5^{3}	$5^{1\frac{1}{2}}$	6	6	Cooke C	7.30

OFF AT 4:17 EDT. Start good, Won easily. Time, :24⅕, :47⅗, 1:11⅗, 1:36⅖, 1:42⅘ Track fast.

$2 Mutuel Prices:				
	5–LADY OF PROMISE	**4.40**	**3.00**	**2.60**
	8–NASTY JAY		**10.80**	**4.20**
	1–AVERELL			**4.00**
	$2 EXACTA 5–8 PAID $74.20.			

Ch. f, by Par Excellent—Land Of Promise, by Promise. Trainer Sheffer J William. Bred by Walker W F (Md).

LADY OF PROMISE, hustled to the front along the rail, was rated down the backstretch and was never challenged while under snug restraint in the stretch. NASTY JAY worked inside horses down the backstretch and finished evenly. AVERELL fell back down the backstretch, eased outside in the upper stretch and finished gamely. CRIMSON APRIL launched a bid outside on the far turn and steadily fell back thereafter. JAMILA KADIR was through after a half mile. PRETTY DOES was not a factor.

Owners— 1, Walker W F; 2, Edwards K J; 3, Sharp B; 4, Zarin B; 5, Bogley Mrs S E; 6, Retter Mrs R.

Trainers— 1, Sheffer J William; 2, Brice Harold B Jr; 3, Peoples Charles; 4, Alfano Ronald A; 5, Field Thomas E; 6, Kousin Jack.

Overweight: Jamila Kadir 1 pound.

Scratched—Euphrosyne (20Jun81 ^{8}Bel^{4}); Foolish Spoon (1Jly81 ^{7}Pim^{6}); Lady Lobbyist (6Jun81 ^{8}Mth^{4}).

Sometimes I am astonished by the effect that the routine development of races can have on the relative performance of horses. Lady of Promise took the lead on the inside, enjoyed a perfect trip, and coasted to a six-length victory. Pretty Does lost ground most of the way and finished 19 lengths behind.

In addition to noting who saves and loses ground on the turns, I look for horses who make strong, decisive, eye-catching moves. In harness racing, a horse's ability to unleash a burst of speed for an eighth or a quarter of a mile and take command of a race is considered much more important than his final time. Relatively few thoroughbreds have this capacity for sudden acceleration, but those who can display it, making the horses around them look as if they are standing still, are revealing signs of quality that may not otherwise be reflected in their speed figures or their past performances. Pleasant Colony was such a horse. In the Wood Memorial Stakes at Aqueduct, he was just getting into contention as he entered the final turn. By the time he turned into the stretch, he had seized control of the race with one explosive move. Two weeks later, he made the same kind of swift, decisive move to capture the Kentucky Derby. When I see a horse accelerate impressively, I write "Move" in my notes. If I am really dazzled, I might write "Zoom." Conversely, if a horse gets the lead merely by taking over from an exhausted leader, I will write, "Inherit," and possibly downgrade the performance a bit.

As many horses attempt to accelerate on the turn, some will have room to run and others won't. If a horse has to steady, awaiting room, I try to judge the extent of his trouble the same way I do at the other stages of the race, and estimate how many lengths he may have lost. But I know that, as often as not, this trouble is deceptive. Just because a horse is blocked does not mean he would run well if he were clear. And the horses who do get into traffic trouble on the turn are usually racing on the inside, saving ground. A horse who has two lengths of interference on the rail is still better off than a rival who has clear sailing in the 5-path.

The turn is the best place to judge the intentions of jockeys. A rider may have his mount under a snug hold on the backstretch because he is rating him and wants to make his run late. A rider might not be persevering in the stretch because his mount is exhausted and he sees no reason to beat the proverbial dead horse. But if a jockey isn't on his belly and doesn't have his whip cocked on the turn, I will write "NPT" — no push turn — in my notes and begin to harbor dark suspicions.

There are few aspects of race-watching as important or as tricky as detecting jockeys who aren't trying to win. Larceny doesn't occur with such frequency that the game is rendered indecipherable or that horseplayers should feel paranoid whenever they place a bet. But it does happen often enough that an observant handicapper must watch for it and try to profit from it.

Uninformed horseplayers usually overreact to jockeys' use (or nonuse) of the whip. They will often accuse a jockey of stiffing a horse even if he has been pushing and shoving every step of the way, giving a vigorous and effective hand ride. Instead of watching the whip so much, they should concentrate on the jockey's hands and arms. When a rider is asking a horse for a response, he is thrusting forward; his arms are doing much of the work. If there is no forward thrust, he has the horse in a neutral gear. And occasionally a jockey will look as if he is trying to put his mount into reverse. He will visibly restrain the animal, taking a tight hold of the reins. He may have a posture that my colleague Clem Florio, a sagacious student of thievery, describes as "having his feet in the dashboard."

The most sophisticated dishonest riders will accomplish their objectives without putting horses under a blatant hammerlock. They will go unnecessarily wide on the turn or into the midst of heavy traffic where there is no room to run. Because such larceny can be so subtle, it is helpful if a handicapper has some forewarning so he can watch for it. He may anticipate that horses will be stiffed because they are being prepared for some future objective. First-time starters are the most likely candidates. So are horses who have been laid off, and ones who are clearly pointing for a more appropriate spot, such as distance horses in sprint races, stakes horses in allowance races, grass horses entered on the dirt.

Sometimes even a nonparanoid horseplayer will be deceived by what he thinks is larceny. He may watch the stretch run of a race on television and think that the jockey isn't trying when in fact he is whipping with his left hand. He may observe a rider keeping his mount under a snug hold all the way around the track and conclude that a betting coup is in the offing, when in fact the horse is so infirm that the jockey doesn't want to risk life and limb by asking him to run. Even if a handicapper is convinced that a horse was stiffed, the possibility exists that he doesn't possess much ability anyway. What does a horseplayer do when a horse who has been strangled is entered against a rival with solid credentials?

I encountered this dilemma at Gulfstream Park in a race that offered the opportunity for a major killing. The names must be changed, much as I would like to besmirch the name of the thieving rider I will hereafter refer to as Ganef.

Jockey Ganef is one of the best-known members of his profession in America. He has won at least one Triple Crown event, and his mounts earn millions a year, but that does not deter him from giving frequent rides that could only be admired by the Boston Strangler. I had already collected several sizable payoffs that resulted from his stiff jobs, and so I was watching closely when he rode a first-time starter named Peach Cobbler at Hialeah. Peach Cobbler showed good speed and raced abreast of the leaders down the backstretch, but as I watched Ganef's hands I saw he wasn't asking her for anything. The filly was doing everything under her own power. As she reached the turn, Ganef still looked as if he were afflicted by rigor mortis. Then, as the filly turned into the stretch, Ganef reached up on the reins and applied his hammerlock. Peach Cobbler was beaten by more than 15 lengths.

When I saw her name in the Gulfstream entries a month later, I hoped that she would be meeting a weak maiden field where I could bet without fear. Unfortunately, Peach Cobbler did have one formidable rival. Pillbox was a well-bred filly who had made one start in her career in New York and showed high speed before she tired. She had now drawn the inside post position on a track where the rail seemed to be advantageous. She was trained by a sharp man. But what confounded me was the jockey assigned to ride Pillbox: Jockey Ganef.

His choice of this mount presumably meant that he preferred her chances to those of Peach Cobbler, but I couldn't be sure. I didn't know how to play the race. Finally I decided to bet a pair of $200 exactas, with Peach Cobbler on top of Pillbox and vice versa.

Pillbox broke alertly and took a brief lead, but when Peach Cobbler moved up on the outside I saw — or at least I thought I saw — Ganef glance over and then take a firmer hold of his mount's reins, permitting his principal rival and one other longshot to spurt in front of him. When he reached the turn on this rail-favoring track, he swung needlessly into the 6-path. Only the tiring longshot was between Peach Cobbler and Pillbox, between me and a $14,000 exacta payoff. But Ganef waited — or at least I thought he waited — until Peach Cobbler was safely several lengths in front before he asked Pillbox for any response. By the time he applied the whip it was too late to overhaul the other horse for second place. Peach Cobbler paid $29.40 to win, Pillbox ran third and I collected nothing.

I rushed into the stewards' stand and shouted to state steward Walter Blum, "That's the worst thing I've ever seen!" Indulgently he called for a videotape replay of the race and pointed out that Ganef had indeed been whipping through the stretch run. He looked at me as if I were a crazy, paranoid horseplayer. That night I went to a party, intending to drown my sorrows, and ran into the trainer of Pillbox. What, I asked, had he thought of her performance? "She's a little green," the trainer said. "Ganef said he was having a little trouble with her on the turn." Had I been wrong? Or paranoid? This is always a danger when a horseplayer is attempting to detect larceny. But this was a case, I still believe, where I was neither wrong nor paranoid; I was robbed.

IN THE STRETCH

As horses drive to the wire, the eyes of most spectators will be riveted on the leaders. But a conscientious trip handicapper will be watching the horses in the middle and the rear of the pack.

As a rule, not much can be learned by watching the winner cross the finish line, not even the thing that so many horseplayers attempt to judge: the ease of his victory. The chart-callers for the *Daily Racing Form* use the terms *driving, handily, ridden out,* and *easily* to categorize every winning performance according to the amount of pressure the jockey was applying. This is usually misleading. When a horse wins a race by 10 lengths, his rider will rarely be whipping him or even pushing him hard. The animal will give the impression that he is doing everything easily, that he has much more energy in reserve. In fact, horses who win "easily" rarely run much faster when they are subjected to pressure.

To spot horses who win with speed in reserve, handicappers should look to the early stages of a race instead of the finish. If a jockey restrains his mount much of the way, and then lets him accelerate just enough to win, it is quite possible that he could have run better if he had commenced his move sooner. When Forego was the dominant handicap horse in America, and Bill Shoemaker did not want to pick up heavier weight assignments by winning too impressively, he would time the old gelding's stretch run so that he would win by less than a length — even against fields he could have demolished. But once a half-ton animal is in high gear, there is little that a 110-pound jockey can do to slow his momentum, and when the jockey seems to "ease" a winner at the end it is usually just an illusion.

If a horseplayer looks up the track at the also-rans, he may find the keys to future bets. When a horse has been battling for the lead and then has begun to tire, I like to observe just how long he managed to stay in contention. And after he is clearly beaten, I watch to see if the jockey eases him in a fashion that will make his finish look deceptively terrible. At Hialeah in 1982 I bet a sprinter named Wiggles Not Holme in a route race, thinking that he could get loose on the lead. He couldn't. He engaged in an all-out, head-and-head battle and got tired. As soon as it was obvious that he was going to lose, jockey Roger Danjean wrapped up on him entirely. Instead of losing by a respectable eight or ten lengths, Wiggles Not Holme lost by 32. (My notes read, "2B hard duel, eased S." He had fought for the lead in the 2-path on the backstretch and was eased in the stretch.) A week later he was back in a sprint, where he belonged, and because of that horrendous finish he paid $46 when he won.

A jockey who has had no interest in winning a race will often turn his mount loose late in the stretch. Riders are supposed to look as if they are trying when they are in front of the grandstand. Besides, if they are preparing a horse for a future objective, they may want to get some indication of his ability. So if a bettor has noticed a horse being restrained on the backstretch or the turn, he ought to keep his binoculars on that animal through the stretch.

Paul Cornman once found a memorable betting opportunity when he did this and kept his eyes on a maiden named Royal Accomplice at Belmont Park. "The horse was trained by John Russell, who I knew liked to educate his young horses before he really asked them to run," Cornman said. "Royal Accomplice had sprinted three or four times and hadn't done anything. One day I was watching him and I saw on the turn that the jockey wasn't asking him to run. Then I picked him up again in the last sixteenth of a mile. There were three horses in the back of the pack together; when the jockey brushed Royal Accomplice with the whip he ran away from that pack by four lengths. It was the first time he'd ever been really asked to do anything — and he did it big."

Although Paul had been visually impressed, the colt's running line looked dismal:

$$11^{11} \qquad 11^{16} \qquad 9^{17} \qquad 9^{15}$$

Ten days later, on July 14, 1977, he was entered at a mile and one sixteenth, and Paul assumed that this was the spot for which he had been preparing all along. A son of Buckpasser, Royal Accomplice was bred for distance races, not sprints. The competition looked weak, and Paul decided to go to the bank and be prepared to bet more than $100 on a horse for the first time in his life.

Students of trivia may remember July 14, 1977, as something other than the date of Royal Accomplice's first route race. It was the day after the night the lights went out in New York City; the famous blackout had triggered widespread looting and violence. The next morning, the city was in a state of shock and paralysis, and most businesses and institutions were closed — including the banks. Still, Paul didn't panic. The racing community is a chummy one, and Paul assumed he would be able to find friends who could loan him the money for his bet. But when he got to the track, he said, "It was one of those days when nobody was there. Most people, I think, thought that the races would be canceled because of the blackout. I didn't see a familiar face." Paul had $20 in his pocket and bet it all on Royal Accomplice. When the colt won by a nose, paying $46 to win, Paul did not know whether to cheer or cry.

•   •   •

To develop race-watching skills as acute as Paul's is not easy. For me, I suspect, it is practically impossible. I do not possess naturally good powers of observation. When I meet someone, I won't be able to remember five minutes later what color tie he was wearing. Or whether he was wearing a tie. So as I attempted to learn about trip handicapping, I doubted whether it would ever be especially useful to me.

What I did at the outset was to force myself to write down everything I saw in the running of a race, whether it seemed likely to have any future significance or not. Before I studied each day's card, I dutifully transcribed my trip notes into my *Racing Form*, even though most of the time that information would have no bearing on my handicapping judgment. At best, I thought, I might be able to profit occasionally from observations that horses had encountered very serious trouble or had gone extraordinarily wide in their previous races.

But as I watched more and more races, I found that my powers of observation were improving. I still had trouble disciplining myself to concentrate on the rear of the field, instead of the horse I had bet, but I was nevertheless starting to see things that I could not have seen before. My observations were beginning to contribute to my handicapping judgment more frequently. And occasionally I would encounter one of those revelatory situations in which trip notes contained the key to a race that would have been otherwise indecipherable, such as the second race at Saratoga on August 15, 1980.

2 **SARATOGA**

INNER TURF COURSE
1 1-16 MILES
SARATOGA
START FINISH

1 1/16 MILES. (INNER-TURF). (1.42) MAIDEN SPECIAL WEIGHT. Purse $18,000. Fillies, 2-year-olds. Weight, 117 lbs.

Coupled—Seaholme and Fabled Morn.

M. For Mary B. f. 2, by Minnesota Mac—Mile Barker, by Mossborough
Own.—Burke W P Br.—Burke W P (Fla) Tr.—Pierce Joseph H Jr **117**
St. 1st 2nd 3rd Amt. 1980 3 M 0 2 $2,625

7Aug80- 5Mth fst 5½f :22⅗ :46⅗ 1:05⅗ ⒻMd Sp Wt 5 3 6⁶½ 6⁵¾ 4⁷ 3¹⁰ Perret C 117 3.20 77-20 Muchisma 112no Drop A Gem 117¹⁰ M. For Mary 117¾ No threat 9
29Jly80- 3Mth sly 5½f :23⅗ :47⅘ 1:07⅕ ⒻMd Sp Wt 1 4 4¹½ 6⁷ 4¹¹ 4⁸¼ McCauley W H 117 *2.00 71-19 Sum Of'EmDo117¹ChangePlaces117⁷ⒹMusicCamp117nk Checked 7
29Jly80-Placed third through disqualification
18Jly80- 5Mth fst 5½f :22⅗ :47 1:07⅕ ⒻMd Sp Wt 10 5 6⁴¾ 4⁴ 4⁴½ 5⁴ McCauley W H 117 *3.00 75-22 Eloqueen 117½ Laura's Recipe 117½ Lovely Lei 117nk Wide 10
LATEST WORKOUTS Jly 26 Mth 4f fst :49⅖ b Jly 17 Mth 3f my :37 b Jly 11 Mth Ⓣ 7f fm 1:35 b (d) Jly 2 Mth 5f fst 1:01 hg

Laurial B. f. 2, by Apalachee—Lady Noholme, by Noholme II
Own.—Regent Farm Br.—Regent Farm (Ky) Tr.—Laurin Roger **112⁵**
St. 1st 2nd 3rd Amt. 1980 1 M 0 0

3Aug80- 4Sar fst 6f :21⅘ :45 1:11⅖ ⒻMd Sp Wt 5 8 8¹¹ 8¹³ 8¹⁵ 8¹⁹ Venezia M 117 6.10 64-12 Expressive Dance [illegible] FinalDecision117² Outrun 9
LATEST WORKOUTS Aug 11 Sar Ⓣ 4f fm :50⅖ b Jly 30 Sar 5f fst 1:00⅖ h Jly 23 Bel 5f sly :59⅕ h Jly 17 Bel 4f fst :47⅗ h

Zimbaba
Dk. b. or br. f. 2, by Bravest Roman—Speedy Jodee, by Count Flame — Br.—Victor G (Ky) — Tr.—DiMadro Stephen — **117**
Own.—Carl Suzanne F
Turf Record: St. 1st 2nd 3rd — 1 0 0 0
St. 1st 2nd 3rd Amt. — 1980 3 M 0 1 $3,060
4Aug80- 6Sar fm 1 Ⓣ:48⅗ 1:13⅗ 1:38 ⒻMd Sp Wt 3 6 75 66½ 35 55¼ Fell J 117 13.40 84-12 Bravo Native 117¾ Wayward Lass 117² Seaholme 117½ Weakened 9
23Jly80- 4Bel sly 7f :23⅗ :47⅕ 1:24⅘ ⒻMd Sp Wt 4 3 1½ 1½ 36 315 Vasquez J 117 4.90 65-22 Heavenly Cause 117⁹ Wayward Lass 117⁶ Zimbaba 117⁴½ Weakened 8
11Jly80- 4Bel fst 6f :23 :48 1:12 ⒻMd Sp Wt 7 10 86½ 74½ 65¾ 49½ Vasquez J 117 23.30 73-16 DeLaRose 117¾ BravoNative 117⁵¾ CircleGme 117hd L'cked room st. 11
LATEST WORKOUTS Jly 18 Bel tr.t 4f fst :49 b — Jly 7 Bel 5f fst 1:01⅘ bg — Jly 1 Bel 5f fst 1:01⅗ b — Jun 26 Bel 6f fst 1:17 b

Hazy Forest
Gr. f. 2, by Cloudy Dawn—Penny Bryn, by Tulyar — Br.—Pen-Y-Bryn Farm (Ky) — Tr.—Barrera Luis — **112⁵**
Own.—Harbor View Farm
St. 1st 2nd 3rd Amt. — 1980 1 M 0 0
10Aug80- 6Sar fst 6f :22⅘ :45⅗ 1:11 ⒻMd Sp Wt 8 11 1317 1118 916 718 Lovato F Jr5 112 29.50 67-14 Prayers'nPromises 117⁸¾ DarkRelity 117nk Hgley'sPoint 117³ Outrun 13
LATEST WORKOUTS Aug 7 Sar Ⓣ 5f fm 1:01 h — Aug 1 Sar tr.t 4f fst :50 b — Jly 26 Sar tr.t 4f fst :49⅘ h — Jly 22 Bel tr.t 4f fst :51⅕ b

Simba Sara
Ch. f. 2, by Cougar II—Saracen Summer, by Bagdad — Br.—Taylor Mrs W J (Ky) — Tr.—Maloney James W. — **117**
Own.—Taylor Shirley H
St. 1st 2nd 3rd Amt. — 1980 1 M 0 0
10Aug80- 4Sar fst 6f :22⅕ :45⅘ 1:10⅘ ⒻMd Sp Wt 3 10 1314 1317 1321 1329 Hernández R 117 38.70 57-14 Hope She's Bold 117²¾ Temple Bells 117no Artmatic 117⁶¾ Outrun 13
LATEST WORKOUTS Aug 6 Sar 5f fst 1:01⅗ hg — Aug 3 Sar 3f fst :36 h — Jly 31 Sar 3f fst :37⅘ b — Jly 16 Bel 4f fst :50⅕ bg

Wayward Lass
Dk. b. or br. f. 2, by Hail the Pirates—Young Mistress, by Third Martini — Br.—Luro H A (Fla) — Tr.—Martin Jose — **117**
Own.—Flying Zee Stable
Turf Record: St. 1st 2nd 3rd — 1 0 1 0
St. 1st 2nd 3rd Amt. — 1980 4 M 2 2 $11,780
4Aug80- 6Sar fm 1 Ⓣ:48⅗ 1:13⅗ 1:38 ⒻMd Sp Wt 6 2 11½ 13 2hd 21¾ Cordero A Jr 117 *1.70 87-12 Bravo Native 117¾ Wayward Lass 117² Seaholme 117½ 2nd best 9
23Jly80- 4Bel sly 7f :23⅗ :47⅕ 1:24⅘ ⒻMd Sp Wt 3 4 2½ 2½ 24 29 Cordero A Jr 117 *1.50 71-22 Heavenly Cause 117⁹ Wayward Lass 117⁶ Zimbaba 117⁴½ 2nd best 8
2Jly80- 3Bel fst 5½f :22⅘ :45⅘ 1:05⅕ ⒻMd Sp Wt 8 6 32½ 45½ 47½ 35 Cordero A Jr 117 4.40 84-17 PrimeProspect 117½ QueenDesignate 112¾ WaywardLass 117 Wide 9
23Jun80- 4Bel fst 5½f :22⅘ :46⅖ 1:05⅘ ⒻMd Sp Wt 3 8 46 47 37½ 36 Cordero A Jr 117 6.30 82-15 Famous Partner 117² Shalomar 117⁴ Wayward Lass 117½ Rallied 9
LATEST WORKOUTS Jly 31 Sar 4f fst :48 b — Jly 21 Bel tr.t 4f fst :48⅘ b — Jly 16 Bel tr.t 4f fst :48⅘ b — Jly 11 Bel tr.t 4f fst :48 h
2FT Rail B.D.S

This One's Mine
Ch. f. 2, by One For All—Swizzle, by Nearctic — Br.—Jonabell Farm (Ky) — Tr.—Freeman Willard C — **117**
Own.—Bell J A III
St. 1st 2nd 3rd Amt. — 1980 1 M 0 0
1Aug80- 3Sar sly 6f :22⅕ :46⅕ 1:12⅘ ⒻMd 50000 7 10 106½ 109½ 89 79½ Skinner K 117 16.70 68-21 Picture Pretty 112½ Years Of Joy 117²¾ Miss List 115² Outrun 12
LATEST WORKOUTS Aug 9 Sar 5f fst 1:03 b — Jly 31 Sar 3f fst :37⅘ b — Jly 27 Sar 6f fst 1:15 b — Jly 23 Aqu ⊡ 6f sly 1:17⅘ b

Seaholme
B. f. 2, by Noholme II—Tim Pam, by Tim Tam — Br.—Live Oak Stud (Fla) — Tr.—Kelly Patrick J — **117**
Own.—Live Oak Plantation
Turf Record: St. 1st 2nd 3rd — 1 0 0 1
St. 1st 2nd 3rd Amt. — 1980 4 M 0 1 $3,180
4Aug80- 6Sar fm 1 Ⓣ:48⅗ 1:13⅗ 1:38 ⒻMd Sp Wt 9 8 86 56 55¾ 33¾ Cauthen S 117 12.00 85-12 Bravo Native 117¾ Wayward Lass 117² Seaholme 117½ Wide 9
23Jly80- 4Bel sly 7f :23⅗ :47⅕ 1:24⅘ ⒻMd Sp Wt 5 6 63½ 88½ 413 420 Maple E 117 20.50 60-22 Heavenly Cause 117⁹ Wayward Lass 117⁶ Zimbaba 117⁴½ Outrun 8
11Jly80- 4Bel fst 6f :23 :48 1:12 ⒻMd Sp Wt 11 6 64½ 86½ 712 817 Imparato J 117 21.40e 65-16 De La Rose 117¾ Bravo Native 117⁵¾ CircleGame 117hd Tired, wide 11
23Jun80- 4Bel fst 5½f :22⅘ :46⅖ 1:05⅘ ⒻMd Sp Wt 2 2 816 819 716 613 Saumell L 117 16.60e 75-15 Famous Partner 117² Shalomar 117⁴ Wayward Lass 117½ Outrun 9
LATEST WORKOUTS Aug 11 Sar 6f fst 1:14 h — Jly 31 Sar Ⓣ 6f fm 1:13⅘ h — Jly 19 Bel 5f fst 1:00⅕ h — Jly 5 Bel 5f fst 1:00 h
4T Move

Gdynia
Ch. f. 2, by Sir Ivor—Classicist, by Princequillo — Br.—Gaines & Johnson (Ky) — Tr.—Stephens Woodford C — **117**
Own.—Dekwiatkowski H
Turf Record: St. 1st 2nd 3rd — 1 0 0 0
St. 1st 2nd 3rd Amt. — 1980 2 M 0 0
4Aug80- 6Sar fm 1 Ⓣ:48⅗ 1:13⅗ 1:38 ⒻMd Sp Wt 1 5 64½ 87½ 77¾ 66¼ Maple E 117 3.90 82-12 Bravo Native 117¾ Wayward Lass 117² Seaholme 117½ Outrun 9
23Jly80- 4Bel sly 7f :23⅗ :47⅕ 1:24⅘ ⒻMd Sp Wt 1 7 31 44½ 514 625 McKnight R E 117 5.30 55-22 Heavenly Cause 117⁹ Wayward Lass 117⁶ Zimbaba 117⁴½ Slow start 8
LATEST WORKOUTS Aug 11 Sar 5f fst 1:00⅘ h — Jly 30 Sar 5f fst 1:00⅘ h — Jly 22 Bel 3f fst :34⅘ h — Jly 19 Bel 4f fst :48⅕ h
Rail

Lucky Ice
Ro. f. 2, by Icecapade—Lucky Jo Jo, by Mito — Br.—Thoroughbred Farm Inc (Ky) — Tr.—Barrera Albert S — **117**
Own.—Hughes L
St. 1st 2nd 3rd Amt. — 1980 1 M 0 0
26Jly80- 4Bel fst 6f :22⅘ :46⅗ 1:12⅘ ⒻMd Sp Wt 6 10 1111 1114 1119 1121 McHargue D G 117 19.60 59-16 Reality Island 117²¼ Bravo Native 117³½ Noura 117½ Outrun 11
LATEST WORKOUTS Aug 13 Sar tr.t 4f fst :50 b — Aug 6 Sar tr.t 4f fst :49⅘ b — Jly 21 Bel 4f fst :49⅘ bg — Jly 7 Bel 6f fst 1:18 b

In this grass race for maiden 2-year-olds, the only fillies who had displayed any signs of ability were the ones who had run against each other on August 4: Wayward Lass, Seaholme, Gdynia, and Zimbaba. While a handicapper might have stretched a point and looked for wakeups by some of the fillies who were making their debuts on the turf and were bred for it (M. for Mary, Laurial, Simba Sara, This One's Mine), I had nothing positive in my notes about any of them. And none of them was getting any notable betting action. Wayward Lass was the 6-to-5 favorite on the basis of her second-place finish in this company last time. Seaholme, who had lost to her by two lengths, was the 3-to-1 second choice. Gydnia was 6 to 1. To a student of the past performances, these prices would have seemed very reasonable. But any trip handicapper who had watched these horses run knew that the odds were dead wrong. My notes from the August 4 race read:

Wayward Lass	**2FT, rail B,T,S**
Seaholme	**4T move**
Gdynia	**rail**

In that race, Wayward Lass briefly stalked a longshot, took over from her, and moved to the rail, saved ground on the tight turns of Saratoga's inner turf course — and still lost after this easy trip. Gdynia had absolutely nothing to recommend her. But Seaholme had plenty of virtues. After breaking from the outside post position and trailing early, she had accelerated strongly while racing in the 4-path all the way around the turn. Even according to the crude rule of thumb that a horse loses a length for each path by which he is removed from the rail on the turn, Seaholme figured to improve by three lengths vis-à-vis Wayward Lass. In fact, ground loss on the sharp turns of the turf course is probably more significant than that. Moreover, the fillies' rematch was being run at $1\frac{1}{16}$ miles, giving Seaholme an extra sixteenth of a mile in which to catch Wayward Lass. Which she did.

SECOND RACE **$1\frac{1}{16}$ MILES.(Inner-turf). (1.42) MAIDEN SPECIAL WEIGHT. Purse $18,000. Fillies, 2-year-olds. Weight, 117 lbs.**

Saratoga

AUGUST 15, 1980

Value of race $18,000, value to winner $10,800, second $3,960, third $2,160, fourth $1,080. Mutuel pool $113,507, OTB pool $137,937. Track Quinella Pool $98,669. OTB Quinella Pool $172,369.

Last Raced	Horse	Eqt.A.Wt	PP	St	¼	½	¾	Str	Fin	Jockey	Odds $1
4Aug80 ^{6}Sar^3	Seaholme	2 117	8	9	$8^{\frac12}$	7^1	5^4	$1^{1\frac12}$	$1^{4\frac12}$	Fell J	3.20
4Aug80 ^{6}Sar^2	Wayward Lass	2 117	6	3	1^3	$1^{1\frac12}$	1^1	$2^{\frac12}$	$2^{2\frac14}$	Cordero A Jr	1.20
4Aug80 ^{6}Sar^5	Zimbaba	2 117	3	2	$2^{\frac12}$	2^{hd}	3^4	3^2	$3^{1\frac12}$	Vasquez J	15.40
7Aug80 ^{5}Mth^3	M. For Mary	2 117	1	1	6^2	$5^{\frac12}$	4^2	5^7	$4^{\frac12}$	Miranda J	5.30
4Aug80 ^{6}Sar^6	Gdynia	2 117	9	6	4^1	3^5	2^1	$4^{1\frac12}$	$5^{8\frac12}$	Maple E	6.50
1Aug80 ^{3}Sar^7	This One's Mine	2 117	7	4	3^1	$4^{\frac12}$	$7^{\frac12}$	7^2	$6^{2\frac14}$	McHargue D G	22.10
10Aug80 ^{4}Sar^{13}	Simba Sara	2 117	5	5	$7^{\frac12}$	$8^{\frac12}$	$8^{1\frac12}$	$6^{\frac12}$	$7^{2\frac14}$	Hernandez R	49.20
26Jly80 ^{4}Bel^{11}	Lucky Ice	b 2 117	10	10	10	10	10	$8^{\frac12}$	$8^{\frac12}$	Martens G	57.70
10Aug80 ^{6}Sar^7	Hazy Forest	2 112	4	8	9^2	9^1	$9^{\frac12}$	10	9^{nk}	Lovato F Jr^5	19.90
3Aug80 ^{4}Sar^8	Laurial	2 117	2	7	5^2	6^3	6^2	$9^{\frac12}$	10	Venezia M†	23.80

OFF AT 2:06, EDT. Start good, Won ridden out. Time, :24$\frac15$, :48$\frac25$, 1:13, 1:39$\frac35$, 1:46$\frac25$ Course good.

$2 Mutuel Prices:				
	1-(H)-SEAHOLME	**8.40**	**3.60**	**3.00**
	7-(F)-WAYWARD LASS		**2.80**	**2.40**
	4-(C)-ZIMBABA			**4.20**
	$2 QUINELLA 1-7 PAID $7.60.			

B. f, by Noholme II—Tim Pam, by Tim Tam. Trainer Kelly Patrick J. Bred by Live Oak Stud (Fla).

SEAHOLME, outrun early, moved boldly along the inside to catch the leaders approaching the final furlong and drew away. WAYWARD LASS made the pace into the stretch but was no match for the winner. ZIMBABA, close up early, split horses to make a bid leaving the far turn but tired during the drive. M. FOR MARY failed to be a serious factor. GYDNIA went after WAYWARD LASS racing into the far turn, remained a factor to the stretch and gave way. THIS ONE'S MINE was finished early. LAURIAL was finished early.

Owners— 1, Live Oak Plantation; 2, Flying Zee Stable; 3, Carl Suzanne F; 4, Burke W P; 5, Dekwiatkowski H; 6, Bell J A III; 7, Taylor Shirley H; 8, Hughes L; 9, Harbor View Farm; 10, Regent Farm.

Trainers— 1, Kelly Patrick J; 2, Martin Jose; 3, DiMauro Stephen; 4, Pierce Joseph H Jr; 5, Stephens Woodford C; 6, Freeman Willard C; 7, Maloney James W; 8, Barrera Albert S; 9, Barrera Luis; 10, Laurin Roger.

† **Apprentice allowance waived:** Laurial 5 pounds.

Scratched—Special Edition (1Aug80 ^{3}Sar^6); Fabled Morn (23Jun80 ^{4}Bel^7).

Seaholme had a relatively easy trip this time, getting through on the inside to win by 4½ lengths and pay $8.40. The result, by the way, did not have much predictive value for the horses' futures. Seaholme was never more than an average allowance-class runner, while Wayward Lass went on to be voted the champion 3-year-old filly in America the next season.

Pure trip-handicapping plays like this one don't materialize every day. Neither do situations where a horse has had such a blockbuster trip — a staggering amount of trouble, a blatant stiff job — that he deserves an automatic bet. But there are times when a handicapper's trip notes will become the basis of many wagers a day, when they will enable him to capitalize on the most profitable circumstances that the racing game can offer. Trip notes are indispensable and invaluable whenever a handicapper encounters a track bias.

THREE

Trips and Track Biases

O N THE THIRD WEEKEND in May 1982, the attention of the racing world was focused on Pimlico, where the Preakness Stakes was expected to confirm that Linkage was the best 3-year-old in America. Instead, the Preakness demonstrated something quite different: that the characteristics of a racing strip — its tendency to favor horses with certain running styles, posts, or positions on the track — can at times be the most important factor in the sport.

The inside part of the Pimlico track periodically seems to become harder and faster than the outside, so that the horse who gets to the rail first is an almost automatic winner. In 1977 I had enjoyed a spectacularly successful season at the Baltimore track by betting on horses with early speed and inside post positions. But Pimlico officials do not want these unfair conditions to mar their most famous race, and so they usually work on the track before the Preakness to make it uniform. These efforts appeared to have succeeded in 1982; two days before Linkage was expected to go to the post as an odds-on favorite the track was perfectly normal.

So no one could have anticipated what was going to happen on the afternoon before the Preakness. In the first race, the odds-on favorite led all the way to win. In the second race, a maiden named Work of Art, who had tired and lost a sprint by 16 lengths in her last start, was now attempting to go $1\frac{1}{16}$ miles. Breaking from post position two, she took the lead on the rail (which was expected), but when the stretch-runners moved outside her on the final turn, she brushed off their challenges and drew away to a decisive victory (which was amazing). Logical front-runners won the third, fourth, fifth, and sixth races. In the seventh race a colt named Beam Reach, who had tired and lost by 15 lengths against the same company a week earlier, broke from the No. 1 post position and led until the stretch. Then Ballroom Dancer, who had trounced Beam Reach in their previous meeting, made a powerful move in the 4-path and looked as if he were going to run away with the race. But Beam Reach bounded along the rail, regained command, and won by half a length. The evidence was incontrovertible: This racetrack had a powerful bias that would carry to victory almost any horse who got the lead on the rail.

On the day of the Preakness the bias still existed, although the evidence of it was not quite so obvious. Two horses did manage to win on the outside that day, but both were overwhelmingly superior to their opposition — stakes horses running in allowance company — and could have won if they had to run through a swamp. To the handicappers who recognized the strength of the bias, it was apparent that the outcome of the Preakness was going to be determined by the riders' tactics. Aloma's Ruler was the quickest horse in the field; if he had been breaking from an inside post position he might have merited an automatic play. Instead he was starting from the outside post, No. 7. Linkage, who also possessed early speed, was starting from the stall just inside him. Would Linkage and jockey Bill Shoemaker get to the rail and keep Aloma's Ruler off the favorable path? Or would jockey Jack Kaenel try to get Aloma's Ruler to the rail?

Every serious Pimlico regular understood the issues involved in the Preakness. The cognoscenti at the track are so attuned to the importance of biases that horses who lost their last starts by 20 or 30 lengths will often be favored if they figure to get the lead on the rail. But the majority of people in the crowd of 80,000 and the millions who were watching on television had no idea what was happening. ABC's commentators, Howard Cosell and Bill Hartack, made no reference to the most important factor in the race. Henry Clark, Linkage's veteran trainer, didn't know about the track bias. Neither did the legendary Shoemaker, who had ridden one of the two superior horses who had managed to win on the outside earlier in the day and thus misread the nature of the track.

Kaenel, the graduate of bush tracks in places like Rocky Ford, Colorado, had grown up with the credo that speed wins races, and since coming to Maryland he had learned that speed wins races at Pimlico especially often. So he hustled Aloma's Ruler out of the gate while Shoemaker played it cool, keeping Linkage under restraint. As Aloma's Ruler sprinted to the lead and dropped over to the rail at the first turn, Shoemaker kept Linkage in the 3-path and offered no resistance. Handicappers attuned to the importance of the bias knew that the 107th Preakness was history; what happened thereafter was a foregone conclusion. Aloma's Ruler stayed on the rail and led all the way. Linkage struggled in vain to overcome the bias and missed by half a length.

Three months later another colt, Conquistador Cielo, was trying to verify in the Travers Stakes at Saratoga that he was the best 3-year-old in America. He had won seven races in a row, by a combined total of 44 lengths; he was being widely hailed as a superhorse; he had recently been syndicated for the astonishing sum of $36.4 million, making him the most valuable thoroughbred in history. Despite his lofty reputation, some handicappers still harbored doubts about his ability to go the Travers distance, 1¼ miles, if he were pressured by Aloma's Ruler, who was once again cast in the role of a spoiler. When bias-oriented handicappers observed the nature of the racing strip on the day of the Travers, they could easily envision a scenario for Conquistador Cielo's defeat.

In the third race that day, an overwhelmingly superior 3-to-5 shot, Middle Stage, raced along the rail all the way and suffered a seemingly inexplicable defeat. In the fifth race, a solid figure horse named Prosper got through along the inside and momentarily looked like a winner, but faded badly as Dedicated Ruler rallied in the 5-path to score an easy victory. In the sixth race Timely Hitter swooped around the field to win, while the odds-on favorite Rising Raja ran a disappointing race in the 2-path. Nobody won on the rail all day; the Saratoga track was the very antithesis of Pimlico's.

Not only did observant horseplayers recognize that the rail was a disadvantage, but so did one jockey, Angel Cordero Jr. No rider in America is a keener student of track biases; no rider is more adept at maneuvering horses to take advantage of them. In the Travers he had the perfect opportunity to do so, for he was riding Aloma's Ruler and breaking from the outside post, No. 5, with Conquistador Cielo just inside him. The two colts raced abreast of each other to the first turn, and when they got there Cordero had pinned Conquistador Cielo and his jockey Eddie Maple on the rail. There was nothing Maple could do to extricate himself from this position, and so Conquistador Cielo stayed on the rail and Aloma's Ruler remained in the 2-path all the way around the track. Cordero's tactics won the battle but lost the war. While Aloma's Ruler beat Conquistador Cielo, longshot Runaway Groom stayed well away from the rail all the way, rallied in the 4-path through the stretch, and beat them both.

At the Travers and especially at the Preakness, good handicappers found themselves in a position that beginning horseplayers can scarcely imagine. When a newcomer gets involved in the game, he looks on insiders as all-knowing and all-powerful. He may believe that the only way to beat the game is to know what owners, trainers, jockeys, and their agents are thinking and doing and betting. Indeed, there are many circumstances when these insiders do possess crucial information — about the ability of a first-time starter, the condition of a horse who has been laid off, the health of a claiming horse who is being dropped in class sharply. Because the parimutuel system is a competition among bettors, the insiders do possess an edge in these circumstances; but when a bias exists, insiders usually don't have the perspective to deal with it because they are so wrapped up with their own horses. Never have I heard a trainer say, "I've got the best horse and he's in great shape, but I don't think he can overcome the bias." Neither Linkage's Hall-of-Fame trainer nor his Hall-of-Fame jockey was capable of making that observation. When a bias exists, it is the outsiders — the good handicappers — who have the edge.

The greatest winning streaks of my life have all occurred during a prolonged track bias: at Pimlico in 1977, Hialeah in 1979 and 1980, Saratoga in 1981. I have often thought that a gambler singlemindedly determined to make money playing the horses would be wise to monitor the results at tracks around the country, to go wherever he found a strong bias and stay there as long as it lasted. Lack of familiarity with the track would not hurt him much, because a horseplayer does not need an especially wide range of handicapping skills to win under such conditions. What he does need is the ability to watch races perceptively and the diligence to take thorough notes on them. This is where trip-handicapping skills pay off.

The first step in making money from a track bias is to recognize its existence — which is often not easy. Biases are mysterious and elusive phenomena; even professional track superintendents have difficulty explaining why they appear and disappear. I can only guess that one of the reasons for their existence is the fact that all race-tracks are banked, causing loose soil to drift and moisture to drain toward the rail. Another factor is the soil composition of the track. Moisture may have the same effect on a sandy racing strip that water does when it washes up on a beach, packing it down, making it hard. If moisture collects on the inside of a track with a high clay content, it may turn the rail into a big mudpie. But while biases often appear after a rainstorm, they sometimes occur without any change in the weather; there wasn't a cloud in the sky on the weekend when Aloma's Ruler won the Preakness. A horseplayer must judge the nature of a track by watching the way races are run over it.

This is one of the most fundamental parts of the whole handicapping process. The most frustrating and costly periods of my gambling life have usually come when I wasn't quite sure of the nature of the track where I was operating, when I wasn't sure whether a bias existed or not. I can deal reasonably well with any type of track — as long as I can identify the type. Either a track is normal or else it has a bias that will fall into one of four or five basic categories.

GOOD RAIL

When the inside part of a track is especially favorable, the signs of it are easy to detect. The majority of races are won by the horse who takes the lead and gets to the rail. Occasionally a come-from-behind runner may sneak up the rail, but typically such horses are forced to make their moves on the outside. When strong stretch runners swing into the 3- or 4-path on the turn as if they are about to make a big move, and then look as if they are running on a treadmill, a bias almost surely exists.

The most reliable indications of a rail bias are performances by horses that seem to contradict handicapping logic. It is theoretically possible, for example, that the best horse in most of the races on a day's card would happen to be a superior front-runner breaking from an inside post. Even if the track were perfectly uniform, a handicapper might easily form the conclusion that a bias existed. On August 5, 1982, at Saratoga, five races were run on the main track, and all five were won by horses who led all the way along the rail. I promptly concluded that we had seen a powerful track bias. Both Paul Cornman and Joe Cardello pointed out to me that four of the five winners were favorites, and that all the results made sense, but I was unswayed.

Maudlin, one of the horses who had won on the rail that day, was entered a week later against a rival he had narrowly beaten, Castle Knight. The track was normal now, and Castle Knight was sure to turn the tables. I was the guest handicapper that day at Saratoga's Paddock Club, where I was asked to analyze this race, and I warmed to the task. "I cannot bet Maudlin at 4 to 5!" I told the audience. "He cannot win! He will not win!" Maudlin promptly won by 8¼ lengths over Castle Knight, missing the track record by only two fifths of a second and suggesting that his victory the previous week had not been a bias-created fluke. Two of the other horses who had won on the rail that day came back to win subsequently, too. The track had indeed been normal.

The key to identifying a bias, then, is not to observe a preponderance of speed-on-the-rail victories, but rather speed-on-the-rail performances that don't make sense. On the day before the Preakness, the victory by Work of Art, the sprinter who was suddenly able to go 1¹⁄₁₆ miles, was the kind of strange result that strongly suggests the existence of a bias. The victory by the faint-hearted Beam Reach, who stayed on the rail to defeat a stretch-runner who had trounced him the week before, was another. When clearly superior horses cannot get past inferior horses on the rail, a bias is probably stopping them.

BAD RAIL

Sometimes the inside part of a track will be so disadvantageous that a bias is obvious. No horse can win anywhere near the rail. Horses

circling the field in the 8-path win race after race. More often, however, the evidence is somewhat subtle because the effects of a bad
rail will be offset to some extent by the advantage of saving ground
on the turns.

While the existence of a good rail can sometimes be deduced
from the implausible result of a single race, a handicapper needs an
accumulation of evidence before he can conclude that a rail is bad.
On many days at Saratoga in 1982, my roommates and I would come
home from the track in a state of bewilderment and ask each other,
"What happened today?" "Was the rail bad?" We would review our
trip notes, looking at the paths in which the winners had run, looking at the performances of horses who had been on the rail. If a bias
existed, horses in outside posts would usually outbreak those on the
inside. Horses would frequently make winning moves in the 3-path,
the 4-path, and beyond. Horses who appeared to take command and
then angled to the rail would falter. Stretch-runners who attempted
to rally on the inside would not be able to sustain their moves. When
two or three horses battled through the stretch, the one on the outside would usually prevail.

Even after all our analysis, though, the evidence sometimes remained ambiguous or misleading. More than once I decreed that the
track had been normal, only to see that horses who had raced on the
rail came back to improve sharply in their subsequent starts. Sometimes the only way to recognize a bad rail is with the benefit of such
hindsight.

SPEED-FAVORING TRACKS

After the first three days of the 1981 Saratoga season, the meeting
that was to prove the most lucrative of my life, I was losing $8000
and I couldn't understand why. The track seemed to be favoring
speed on the rail, just as Pimlico usually did, and I always expect to
win under such conditions. So I pored over the results and tried to
comprehend what was happening.

I have always understood rail-favoring biases, because I realize
that it is easily possible for the inside part of the track to become
harder and faster than the outside. I know that under such circumstances the horse who is fast enough to get to the lead on the rail

will usually be the winner. Even though speed horses win most of the time, this is still a rail bias, not a speed bias.

But at Saratoga in 1981 I was seeing a pure speed-favoring track. The racing strip was perfectly uniform from inside to outside, and yet the horse who took the early lead couldn't be caught. I can't conceive of an explanation for this phenomenon. I doubt that any track superintendent could identify a characteristic of soil that keeps even inferior, chronically faint-hearted horses from getting tired. Yet the condition existed, indisputably. Casual racing fans who followed the results at Saratoga that season from afar might have wondered how the lowly New York–bred Fio Rito beat stars like Winter's Tale and Noble Nashua in the Whitney Stakes. Or how the gutless 2-year-old Mayanesian beat Conquistador Cielo in the Sanford Stakes. Or how the untalented Willow Hour upset Pleasant Colony and Lord Avie in the Travers. They were all front-runners, and on that track they never got tired. On the day of Mayanesian's victory, every race on the main track was won by the horse who broke out of the gate on top. And in almost every race the horse who broke second maintained that position all the way around the track to finish second.

It is easy to spot a bias this strong, but it is important to distinguish it from a rail bias. If the rail is advantageous, a speed horse who duels for the lead on the outside is in the worst possible position. He will be parked away from the rail and will usually lose badly, not only to the front-runner inside him but also to horses in the second flight who rally up the rail. On a pure speed-favoring track, horses on the outside run as well and win as often as those on the inside.

Even when a powerful speed bias does exist, its effect can be somewhat negated by riders' recognition of it. At the California tracks, where every member of the jockey colony knows that front-runners have an advantage, horses are regularly hustled to get the lead in seemingly insane fractions. It is common to see claiming horses battling through a half mile in 44 seconds or so. Under such extreme pressure, horses may collapse — even on a speed-favoring surface — and lose to stretch-runners. But not very often.

CLOSERS' TRACKS

If a racing strip can favor speed horses, it seems logical that the converse should be possible: that there will be racing strips where stretch-runners dominate. In fact, they don't materialize very often. At Belmont Park in 1976 there was a 10-day period when not a single speed horse led all the way to win, but such conditions are extraordinary. The American racing game favors speed so much that I find it almost impossible to imagine a track where I would not bet on a superior horse because he was a front-runner.

CONTOUR BIASES

While most biases are due to idiosyncrasies in the racing surface, many tracks have shapes that influence the results. At tracks less than a mile in circumference, the sharp turns and short stretch almost always work to the advantage of front-runners and horses on the inside.

Almost any race that starts near a turn will favor horses on the inside. Even if there is a long race and a long stretch ahead — as in $1\frac{1}{8}$-mile races at Aqueduct or $1\frac{1}{16}$-mile races at Pimlico — the ground that horses save or lose on the first turn will often prove decisive. A few years ago I took a vacation to the Far East, where I lost a few thousand baht at the Royal Bangkok Turf Club but managed to recoup at the Macao Canidrome, the dog track on an island near Hong Kong. Although most of the past performances were in Chinese, I was able to win with an elementary perception, and then sent all my friends a post card of the dog track with the same message: "I have come halfway around the world to discover one of the eternal verities. When there is a short run to the first turn, bet speed on the rail."

Biases, of course, can come in many degrees of strength, from those that may affect the performances of horses slightly to those that can stop a Conquistador Cielo. But a handicapper cannot realistically hope to evaluate their relative strength with any precision — on a 1-to-10 scale, for example. I try only to divide them into two classes: biases that affect the outcome of races, and those so strong they virtually dictate the results. I maintain a notebook in which I list biases, day by day. When I start to handicap, I transcribe this information into my *Racing Form,* jotting it by the date of the horse's previous race in his past performances. For simplicity's sake I use the following designations:

GR	Good rail.
GR+	Very strong good rail.
BR	Bad rail.
BR+	Very strong bad rail.
S	Speed-favoring track.
S+	Very strong speed-favoring track.
C	Track that favors closers.

To evaluate any horse's trip, a handicapper must consider it in the context of the track over which he ran. If his trip notes read "3B 2T 3E" — meaning that a horse was running in the 3-path on the backstretch, the 2-path on the turn, and the 3-path as he entered the stretch — this would hardly be earth-shaking information if the track had been normal. But if the horse had run on a track with a GR+ bias, he had an eventful and difficult trip, being kept off the rail all the way. If he had run the same race on a track with a BR bias, he may have had a nearly perfect trip, staying off the rail without losing too much ground, either.

With this information, a handicapper will be able to see horses' past performances in a new and revealing light. Its applications should be readily apparent.

If a horse ran well with a bias in his favor, his performance should be substantially discounted. Victories by horses who lead all the way on the rail over tracks with an inside-speed bias should be ignored. It is often profitable to bet against such horses when they run again.

If a horse shows nothing while running against a bias, that loss can be ignored, and he can be evaluated on the basis of his previous starts.

If a horse raced creditably against a bias, he may deserve to be bet when he runs again. And if he raced impressively under adverse conditions, he may offer a sensational opportunity. Such opportunities can take many forms, but they are often both obvious and lucrative.

Nice Sailing — Ch. g. 6, by Sail On-Sail On—Nice To Us Kids, by Mighty Fennec
$20,000 Br.—Curley Mollie A (Md)
Own.—D & S Stable Inc — Tr.—Dutrow Richard E
115

Lifetime							
65 13 9 8	1982	7	2	1	1	$13,722
$119,990	1981	27	8	5	3	$67,630
	Turf	4	0	0	1	$1,338

GR	5May82- 4Pim	fst	1 1/16	:48⅕	1:12⅘	1:44⅕	Clm 14500	5	1	1 2½	1 6	1 8	1 18	Pino M G	114	2.60	84-23	Nice Sailing 114 18 Be A Joy 114 1½ February Thaw 107 4	Easily	6
	21Apr82- 9Pim	fst	1 1/16	:46⅖	1:10⅗	1:42⅗	Clm c-11500	1	1	1 1	1 ½	2 hd	1 1	Grove P	114	8.20	92-15	Nice Sailing [illegible] Bade's Ace 114 2¼ Fellow Heir 114 4	Driving	11
	15Apr82- 9Pim	fst	1 1/16	:47⅗	1:11⅗	1:44⅖	Clm c-8500	1	1	1 1½	1 1	1 1½	2 1	Pino M G	114	*2.40	82-14	Rollo 114 1 [illegible] nk Grasp 105 2½	Weakened	7
	29Mar82- 1Aqu	fst	1⅛	:49⅗	1:15⅕	1:55⅗	Clm 7500	3	3	2 1½	2 1	5 5½	6 9½	Santagata N	117	3.20	47-29	Paris Station 109 1 Surgeon Nate 112 no Ohno 117½	Tired	11
	27Feb82- 1Aqu	fst	1⅛	[•]:47⅖	1:13	1:53⅖	Clm 12500	1	6	6 13	6 8½	8 7¾	8 8½	Borden D A	117	11.40	70-16	Worthy of Praise 117 3½ Lancer's Pride 119¾ Catiline 112¾	Outrun	10
	3Feb82- 2Aqu	sly	1⅛	[•]:49⅘	1:16⅕	1:58⅘	Clm c-10000	2	1	1 hd	3 2½	7 12	10 21	Santagata N	117	6.70	31-37	Milliard 112 5¾ Prince Quince 115 1½ Worthy ofPraise108½	Stopped	10
	16Jan82- 1Aqu	fst	1⅛	[•]:49	1:13	1:53⅕	Clm 10500	7	2	2 1½	2 2	1 1½	3¾	Santagata N	113	14.90	79-10	Dumbo 114 hd Koru 117¾ Nice Sailing 113 2¾	Weakened	10
	19Nov81-10Med	fst	170	:46⅗	1:12	1:42⅘	3↑ Clm 10000	5	1	1 2	1 1	4 5	4 7½	Quinones F5	111	4.90	79-16	Super Sting 111½ Stevrullah 114 1½Lambidextrous109 5¾	Weakened	10
	7Nov81- 4Med	fst	1 1/16	:48	1:13	1:45⅕	3↑ Clm c-8000	7	1	1½	2 1½	3 5½	3 15	Lopez C C	116	*2.20	68-22	Super Sting 111 12 Stevrullah 119 3½ Nice Sailing 116 2½	Tired	9
	31Oct81- 4Med	fst	1 1/16	:48⅗	1:13⅘	1:46⅖	3↑ Clm 10000	9	10	11 11	7 5½	7 5¾	5 5¾	Lopez C C	115	*2.10	71-19	Millenium Falcon 118 nk LyricEcho115 3½PullACutie118 2	No threat	11

LATEST WORKOUTS May 19 Pim 5f fst 1:06 b

Ballroom Dancer * — B. g. 7, by Bold Hour—Gracefully, by Gallant Man
$25,000 Br.—Davison Mrs R (Md)
Own.—Cables H S Jr — Tr.—Patterson Pat
115

Lifetime						
46 10 8 8	1982	7	1	2	0	$13,568
$82,806	1981	13	3	2	3	$24,200
	Turf	7	0	0	2	$430

GR+	14May82- 7Pim	fst	1 1/16	:47⅕	1:12⅗	1:45	Alw 14600	5	6	7 8½	5 2¼	1 hd	2½	Cooke C	113	10.30	79-21	Beam Reach 113½ Ballroom Dancer 113 no Haligoluk 114 4½	Wide	7
	4May82- 8Pim	fst	1 1/16	:47	1:12⅗	1:45⅘	Alw 14600	1	8	6 13	6 3¾	4 2	4 5¼	Cooke C	113	5.50	71-27	Ixatapa 114[illegible] Brave Bar 116 no [illegible] Sale 119 3½	Outrun	8
	1Apr82- 8Pim	fst	1 1/16	:46⅕	1:11	1:43⅘	Alw 12000	2	6	7 21	5 7½	3 6	4 3¾	Ford E	113	12.00	82-29	Pol Luka113[illegible]Renunciator118½Crown[illegible]Cross112 nk	Clipped heels	7
	26Feb82- 7Bow	fst	1 1/16	:47⅘	1:12⅘	1:45⅗	Clm 32500	2	7	7 15	7 11	5 6	4 8¼	Ford E	113	16.10	70-28	ForcedBusing107 5SanguineSword114 nkLederOfThePck119 3	Wide	8
	8Feb82- 6Bow	fst	1 1/16	:48⅖	1:13⅖	1:46⅘	Clm 23500	5	7	7 11	6 6¼	3 1	1 no	Ford E	114	3.60	72-24	BallroomDancer114 noTheAustrinCount114 3Hligoluk114 nk	Driving	8
	27Jan82- 8Bow	fst	1 1/16	:48⅘	1:12⅖	1:43⅘	Alw 13500	2	7	7 9	7 14	7 9¼	6 2¾	Ford E	113	5.00	84-15	Dawn Parade 109 nk Preconsent 116 1 Wargate 113½	Swung out	7
	6Jan82- 7Bow	fst	1 1/16	:50⅕	1:15⅖	1:47⅗	Alw 13500	1	6	5 4	4 4	3 2	2 2¼	Ford E	113	4.70	66-33	BlackieDaw119 2¼BallroomDancer113 1CrftyExchnge113 2½	Gamely	6
	26Dec81- 4Lrl	fst	1	:48	1:14	1:39⅘	3↑ Clm 25000	2	6	6 4½	1 1½	1 1	2 hd	Ford E	119	2.70	73-22	Best Man 113 hd Ballroom Dancer 119 2½Simetrico112 nk	Just failed	6
	5Dec81- 9Lrl	gd	1	:47⅖	1:13⅘	1:40	3↑ Clm 25000	6	9	7 6¼	5 1¼	3 2½	3 4	Ford E	119	9.30	68-25	StrightSets115 3Terullh113 1BllroomDncer119 2¾	Poor st.,lost whip	9
	26Nov81- 5Lrl	fst	1	:47⅗	1:13⅖	1:40⅖	3↑ Clm 22000	4	8	7 10	7 5¾	3 2	1½	Ford E	115	6.30	70-29	BllroomDncer115½VirginTerritory108 hdPlyfulChester112 nk	Driving	8

Nice Sailing and Ballroom Dancer were the principal contenders in the 1 1/16-mile eighth race at Laurel on May 25, 1982. On the surface, Nice Sailing had the more glittery credentials. He had won his last start by 18 lengths, and his final time was worthy of a $50,000 animal. My speed figures gave him a 3½-length edge over Ballroom Dancer.

But Nice Sailing had run this race over a rail-favoring track and had taken the lead on the inside without any difficulty or pressure. He had scored his previous victory over a normal track, but he had broken from post position one and stayed inside all the way at the 1 1/16-mile distance at Pimlico, where horses with speed and inside posts always fare well. Two victories, two perfect trips.

Ballroom Dancer, by contrast, had had nothing but bad trips. On April 1, according to the past performances, he "clipped heels." On May 4, over a rail-favoring track, he had started from post one, but my notes read "4T 5E"; he had been parked four-wide around the turn but had still managed to finish respectably well. Ballroom Dancer's most recent race was positively sensational. On the day before the Preakness, over a track that could be rated GR+ if there ever was one, my notes said "4T move." Ballroom Dancer had accelerated boldly in the 4-path and had lost by only a half length to a rival who was hugging the rail. He was virtually the only horse all day who gave a good performance while racing so wide. Yet the betting public couldn't perceive his virtues on the basis of the past performances. Ballroom Dancer was 4 to 1, with Nice Sailing the even-money favorite.

Ballroom Dancer rallied to win in a photo finish over an out-of-town invader and paid $10.20. Nice Sailing finished third, seven lengths farther back, without a bias to help him.

•   •   •

Graustell	B. c. 3, by Graustark—Tales To Tell, by Donut King					
Own.—Andrade F	Br.—Jones Aaron U (Ky) Tr.—Azpurua Leo		119		St. 1st 2nd 3rd	Amt.

Entered 26Jan79- 5 GP

16Jan79- 5GP fst 1 1/16 :48 4/5 1:14 2/5 1:46 4/5	Md Sp Wt	9 2 1hd 64 511 516	Lopez R D	b 119	40.70	51-28 Son Of Glad 1181 Dragon Slayer 1198 King of Jig 1102	Tired 11
6Jan79- 3Crc fst 6f :23 :46 4/5 1:11 4/5	Md Sp Wt	6 9 89 713 69 69	Lopez R D	b 122	50.20	84-11 Mark Son	Outrun 12
29Dec78- 4Crc fst 6 1/2f :22 3/5 :45 4/5 1:20	Md Sp Wt	3 7 89 916 811 89 3/4	Smith A Jr	b 120	17.90	76-14 Denny's Choice 120hd Jordann 120hd Linda 120no	No factor 12
30Aug78- 5Crc fst 6f :23 1/5 :46 4/5 1:13 1/5	Md Sp Wt	2 7 812 813 813 713	Guzman R	118	4.60	73-15 Three Fold 1181 1/4 BeauBegga 110 Cooma	Swerved in 8

LATEST WORKOUTS   Dec 23 Crc 7f fst 1:31 3/5 b   Dec 20 Crc 3f fst :36 h   Dec 9 Crc 5f fst 1:02 b

There weren't many virtues evident in the past performances of Graustell, but when he appeared in a seven-furlong maiden race at Gulfstream I saw a chance not only to make money for myself but to help a friend.

My pal Carlos was vacationing in Miami, but on the previous day at the track his net assets had dropped to $1.90 and he was preparing to go back to Washington. On the morning of Graustell's race, however, I called him at the motel where he was packing and said, "Scrape up a few dollars somehow. We can make money today."

Carlos showed up at the track along with another Washington visitor named Mitch, and I proceeded to expound on Graustell's merits. During the early stages of the Gulfstream meeting, the rail had been so deep that even newspaper turf writers were making an uproar about it. All the winners were making their moves in the 3-path, the 4-path, and beyond. Graustell had run on one of these biased tracks, and my notes read, "Strong move rail to lead." I told Carlos, as Mitch listened attentively, that this was one of the very few horses who had accelerated strongly on the inside at the whole meeting; most horses weakened as soon as they got near the rail.

When Graustell paid $48.40 to win and produced an exacta pay-off of $998.20, Carlos had recouped the costs of his vacation. But the greatest beneficiary of my opinion was Mitch, who left the track that day with several thousand dollars. While serious handicappers share their opinions with each other freely, a novice who benefits from someone else's cerebration is expected to show his gratitude in some tangible way. Racetrack etiquette demands it. I decided that when Mitch asked me what would be appropriate, I would mention that I had seen in a Washington jewelry store a lovely pair of cufflinks, consisting of 18-karat gold horse heads embedded with little diamond eyes. As we celebrated our triumph at dinner that night, however, Mitch didn't ask the question for which I had prepared my answer. In fact, he didn't even volunteer to pick up the dinner check.

I didn't make a vulgar scene. Instead I merely wrote a column for the *Washington Post* on the general topic of racetrack etiquette, citing Mitch's ingratitude as the most despicable behavior I had ever witnessed. He moved from Washington not long after that. I hope he took with him more than an appreciation of the importance of watching horses who make big moves on bad rails.

• • •

After losing much money in the first few days of the 1981 Saratoga meeting, I realized that I had failed to perceive the existence of a pure speed-favoring bias. But I belatedly got the chance to capitalize on this phenomenon on August 6, when the track had temporarily returned to normal and Royal Jove was entered in a seven-furlong race.

Royal Jove had run only four days earlier and had raced in the 5-path all the way around the turn — a trip that would have been tough on any type of track. But on that highly speed-favoring surface, his chances of coming from behind with such a move were nil. Under the circumstances, his four-length loss was not a bad performance. (His previous start was much better than it looked, too; my notes said "Check B sharply.") I bet a cold daily double combining Royal Jove with a Monmouth shipper I loved in the second race. When Royal Jove won and paid $11.40 and the double returned $91.80, I was off and running at Saratoga.

• • •

Brasher Doubloon — B. c. 3, by Riva Ridge—Clear Copy, by Copy Chief
Own.—Brant P — Br.—Brant P M (Ky) — Tr.—Martin Frank — **113**

	St.	1st	2nd	3rd	Amt.
1981	11	2	2	0	$31,480
1980	0	M	0	0	

GR	28Aug81- 7Bel	fst	6f	:22⅖	:45	1:10⅕	3↑ Allowance	5	5	67¼	56½	55	53½	Maple E	114	2.50e	87-18	Delay of Game 122^{3} Carte Blanche 117^{nk} Sly Flyer 117no	Wide	8
S+	12Aug81- 7Sar	gd	6f	:22⅕	:45	1:09⅗	3↑ Allowance	2	7	64	64	67¼	49¼	Vasquez J	117	*2.40	83-12	Band Practice 113¾ [illegible] Dance 117^{4¾} Copper Mine 112¾	Rallied	7
S	1Aug81- 6Sar	fst	7f	:23⅕	:45⅖	1:21⅘	3↑ Allowance	3	6	64¼	52	43¼	45½	Maple E	117	3.50	87-12	LordDarnley112^{nk} [illegible]H.1124¼ Cinnmon'sChoice114^{1}	Hit gate	6
	18Jly81- 4Bel	fst	6f	:22⅖	:45⅗	1:10⅖	3↑ Allowance	5	2	87¾	72¾	11	12	Maple E	116	5.80	90-15	BrsherDoubloon116^{2} [D] WsHeFuzzy1112¼ AcdmyH.114^{hd}	Drew clear	9
	29Jun81- 3Bel	fst	7f	:23⅕	:46⅕	1:23⅘	3↑ Md Sp Wt	2	6	42	52	1hd	11¼	Maple E	114	3.50e	83-15	BrsherDoubloon1141¼ FelGood1143½ StonwllChmp114^{hd}	Drew clear	10
	5Jun81- 6Bel	fst	6f	:22⅗	:45⅘	1:10⅘	3↑ Md Sp Wt	2	8	97¼	96¼	52½	21	Pincay L Jr	117	5.80	87-17	RedWingPrince114^{1} BrsherDoubloon117^{no} SecretSilvr114^{no}	Rallied	13
	20May81- 6Bel	fst	7f	:23	:45⅘	1:24⅕	3↑ Md Sp Wt	1	2	11½	1½	3½	56	MacBeth D	113	4.70	75-20	John Casey 124½ Quarter Move 113¾ Acaroid 113½	Weakened	12
	2May81- 4Aqu	gd	7f	:23⅕	:47	1:24	Md Sp Wt	9	1	31½	22	24	25	Migliore R^{5}	117	5.60	76-19	BestCannon122^{5} BrsherDoubloon117^{nk} Mre'sPlesure122^{2}	Game try	9
	16Apr81- 5Aqu	fst	7f	:22⅘	:45⅗	1:25⅖	Md Sp Wt	3	5	1hd	2hd	717	719	Fell J	b 122	10.80	55-25	Adventure 122¾ Prince Merlin 122^{hd} Emperor's Lad 122½	Tired	7
	8Apr81- 5Aqu	fst	6f	:22⅖	:46	1:11⅗	Md Sp Wt	5	5	53½	45	57½	615	Fell J	122	2.60	69-22	San Saba 122^{6} Turn For More 122^{3} B. K. Todd 117^{2}	No factor	7

LATEST WORKOUTS ●Sep 5 Bel tr.t 4f fst :46 h ●Aug 26 Bel tr.t 4f fst :47 h ●Aug 19 Sar 4f fst :46⅘ h Aug 8 Sar 5f fst :59 h

4T

Sometimes a succession of bad trips can obscure a horse's ability almost beyond recognition. Just about anyone studying the past performances of Brasher Doubloon would conclude that he had gone off form after winning two races in the summer of 1981. A trip handicapper knew otherwise.

On August 1, another of those speed-favoring days at Saratoga, Brasher Doubloon had an impossible trip. My notes said: "Check G (2L) 4T vs no pace." He had trouble at the start, breaking two lengths behind the field; the *Racing Form*'s chart-caller saw what I didn't, that he had hit the side of the gate. Brasher Doubloon tried to rally in the 4-path on the turn, but in vain. Not only was the track speed-favoring, but the front-runners were setting a very slow pace and they would have been hard to catch under any circumstances. The next time he ran, August 12, I wrote a column in the *Washington Post* describing the awful things that had happened to Brasher Doubloon and advising my readers to mortgage their homes and bet on him. By the time of the race, however, I knew he had no chance. I had never seen a track so speed-favoring; I would have rated it S+++ if I had such a designation. This was the day when every race was won by a horse leading from wire to wire, when Mayanesian beat Conquistador Cielo. With his stretch-running style, Brasher Doubloon had no chance.

So I looked forward to seeing him at Belmont Park, where stretch-running horses have traditionally performed well, and when he was entered there on August 28 I flew to New York for the occasion. To my chagrin, a rail bias materialized from out of the blue that day. Almost every race was won by a horse on the rail; nobody won outside the 2-path; speed horses were dominant. Brasher Doubloon tried to rally in the 4-path on the turn and, as usual, could not overcome the bias.

When he finally got a chance to run on a normal track in a seven-furlong allowance race on September 7, Brasher Doubloon's form was so well-concealed that he could have paid a tremendous price. But fate wasn't kind to the trip handicappers who had been watching all his travails. Trainer Frank Martin had entered him in the race with a stablemate, Hit the Road Jack, who had run six furlongs in 1:10⅗ in his last start and whose merits were readily apparent to any casual handicapper. When Brasher Doubloon won by two lengths, with his stablemate second, he paid a measly $8.60, rewarding the people who had liked Hit the Road Jack equally with those who had been following Brasher Doubloon for weeks. Who says there is justice in the world?

• • •

Pollster was another horse whose ability was hidden almost beyond recognition. I had to do plenty of work in order to detect it.

The year before, in 1981, I had made my annual foray to Florida just in time for the opening of the Gulfstream season. I had compiled sets of speed figures that would enable me to compare invaders from New York, Kentucky, Illinois, New Jersey, and Maryland with the resident Florida horses who had been campaigning at Calder. I had done extensive analyses of the trainers who would be operating there. But all this preparation had not helped me a bit. For more than two months, a strong rail-favoring bias had existed at Calder, and it was virtually impossible to evaluate any of the horses who had raced there without knowing where they had been on the track. I handicapped ineffectually as a result, but I vowed that this wouldn't happen again. When I saw in November that the same type of bias had reappeared at Calder, I went there in December to do my homework. I didn't bet much, but I watched every race closely and made note of every horse's position on the biased track. When the prime part of the Florida season began at Hialeah, I was prepared.

I had seen Pollster have an extremely difficult trip on December 26. My notes said "4FT held out there 3T." After breaking from the No. 11 post position, he had raced in the 4-path all around the first turn, without being able to drop to the inside. He advanced into contention, but then had to race three-wide around the final turn and dropped out of it. In his two other recent races, he had the disadvantage of breaking from posts 11 and 10. When he was entered in a seven-furlong race on January 20, I could not make a case that he was a cinch, but I knew that he was much better than a 20-to-1 proposition. When he won clearly and paid $42.40, I felt that my diligence had been properly rewarded.

In order to handicap properly on a biased track, a horseplayer must know more than the nature of the trips the horses have had in their previous starts. He must anticipate what kind of trips they will have today. A horse like Brasher Doubloon may have had an impossibly difficult trip in his last start, but he cannot be bet if he is going to be parked wide on an inside-speed track again.

When the rail is bad, there will rarely be one clear standout on the basis of a bias. A handicapper may feel safe in disregarding speed horses with inside post positions, but several horses will probably be eligible to make moves on the outside. A bettor will have to employ all the usual fundamentals of handicapping to decide who is best.

On a strong rail-favoring or speed-favoring track, however, he must try to forget the fundamentals, to disregard most of his usual handicapping methods, and look single-mindedly for the horse who will be able to capitalize on the bias.

When there is only one speed horse in a field, he will usually deserve an automatic bet. When there is more than one speed horse, a handicapper must decide if one has superior quickness that will enable him to get clear of the rest. To make this judgment I do not rely solely, or even principally, on the fractional times of horses' previous races. I look for horses who get to the front frequently. I examine their previous races to see whom they have dueled with or outrun. In route races, I prefer horses who have been running in sprints recently.

If two or more horses competing on a rail-favoring track seem to have roughly equal speed, the one breaking from the innermost post position has a significant advantage. In order to get to the rail from the outside, a horse must outrun his rivals by about two lengths before he can get clear and drop over. That is not easy to do.

One other important factor in determining the horse likely to take advantage of a bias is the jockey. Some riders are keenly aware of what they must do to win on an inside-speed track. Angel Cordero was once riding a plodder who was breaking from post No. 7 on a rail-favoring track at Saratoga and figured to have absolutely no chance because of the bias. With any other jockey, he wouldn't have. But Cordero warmed him up vigorously before the race, and when the gate opened he whipped the horse about 20 times in the first eighth of a mile. The startled animal went to the lead for probably the first time in his life, dropped over to the rail, and led all the way. But there aren't many Corderos. There are also riders like Jeffrey Fell and Mickey Solomone who have such a fondness for the 6-path that they often find a way to get there with a speed horse breaking from the inside post.

Nothing frustrates a bias-oriented handicapper so much as finding a horse has the capability to get to the lead on the rail, and then watching the jockey fail to capitalize on the advantage he has. While an extreme rail bias existed at Hialeah, Paul Cornman felt he was being victimized with unusual frequency by the misjudgment of his jockeys, and he attempted to remedy the problem in a way that other horseplayers might consider.

"I liked a horse named Sib's Future, who had some speed and had the ability to get the lead on the rail," Paul recalled. "But the jockey was Brian Long and he had shown through his riding that he didn't understand the track. I wanted to tell him but I knew I couldn't yell at him or I'd just sound like another one of the irate fanatics. So when he was going out to the track from the paddock I said as calmly as possible, 'Every winner has been on the inside. You're 20 to 1 but if you hustle to the rail you'll win.' "

Long hustled, got Sib's Future to the rail, and led all the way, returning a $43.20 payoff that got Paul out of the doldrums. As Long walked back to the jockeys' room he gave Paul a little nod, as if to acknowledge that he appreciated the advice.

Encouraged by this success, Paul offered the same kind of assistance a couple of days later to jockey David Dennie, who had also been displaying a lack of awareness of the bias. Dennie proceeded to stay in the 3-path all the way around the track and lost with a horse who was many lengths the best, forcing Paul to fall back on the forms of discourse that usually characterize bettors' communication with jockeys: abuse, invective, and character assassination.

Even though a horseplayer will inevitably lose some decisions that he deserved to win, he will prosper on a biased track if he steadily and consistently plays horses who will take advantage of the conditions. While the rail bias existed at Hialeah in 1979 I was in such a groove, handicapping every race by trying to diagnose the horse who would take the lead on the rail. Sometimes this analysis would produce betting opportunities that looked almost ironclad, as in the second race on March 27.

② HIALEAH 〔7 FURLONGS〕

7 FURLONGS. (1.20⅘) CLAIMING. Purse $3,500. 4-year-olds and upward. Weights, 122 lbs. Non-winners of two races since January 17 allowed 3 lbs. A race since then 5 lbs. A race since January 3 8 lbs. Claiming Price $3,500.

Occult

Dk. b. or br. g. 4, by Jacinto—Amalesian, by Ambiorix
$3,500
Own.—Merrill Mrs F H
Br.—Claiborne Farm (Ky)
Tr.—Merrill Frank H

								St. 1st 2nd 3rd	Amt.
						119	1979 2 1 0 1	$3,300
							1978 16 2 3 3	$14,069

LATEST WORKOUTS Feb 22 GP

*Malalhue

Ch. g. 5, by Naspur—Managua, by Mataslete
$3,500
Own.—Hays T E
Br.—Haras El Bosque (Chile)
Tr.—Plesa Edward Sr

			Turf Record			St. 1st 2nd 3rd	Amt.
		114	St. 1st 2nd 3rd		1979 3 0 0 0	$140
			12 2 0 0		1978 13 2 0 1	$1,367

LATEST WORKOUTS Mar 3 Crc

Peludo

Ch. c. 4, by Viejo & Peludo—Pot Pocker, by Third Martini
$3,500
Own.—Peppermint Racing Stable
Br.—Peppermint Farm Inc (Fla)
Tr.—Opperman Wayne

					St. 1st 2nd 3rd	Amt.
		114			1979 1 0 0 0	$210
					1978 6 0 0 0	$2,737

LATEST WORKOUTS Mar 23 Crc

Hi Neck Ken

Dk. b. or br. h. 6, by Big Burn—Sugar River, by Flying Relic
$3,500
Own.—Bee Bee Stables Inc
Br.—Callahan J (Fla)
Tr.—Tortora Emmanuel

					St. 1st 2nd 3rd	Amt.
		112			1979 6 0 1 0	$878
					1978 14 1 3 2	$4,506

LATEST WORKOUTS Mar 19 Crc

Baywood's Magnum

Ch. g. 6, by Watch Your Step—Run the Table, by Beau Gar
$3,500
Own.—Cataldi T
Br.—Neubeck E Jr & Harriet (Fla)
Tr.—Cataldi Tony

					St. 1st 2nd 3rd	Amt.
		119			1979 5 1 0 0	$2,445
					1978 21 3 4 2	$12,353

LATEST WORKOUTS Feb 28 GP

Watanagreement

B. g. 6, by Hard Work—Fair Fashion, by Rippey
$3,500
Own.—Hobojo Racing Stable
Br.—Prox J (Ky)
Tr.—Hough Stanley M

					St. 1st 2nd 3rd	Amt.
		109 5			1979 1 0 0 0	$44
					1978 21 1 2 9	$7,775

LATEST WORKOUTS Mar 24 Crc

Bella Pruner — B. c. 4, by The Pruner—Zabel, by Crazy Kid — $3,500 — Br.—Burbank L D (Fla) — Tr.—Yowell Edward — 109^5
Own.—Sturz & Theobald

	St.	1st	2nd	3rd	Amt.
1979	1	M	0	0	$48
1978	4	M	0	0	$195

Date/Race	Cond	Dist	Fractions	Class	PP St Calls Fin	Jockey	Wt	Odds	Speed	Company	Comment
21Feb79- 1GP	fst	7f	:23 :46⅕ 1:24⅗	Clm 5000	1 12 9^4 12^15 11^22 11^25	Milonas J	b 114	69.90	57-13	Holiday Prince 119¾ Junior Hop 116^1½ Tony's Game 114¾	Outrun 12
22May78- 2Crc	fst	6f	:22⅘ :46⅘ 1:13⅗	3↑ Md 5000	6 10 10^8½ 9^14 6^7½ 5^6	Giovanni J	116	11.80	78-15	Daughter Ange 114^1 MeanSea106^1½ DollyO'Donovan111½	No threat 10
8May78- 1GP	fst	6f	:22⅗ :45⅘ 1:11⅗	3↑ Md 10000	9 12 12^8¾ 11^9½ 11^16 10^17	MacBeth D	b 115	25.30	64-17	TitleBsin115^3 ActsLikeAJudge110^2½ SevntysixthFloor115^1½	Outrun 12
4Apr78-10GP	fst	6f	:22⅗ :46 1:10⅘	Md 13000	5 11 11^12 10^18 10^21 8^22	Fell J	b 117	36.20	63-23	Inkolater 120^2 High Asthe Sky 111^5 FatherHalford120^2	No factor 12
10Mar78- 3GP	fst	7f	:22⅘ :45⅘ 1:24⅕	Md 25000	12 8 8^5¾ 8^7 8^9 8^11	Stahlbaum G	b 117	80.90	72-21	No Moleste 117^3½ Rolla'sDancer117¾ BornDictator120^2½	No factor 12
2Dec77- 1Crc	fst	7f	:23⅗ :47⅗ 1:28⅘	Md 12500	6 1 1^hd 4^2½ 8^7½ 7^7½	Smith A Jr	b 120	15.00	66-19	Young Whiz 120^1½ Pazzo 120½ Ramblin Dude 120^1½	Early speed 8
18Nov77- 3Crc	fst	7f	:23⅕ :47 1:27⅘	Md 15000	9 1 3^2½ 4^3½ 7^6½ 8^8	Jimenez I J^5	b 115	11.90	71-13	Marion's Bliss 108½ Mighty Behaving 120½ Sensinita 120½	Tired 12
7Nov77- 3Crc	fst	1	:48⅗ 1:14⅗ 1:41	Md Sp Wt	1 1 1^2 3^2½ 5^6¼ 5^12	Castaneda K	b 118	18.60	72-11	Kuma San 118^1 Dylan 118^6 Notable Attire 118^2½	Tired 9
19Oct77- 5Crc	fst	6f	:23⅕ :46⅘ 1:12⅗	Md 22000	9 1 2½ 5^7 9^15 9^21	Jimenez I J^7	b 113	10.10	69-11	Viscount Scope 120^3½ Crafty Bull 120^3½ Dylan 120^3	Tired 9
3Oct77- 3Crc	fst	6f	:23 :47⅗ 1:13⅘	Md Sp Wt	7 4 5^4 5^10 6^11 6^13	Cespedes R	b 120	37.10	71-15	GentlemanPlus120^no RedLicorice120^4 ReggieF.120^nk	Shuffled back 8

LATEST WORKOUTS Mar 24 GP 5f fst 1:01 hg Mar 19 GP 3f fst :36 hg Mar 14 GP 5f fst 1:02 hg Mar 10 GP 3f fst :37⅘ bg

Hidden Proof — Blk. g. 4, by Issue—Popeyes Proof, by Prove It — $3,500 — Br.—Hidden Lane Stables (Md) — Tr.—Maziarz Henry — 104^10
Own.—North Cove Stable

	St.	1st	2nd	3rd	Amt.
1979	2	0	1	1	$1,180
1978	12	1	1	1	$4,808

Date/Race	Cond	Dist	Fractions	Class	PP St Calls Fin	Jockey	Wt	Odds	Speed	Company	Comment
14Mar79- 1Hia	fst	6f	:22⅘ :46⅗ 1:13⅗	Clm 3500	6 5 3^2 4^2½ 3^nk 2^nk	Riera R Jr	114	3.20	76-15	Noble Landing 114^nk Hidden Proof 114^1½ Peludo 114^2½	Sharp 11
5Mar79- 1GP	fst	7f	:22⅕ :46 1:26⅗	Clm 3500	11 2 4^2½ 2½ 2^hd 3^2½	Riera R Jr	114	13.70	69-24	Little Cawky 117¾ ALittleBold114^hd HiddenProof114^nk	Weakened 12
16Dec78- 7Suf	fst	6f	:22⅘ :46⅘ 1:12⅘	3↑ Clm 5500	1 5 4^nk 5^3 6^6½ 7^5½	Feagin C	b 112	4.00	72-24	Broadwayat[illegible] 11[illegible] Ichabod 114^2 [illegible]joe 115no	Tired 11
7Dec78- 7Suf	sl	6f	:22⅗ :47⅕ 1:14⅗	3↑ Clm 6250	5 4 6^8 6^10 6^7½ 5^5½	Swatman W	b 115	6.60	62-41	Belmont T[illegible] Diamond J[illegible] 117^1½ [illegible]pleScore116^1½	Outrun 7
27Nov78- 4Suf	fr	6f	:22⅗ :45⅗ 1:10⅕	3↑ Clm 7500	5 1 2^1 3^3½ 4^4 5^6½	Swatman W	b 112	8.10	83-14	Foxy Raja 117^1½ Bompie 114^2¾ Liberty's Host 115¾	Tired 8
16Nov78- 8Suf	fst	6f	:22⅗ :46⅕ 1:12⅘	3↑ Clm 7500	3 4 5^8 6^10 7^8¾ 5^6½	MacCormack R^5	111	9.00	72-28	Syntab 114¾ Bompie 114^2¾ Liberty's Host 115no	Outrun 7
6Jly78- 7Rkm	fst	6f	:22⅘ :45 1:09⅘	3↑ Clm c-5500	8 3 3½ 5^6 7^11 6^14	Carrozzella M	b 109	2.20	81-12	Arthur Boy 114^4½ Poker Chief 114^nk Signal Keys108^5	Brief speed 10
18May78- 2Pim	my	6f	:23⅘ :47⅗ 1:14⅕	Clm 6500	7 2 7^6½ 7^5½ 5^5 5^3½	Gilbert R B	b 119	4.50	72-33	Rough Devil 114^1 Icy Behavior 114^1 Twin Tee's 109^1	No mishap 7
9May78- 5Pim	gd	6f	:23⅗ :47⅗ 1:13⅘	Clm 6000	6 1 3^1 4^1½ 2^hd 1^2	Gilbert R B	b 112	2.80	77-24	Hidden Proof 112^2 Oat Duster 114^1 Bold Vicar 109^1½	Drew clear 8
25Apr78- 2Pim	fst	6f	:23⅗ :47 1:12⅘	Clm 5000	6 3 5^3¾ 4^6½ 3^5 2^4	Drury M A	b 112	8.80	80-24	Twin Tee's 112^4 Hidden Proof 112^1 Serene Road 107^7	Gamely 10

LATEST WORKOUTS Mar 3 GP 5f fst 1:02⅘ bg Feb 24 GP 3f fst :38⅘ b Feb 19 GP 5f fst 1:01⅗ b

Prontian — B. g. 5, by Indian Chief II—Candy Aglo, by Candy Spots — $3,500 — Br.—Kingwell R A (Fla) — Tr.—Geiger Larry — 114
Own.—Kaytes Adrienne

Turf Record	St.	1st	2nd	3rd
	7	0	0	1

	St.	1st	2nd	3rd	Amt.
1979	3	0	0	0	$143
1978	18	1	2	1	$5,712

Date/Race	Cond	Dist	Fractions	Class	PP St Calls Fin	Jockey	Wt	Odds	Speed	Company	Comment
22Feb79- 2GP	fst	1¼	:46⅘ 1:38 2:03⅘	Clm 3500	2 4 4^11 4^12 5^12 6^19	Aviles O B	b 114	9.50	59-20	Harmony T. 114^8½ Parisino 119½ Pure Silk 112^3¾	Tired 10
9Feb79- 4GP	fst	1¼	:48⅕ 1:40⅗ 2:06⅘	Clm 5000	3 6 5^5½ 6^4½ 7^9¾ 10^17	Giovanni J	b 114	9.20	46-29	Don Lunes 114^2½ Macao III 122^2 Pumpernickle 117^nk	Outrun 12
13Jan79-11Crc	fst	1⅛	:48⅗ 1:14 1:53⅘	Clm 6000	2 6 6^4½ 6^4 5^4½ 5^3½	Aviles O B	116	16.30	82-12	Jolly Host 105^hd Fair Sport 116^3 Lead OnMcduff110^nk	no mishap 9
30Dec78-10Crc	fst	1 1/16	:49 1:14 1:47⅕	3↑ Clm 6500	5 6 6^5½ 6^7 5^5 4^5	Aviles O B	116	27.10	78-10	Force Seven 109^1½ Dr.Sprunt111^2 Pumpernickle116^1½	Lacked rally 10
19Dec78-10Crc	fst	1 70	:47⅗ 1:13⅗ 1:44⅗	3↑ Clm 7500	6 6 4^6½ 7^7½ 8^8¾ 8^8¼	Aviles O B	b 116	11.90	80-13	April's Hideaway 113^1½ Royal A. 113½ Batekoa 119^nk	Tired 11
10Nov78-10Crc	gd	*1 ①	1:41⅗	3↑ Allowance	3 5 5^4½ 5^5½ 7^6½ 6^7	Bailey J D	b 118	11.60	75-18	Splode 117^1 [DH]Ceeaye 108 [DH]Yellow Ribbon II 116^1	Tired 8
3Nov78- 9Crc	fm	*1 ①	1:39⅗	3↑ Allowance	4 6 6^6½ 6^6½ 5^6½ 4^7	Aviles O B	b 118	30.90	84-12	[D]VorheesDiplomt118^hd ErlofSpokne107^6 SummerBrez113^1	Outrun 6
12Oct78-10Crc	fst	1 70	:49⅕ 1:15⅕ 1:47	3↑ Md 5000	1 3 4^2 2^3 2^1 1^4	Bailey J D	b 122	*1.70	76-18	Prontian 122^4 Audrey's Boots 115no [DH]Pumpernickle 117	Driving 12
28Sep78-10Crc	fst	1 1/16	:48⅗ 1:14 1:48⅗	3↑ Md 5000	3 8 6^8¾ 7^10 5^8½ 4^7½	Aviles O B	b 122	*1.40	69-16	Willy Dude 116^4 Not That Brave 116^2 DaccaDelta106^1½	No threat 11
24Aug78-10Crc	fst	1 1/16	:49⅗ 1:15⅘ 1:49	3↑ Md 5000	9 10 6^4 4^4½ 3^1½ 2no	Aviles O B	b 122	*1.20	74-16	Rangle's Edition 114no Prontian 122^1½ NotThatBrave114^1½	Missed 12

LATEST WORKOUTS Mar 25 Crc 3f fst :37 b Mar 19 Crc 3f fst :38 b Mar 9 Crc 5f fst 1:04 b Mar 3 Crc 3f fst :37 b

Half Greek — B. g. 4, by Greek Page—My Half, by Anzio Landing — $3,500 — Br.—Blythe & Mullen & Wood III (Ind) — Tr.—Garcia Mario — 114
Own.—Norton Farm

	St.	1st	2nd	3rd	Amt.
1979	4	0	0	0	$167
1978	15	1	1	2	$3,886

Date/Race	Cond	Dist	Fractions	Class	PP St Calls Fin	Jockey	Wt	Odds	Speed	Company	Comment
12Mar79- 2Hia	fst	1⅛	:47⅗ 1:12⅗ 1:51⅗	Clm 3500	8 3 3^1½ 7^14 11^24 11^34	Garcia J O	b 114	102.50	40-21	Simply Dynastic 114^1 Joan's Boy 114^5 Malign 114^2½	Tired 12
15Feb79- 1GP	fst	1 1/16	:47⅘ 1:12⅕ 1:44⅕	Clm 3500	4 8 8^15 8^9½ 8^20 9^23	Garcia J O	b 114	123.30	57-21	Parisino 114^5 Like Daddy 114no Bruce Trail 114^2½	Outrun 12
1Feb79- 1GP	fst	1 1/16	:48⅕ 1:13⅗ 1:46⅘	Clm 3500	10 8 6^8½ 10^9¾ 11^8½ 10^12	Garcia J O	b 114	88.80	55-19	El Penquista 114^4 Diaghilev 119^1½ FiddleDumbDee109¾	No factor 12
11Jan79- 5Crc	fst	6f	:22⅕ :45⅘ 1:12⅗	Clm 4000	7 8 10^16 10^22 10^12 7^12	Garcia J O	b 116	282.00	77-15	Golden Sherry 116^2 First Watch 116^2 Flint Star 112^3	No factor 12
26Dec78- 1Crc	fst	1 70	:48⅕ 1:14⅕ 1:45⅗	3↑ Clm 5000	11 7 9^11 8^9½ 10^12 10^7½	Garcia J O	b 115	102.90	75-15	Francis Light 118^1 Structural 118^1½ AdvanceDancer111^1	No speed 12
16Dec78- 4Crc	fst	7f	:23⅕ :46⅗ 1:27	3↑ Clm 5000	11 10 9^10 10^14 9^18 9^13	Garcia J O	b 116	98.80	68-13	Cheerful Steve 118^1 Structural 118^hd Flint Star 113^3	Outrun 12
20Nov78- 2CD	fst	1⅛	:50 1:16 1:55⅕	3↑ Clm 3000	3 2 2^1½ 2^hd 2^hd 2^2	Espinoza J C	b 114	7.30	64-23	Bosun Talks 117^2 Half Greek 114^1½ Ligur 119^3	Gamely 12
15Nov78- 2CD	sly	1 1/16	:49⅘ 1:16⅘ 1:51⅘	3↑ Clm 3250	12 12 12^17 11^9½ 11^18 11^18	Espinoza J C	b 115	18.90	31-29	Restless Energy 117½ Regal Rose 110^2 J. Artest 120^2½	No factor 12
6Nov78- 4CD	fst	1 1/16	:48⅕ 1:14⅕ 1:49⅗	3↑ Clm 3000	9 5 5^8 3^7 1^hd 5^4½	Espinoza J C	114	4.80	55-25	KingofAction119^hd MidnightAmber117^1½ TioWilson114^nk	Gave way 12
1Nov78- 2CD	fst	1 1/16	:48⅘ 1:15⅕ 1:49⅕	3↑ Clm 3250	9 9 8^13 9^8¾ 11^12 11^18	Espinoza J C	b 115	3.80	44-23	Rullah Judy 112^1 DashingPhil122^5 Woudn'tChuckIt119^1	No factor 12

LATEST WORKOUTS Feb 10 Hia 4f fst :48 b

Occult had run impressively in his first start of the year, winning by five lengths against the same $3500 claiming company he was facing now. His subsequent nine-length defeat may have looked on the surface like a poor performance, but trip handicappers knew otherwise. On a rail-favoring track, Occult broke from the No. 11 post position, raced in the 5-path around the turn, and was carried even wider as he turned into the stretch. Under the circumstances, his effort was not a bad one at all. He was clearly the superior horse in the field and figured to win — if he got a decent trip.

Occult was breaking from post position three, and the two horses inside him were so hopelessly slow that they could not prevent him from getting to the rail. Nor did any of the horses on the outside appear fast enough to outrun Occult and drop over to the rail. Baywood's Magnum did not have sprint-quality speed. Watanagreement had some early foot, but the combination of a three-month layoff and a drop in class made his physical condition highly suspect. Occult figured to hold the rail all the way, and when a superior horse has a bias in his favor he almost never loses. Yet the crowd was betting Hidden Proof, who had absolutely no chance; the No. 10 post position would insure that he had a bad trip, and his speed figures suggested that he was 10 lengths inferior to Occult anyway.

SECOND RACE

Hialeah Park

MARCH 27, 1979

7 FURLONGS. (1.20⅗) CLAIMING. Purse $3,500. 4-year-olds and upward. Weights, 122 lbs. Non-winners of two races since January 17 allowed 3 lbs. A race since then 5 lbs. A race since January 3 8 lbs. Claiming Price $3,500.

Value of race $3,500, value to winner $2,100, second $630, third $350, fourth $140, balance of starters $35 each. Mutuel pool $37,494. Perfecta Pool $31,115. Trifecta Pool $24,518.

Last Raced	Horse	Eqt.A.Wt	PP	St	¼	½	Str	Fin	Jockey	Cl'g Pr	Odds $1
10Mar79 2Hia3	Occult	b 4 119	3	7	3½	2¹	1½	1¹	Claessens N.	3500	3.10
12Mar79 1Hia1	Baywood's Magnum	b 6 119	7	5	1¹½	1hd	2²	2nk	Gaffglione R	3500	6.90
17Mar79 12Hia11	Malalhue	5 114	4	8	5¹	4¹	5⁴	3¹	Capodici J	3500	19.10
28Feb79 1GP9	Hi Neck Ken	b 5 112	6	11	6¹	5¹½	4½	4¹½	Lewis C D7	3500	46.90
14Mar79 1Hia2	Hidden Proof	b 4 107	10	1	7hd	9¹½	6¹½	5no	Ussery R A10	3500	3.00
5Jan79 4Crc6	Watanagreement	b 6 109	8	6	2hd	3⁴	3½	6³	Penna D5	3500	5.10
22Feb79 2GP6	Prontian	b 5 114	11	4	10hd	117	8½	7¾	Aviles O B	3500	23.20
12Mar79 2Hia11	Half Greek	b 4 114	12	2	116	10½	106	8nk	Gavidia W	3500	146.10
21Feb79 1GP11	Bella Pruner	b 4 109	9	3	4½	6¹½	9½	9²½	Guerra W A5	3500	32.70
14Mar79 1Hia3	Peludo	b 4 114	5	9	8¹	7³	7¹½	108	Danjean R	3500	3.00
21Mar79 2Hia9	Mrs Rosena O.	4 109	1	10	9³	8hd	11	11	Lee M A	3500	60.30
14Mar79 1Hia7	Homer's Jenny	7 104	2	12	12	12	—	—	Bueno O K Jr10	3500	38.70

Homer's Jenny, Bled.

OFF AT 1:45 EST. Start good, Won driving. Time, :23⅗, :46⅗, 1:13, 1:27 Track fast.

$2 Mutuel Prices:			
3-OCCULT	8.20	6.00	4.00
7-BAYWOOD'S MAGNUM		5.80	4.20
4-MALALHUE			9.00

$2 PERFECTA 3-7 PAID $53.40. $2 TRIFECTA 3-7-4 PAID $561.00.

dk b or br. g, by Jacinto—Amalesian, by Ambiorix. Trainer Merrill Frank H. Bred by Claiborne Farm (Ky).

OCCULT raced along the inside, gained the advantage in midstretch and continued on determinedly to the finish. BAYWOOD'S MAGNUM moved to a clear early lead, but could not keep pace with the winner in the final sixteenth. MALAHUE raced forwardly and was gaining slowly at the finish between horses. BI NECK KEN raced forwardly, but could not appreciably gain ground in the final eighth. HIDDEN PROFF had a mild stretch response. WATANAGREEMENT could not keep pace. PELUDO lacked a rally. HOMER'S JENNY bled and fell in midstretch.

Owners— 1, Merrill Mrs F H; 2, Cataldi T; 3, Hays T E; 4, Bee Bee Stables Inc; 5, North Cove Stable; 6, Hobojo Racing Stable; 7, Kaytes Adrienne; 8, Norton Farm; 9, Sturz & Theobald; 10, Peppermint Racing Stable; 11, Rodriguez Mrs E; 12, Clevenger L P.

Trainers— 1, Merrill Frank H; 2, Cataldi Tony; 3, Plesa Edward Sr; 4, Tortora Emanuel; 5, Maziarz Henry; 6, Hough Stanley M; 7, Geiger Larry; 8, Garcia Mario; 9, Yowell Edward; 10, Opperman Wayne; 11, Rodriguez Eugene; 12, Clevenger Lawrence P.

Overweight: Hidden Proof 3 pounds.

Occult was claimed by Kern H; trainer, Edmundson Samuel M; Hidden Proof was claimed by David & Demora; trainer, David Samuel B Sr.

Scratched—Gracious Sage (19Mar79 1Hia11); Praise Maker (17Feb79 2OP10); Dasher Don (14Mar79 1Hia8); Flying Ambassador (8Mar79 2Hia11); Gallant Crew (15Mar79 1Hia5).

$2 Daily Double 1–3 Paid $29.80. Daily Double Pool $68,982.

Results like the $8.20 payoff on Occult (as well as the $53.40 exacta with Baywood's Magnum) made the 1979 Hialeah season a very profitable one for me, and I hoped that the bias would reappear the next season. My prayers were answered; during the first few weeks of the 1980 meeting the bias was as strong as ever.

One day during this period a mutual friend introduced me to Frederick Exley, author of the autobiographical novel *A Fan's Notes,* which the *Washington Post*'s book critic puts in his list of the best works of fiction written by an American in this century. I was somewhat awed to be in the presence of such a literary giant and a bit apprehensive when the giant asked me if I liked anything on the day's program. My record as a tout leaves something to be desired; whenever I try to pick a winner for a boss, a pretty girl, or someone I'd like to impress, fate usually intervenes to make me look foolish. But I opened the *Racing Form* to the past performances for the second race and gave Exley a brief lecture on track-bias handicapping.

2 HIALEAH — START — 6 FURLONGS HIALEAH — FINISH

6 FURLONGS. (1.08⅗) CLAIMING. Purse $5,000. Fillies, 3-year-olds. Weight, 121 lbs. Non-winners of three races since January 8 allowed 2 lbs. Two races since then, 4 lbs. A race since then, 6 lbs. Claiming price $11,500; for each $500 to $9,500 allowed 1 lb. (Races where entered for $7,500 or less not considered.)

Amber Maid — Ch. f. 3, by Good Knight—Classy Terry, by Solicitor — $9,500 — Br.—Twin Pine Farm Inc (Fla) — Tr.—Rigione John H — Own.—South Shore Stable — 111

Turf Record	St.	1st	2nd	3rd			St.	1st	2nd	3rd	Amt.
	1	0	0	0		1980	3	0	0	0	$180
						1979	12	2	2	0	$8,750

15Feb80-10Hia	gd 6f	:22⅖ :46 1:11⅗	ⒻClm 10000	8 7	88½ 88¾ 58½ 59¾	Williams L R		115	37.80	76-15	Pleasure Jennie 1154½ Solo Et 1151¾ Go Pride 115no	No threat	12
25Jan80- 2Hia	fst 6f	:22⅗ :46⅘ 1:12⅘	ⒻClm 8000	4 10	97¼ 96¾ 58½ 515	Ashcroft D		104	7.50	64-22	PermanentSolution1173PleasureJennie11510RedGp117¾	No factor	12
16Jan80- 6Hia	fm 1 1/16 Ⓣ	1:42⅖	ⒻClm 22500	1 8	89¾ 1117 1125 1128	Brocklebank J	b	112	42.10	58-10	Knightly Noble 1161¼ Romantic Mood1147LondonAce1121	Outrun	12
6Dec79- 5Crc	fst 7f	:23⅖ :47⅕ 1:28⅖	ⒻClm 15000	3 6	53½ 54½ 47½ 412	Vasquez J	b	115	5.00	62-20	Good and Hasty 1092½ Chula 1145CaptivatingDiana1144	No factor	6
22Nov79- 2Crc	fst 170	:48⅕ 1:13⅘ 1:45⅘	ⒻAllowance	9 2	42½ 57½ 714 820	Breen R	b	113	64.80	61-18	Jill's Glory 1122 Country Skooter 114no Tibb's Girl 1142	Tired	9
16Nov79- 5Crc	fst 170	:49 1:15⅗ 1:48⅖	ⒻClm 11500	3 3	31½ 11½ 12 1hd	Vasquez J	b	115	3.90	68-20	Amber Maid 115hd Proud Gambler 114nkBelleMaryse1162	Driving	6
8Nov79- 6Crc	fst 6f	:22⅘ :46⅘ 1:13	ⒻClm 12500	3 5	54½ 55 45 48¼	Hilburn K D5	b	111	25.60	79-16	Clara's Bid 1144½ Rough Stepping 1143½GreekArk112nk	No factor	9
25Oct79- 3Crc	fst 6f	:23⅗ :48⅕ 1:15⅕	ⒻMd 10500	3 1	1hd 1hd 13 18	Hilburn K D5	b	109	2.30	76-20	Amber Maid 1098 Sunny O. 11610 Nomorefreebees 11416	Handily	4
28Sep79- 6Crc	fst 6½f	:23 :47⅕ 1:21⅖	ⒻMd 10500	8 1	12 21 67¼ 712	Jimenez I J	b	113	9.60	66-20	Proud Gambler115nkCaptivatingDiana1172½Degustation117½	Tired	9
22Aug79- 4Crc	fst 6½f	:23⅖ :47⅕ 1:21⅖	ⒻMd 12500	8 7	41½ 53½ 1012 1110	Jimenez I J	b	117	7.60	68-12	Greek Ark 1122 Buckalassie 110nk Country Skooter 110hd	Tired	11

LATEST WORKOUTS Feb 14 Hia 3f fst :35⅖ h — Feb 5 Hia 5f fst 1:04 b — Jan 9 Hia 4f fst :48⅗ h — Jan 5 Hia 3f fst :37 b

Don'Tu Just Luvit — Ro. f. 3, by Cutlass—Syncom, by Old Pueblo or Nashville — $11,500 — Br.—Equidae Stables (Fla) — Tr.—Draper Manley — Own.—Rogers A S & R — 108[7]

Turf Record	St.	1st	2nd	3rd			St.	1st	2nd	3rd	Amt.
	1	0	0	0		1980	3	1	0	0	$3,065
						1979	17	1	2	6	$9,997

12Feb80- 2Hia	fst 6f	:23 :46⅖ 1:12⅕	ⒻClm 14000	8 3	75¾ 711 613 715	Brumfield D		114	17.40	67-20	She's The One 1091½ Taradith 114hd Becky Bumps 11510	Outrun	11
29Jan80- 8Hia	fm *1⅛ Ⓣ	1:50	ⒻAllowance	7 4	54 98½ 910 925	Lee M A	b	114	92.60	57-12	Arisen 1141½ Erin's Word 1181 Esdiev 1143½	Tired	9
11Jan80- 4Crc	fst 7f	:23⅕ :47⅖ 1:28⅘	ⒻClm c-10000	8 2	22 3nk 1hd 11½	Hussey C	b	114	*1.60	72-19	Don'TuJustLuvit1141½BisquitDncr116noMyRdWing118hd	Drew out	8
26Dec79- 3Crc	fst 170	:49 1:15⅘ 1:47⅗	ⒻClm 14000	3 2	1hd 1hd 32 35	Lee M A	b	114	*1.20	67-18	Fan For Air 1143LondonAce1152Don'TuJustLuvit1141½	Weakened	6
8Dec79- 9Crc	sly 1 1/16	:47⅗ 1:13⅘ 1:46	ⒻMiss Dade	2 11	1115 1112 1018 927	Smith A Jr	b	112	121.70	62-14	Sober Jig 1195 Sweet Audrey 116½ Karla's Enough 119nk	Outrun	11
8Nov79- 9Crc	fst 170	:48⅕ 1:14⅕ 1:46	ⒻAllowance	5 5	57½ 57½ 56¼ 35	Smith A Jr		112	50.40	75-16	Knightly Noble 1141Tibb'sGirl1144Don'TuJustLuvit112hd	Mild bid	6
11Oct79- 7Crc	fst 7f	:23⅘ :48⅕ 1:27⅘	ⒻClm 10000	6 3	32 32½ 23 27	Bailey J D	b	114	2.60	70-19	Rizzo'sBest1147Don'TuJustLuvit114¾BllMrys114nk	Best of others	6
2Oct79- 1Crc	fst 6½f	:23⅖ :47⅗ 1:21	ⒻClm 12500	4 2	31 44½ 56 43	Guerra W A5	b	109	2.60	77-17	Alysia N. 1162½ My Red Wing 114hd Buckalassie 116½	Tired	7
24Sep79- 6Crc	fst 6f	:22⅗ :46⅗ 1:13⅖	ⒻClm 14000	7 7	76¼ 77¼ 46 36½	Smith A Jr	b	114	6.00	78-17	Jill's Glory 1153½ Clara's Bid 1143Don'TuJustLuvit114¾	No threat	8
31Aug79- 8Crc	fst 6½f	:22⅘ :46⅘ 1:20⅗	ⒻClm 16000	8 9	912 89½ 58½ 57	Vergara O	b	115	4.40	75-16	Tomar's Love 1143½ Set The Hop 1161 Greek Ark 1111	Outrun	9

It Was There — B. f. 3, by Highbinder—Chives, by Roman Patrol — $11,000 — Br.—Rosoff A (Fla) — Tr.—Edmundson Samuel M — Own.—Lorraine & Cindy Stable — 107[7]

	St.	1st	2nd	3rd	Amt.
1980	1	M	0	0	$110
1979	0	M	0	0	

30Jan80- 8Hia	fst 7f	:23⅖ :46⅗ 1:24⅖	ⒻAllowance	11 2	95 1119 1128 1132	Guerra W A		115	164.80	49-22	Cerada Ridge 1156 PollyannaPatrick1151RoseOfMorn121½	Outrun	11

LATEST WORKOUTS Jan 6 Crc 3f fst :39⅖ b — Jan 3 Crc 5f fst 1:03⅘ b — Dec 22 Crc 3f fst :39⅗ b

Red Gap
Own.—3 T's Stable $9,500
Dk. b. or br. f. 3, by Stopgap—Red Fog, by Old Man Red
Br.—Three T's Stable (Fla)
Tr.—Pierce Joseph H Jr

			St.	1st	2nd	3rd	Amt.
111		1980	2	1	0	1	$3,020
		1979	8	M	0	3	$1,928

25Jan80- 2Hia fst 6f :22½ :46½ 1:12½ ⓕClm 10000 5 8 86½ 53½ 37 31³ Anderson J 50 117 21.10 66-22 PermanentSolution117³PlesureJennie115¹⁰RedGap117³ No mishap 12
11Jan80- 2Crc fst 6f :23 :47½ 1:22¾ ⓕMd 7500 7 6 44½ 66½ 31½ 11 Anderson J 120 11.10 72-19 Red Gap 120¹ Go Ride 120ⁿᵒ Procession 120³ Driving 11
26Dec79- 2Crc fst 6f :23¾ :48½ 1:15½ ⓕMd 7500 8 2 51½ 31½ 2½ 3³ Anderson J R b 119 5.40 73-18 Spanish Throw 119ⁿᵒHint 119ⁿᵒRed Gap 119⁴ Hung 10
13Dec79- 2Crc fst 6f :23½ :47½ 1:20½ ⓕMd 7500 9 3 31½ 22 2⁵ 41³ Anderson J R b 119 3.50 68-16 Az 1 Honey 117¹Estrey¹⁴⁹¹¹ Minna 116² Weakened 9
21Nov79- 4Crc fst 6f :23½ :47½ 1:14¾ ⓕMd 6500 7 9 42½ 33 2⁵ 7¹ Langone R⁷ b 111 5.20 72-18 Rio Lady 109⁴ Nahua 115²½ Red Gap 111ʰᵈ Evenly 12
28Sep79- 4Crc fst 6f :23 :47½ 1:21¾ ⓕMd 10500 6 5 65½ 67 89½ 81³ Hilburn K D⁵ b 108 13.70 65-20 ProudGambler115ⁿᵏCaptivtingDin117²½Degusttion117½ No factor 12
19Sep79- 4Crc fst 6f 1:14 ⓕMd 10000 9 1 31½ 44½ 64½ 67½ Danjean R b 117 4.30 75-13 Blessed Dancer 113¹½ Tiny Tiny117¹M.B.'sRuler113ⁿᵏ Sp'd for 1/2 11
31Aug79- 6Crc fst 6f :22½ :46½ 1:13½ ⓕMd 20000 7 6 64½ 44½ 61¹ 81² Danjean R b 117 10.20 74-16 Alysia N. 113¹½ Money Does All1157⁵CountessSatan117½ No factor 8
15Aug79- 4Crc fst 6f :22½ :46½ 1:14 ⓕMd 20000 1 6 42½ 42½ 2³ 34½ Gaffalione S⁵ b 112 15.10 77-14 Knightly Noble 117¹ Evening Gambler 112³½RedGap112ⁿᵏ Rallied 8
8Jun79- 6Crc fst 5½f :22¾ :46½ 1:06½ ⓕMd Sp Wt 6 9 76½ 71² 6¹³ 51⁷ Gaffalione S⁵ b 111 62.20 77-13 PrivteAudition119½Tibb'sGirl116¹WeilKtPrincess116³½ No factor 10
LATEST WORKOUTS Jan 5 Crc 4f fst :49½ b

My Red Wing
Own.—Daybreak Farm $11,500
Ch. f. 3, by Wing Out—Majestic Hostess, by Majestic Prince
Br.—Daybreak Farm (Fla)
Tr.—Kelley Bill P

			St.	1st	2nd	3rd	Amt.
110⁵		1980	2	0	0	1	$641
		1979	3	1	0	0	$8,332

GR 12Feb80- 2Hia fst 6f :23 :46¾ 1:12½ ⓕClm 14000 10 9 97½ 69½ 411 61³ Long B⁵ 47 109 43.70 69-20 She's The One 109¹½ Taradith 114ʰᵈ BeckyBumps115¹⁰ No threat 11
11Jan80- 4Crc fst 7f :23½ :47½ 1:28¾ ⓕClm 10000 3 5 32 1ʰᵈ 43½ 3¹½ Bailey J D 55 115 9.50 70-19 Don'TuJustLuvit114¹½BsqutDncr116ⁿᵒMyRdWng118ʰᵈ Came again 8
27Dec79- 1Crc fst 6f :22½ :47½ 1:15 ⓕClm 7500 3 7 74½ 63½ 3ⁿᵏ 1¹ Bailey J D b 112 2.30 77-17 My Red Wing 112¹ Horty 116ⁿᵏ Morn o' Goshen 112¹ Driving 9
19Oct79- 1Crc fst 6f :21½ :46½ 1:12½ ⓕClm 12000 2 7 61⁴ 61⁰ 47 49½ Breen R b 113 23.50 78-16 Jill's Glory 111² Rizzo's Best 116⁵½ Clara's Bid 108² Outrun 7
11Oct79- 7Crc fst 6f :23½ :47½ 1:27¾ ⓕClm 10000 5 6 53½ 53½ 46½ 48 Guerra W A⁵ b 109 *1.40 69-19 Rizzo's Best114⁷Don'TuJustLuvit114²½BelleMaryse114ⁿᵏ No factor 9
20ct79- 1Crc fst 6½f :22¾ :47½ 1:21 ⓕClm 12500 1 7 53½ 66½ 35 22½ Breen R b 114 9.60 77-17 Alysia N. 116²½ My Red Wing 114ⁿᵏ Buckalassie 116½ Rallied 7
24Sep79- 4Crc fst 6f :22½ :46½ 1:13¾ ⓕClm 16000 4 5 43½ 46½ 67½ 57¾ Woodhouse R b 114 8.40 77-17 Jill's Glory 115³½ Clara's Bid 114³ Don'Tu Just Luvit 114½ Tired 8
31Aug79- 8Crc fst 6f :22½ :46½ 1:20¾ ⓕClm 16000 4 8 78½ 91¹ 71⁰ 45½ Breen R b 114 20.10 76-16 Tomar's Love 114¹½ SetTheHop116¹GreekArk111¹ Altered course 9
22Aug79- 3Crc fst 6f :22¾ :46½ 1:20¾ ⓕClm 21500 1 6 65 59½ 58 51⁰ Winant R b 113 11.90 72-13 Mom's Jewel 114² Sage Advice 107¾ Ell'sKatyDuz116⁴ No factor 7
3Aug79- 4Crc fst 6f :22½ :46½ 1:20¾ ⓕClm 16000 2 6 76 71² 6¹³ 517 Winant R b 115 12.10 75-15 GoandHsty115¹½SweetShkeeFnny114²Clr'sBid118¹½ No factor 7
3Aug79-Placed fourth through disqualification
LATEST WORKOUTS Jan 26 Hia 4f fst :50 b Dec 22 Hia 6f fst 1:17 b

Blessed Dancer
Own.—Allen Curley $11,500
Dk. b. or br. f. 3, by Bless Business—Nat A Dancer, by Natidan
Br.—Sikorski E (Fla)
Tr.—Rose Harold J

			St.	1st	2nd	3rd	Amt.
115		1980	1	0	0	0	$200
		1979	3	1	0	0	$2,803

25Jan80- 2Hia fst 6f :22½ :46½ 1:12½ ⓕClm 10000 2 4 42 43 47 41⁴ Danjean R 49 115 33.70 65-22 Permanent Solution 117³ Pleasure Jennie115¹⁰RedGap117½ Tired 12
16Oct79- 7Crc fst 6½f :23 :47½ 1:21½ ⓕClm c-6500 5 2 1½ 3ⁿᵏ 69 616 Capodici J 116 *1.10 61-19 High Class 116³½Fist Chic112²Tammie AnnJr.109³½ Tired 6
24Sep79- 6Crc fst 6f :22½ :46½ 1:13¾ ⓕClm 16000 6 2 3ⁿᵏ 56½ 816 819 Capodici J 114 7.60 66-17 Jill's Glory 116¹ Clara's Bid 114⁴ Don'TuJustLuvit114½ Gave way 8
19Sep79- 4Crc fst 6f :22½ :46½ 1:14¾ ⓕMd 9000 2 3 11½ 11½ 12 11½ Capodici J 113 38.60 82-13 Blessed Dancer 113¹½ Tiny Tiny 117¹ M. B.'s Ruler 113ⁿᵏ Driving 11
LATEST WORKOUTS Feb 7 GP 4f fst :50½ b Jan 3 Crc 4f fst :50 b Dec 28 Crc 3f fst :36 h

French Dressing
Own.—Dogwood Stable $11,500
Ch. f. 3, by Hearts of Lettuce—Parlez Valentine, by Needles
Br.—Leon Mr-Mrs R (Ky)
Tr.—Alexander Frank A

			St.	1st	2nd	3rd	Amt.
114		1980	2	1	0	1	$3,250
		1979	7	1	0	0	$4,805

4Feb80- 2Hia fst 6f :23½ :48½ 1:27½ ⓕClm 11000 6 7 21½ 11½ 24 38½ Rivera M A 48 114 4.60 55-29 AllezYane112⁶½FeatherReward112²FrenchDressing114² Weakened 12
7Jan80- 4Crc fst 6½f :23 :47 1:20¾ ⓕClm 7500 8 6 33½ 2ʰᵈ 14 14 Rivera M A 74 114 4.10 83-18 FrnchDrssing114⁴PrmnntSoluton112¾BsqutDncr113³ Ridden out 11
25Dec79- 2Crc fst 6f :22½ :47½ 1:28¾ ⓕClm 12500 4 4 22 22½ 36 47½ Rivera M A 58 114 5.00 74-19 She's The One 112²½ HoneyMaudie114¹¹HalterQueen113¹½ Weakened 7
6Dec79- 5Crc fst 7f :23½ :47½ 1:28¾ ⓕClm 16000 5 4 43 4³ 6¹³ 517 Rivera M A b 114 7.70 57-20 Good and Hasty116²Fencings Fina113²½Dancerina110 Stumbled st. 6
17Nov79- 3Med fst 6f :23½ :47½ 1:15½ ⓕMd 16000 1 2 1³ 12 11½ 1½ Rocco J⁵ b 113 5.10 69-23 French Dressing 113½ Nosey Flane 118¹½ Tu Lovely 118²½ All out 6
22Oct79- 4Med fst 6f :23½ :47 1:20½ ⓕMd 20000 4 9 53½ 56 612 62¹ Saumell L b 118 5.40 61-19 Skip A Grade 111¹⁰ Penrage Queen 113⁵ Kella Rich 116½ Tired 9
12Oct79- 3Med sly 6f :22½ :47½ 1:12½ ⓕMd Sp Wt 5 3 21½ 46 59 616 MacBeth D b 118 9.50 68-18 Nijit 118⁶ Full Tigress 118ⁿᵒ Dunloe Lady 118³½ Tired 7
30ct79- 9Med my 6f :22½ :47¾ 1:14 ⓕMd Sp Wt 8 2 21½ 22 64½ 79¾ MacBeth D b 118 4.20 64-19 Peace Holder 118⁴ Reads Good 118¹ Two On One 118³ Tired 9
17Sep79- 3Med fst 6f :23½ :45½ 1:12½ ⓕMd Sp Wt 9 1 54½ 41½ 51⁷ 516 Fann B 118 7.60 68-13 Patt King 118⁶ Great Dialogue 118³ Space Of Time 118½ Evenly 9
LATEST WORKOUTS Jan 26 Hia 5f fst 1:02½ b Jan 19 Hia 3f fst :36½ hg

Honey Dana
Own.—J E Stable $11,500
B. f. 3, by Honey Jay—Smartrail, by Smart
Br.—Stevens L T (Ky)
Tr.—Cole William A

			St.	1st	2nd	3rd	Amt.
108⁷		1980	2	0	0	0	$315
		1979	10	2	1	0	$8,980

18Jan80- 4Hia fst 6f :22½ :45½ 1:13 ⓕClm 16000 11 7 10¹²10¹² 64½ 61½ Rolfe D L 52 115 18.20 68-23 Jane Lake 108³ Set The Hop 115¹½ Taradith 71ⁿᵏ No threat 12
3Jan80- 1Crc fst 6½f :22½ :46½ 1:21¾ ⓕClm c-11500 6 8 82½ 67½ 41½ Sellers M 52 114 7.20 74-17 Miss Maudie 115ⁿᵏ Halter Queen 114ⁿᵒ M.B.'s Ruler 111¹ Rallied 9
26Dec79- 3Crc fst 1 70 :49 1:15½ 1:47¾ ⓕClm 14000 4 3 43 43½ 53½ 46½ Guerra W A 114 5.50 65-18 Fan For Air 111³LondonAce115²Don'TuJustLuvit114½ Weakened 6
30Nov79- 7Med fst 1 70 :47½ 1:14 1:46¾ ⓕAllowance 1 6 712 714 718 720 Brumfield D b 115 19.90e 48-26 Omaha Jane 120³ Herald Princess 120⁴ Peace Holder117½ Outrun 7
24Oct79- 5Key fst 6f :22½ :46½ 1:20¾ ⓕClm 18000 8 6 67 68½ 79¼ 47 Tejeira J b 116 3.00 63-29 Don'tBeDaft116³½FncysRogue107³SocksOnSocks112½ No mishap 8
16Oct79- 7Med fst 6f :23 :47½ 1:14½ ⓕClm 16000 8 2 74½ 64½ 42½ 34½ MacBeth D b 117 2.80 72-20 NorthernRipple112½HoneyDana117ⁿᵏJessicaBby115³ Up for place 9
26Sep79- 8Med fst 6f :23 :47½ 1:13½ ⓕClm 22500 6 4 69½ 51¹ 51¹ 45½ McCauley W H b 113 3.40e 74-19 Still Blue 121½TestTubeBaby117⁴½SharonsFareWell113¹½ Late bid 9
14Sep79- 4Del fst 6f :22½ :46½ 1:11¼ ⓕClm c-14500 2 3 74½ 44½ 2ʰᵈ Adams J K b 117 5.50 79-16 Sharons Fare Well 117¹ Honey Dana 117²½ Me Voy117¹½ 2nd best 5
3Sep79- 4Del fst 6f :22½ :46½ 1:14 ⓕMd c-11500 9 2 42½ 41 1³ 1ⁿᵏ Pino M G⁵ b 115 9.20 71-18 Honey Dana 115ⁿᵏ Roose Dream 120⁸ Brave Gladys 120¹ Driving 9
14Aug79- 9Del fst 6f :22½ :46½ 1:14½ ⓕMd 12500 2 6 5½ 44½ 32 2ⁿᵒ Fann B b 118 8.80 72-20 Me Voy 120ⁿᵒ Honey Dana 119³ Gallant Too 115½ Missed 9
LATEST WORKOUTS Feb 9 GP 4f fst :50½ b Feb 5 GP 4f fst :52 b

High Pronto
Own.—Noonan H B $11,500
Ch. f. 3, by High Echelon—Mischief, by Pronto
Br.—Noonan H B (Ohio)
Tr.—Sonnier J Bert

			St.	1st	2nd	3rd	Amt.
115		1980	1	M	0	0	$67
		1979	5	M	0	0	$362

GR 15Feb80- 2Hia gd 6f :22½ :45½ 1:10¾ ⓕClm 18000 2 6 91³ 916 812 710 Intelisano 56 115 75.40 80-15 Dancing Tesse 115¹ Jane Lake 111¾ Jill's Glory 108ⁿᵒ No threat 12
27Dec79- 1Crc fst 6½f :23½ 1:21 ⓕMd 15000 6 5 76½ 69 61⁰ Faine C⁷ 45 118 23.20 69-19 Val Cyn 119⁵½ Its In The Stars 119²½ Fast and Crafty119² Outrun 9
18Dec79- 3Crc fst 7f :23¾ :47¾ 1:28½ ⓕMd 15000 2 8 77½ 71½ 61⁹ 51⁹ Intelisano G P Jr 115 5.20 61-16 Serene Tanya 105²½ Fast Tracie 116⁵½ Loyal Liberal 115¹½ Outrun 8
30Nov79- 2Crc fst 1 70 :49½ 1:15½ 1:46¾ ⓕMd Sp Wt 7 7 10¹² 915 916 918 Intelisano G P Jr 117 17.60 58-17 AfeelyaPulse117³½Getoffofmycloud112¹GleamingCap117¹ Outrun 10
16Nov79- 4Crc fst 6f :22½ :47½ 1:13¾ ⓕMd 12500 11 6 77½ 66 57½ 58½ Pollard L S 118 7.00 69-20 My Glimpse 118⁸CollectorsDream118¹½LooseyVee114ⁿᵏ No factor 11
18Sep79- 4AP fst 6f :22½ :47½ 1:13¾ ⓕMd 10000 4 7 65½ 65½ 56½ 58½ Fires E 119 *1.50 66-18 Princess Sable 110⁶ Leeantrew 119¹½ Gloria Lori 115½ No factor 9
LATEST WORKOUTS Feb 13 GP 4f fst :49 b Feb 7 GP 5f fst 1:04 b

---

"For the last three weeks," I said, "just about every race here has been won by the horse who gets to the lead on the rail. Figuring out who that horse is going to be is more important than every other handicapping factor combined. In the second race I think I know who it's going to be. Blessed Dancer has got pretty good speed, and none of the five horses inside her is going to keep her from getting over to the rail. Her last race was her first start in months, and the horse she was chasing, Pleasure Jennie, is pretty fast. Even though she tired and got beat by 14 lengths, her final time still wasn't so bad. There's only one other horse in this field with any speed or any ability — French Dressing. You can take the two horses back and forth in the exacta if you want to be safe, but French Dressing doesn't look quick enough to get past Blessed Dancer and get over to the rail."

SECOND RACE
Hialeah Park
FEBRUARY 22, 1980

6 FURLONGS. (1.08⅗) CLAIMING. Purse $5,000. Fillies, 3–year–olds. Weight, 121 lbs. Non–winners of three races since January 8 allowed 2 lbs. Two races since then, 4 lbs. A race since then, 6 lbs. Claiming price $11,500; for each $500 to $9,500 allowed 1 lb. (Races where entered for $7,500 or less not considered.)

Value of race $5,000, value to winner $3,000, second $900, third $600, fourth $250, balance of starters $50 each. Mutuel pool $53,172. Perfecta Pool $67,484.

Last Raced	Horse	Eqt.	A.Wt	PP	St	¼	½	Str	Fin	Jockey	Cl'g Pr	Odds $1
25Jan80 ^{2}Hia^{4}	Blessed Dancer		3 115	6	2	1^{1}	1^{hd}	$1^{\frac{1}{2}}$	1^{1}	Anderson J R	11500	10.10
4Feb80 ^{2}Hia^{3}	French Dressing	b	3 114	7	1	$2^{\frac{1}{2}}$	$2^{1\frac{1}{2}}$	2^{3}	2^{4}	Rivera M A	11000	1.50
25Jan80 ^{2}Hia^{3}	Red Gap	b	3 113	4	3	$5^{1\frac{1}{2}}$	3^{4}	3^{3}	$3^{2\frac{1}{2}}$	Cordero A Jr	9500	5.10
12Feb80 ^{2}Hia^{6}	My Red Wing	b	3 110	5	4	6^{3}	5^{2}	4^{2}	4^{1}	Long B^{5}	11500	9.00
15Feb80 ^{2}Hia^{7}	High Pronto	b	3 115	9	6	$8^{\frac{1}{2}}$	$8^{1\frac{1}{2}}$	$6^{\frac{1}{2}}$	5no	Danjean R	11500	11.60
18Jan80 ^{4}Hia^{6}	Honey Dana	b	3 108	8	5	7^{2}	6^{3}	5^{2}	$6^{\frac{1}{2}}$	Cohen G^{7}	11500	5.80
12Feb80 ^{2}Hia^{7}	Don'Tu Just Luvit	b	3 110	2	9	9	9	8^{1}	7^{3}	Ashcroft D C^{7}	11500	48.80
30Jan80 ^{8}Hia^{11}	It Was There		3 107	3	7	4^{hd}	$7^{1\frac{1}{2}}$	9	$8^{2\frac{1}{2}}$	Milner J A^{7}	11000	39.10
15Feb80 ^{10}Hia^{5}	Amber Maid	b	3 111	1	8	$3^{1\frac{1}{2}}$	4^{hd}	$7^{\frac{1}{2}}$	9	Williams L R	9500	16.90

OFF AT 1:30 EST. Start good, Won driving. Time, :22⅘, :46⅖, 1:12⅗ Track fast.

$2 Mutuel Prices:			
6–BLESSED DANCER	22.20	10.40	4.60
7–FRENCH DRESSING		3.20	2.60
4–RED GAP			3.40

$2 PERFECTA 6–7 PAID $84.20.

Dk. b or Br. f, by Bless Business—Nat A Dancer, by Natidan. Trainer Rose Harold J. Bred by Sikorski E (Fla).

BLESSED DANCER saved ground while showing speed, responded readily when challenged by FRENCH DRESSING nearing the stretch and proved best. The latter went up after BLESSED DANCER nearing the stretch but wasn't good enough. RED GAP made a bid nearing the stretch and weakened. MY RED WING lacked a rally. HONEY DANA was always outrun. DON'TU JUST LUVIT showed nothing. IT WAS THERE was finished early. ASMER MAID tired badly.

Owners— 1, Allen Curley; 2, Dogwood Stable; 3, 3 T's Stable; 4, Daybreak Farm; 5, Noonan H B; 6, J E Stable; 7, Rogers A S & R; 8, Lorraine & Cindy Stable; 9, South Shore Stable.

Trainers— 1, Rose Harold J; 2, Alexander Frank A; 3, Pierce Joseph H Jr; 4, Kelley Bill P; 5, Sonnier J Bert; 6, Cole William A; 7, Draper Manley; 8, Edmundson Samuel M; 9, Rigione John H.

Overweight: Red Gap 2 pounds.

Honey Dana was claimed by Baer S M; trainer, Pierce Joseph H Jr; Don'Tu Just Luvit was claimed by Benjamin C B; trainer, Kelley Thomas W.

Scratched—Faygele (12Feb80 ^{2}Hia^{5}).

Like so many races on a biased track, this one followed the script perfectly. Blessed Dancer popped out of the gate, went to the rail, and led French Dressing all the way around the track to win at 10 to 1, earning me Exley's thanks and admiration. All things considered, I would rather have looked dazzlingly brilliant for Candice Bergen than Exley, but the author paid me back as best he could. A year later he was reviewing for *New York* magazine the racetrack book *Laughing in the Hills,* in which author Bill Barich makes a couple of passing references to my speed-handicapping methods. Exley seized the opportunity to mention our meeting. "The first time Beyer marked my card at Hialeah," he wrote, "he told me to bet the daily double and an exacta in the second. Whereas for $14 I made $450, Beyer made $16,000. When I rushed back into the press box, extended my hand and shouted, 'Andy, you're the greatest!' Beyer reddened shyly, smiled a wonderfully toothy smile, and said, 'I know it.' At that moment Beyer was at one with the universe."

Indeed, that was the way I felt. Most of the time, a horseplayer will perceive the racing world as being as chaotic and incomprehensible as the real world. He will be dealing with considerations of speed, trips, class, jockeys, and trainers and will never be sure how to assess the relative influence of all these different factors. But when a strong bias exists, it becomes the paramount factor, rendering all the others secondary and giving a horseplayer the rare and wondrous sense that he knows exactly what makes the universe tick.

FOUR

Trips and Pace

A HORSEPLAYER WILL LEARN most of his lessons about handicapping from an accumulation of observations and experience over a period of years. But occasionally a lesson may be etched forever in his mind by a single race that demonstrates a principle vividly and incontrovertibly. My view of the sport was permanently altered at Churchill Downs on the first Saturday in May 1981.

In *Picking Winners* I had questioned the traditional assumption that the early pace of a race can have a significant effect on its outcome. "A horse's fractional times do not affect his final time," I declared. "Horses are never 'burned up' by fast fractions. There is no such thing as a 'killing pace' . . . I ignore it when I am handicapping." What I had really ignored, of course, was the mountain of evidence that contradicted this point of view. I am sure I could have found contradictions every day if I had been looking for them, but the one that hit me like a bolt of lightning was the Kentucky Derby won by Pleasant Colony.

If I had wanted to test the influence of pace, I might have designed an experiment like this: Have the early leaders in the Kentucky Derby run the fastest first quarter mile in the history of the race and judge its effect. As a control experiment, take roughly the same group of horses and have them run an extraordinarily slow first quarter in the Preakness. Then compare the results of the two races.

That experiment was conducted in the laboratories of Louisville and Baltimore. The Derby field was filled with brilliant speed horses, notably Proud Appeal and Cure the Blues. They all went charging for the lead, and a bullet named Top Avenger got it, running the quarter in :21$\frac{4}{5}$ seconds — the fastest fraction at Churchill Downs in 107 years — and the half mile in a swift :45$\frac{1}{5}$. Every horse who was near this breathtaking pace collapsed. The horses who were running 1–2–3–4–5 after three quarters of a mile finished 19–10–18–16–17. As they backed up, all the stretch-runners and plodders passed them. The first five finishers at the end of the Derby were horses who had been running 15–19–10–17–20 after three quarters. The winner, Pleasant Colony, was a genuinely good horse, but nondescript plodders like Woodchopper and Television Studio had rallied to finish ahead of superior horses like Cure the Blues and Proud Appeal by margins of 20 or 30 lengths. The outcome of the Derby seemed to have relatively little to do with the ability of the horses; it was much more the result of pace.

Under the circumstances, the horse who had impressed me most in the Derby was the tenth-place finisher, Bold Ego. He had dueled with Top Avenger for three quarters of a mile and had taken the lead on the final turn. When the first wave of stretch-runners started making their moves, they couldn't get past him. Bold Ego fought back and stayed in contention long after all the other speed horses had collapsed, but he finally weakened in the last eighth of a mile. I didn't know if he could win the Preakness, but I felt confident that he would run much better.

Indeed, Bold Ego did not win at Pimlico, but his strong second-place finish demonstrated what a profound difference pace can make. In the wake of the Derby, all the jockeys in the Preakness field wanted to avoid getting into another suicidal speed duel. The rider of Top Avenger, the Derby pacesetter, put him under a virtual stranglehold as soon as the gate opened. Bold Ego was able to take the lead while running the first quarter in 23$\frac{4}{5}$ seconds, the slowest such fraction in the Preakness in 17 years. He reached the half-mile mark in a slow :47⅗. In marked contrast to the Derby, the horses who were running 1–2–3 after this half mile finished 2–3–4. Pleasant Colony did win again, verifying his superiority to this whole group, but Bold Ego finished 10 lengths closer to him than he had at Churchill Downs, and the performance of all the other horses further convinced me of the importance of pace. I had rediscovered the wheel.

I realized now that a horse's trip has three important components. The essence of it, of course, is the way he actually runs — the ground he loses on turns, the trouble he encounters, the general impression he conveys. But the way he runs must be viewed in the context of the racing strip over which he is competing. And it must be viewed in the context of the pace of the race. A horse may save ground on the rail all the way, but if he is battling through a quarter mile in :21⅘ and a half in :45⅕ he is certainly not enjoying an easy trip. A horse may make a strong move in the 4-path to take command of a race, but that accomplishment may not be so impressive if the three horses in front of him have annihilated each other in an all-out speed duel.

After I started paying attention to pace, I began to see how often it explained the outcome of races when my beloved speed figures couldn't. A textbook illustration arose in the 1982 Hopeful Stakes at Saratoga. These were the most recent fractions and final times of the contenders (after they had been adjusted to take into account the speed of the racetracks over which the horses had run):

Copelan	:22	:44 4/5	1:10 4/5
Pax in Bello	:23	:46 3/5	1:10 4/5
Victorious	:22 4/5	:46 3/5	1:11

Once I would have viewed the Hopeful as indecipherable, because all the contenders' final times were about the same. I would have concluded that they were therefore of similar ability. But now I was able to perceive that Copelan was the vastly superior horse. Pax in Bello had earned his final time the easy way, racing close to a slow early pace. Victorious had rallied after the leaders in front of him had engaged in a suicidal speed duel. But Copelan had recorded his final time of 1:10⅘ the hard way, battling for the lead at a fast pace that might have caused a lesser horse to collapse. In the Hopeful he verified his superiority, beating Victorious by 3¼ lengths and Pax in Bello by four, and paid $8.60 to win.

It had occurred to me that there might be some way to evaluate horses' fractional times mathematically, to express Copelan's superiority over Pax in Bello and Victorious with some kind of sophisticated number. I had seen various pace-rating methods published in handicapping books, but all of them looked uselessly simplistic. Then one day at Saratoga I received a call from a young man who introduced himself as Steve Scharff and didn't waste time with small talk. "I have the answer," he said, and the tone of his voice told me that he meant he had the Answer, the solution to all the mysteries of handicapping. "Write this down: V3 equals C times minus E to the VI power, where E is a universal constant with the value of 2.718 . . ."

Scharff had done five years of graduate study in mathematics and physics, specializing in general relativity, and was teaching statistics and probabilities in college. When he started taking an interest in racing, he naturally looked for a way to apply his mathematical expertise. He perceived that the most efficient way for a horse to run is to maintain a fairly even rate of speed throughout, decelerating slightly toward the end of the race. But the more a horse deviates from this ideal pattern, running a very fast fraction somewhere — as Copelan did — the more impressive his performance is. This was a rather good summation of the whole theory of pace, and Scharff set out to express it in a formula. What he did, basically, was to calculate the horse's average speed for each quarter of a race and add those figures together to produce his pace rating. Compare, for example, two horses who ran six furlongs this way:

Horse A	**:23**	**:47**	**1:11**
Horse B	**:22**	**:44**	**1:11**

Horse A covered the first two furlongs in 23 seconds; 2/23 equals .0869 furlongs per second. He ran the next two quarters in 24 seconds each; 2/24 equals .0833 furlongs per second. Adding 869, 833, and 833, his rating is 2535. Using similar arithmetic, Scharff would give Horse B a rating of 2558, clearly superior to A's despite their identical final times. This is a considerable simplification of Scharff's method, because much of the mathematics involved was beyond my comprehension, but I thought at length about the ideas behind his figures. As I did, I realized what was wrong with mathematical analyses of pace, and what was the right way to deal with this important handicapping factor.

Many technical difficulties confuse efforts to analyze fractional times with precision. In particular, the distance from the starting gate to the beam of light that activates the electric timer varies at different tracks. At Monmouth Park, there is an unusually long run to the point where the race officially begins, and because horses get a flying start they run fast opening quarters. At Pimlico there is no long run to the beam. So a horse who goes :21⅘, :44⅘, 1:11 at Monmouth might go :23, :45⅘, 1:11 at Pimlico. His performance may be identical but the recorded fractions are much different.

Even if a handicapper has easily comparable fractions with which to work, they may be deceptive. Fast fractions don't hurt speed horses as much as pressure does. An animal may run a quarter mile in 22 seconds, opening a clear lead over his opposition, reach the half mile in :45 flat, and go on to win with ease. But if the same horse engages in a head-and-head duel in :22 and :45, he may collapse. There are many cases, too, in which horses will vie for the lead in fractions that don't appear fast, but one of them will seem to crack under pressure, anyway. The explanation may be that somewhere during the course of that duel, one of the speedballs accelerates and runs a sixteenth of a mile in 5⅗ seconds, delivering a swift (but barely perceptible) knockout punch. Although I remain somewhat intrigued by the possibility of analyzing fractional times mathematically, the best way to judge the effects of pace is the way trip handicappers do: to watch races intelligently and perceptively.

I look for indications, in addition to the fractional times, that the front-runners may be engaging in a harmfully tough battle for the lead. I watch for horses who are being pushed hard by their riders in the early stages of a race. I look for battles involving horses whose records indicate that they possess high speed, and who may be throwing those :05⅗ sixteenths at each other. I look for races in which all the speed horses collapse, as they did in the 1981 Derby.

Making these subjective judgments is especially important on turf courses, such as those in New York, which don't have electric timers.

When I see what appears to be a hard battle for the lead, I write "Duel" by the names of the horses involved and "Stalk" by the names of the horses sitting within easy striking distance of them. I note horses who break a bit tardily and are rushed up to compete with a fast pace, or those who make premature moves on the backstretch while the leaders are in high gear. Other information that a trip handicapper regularly records in his notes may take on special significance if the pace is hot. It is tough enough to engage in an all-out battle for the lead under any circumstance, but if a horse is doing it while parked in the 3- or 4-path all the way around the turn, losing ground while he is trying to keep up, he is facing an especially difficult task.

All this may seem elementary to a horseplayer who appreciates the importance of pace. Often it is. Anyone can look at the past performances of a horse who was running second by a neck after a half mile in :44 flat and conclude that he was in a tough speed duel. But it would take a good trip handicapper to evaluate a horse like Dowdstown Miss.

When I first looked at the record of Dowdstown Miss in a 1½-mile grass race for maidens at Saratoga on August 7, 1981, I did not consider her a serious contender. She had tired badly in her last start at Belmont Park, after running fractions that were respectable but could hardly be considered destructive, and now was attempting to go a longer distance. But Joe Cardello had seen her race, and his view of it was entirely different from what the past performances suggested. Dowdstown Miss was his type of horse. "Trip handicappers," he has said to me more than once, "are always looking for dramatic bits of trouble — horses getting blocked or checked — but most of the time something as unspectacular as a premature or ill-timed move is much more significant." Dowdstown Miss had been running against two speedballs who were fast enough to have taken the lead in sprint races. But instead of letting these speedsters go, Joe told me, jockey Richard Migliore was pushing Dowdstown Miss as soon as she left the gate in order to keep up with them. The three leaders raced abreast of each other, alternating for the lead for nearly a mile, when Dowdstown Miss put them away. The other fillies faded to finish last and next-to-last after their exertions. But as soon as Dowdstown Miss had taken command, the stretch-runners who had been sitting patiently behind this battle began to make their moves. Dowdstown Miss offered some resistance, but finally faded in the stretch. Still, Joe persuaded me, the race hardly provided evidence that she was incapable of going a longer distance.

He was right. This time Migliore rated her, choosing to use her speed in a more judicious fashion, and Dowdstown Miss took the lead after a mile. She raced to an easy three-length victory, paying $19.80. One of the stretch-runners who had beaten her in her previous start was 14 lengths behind this time.

While a fast pace that kills off speed horses is obvious to most racing fans, a slow pace and its effects are often more subtle — and, to good trip handicappers, more profitable.

When a single horse manages to take a clear lead while setting a slow early pace, those circumstances may change his entire character. Quitters can become world-beaters. Horses can give performances of which they would never otherwise be capable. Nice Sailing, the $20,000 claimer cited in the previous chapter, was able to win by 18 lengths and finish in a time worthy of a $50,000 horse when he was able to get loose in extremely slow fractions. Novices may look at such past performances and conclude that the horse might run even better if he were put under pressure, but that is almost never true. Whenever Nice Sailing was pressured, he was worth $20,000 — or less.

Sometimes the entire nature of a race can be changed by something as seemingly inconsequential as a slow first quarter. When Affirmed and Seattle Slew had their long-awaited confrontation in the 1⅛-mile Marlboro Cup, Affirmed's jockey permitted Slew to take a two-length lead while running the first quarter mile in 24 seconds. Neither horse had had to exert himself yet, and so that slow quarter essentially transformed the Marlboro into a seven-furlong race in which Seattle Slew had a two-length head start. The outcome was never in doubt after that. Affirmed, though, was more often the beneficiary of such circumstances. When he beat Alydar in the Belmont Stakes and again when he beat Spectacular Bid in the Jockey Club Gold Cup, he got away with a slow first half mile that forced his rival to make a premature move and chase him. I argue (usually in vain) that Affirmed's victories in these famous confrontations were due less to his ballyhooed courage and competitiveness than to the advantageous trips he had.

If a stretch-runner falls too far behind a slow pace, making up ground can become a physical impossibility — even if the stretch-runner happens to be one of the best horses in the world.

FIFTH RACE
Laurel
NOVEMBER 9, 1974

1 ½ MILES.(turf). (2.23⅘) WASHINGTON D C INTERNATIONAL. Purse $150,000. (By invitation only) 3-year-olds and upward. $150,000 of which $100,000 to first, $25,000 to second, $10,000 to third, $5,000 to fourth, $5,000 to fifth and $5,000 to sixth. Weights, 3-year-olds, 120 lbs. older, 127 lbs. Fillies and Mares, 3 lbs allowance. Starters to be named through the entry box Thursday, November 7 by the usual time of closing. The Laurel Race course, Inc., will present trophies to the winning owner, trainer and jockey.

Value of race $150,000, value to winner $100,000, second $25,000, third $10,000, fourth $5,000, fifth $5,000, sixth $5,000. Mutuel pool $325,981. Exacta Pool $152,835.

Last Raced	Horse	Eqt.	A.	Wt	PP	¼	½	1	1¼	Str	Fin	Jockey	Odds $1
20Oct74 ^{4}Lon^6	Admetus		4	127	5	8^3	$7^{1\frac{1}{2}}$	4^{hd}	4^1	2^{hd}	$1^{\frac{3}{4}}$	Philipperon M	31.00
26Oct74 ^{7}Kee^2	Desert Vixen		4	124	6	1^5	$1^{2\frac{1}{2}}$	1^1	$1^{2\frac{1}{2}}$	1^2	$2^{\frac{3}{4}}$	Turcotte R	5.50
27Oct74 ^{7}WO^1	Dahlia		4	124	3	7^{hd}	8^2	8^1	6^2	$5^{1\frac{1}{2}}$	$3^{1\frac{3}{4}}$	Piggott L	.60
12Oct74 ^{8}Bel^4	Golden Don	b	4	127	8	$2^{1\frac{1}{2}}$	$3^{\frac{1}{2}}$	$3^{\frac{1}{2}}$	$2^{\frac{1}{2}}$	3^1	$4^{1\frac{1}{4}}$	Cruguet J	14.60
6Oct74 ^{4}Lon^3	Margouillat		4	127	9	$3^{\frac{1}{2}}$	$2^{1\frac{1}{4}}$	$2^{\frac{1}{2}}$	3^1	6^2	$5^{1\frac{1}{2}}$	Doleuze G	7.80
19Oct74 ^{2}New^6	Coup de Feu		5	127	1	$4^{2\frac{1}{2}}$	$6^{\frac{1}{2}}$	7^1	5^2	$4^{\frac{1}{2}}$	$6^{\frac{1}{2}}$	Barclay S	101.50
27Oct74 ^{7}WO^2	Big Spruce		5	127	4	$5^{\frac{1}{2}}$	$4^{\frac{1}{2}}$	6^{hd}	$7^{\frac{1}{2}}$	$7^{1\frac{1}{2}}$	$7^{2\frac{1}{4}}$	Hole M	5.20
20Oct74 ^{5}Mil^4	Mistigri	b	3	120	2	9	9	9	8^3	8^7	8^{12}	Taylor B	63.90
13Oct74 ^{6}Kol^3	Marduk		3	120	7	$6^{1\frac{1}{2}}$	5^1	$5^{\frac{1}{2}}$	9	9	9	Remmert P	61.50

OFF AT 2:42, EST. Start good for all but MARDUK, Won driving. Time, :27⅕, :51⅘, 1:17⅕, 1:42, 2:06⅖, 2:29⅗, Course firm.

$2 Mutuel Prices:			
5-(A)-ADMETUS	64.00	22.20	6.40
6-(H)-DESERT VIXEN		7.80	3.80
3-(D)-DAHLIA			2.60

$2 EXACTA 5-6 PAID $711.20.

Ch. g, by Reform—La Milo, by Hornbeam. Trainer Cunnington J Jr. Bred by Ballymacoll Stud Farm Ltd (Fra.).

ADMETUS, unhurried early, advanced to contention between rivals leaving the backstretch the second time, and patiently awaited room behind the first flight entering the stretch. Jockey Philipperon swung him out approaching the furlong grounds and, in response to brisk handling, ADMETUS outfinished DESERT VIXEN. The latter easily took a long early lead under snug restraint as Turcotte slowed down the pace. When the field closed the margin leaving the backstretch, she responded willingly to increase her lead around the far turn, but could not keep pace with the winner while drifting out in the final eighth in a game performance. DAHLIA, snugly reserved along the rail early, swung extremely wide when lodging her bid entering the stretch and could not wear down the top pair in a determined effLDEN DON, reserved while saving ground early, rallied into the stretch and hung. MAGOUILLAT was rated in good striking position but lacked the needed late response. COUP DE FEU saved ground to no avail. BIG SPRUCE gradually weakened. MISTIGRI was outrun. MARDUK dwelt at the start to be off well behind the field, advanced to contention before a half, and gave way readily after a mile.

Owners— 1, Sobell & Weinstock; 2, Mangurian H T Jr; 3, Hunt N B; 4, Donaldson A R; 5, de Moussac Paul; 6, Sasse F H; 7, Elmendorf; 8, O'Ferrall E R More; 9, Batthyany Countess M.

Trainers— 1, Cunnington J Jr; 2, Root T F; 3, Zilber M; 4, Jensen K E; 5, Mony-Pajol R de; 6, Sasse D J G; 7, Nickerson V J; 8, Prendergast P J; 9, Bollow H.

Dahlia was one of the two best fillies I have ever seen (the other being Ruffian), but she was placed in impossible circumstances when she attempted to win the Washington, D.C., International for the second straight year. The early pace was absurdly slow — a half mile in :51⅘, three quarters in 1:17⅕ — but jockey Lester Piggott kept Dahlia far behind. With a quarter mile to run, she still trailed the leader by seven lengths. Because of the slow pace, the final quarter of the International was run in an extraordinary :23⅕. In order to make up those seven lengths, Dahlia would have had to run the final quarter in :21⅘, something I doubt any horse in history has ever done. That she came so close was a tribute to her greatness.

While the effect of a slow pace will rarely be so dramatic or obvious, trip handicappers will have many occasions to note that a slow pace has compromised the chances of stretch-runners. The handicappers who are graduates of harness tracks know that one such situation is especially significant and profitable.

Pace is, of course, a vital factor in harness racing. So is the ability of horses to accelerate at top speed for a quarter mile or so. When a standardbred makes this move at the proper time, he can seize command of a race. But sometimes he will make his move and it will barely be visible. It happens every night: The leaders cut a half mile in a slow 1:02. Now a superior horse capable of pacing a quarter in 29 seconds pulls out to make his move. But the leaders are strong and they start to accelerate at the same time, pacing their third quarter in :29⅗. The superior horse isn't able to blow past them. Because he will be racing wide, losing ground, he may not be gaining an inch, and his performance will look like a very dull one.

Thoroughbreds are different from standardbreds, and pace is less important in thoroughbred races, but the same situation often arises. The early pace is slow, and just when a stretch-runner starts to make his move the leaders accelerate, too. Commonly the stretch-runner will try to swoop around the leaders on the turn, but instead will find himself hung wide all the way around. Because moves like this frequently point out horses ready to win their next starts, I have a special (if somewhat cumbersome) notation to describe them: "MIHP," for Move Into Hot Pace.

Brasher Doubloon, the colt cited in the previous chapter, made such a move in a race at Saratoga that vividly demonstrated the effects of a slow pace.

SIXTH RACE
Saratoga
AUGUST 1, 1981

7 FURLONGS. (1.20$\frac{2}{5}$) ALLOWANCE. Purse $20,000. 3-year-olds and upward which have never won two races other than maiden, claiming or starter. Weights, 3-year-olds, 117 lbs.; older, 122 lbs. Non-winners of a race other than maiden or claiming since July 1 allowed 3 lbs.; of such a race since then, 5 lbs.

Value of race $20,000, value to winner $12,000, second $4,400, third $2,400, fourth $1,200. Mutuel pool $181,134, OTB pool $162,643. Quinella Pool $135,338. OTB Quinella Pool $176,639.

Last Raced	Horse	Eqt.A.Wt	PP	St	¼	½	Str	Fin	Jockey	Odds $1
12Jly81 ^{5}Bel^{2}	Lord Darnley	b 3 112	1	3	2^{hd}	$1^{\frac{1}{2}}$	1^{hd}	1^{nk}	Skinner K	2.90
18Jly81 ^{4}Bel^{2}	Academy H.	3 112	2	2	3^{2}	$2^{\frac{1}{2}}$	2^{3}	$2^{4\frac{1}{4}}$	Asmussen C B	7.50
19Jly81 ^{1}Bel^{4}	Cinnamon's Choice	3 114	5	1	1^{hd}	3^{1}	3^{hd}	3^{1}	Cordero A Jr	1.50
18Jly81 ^{4}Bel^{1}	Brasher Doubloon	3 117	3	6	6	5^{3}	4^{2}	$4^{4\frac{1}{2}}$	Maple E	3.50
23Jly81 ^{7}Bel^{2}	Shahnameh	3 112	4	5	5^{1}	6	6	$5^{1\frac{3}{4}}$	Martens G	9.80
3Dec80 ^{5}Aqu^{1}	Tobruk	3 112	6	4	4^{1}	4^{hd}	$5^{1\frac{1}{2}}$	6	Samyn J L	8.10

OFF AT 4:27, EDT. Start good, Won driving. Time, :23$\frac{1}{5}$, :45$\frac{2}{5}$, 1:09$\frac{2}{5}$, 1:21$\frac{4}{5}$ Track fast.

$2 Mutuel Prices:			
2-(A)-LORD DARNLEY	7.80	5.00	2.80
3-(B)-ACADEMY H.		7.20	3.60
5-(F)-CINNAMON'S CHOICE			2.40
$2 QUINELLA 2-3 PAID $32.20.			

Ch. c, by Arts And Letters—Mary Queenofscots, by Royal Gunner. Trainer Laurin Roger. Bred by Lochleven Stable (Ky).

LORD DARNLEY saved ground while alternating for the lead into the stretch and turned back ACADEMY H. in a long drive. The latter, prominent from the outset, raced outside LORD DARNLEY into the stretch and fought it out gamely. A foul claim against the winner by the rider of ACADEMY H., for alleged interference through the stretch, was not allowed. CINNAMON'S CHOICE showed good early foot, remained a factor to the stretch and weakened. BRASHER DOUBLOON, bounced off the side of the gate at the start, made a run from the outside of the gate at the start, made a run from the outside approaching the stretch but lacked a further response. SHAHNAMEH was always outrun. TOBRUK moved to the inside while rallying approaching the stretch but had nothing left for the drive.

Owners— 1, Getty Mrs G F II; 2, Hooper F W; 3, Calumet Farm; 4, Brant P; 5, Manhasset Stable; 6, Dekwiatkowski H.

Trainers— 1, Laurin Roger; 2, Griffin Mitchell; 3, Veitch John M; 4, Martin Frank; 5, Picou James E; 6, Stephens Woodford C.

Overweight: Cinnamon's Choice 2 pounds.

Scratched—Gallant Dance (19Jly81 ^{1}Bel^{3}); Double Hell (19Jly81 ^{6}FL^{5}); Bottled Water (6Jly81 ^{8}Bel^{5}).

The racetrack on this day was lightning fast; 2-year-old maidens were running the first quarters of their races in 22-and-change. But the leaders in this race crawled the first quarter in :23$\frac{1}{5}$ as Brasher Doubloon trailed them. He moved up on the outside on the backstretch and into the 4-path on the turn, but there was no way he was going to overtake them as they accelerated through the second quarter in a sizzling :22$\frac{1}{5}$ and the third quarter in :24 flat. Brasher Doubloon was parked outside the leaders around the turn without gaining much ground, but this MIHP showed that he had ability that might be used more effectively on another day.

Having come to appreciate the influence of pace rather late in life, I still find myself amazed by what an important factor it is. As I watched the East's best 2-year-old fillies compete in the summer and fall of 1982, starting with the Schuylerville Stakes at Saratoga, I sometimes thought it was the only relevant factor.

EIGHTH RACE
Saratoga
AUGUST 4, 1982

6 FURLONGS. (1.08) 65th Running THE SCHUYLERVILLE (Grade III). Purse $50,000 added. Fillies, 2–year–olds. Weight, 119 lbs. By subscription of $100 each, which should accompany the nomination; $400 to pass the entry box with $50,000 added. The added money and all fees to be divided 60% to the winner, 22% to second, 12% to third and 6% to fourth. Winners of two sweepstakes since June 15 an additional 2 lbs. Non–winners of a sweepstakes allowed 3 lbs. Of a race other than maiden or claiming, 5 lbs. Maidens, 7 lbs. Starters to be named at the closing time of entries. A trophy will be presented to the winning owner. Closed with 32 nominations Wednesday, July 21, 1982.

Value of race $57,700, value to winner $34,620, second $12,694, third $6,924, fourth $3,462. Mutuel pool $139,810, OTB pool $126,902.

Last Raced	Horse	Eqt.A.Wt PP St	¼	½	Str	Fin	Jockey	Odds $1
2Jun82 8Bel2	Weekend Surprise	2 114 7 7	7	6 1½	4 1½	1 1	Velasquez J	b-1.50
17Jly82 6Bel1	Share The Fantasy	2 116 6 1	1 1½	1hd	1 2	2 1	Cordero A Jr	1.30
12Jly82 4Bel1	Flying Lassie	2 114 2 4	3 2½	2½	2 3	3 4¾	Bailey J D	5.20
18Jly82 9Suf1	So Cozy	2 119 5 2	2½	3 4	3½	4nk	MacBeth D	b-1.50
17Jly82 6Bel2	Ultimate Invader	b 2 114 1 5	5½	5 2	6 6	5nk	Fell J	25.50
12Jly82 6Bel1	Winter Queen	2 114 3 3	4 2	4 4	5hd	6 6¼	Vasquez J	6.30
12Jly82 8Bel3	Future Fun	2 114 4 6	6 3	7	7	7	Venezia M	24.80

b-Coupled: Weekend Surprise and So Cozy.

OFF AT 5:28 Start good, Won driving. Time, :22⅕, :45⅖, 1:11 Track fast.

$2 Mutuel Prices:

2-(K)–WEEKEND SURPRISE (b–entry)	5.00	2.60	2.20
3-(I)–SHARE THE FANTASY		2.60	2.20
6-(C)–FLYING LASSIE			2.60

B. f, by Secretariat—Lassie Dear, by Buckpasser. Trainer Carroll Del W II. Bred by Farish W S III & Kilroy W S (Ky).

WEEKEND SURPRISE, outrun to the stretch, finished full fo run while racing wide to wear down SHARE THE FANTASY and won going away. The latter showed good early foot while racing well out from the rail, shook off FLYING LASSIE and SO COZY entering the stretch but wasn't able to withstand the winner. FLYING LASSIE, eased back along the inside soon after the start, moved last from the outside to catch SHARE THE FANTASY on the turn but weakened during the dirve. SO COZY, eased back along the inside nearing the end of the backstretch, made a run between horses on the turn but bore out while tiring. ULTIMATE INVADER saved ground to no avail. WINTER QUEEN tired. FUTURE FUN stumbled slightly after the start and was always outrun.

Owners— 1, Farish W S III; 2, Robins G; 3, Hooper F W; 4, Farish W S III; 5, Sabarese T M; 6, Vanderbilt A G; 7, Tartan Stable.

Trainers— 1, Carroll Del W II; 2, Jolley Leroy; 3, Griffin Mitchell; 4, Carroll Del W II; 5, Parisella John; 6, Whiteley Frank Y Jr; 7, Nerud Jan H.

Scratched—Tarquinia (31Jly82 4Bel1); Blue Garter (12Jly82 8Bel2); Cryptic (23Jly82 6Bel1); Delicate Treasure (27Jly82 9Mth3).

The cold data of the result chart does not fully indicate how hot the pace was in the Schuylerville. My trip notes did:

Winter Queen	GPT behind battle
So Cozy	Rail, took back, 2T, hard battle
Weekend Surprise	2½ T, close vs. dead horses
Share the Fantasy	Rail, hard battle, ran well
Ultimate Invader	Rail T
Flying Lassie	Rail behind duel, rush 3B 3T
Future Fun	1 slo

Share the Fantasy was pressed by So Cozy for a few strides. So Cozy dropped back but quickly moved outside the leader and challenged her again. Flying Lassie was sitting behind them in good position, but moved prematurely to get involved in a three-way fight for the lead. Meanwhile, Weekend Surprise was biding her time. Only after the leaders had done their damage to each other did she blow past them in the stretch. I wasn't impressed by her victory under these optimal circumstances, but I thought that Share the Fantasy had done very well to lose by only a length. Flying Lassie had run well, too.

The Schuylerville had been a prep for Saratoga's principal 2-year-old filly race, the historic Spinaway Stakes. Weekend Surprise, Share the Fantasy, and Flying Lassie were facing each other again and were being challenged by a Monmouth invader, Singing Susan, who I thought was somewhat overrated but did possess high speed. On the basis of what I had seen in the Schuylerville, I thought that Share the Fantasy was the best of the group, but my enthusiasm (and the size of my bet) was considerably tempered by the possibility that she would get involved in another destructive speed duel again. "How much could you bet," another trip handicapper asked, rhetorically, "if you knew they were going to take her off the pace?" As things turned out, the answer to this question was: A whole lot.

EIGHTH RACE
Saratoga
AUGUST 29, 1982

6 FURLONGS. (1.08) 91st Running THE SPINAWAY. $75,000 Added. (Grade I). Fillies, 2-year-olds. Weight, 119 lbs. By subscription of $150 each, which should accompany the nominaiton; $600 to pass the entry box, with $75,000 added. The added money and all fees to be divided 60% to the winner, 22% to second, 12% to third and 6% to fourth. Starters to be named at the closing time of entries. Trophies will be presented to the winning owner, trainer and jockey and mementoes to the grooms of the first four finishers. Closed Wednesday, August 11, 1982 with 32 nominations.

Value of race $83,400, value to winner $50,040, second $18,348, third $10,008, fourth $5,004. Mutuel pool $174,337.

Last Raced	Horse	Eqt.A.Wt	PP	St	1/4	1/2	Str	Fin	Jockey	Odds $1
4Aug82 ^{8}Sar^{2}	Share The Fantasy	2 119	2	3	3^{6}	1^{hd}	$1\frac{1}{2}$	$1^{4\frac{3}{4}}$	Fell J	a-6.70
7Aug82 ^{9}Mth^{1}	Singing Susan	2 119	4	2	1^{hd}	3^{4}	2^{3}	$2\frac{1}{2}$	Passmore W J	.90
16Aug82 ^{8}Sar^{2}	Midnight Rapture	2 119	5	4	$4\frac{1}{2}$	$4\frac{1}{2}$	5^{1}	$3\frac{3}{4}$	MacBeth D	3.80
16Aug82 ^{8}Sar^{4}	Blue Garter	2 119	3	5	6	6	6	4^{nk}	Miranda J	a-6.70
4Aug82 ^{8}Sar^{1}	Weekend Surprise	2 119	1	6	$5^{1\frac{1}{2}}$	5^{1}	$3^{1\frac{1}{2}}$	5^{4}	Velasquez J	2.40
16Aug82 ^{8}Sar^{3}	Flying Lassie	b 2 119	6	1	2^{3}	2^{hd}	$4\frac{1}{2}$	6	Bailey J D	24.50

a-Coupled: Share The Fantasy and Blue Garter.

OFF AT 5:32, Start good, Won handily. Time, :22⅕, :45⅗, 1:09⅘ Track fast.

$2 Mutuel Prices:

1-(B)-SHARE THE FANTASY (a-entry)	**15.40**	**4.00**	**2.60**
3-(D)-SINGING SUSAN		**3.00**	**2.40**
4-(E)-MIDNIGHT RAPTURE			**3.00**

Ch. f, by Exclusive Native—Misukaw, by Northern Dancer. Trainer Jolley Leroy. Bred by Warner M L (Ky).

SHARE THE FANTASY, reserved behind the early leaders, made a run from the outside approaching the stretch, came over slightly on FLYING ALSSIE After straightening away and drew off while being mildly encouraged. THere was a stewards inquiry involving the winner through the stretch before the result was made official. SINGING SUSAN raced well out from the rail while showing speed to midstetch and weakened. MIDNIGHT RAPTURE, wide into the stretch, failed to seriously menace. BLUE GARTER raced very wide. WEEKEND SURPRISE, outrun early, rallied alogn the inside after entering the stretch but lacked a late response. FLYING LASSIE dueled for the lead to the stretch, was steadied slightly between horses near the final three-sixteenths and gave way readily.

Owners— 1, Robins G; 2, Quinichett R; 3, Green Dolly; 4, Brant P M; 5, Farish W S III; 6, Hooper F W.

Trainers— 1, Jolley Leroy; 2, Clarke George; 3, Barrera Lazaro S; 4, Jolley Leroy; 5, Carroll Del W II; 6, Griffin Mitchell.

Share the Fantasy found herself the beneficiary of the quintessential perfect trip. Singing Susan and Flying Lassie got involved in a head-and-head duel for the early lead, while jockey Jeffrey Fell had no trouble rating Share the Fantasy. He was sitting three lengths behind the leaders, within easy striking distance, and six lengths in front of everybody else. As the leaders weakened, Share the Fantasy swooped past them on the turn and drew away to a 4¾-length victory. Weekend Surprise never got close. Share the Fantasy was now being hailed as the East's leading 2-year-old filly, but I knew that if she was better than her defeat in the Schuylerville had suggested, she was not as good as the Spinaway had made her look.

Share the Fantasy made her next appearance in the Matron Stakes at Belmont Park, and she was clearly the fastest member of the five-horse field. Only one of her rivals, Wings of Jove, possessed even moderate speed. But as I tried to anticipate the way the race could develop, I couldn't imagine Jeffrey Fell doing the right thing, hustling Share the Fantasy out of the gate to take command easily.

SEVENTH RACE
Belmont
SEPTEMBER 18, 1982

7 FURLONGS. (1.20⅖) 76th Running THE MATRON. $75,000 Added. (Grade I). Foals of Mares served in 1979. (Filly foals of 1980.) Weight, 119 lbs. By subscription of $25 each if made on or before Tuesday, December 1, 1981 or $50 each on or before Tuesday, March 1, 1982, fee to accompany the nomination. To remain eligible the following payments must be made: $100 on or before Monday, June 1, 1982, $300 to start. The added money together with all nominations fees, eligibility payments, entry and starting fees for The Matron of 1982 to be divided 60% to first, 22% to second, 12% to third and 6% to fourth, after original nominator awards of $5,000 to the winner, $2,500 to second, $1,250 to third. Starters to be named through the entry box at the closing time of entries. Trophies will be presented to the winning owner, trainer and jockey and mementoes to the grooms of the first four finishers. Supplementary nominations may be made at the time of entry by a payment of $3,750 each to pass the entry box and $3,750 to start with the provision that supplementary nominees are excluded from original nominator awards. The nominator awards will be presented to the first three original nominees to finish. Closed with 358 nominations. Closed with 2 supplementary nominees: For Once'N My Life; Share The Fantasy

Value of race $121,000, value to winner $72,600, second $26,620, third $14,520, fourth $7,260. Mutuel pool $459,416, OTB pool $148,259.

Last Raced	Horse	Eqt.A.Wt	PP	St	¼	½	Str	Fin	Jockey	Odds $1
8Sep82 ^{8}Bel^{1}	Wings of Jove	2 119	1	3	$1^{1\frac{1}{2}}$	1^{2}	1^{4}	$1^{3\frac{1}{4}}$	McCauley W H	5.10
29Aug82 ^{8}Sar^{1}	(S)Share The Fantasy	2 119	5	1	3^{2}	3^{4}	3^{4}	$2^{1\frac{1}{4}}$	Fell J	.70
29Aug82 ^{8}Sar^{5}	Weekend Surprise	2 119	2	5	5	5	$4^{1\frac{1}{2}}$	$3^{1\frac{1}{4}}$	Velasquez J	5.40
4Sep82 ^{9}AP^{1}	(S)For Once'n My Life	2 119	4	2	2^{4}	2^{4}	$2^{\frac{1}{2}}$	4^{7}	Maple E	2.90
11Sep82 ^{1}Bel^{2}	Alluring Girl	2 119	3	4	4^{5}	4^{2}	5	5	Bailey J D	27.70

(S) Supplementary nomination.

OFF AT 5:08. Start good, Won driving. Time, :23, :46⅕, 1:11⅖, 1:24 Track fast.

$2 Mutuel Prices:				
	1–(A)–WINGS OF JOVE	12.20	3.60	2.80
	5–(E)–SHARE THE FANTASY		2.60	2.10
	2–(B)–WEEKEND SURPRISE			2.80

Ro. f, by Northern Jove—Regatela, by Dr. Fager. Trainer Sanborn Charles P. Bred by Helmore Farm (KY).

WINGS OF JOVE sprinted clear soon after the start, raced well out from the rail while making the pace, drew off leaving the turn and was kept to pressure to maintain her advantage. SHARE THE FANTASY, wide into the stretch, finished with good energy. WEEKEND SURPRISE, badly outrun early, failed to seriously menace with a mild late response. ALLURING GIRL saved ground to no avail. FOR ONCE'N MY LIFE prompted the pace to midstretch but had nothing left.

Owners— 1, Helmore Farm; 2, Robins G; 3, Kilroy W S; 4, Masterson Joan; 5, Mangurian H T Jr.

Trainers— 1, Sanborn Charles P; 2, Jolley Leroy; 3, Carroll Del W II; 4, Smith Thomas V; 5, Root Thomas F Sr.

Scratched—Magnifique (11Sep82 ^{9}Bel^{2}).

The filly had lost the Schuylerville when she had been hustled; she had scored her most important victory when she had been rated. I had a hunch about what was going to happen — and it happened.

Wings of Jove had been permitted to take a clear lead in :23 flat, while Fell stoutly restrained Share the Fantasy 5½ lengths behind her. The outcome of the race was decided by this slow quarter mile. When Wings of Jove turned into the stretch, she had a four-length lead but was still so untaxed that she was capable of running the last eighth of a mile in 12⅗ seconds. To catch her, Share the Fantasy would have had to cover the last furlong in :11⅘, a feat that might have been beyond the capabilities of Secretariat. Her position was hopeless. About as hopeless, in fact, as that of anyone who would attempt to argue that pace is not an important factor in handicapping.

FIVE

The Flamingo Stakes, 1980

E VERY WINTER the best 3-year-olds in America converge on
Florida for a number of tests that will reveal which are legitimate contenders for the Kentucky Derby and the other classic races.
Events like the Flamingo Stakes at Hialeah and the Florida Derby
at Gulfstream Park expose the 2-year-old stars of the previous season who aren't able to cope with longer distances. They bring to
prominence late-bloomers who don't begin to show signs of ability
until they have turned three. The races focus attention on the trainers of the principal contenders and point out the men who may not
be able to handle the tremendous pressure that the Triple Crown
races create.

A diverse cast of characters came to Hialeah in 1980 for a series
of races that would culminate with the 51st running of the Flamingo.
The most prominent of the horses, Rockhill Native, came with
somewhat implausible credentials. His pedigree was so undistinguished that his trainer had not hesitated to geld him when he was
a yearling. That trainer, Herb Stevens, was a crusty Kentuckian
more accustomed to handling cheap claimers than star stakes horses.
But Rockhill Native had scored six victories in nine races as a 2-

year-old, had won the Eclipse Award as the champion of his generation, and was now the future-book favorite for the Kentucky Derby.

Another of the principal horses at Hialeah was Superbity, who had only started his career on December 1 but had won four straight races at Calder in impressive fashion. His trainer, Melvin (Sunshine) Calvert, had been quietly compiling one of the best winning percentages in the sport over a period of years, impressing racing fans in New Jersey, Maryland, and Florida with his skill and patience. Now Sunshine had the horse who might finally put him in the limelight.

There were plenty of other hopefuls. Irish Tower had shown flashes of brilliance as a 2-year-old and was being trained by Stanley Hough, a young horseman who seemed to be on the brink of stardom. Koluctoo Bay had won one of the richest 2-year-old races of the previous season, but he was plagued by so many infirmities that his 3-year-old season figured to be less a test of his ability than a test of survival.

If this was not a brilliant crop of horses compared to the winters when Alydar and Spectacular Bid were campaigning in Florida, it was at least an interesting group — and, for me, it proved to be a very memorable one. I had already begun learning the principles and techniques of trip handicapping, but I still thought the usefulness of this new discipline was very limited. I knew enough now to spot horses who had been parked in the 6-path around the turn, or ones who had been hindered by a strong track bias, so I could bet them when they ran again. But trip handicapping did not seem to provide an overall understanding of the game as speed handicapping did. With my figures I could measure the ability of every horse in every race. In the 3-year-old stakes races that I was covering for the *Washington Post,* the figures pointed out the horses who were legitimate Kentucky Derby candidates and the ones who were merely pretenders. They helped me spot the lightly raced horses coming out of maiden or low-grade allowance races who had a future in the upper echelon of the 3-year-old ranks. But how, I wondered, could anybody form such judgments with trip handicapping? Did the fact that a horse made a big move in the 4-path at Hialeah mean that he was going to wind up draped with roses on the first Saturday in May?

It was not until 1980 that I was able to appreciate fully the power of trip handicapping. My speed figures did not help me judge the relative ability of the leading 3-year-olds at Hialeah. As often as not the figures were utterly misleading. Only an evaluation of horses' trips could have revealed the significance of the early-season results and pointed out the winner of the Flamingo. The 3-year-old campaign started in earnest with the running of the Bahamas Stakes:

NINTH RACE

Hialeah Park

FEBRUARY 6, 1980

7 FURLONGS. (1.20⅗) 44th Running BAHAMAS. $30,000 Added. 3–year–olds. By subscription of $75 each which shall accompany the nomination, $350 to pass the entry box, starters to pay $350 additiona! with $30,000 added. The added money and all fees to be divided 60% to the winner, 22½% to second, 11% to third, 5% to fourth and 2% to fifth. Weight, 122 lbs. Non–winners of $50,000 twice allowed 3 lbs. $50,000, 5 lbs. A sweepstakes 3 lbs. $9,000 twice, 10 lbs. Starters to be named through the entry box by the usual time of closing. Trophy to winning owner. Closed Wednesday, January 23, 1980 with 26 nominations.

Value of race $36,500, value to winner $21,900, second $8,030, third $4,015, fourth $1,825, fifth $730. Mutuel pool $176,082, Minus show pool $23,319.47. Perfecta Pool $81,891.

Last Raced	Horse	Eqt.A.Wt PP St	¼	½	Str	Fin	Jockey	Odds $1
14Jan80 9Crc3	Irish Tower	b 3 117 6 1	1hd	11½	16	112	Fell J	4.60
14Jan80 9Crc2	Ray's Word	b 3 117 2 6	510	43	412	2nk	Brumfield D	20.80
23Jan80 5Hia1	Rockhill Native	3 122 5 2	31	34	2½	33	Oldham J	30
16Jan80 9Hia1	Native Command	b 3 117 1 3	2½	21½	31½	48	Encinas R I	3.30
19Jan80 5Hia8	Classic Joker	3 117 4 5	6	6	6	58	Solomone M	115.50
22Jan80 8Hia1	Major Run	b 3 117 3 4	41	512	5hd	6	Hirdes R J Jr	80.10

OFF AT 5:08, EST. Start good, Won ridden out. Time, :23, :45⅕, 1:09⅖, 1:22⅗ Track fast.

$2 Mutuel Prices:

6–IRISH TOWER	11.20	5.20	2.10
2–RAY'S WORD		12.00	2.10
5–ROCKHILL NATIVE			2.10

$2 PERFECTA 6–2 PAID $150.40.

Dk. b or Br. c, by Irish Castle—Royal Loom, by Loom. Trainer Hough Stanley M. Bred by Glade Valley Farms Inc (Md).

IRISH TOWER showed good early foot while racing well out in the track, sprinted away from NATIVE COMMAND approaching the stretch and continued to draw off under intermittent urging. RAY'S WORD finished with good energy from the outside to wear down ROCKHILL NATIVE for the place. ROCKHILL NATIVE brushed several times with major run while between horses leaving the chute, wasn't able to stay with the leaders at the turn, was roused sharply entering the stretch but lacked a late response. NATIVE COMMAND tired from his early efforts. CLASSIC JOKER was always outrun. MAJOR RUN brushed with ROCKHILL NATIVE while between horses leaving the chute, was eased back midway along the backstretch and lacked a further response.

Owners— 1, Hough & Winfield; 2, Johnston W E; 3, Oak H A; 4, Hobeau Farm; 5, McCullogh Ruth; 6, Lehmann Verna.

Trainers— 1, Hough Stanley M; 2, Adams William E; 3, Stevens Herbert K; 4, Jerkens H Allen; 5, Ottaway Bernard; 6, Adams William E.

Scratched—I Speedup (25Aug79 8Sar5).

Rockhill Native brought his lofty reputation into the Bahamas Stakes and came out of it with his credibility destroyed. Irish Tower won the race by an incredible 12 lengths, while the Eclipse Award winner finished a dismal third. Even Irish Tower's trainer was stunned by the result. "When I saw him out front that far," Stanley Hough said, "I was speechless." When a horse runs so much better than he has ever run before, the improvement is often due to some highly favorable conditions, such as a strong bias. Irish Tower did get away with a slow first quarter in :23, and the track might have been slightly speed-favoring, but there was no reason to think the outcome of the Bahamas was a fluke. Even though Herb Stevens resorted to the hoariest of excuses to explain Rockhill Native's loss, saying that the track was too deep and "cuppy" for him, it was clear that the little gelding was not as good as he had looked the year before. Irish Tower appeared to be the best 3-year-old in Florida.

NINTH RACE
Hialeah Park
FEBRUARY 15, 1980

1 $\frac{1}{16}$ MILES. (1.40$\frac{3}{5}$) 2nd Running MARION COUNTY HANDICAP. Purse $25 3–year–olds, foaled in Florida and registered with the Florida Thoroughbre Association. By subscription of $75 each, which shall accompany the nominat pass the entry box, starters to pay $300 additional with $25,000 added. The ad and all fees to be divided 60% to the winner, 22% to second, 11% to third, 5 and 2% to fifth. Weights, Saturday, February 9, 1980. Starters to be named through the entry box by the of closing. Trophy to winning owner. Closed Friday, February 1, 1980 with 21 nominations.
Value of race $32,575, value to winner $19,545, second $7,167, third $3,583, fourth $1,629, fifth $651. Mutuel po
Perfecta Pool $96,011.

Last Raced	Horse	Eqt.	A.	Wt	PP	St	¼	½	¾	Str	Fin	Jockey
27Jan80 ^{7}Aqu^{2}	Colonel Moran		3	119	5	5	2^{1}	2^{1}	1^{2}	1^{6}	1^{10}	Velasquez J
2Feb80 ^{2}Hia^{1}	Lord Gallant	b	3	113	3	4	$7^{1\frac{1}{2}}$	$7^{1\frac{1}{2}}$	5^{hd}	$3^{\frac{1}{2}}$	2^{1}	Thornburg B
31Jan80 ^{9}Hia^{4}	Brilliant Company		3	114	7	8	8^{3}	8^{1}	6^{2}	$4^{\frac{1}{2}}$	3^{1}	Fell J
1Feb80 ^{9}Hia^{2}	Sure Spry		3	116	4	2	4^{hd}	5^{3}	$3^{\frac{1}{2}}$	2^{2}	$4^{\frac{1}{2}}$	Maple E
14Jan80 ^{9}Crc^{6}	Roar Of The Crowd	b	3	117	9	9	9	9	9	6^{3}	5^{1}	Rivera M A
1Feb80 ^{9}Hia^{4}	Flashy Mac		3	121	2	3	$5^{1\frac{1}{2}}$	$3^{\frac{1}{2}}$	4^{3}	$5^{1\frac{1}{2}}$	$6^{6\frac{1}{2}}$	Vasquez J
31Jan80 ^{9}Hia^{1}	Pirate Law		3	116	8	7	6^{2}	6^{3}	8^{1}	8^{7}	$7^{\frac{1}{2}}$	Cordero A Jr
1Feb80 ^{9}Hia^{6}	Silver Shears		3	114	1	1	$1^{1\frac{1}{2}}$	1^{1}	2^{1}	7^{2}	8^{14}	Brumfield D
1Feb80 ^{9}Hia^{1}	Creamette City		3	118	6	6	3^{1}	$4^{\frac{1}{2}}$	$7^{\frac{1}{2}}$	9	9	Solomone M

a–Coupled: Sure Spry and Creamette City.

OFF AT 5:07 EST. Start good, Won ridden out. Time, :22$\frac{2}{5}$, :45, 1:09$\frac{2}{5}$, 1:34$\frac{2}{5}$, 1:40$\frac{4}{5}$ Track goo

$2 Mutuel Prices:
5–COLONEL MORAN 4.20 3.8
4–LORD GALLANT 9.8
7–BRILLIANT COMPANY ....
$2 PERFECTA 5–4 PAID $31.60.

B. c, by Sham—Weaving Spider, by Nearula. Trainer Kelly Thomas J. Bred by Martin T B (Fla).
COLONEL MORAN raced in closest attendance to SILVER SHEARS, moved to the fore when rea far turn and drew off rapidly under intermittent urging. LORD GALLANT checked along the inside en backstretch, rallied while racing well out on the track leaving the far turn and finished with good ener the place. BRILLIAN COMPANY, Outrun early, rallied mildly while racing very wide. SURE SPRY, back, made a run nearing the stretch but weakened during the drive. ROAR OF THE CROWD, Outr furlongs, was forced to alter course after entering the stretch and his rider lost the whip inside sixteenth. FLASHY MAC moved up along the inside nearing the far turn but was finished after furlongs. PIRATE LAW failed to be a serious factor. SILVER SHEARS was used up making the pac METTE CITY, wide into the first turn, continued outside horses while remaining a factor to the far had nothing left.
Owners— 1, Martin T B; 2, Appleton A I; 3, Miami Lakes Ranch; 4, Frances A Genter Stable; 5, J F; 6, Elcee-H Stable; 7, Stud Toronado; 8, Zimmerman Mrs M; 9, Frances A Genter Stable.
Trainers— 1, Kelly Thomas J; 2, Goldfine Lou M; 3, Arcodia Antonio; 4, Calvert Melvin; 5, Michael; 6, Gomez Frank; 7, Azpurua Eduardo; 8, Levitch James M Jr; 9, Calvert Melvin.
Overweight: Lord Gallant 1 pound; Silver Shears 2.
Scratched—Lights of London (8Feb80 ^{8}Hia^{4}); Straight Strike (1Feb80 ^{9}Hia^{3}).

A promising colt named Colonel Moran came from New York for some easy pickings in the Marion County Handicap. Not only was this a weak field of Florida-breds, but Colonel Moran was running at a track and distance that gave him an insuperable advantage. The 1¹⁄₁₆-mile races at Hialeah start so close to the turn that horses with early speed and inside post positions win almost all the time. That advantage had now been compounded by the development of a strong rail bias at Hialeah. Colonel Moran raced in the 2-path around the first turn and part of the way down the backstretch, stalking an 82-to-1 sprinter, Silver Shears. When the pacesetter collapsed, Colonel Moran inherited the lead, stayed on the rail the rest of the way, and drew off to a 10-length victory. He missed the track record by only one fifth of a second; his speed figure was sensational. But under the circumstances he almost had to run a race that looked sensational. The bias had been in his favor, and he had an easy trip while most of his rivals had tough trips. (The second-place finisher, Lord Gallant, had been checked on the backstretch and had raced in the 3-path all the way around the turn.) I knew, at the very least, that Colonel Moran was not nearly as good as his figure suggested.

NINTH RACE
Hialeah Park
FEBRUARY 19, 1980

$1\frac{1}{16}$ MILES. (1.40⅗) ALLOWANCE. Purse $11,500. 3–year–olds, which have not won two races other than maiden or claiming. Weight, 122 lbs. Non–winners of $9,000 since January 1 allowed 3 lbs. $7,200 since December 15, 5 lbs. $6,600 since December 1, 7 lbs. (Maiden and Claiming races not considered.)

Value of race $11,500, value to winner $6,900, second $2,185, third $1,380, fourth $575, balance of starters $115 each. Mutuel pool $72,976. Perfecta Pool $85,036.

Last Raced	Horse	Eqt.	A.Wt	PP	St	¼	½	¾	Str	Fin	Jockey	Odds $1
11Feb80 ^{7}Hia^{1}	Prince Valiant		3 110	1	1	1^{hd}	3^{2}	1^{hd}	1^{2}	$1^{4\frac{1}{2}}$	Gonzalez M A^{5}	1.90
3Nov79 ^{6}Med^{1}	Koluctoo Bay		3 115	5	3	3^{1}	4^{1}	4^{hd}	3^{3}	$2^{1\frac{1}{4}}$	Maple E	1.60
31Jan80 ^{7}Hia^{4}	Two's A Plenty	b	3 115	6	6	$2^{1\frac{1}{2}}$	2^{hd}	2^{1}	2^{hd}	3^{3}	Vasquez J	56.10
8Feb80 ^{8}Hia^{1}	Proctor		3 115	3	7	7^{4}	7^{3}	7^{1}	$4^{1\frac{1}{2}}$	4^{2}	Perret C	3.30
17Jan80 ^{8}Hia^{1}	Just A Square	b	3 119	4	2	5^{2}	5^{2}	5^{2}	$5^{1\frac{1}{2}}$	$5^{2\frac{1}{2}}$	Bailey J D	20.70
30Jan80 ^{7}Hia^{4}	Tripack		3 117	7	4	4^{1}	1^{hd}	3^{1}	$6^{1\frac{1}{2}}$	6^{1}	Velasquez J	15.60
19Jan80 ^{5}Hia^{4}	Flying Target	b	3 115	8	5	8	8	8	7^{5}	7^{9}	Thornburg B	25.00
30Jan80 ^{7}Hia^{3}	Buckn' Shoe		3 115	2	8	6^{1}	6^{3}	6^{1}	8	8	Fell J	9.50

OFF AT 5:14, EST. Start good, Won ridden out. Time, :23⅗, :47⅗, 1:12, 1:36, 1:42 Track sloppy.

$2 Mutuel Prices:

1–PRINCE VALIANT	5.80	3.00	2.60
5–KOLUCTOO BAY		3.20	2.60
6–TWO'S A PLENTY			5.40

$2 PERFECTA 1–5 PAID $14.40.

Ch. c, by Stage Door Johnny—Royal Folly, by Tom Fool. Trainer Gaver John M Jr. Bred by Greentree Stud Inc (Ky).

PRINCE VALIANT broke alertly, was rated along while saving ground, shook off TWO'S A PLENTY when roused after entering the stretch and was ridden out to draw off. KOLUCTOO BAY reserved behind the leaders until near the stretch, came out for the drive and finished with good energy. TWO'S A PLENTY dueled with PRINCE VALIANT to the stretch and weakened. PROCTOR angled out while rallying leaving the far turn but lacked a further reponse. JUST A SQUARE saved ground to no avail. TRIPACK reached the front briefly midway along the backstretch but was finished after going six furlongs. FLYING TARGET was always outrun. BUCKIN' SHOE steadied after breaking slowly, moved within easy striking distance at the far turn but had nothing left.

Owners— 1, Greentree Stable; 2, Lightning Stable; 3, Smith A W; 4, Dogwood Stable; 5, Cisley Stable; 6, Bright View Farm; 7, Dixiana; 8, Eblen O.

Trainers— 1, Gaver John M Jr; 2, Ferriola Peter; 3, Buxton Merritt A; 4, Alexander Frank A; 5, Croll Warren A Jr; 6, Bardaro Anthony J; 7, Westler Charles R; 8, Sarazin Ronald J.

The ninth race at Hialeah on February 19 was only an allowance event, but it served as a prep for two Flamingo contenders. Koluctoo Bay was making his first start since winning the $251,600 Young America Stakes at the Meadowlands the previous fall. Prince Valiant was a lightly raced Greentree Stable colt with a growing reputation. Although Koluctoo Bay had greater accomplishments and speed figures, everything seemed to favor Prince Valiant on this day. He was breaking from the inside post position at the $1\frac{1}{16}$-mile distance on another track with a rail bias. Moreover, there was no consequential speed in the field, and while Prince Valiant had a little early foot Koluctoo Bay had none at all. The race developed as I had anticipated for Prince Valiant. He stayed on the rail, and without much urging by jockey Mike Gonzalez he found himself abreast of the leaders while they were going a slow quarter in :23⅗. He dropped back a bit on the backstretch as the pace quickened, but never had to leave the rail. Meanwhile, I was surprised to see what Eddie Maple was doing with Koluctoo Bay. Despite the lack of speed in the race, he had his mount under a hammerlock. I scribbled in my notes, "Hard held early. 2B, 3T." He was obviously a lot less interested in winning this allowance race than he would be in the Flamingo two weeks hence. While Prince Valiant drew away to an easy victory, Koluctoo Bay stayed off the rail and finished 4½ lengths behind. I knew the margin of victory had little to do with the colts' relative ability.

NINTH RACE
Hialeah Park
FEBRUARY 20, 1980

1 ⅛ MILES. (1.46⅗) 34th Running EVERGLADES. $40,000 added. 3-year-olds. By subscription of $100 each which shall accompany the nomination, $400 to pass the entry box, starters to pay $400 additional with $40,000 added. The added money and all fees to be divided 60% to the winner, 22% to second, 11% to third, 5% to fourth and 2% to fifth. Weight: 122 lbs. Non-winnrs of $50,000 twice allowed 3 lbs.; $50,000, 5 lbs. $25,000 twice, 8 lbs.; a sweepstakes, 10 lbs. Starters to be named through the entry box by the usual time of closing. Trophy to winning owner. Closed with 28 nominations.

Value of race $49,200, value to winner $29,520, second $10,824, third $5,412, fourth $2,460, fifth $984. Mutuel pool $123,827. Perfecta Pool $107,972.

Last Raced	Horse	Eqt.	A.	Wt	PP	St	¼	½	¾	Str	Fin	Jockey	Odds $1
6Feb80 ^{9}Hia^{3}	Rockhill Native		3	122	5	3	3^{2}	3^{3}	3^{5}	$1^{\frac{1}{2}}$	$1^{1\frac{1}{4}}$	Oldham J	3.30
6Feb80 ^{9}Hia^{1}	Irish Tower	b	3	114	8	4	1^{hd}	1^{hd}	2^{2}	2^{3}	$2^{2\frac{1}{2}}$	Fell J	1.70
30Jan80 ^{7}Hia^{1}	Inland Voyager		3	112	1	5	6^{hd}	$6^{\frac{1}{2}}$	$6^{\frac{1}{2}}$	4^{2}	$3^{\frac{1}{2}}$	Cordero A Jr	a-9.10
14Jan80 ^{9}Crc^{1}	Superbity	b	3	119	3	2	2^{5}	2^{5}	1^{hd}	3^{3}	$4^{1\frac{1}{4}}$	Vasquez J	1.30
11Feb80 ^{7}Hia^{2}	Starbinia	b	3	112	6	7	7^{2}	7^{2}	7^{4}	$6^{1\frac{1}{2}}$	5^{3}	Rivera M A	a-9.10
6Feb80 ^{9}Hia^{2}	Ray's Word	b	3	117	7	6	5^{4}	5^{5}	4^{hd}	5^{1}	6^{2}	Brumfield D	13.60
31Jan80 ^{9}Hia^{5}	Angry Count	b	3	114	4	8	8	8	8	$7^{\frac{1}{2}}$	7^{nk}	Fires E	122.40
31Jan80 ^{9}Hia^{9}	Rain Prince		3	113	2	1	$4^{\frac{1}{2}}$	4^{hd}	5^{3}	8	8	Maple E	128.10

a-Coupled: Inland Voyager and Starbinia.

OFF AT 5:14 EST Start good, Won driving. Time, :22⅖, :45⅕, 1:09⅖, 1:35⅕, 1:49 Track fast.

$2 Mutuel Prices:				
	5-ROCKHILL NATIVE	**8.60**	**5.20**	**3.80**
	7-IRISH TOWER		**3.80**	**2.80**
	1-INLAND VOYAGER (a-entry)			**3.60**
	$2 PERFECTA 5-7 PAID $44.00.			

Ch. g, by Our Native—Beanery, by Cavan. Trainer Stevens Herbert K. Bred by Carolaine Farm & Thomas (Ky).

ROCKHILL NATIVE allowed to follow the leaders while well in hand, moved fast to reach the front from the outside leaving the far turn and proved clearly best in a stiff drive. IRISH TOWER raced outside SUPERBITY while alternating for the lead to the stretch and fought it out gamely in a long drive. INLAND VOYAGER, unhurried early, rallied entering the stretch and was going well at the finish. SUPERBITY saved ground while vying for the lead with IRISH TOWER, remained prominent to the stretch and weakened. STARBINIA failed to seriously menace. RAY'S WORD had no apparent excuse. ANGRY COUNT showed nothing. RAIN PRINCE failed to be a serious factor.

Owners— 1, Oak H A; 2, Hough & Winfield; 3, Darby Dan Farm; 4, Frances A Genter Stable; 5, Darby Dan Farm; 6, Johnston W E; 7, Floro & Marcocchio & Welsh; 8, Brunton J M.

Trainers— 1, Stevens Herbert K; 2, Hough Stanley M; 3, Rondinello Thomas L; 4, Calvert Melvin; 5, Rondinello Thomas L; 6, Adams William E; 7, Bolero Joseph M; 8, Laurin Roger.

Overweight: Rain Prince 1 pound.

Now that Rockhill Native had lost status, the Everglades Stakes was expected to demonstrate whether Superbity or Irish Tower was the best 3-year-old in Florida. Superbity had shown excellent speed while winning all four of his starts. Irish Tower had been indisputably brilliant in winning the Bahamas, though he had not yet proved he could carry his speed for 1⅛ miles. I could only guess which of them might be faster and gamer, but the crowd settled on Superbity, making him the 6-to-5 favorite.

Both jockeys were determined to use their horses' speed to the fullest advantage. Superbity and Irish Tower raced head-and-head to the first turn, covering the initial quarter mile in a swift 22⅖ seconds. Neither could shake away from the other, and they were still head-and-head after an enervating half mile in :45⅕. Sitting five lengths behind the leaders, with no other horse in the vicinity of him, was Rockhill Native. Jockey John Oldham was quite happy to let the leaders engage in this mutual destruction a while longer, but after they had reached the six-furlong mark in an insane 1:09⅖ he made his move, and Rockhill Native had little difficulty scoring a victory that restored his reputation. But he had barely crossed the finish line when handicapper Jim Packer, who was watching the race next to me in the press box, remarked, "They ought to sell him tomorrow. He'll never have a trip like that again in his life."

Under the circumstances, Rockhill Native had not won as easily as he might have. He defeated Irish Tower by only 1¼ lengths, with Superbity another three lengths back in fourth place. Irish Tower had held on with such remarkable determination after the speed duel that I was convinced he was the best 3-year-old in Florida. Quite probably he was the best 3-year-old in America.

But I never got the chance to prove this thesis. After Irish Tower's heroic second-place finish, Hough said, "He was acting real funny. And the next morning he was hurting." The trainer summoned a veterinarian, and the x-rays he took disclosed that Irish Tower had suffered a chip fracture in his right front knee that would sideline him for at least six months. He would miss not only the Flamingo but the whole Triple Crown series as well. The 3-year-old picture in Florida, which had momentarily seemed so clear, was confused again. When ten horses were entered in the $179,950 Flamingo, no handicapper of any persuasion could have considered it an easy race. These were the past performances:

10 HIALEAH — 1⅛ MILES HIALEAH — START ⤴ ⤳ FINISH

1⅛ MILES. (1.46⅘) 51st Running THE FLAMINGO STAKES (Grade 1). $125,000 Added. 3-year-olds. By subscription of $250 each, which shall accompany the nomination, by Saturday, January 5, 1980, or by supplementary nomination of $5,000 each by Monday, March 3, 1980. $1,500 to pass the entry box, starters to pay $1,500 additional with $125,000 added. The added money and all fees to be divided 60% to the winner, 22% to second, 11% to third, 5% to fourth and 2% to fifth. weights, 122 closing. Flamingo cup to winning owner. Closed Saturday, January 5, 1980 with 99 nominations. Supplementary nominations of $5,000 each may be made at closing time of entries.

Colonel Moran
Own.—Martin T B
B. c. 3, by Sham—Weaving Spider, by Nearula
Br.—Martin T B (Fla)
Tr.—Kelly Thomas J
122

	St.	1st	2nd	3rd	Amt.
1980	3	2	1	0	$57,795
1979	2	1	1	0	$10,660

Roar Of The Crowd
Own.—Edwards J F
B. c. 3, by Hold Your Peace—Little Niki, by Time Tested
Br.—Burke W (Fla)
Tr.—Passarelli Michael
122

	St.	1st	2nd	3rd	Amt.
1980	3	0	1	0	$7,383
1979	9	2	2	3	$15,554

1.Jan80—Run in Two Divisions 7th & 9th Races.

Inland Voyager
Own.—Darby Dan Farm
B. c. 3, by Roberto—Shearwater, by Sea-Bird
Br.—Galbreath Mrs J M (Ky)
Tr.—Rondinello Thomas L
122

	St.	1st	2nd	3rd	Amt.
1980	3	2	0	1	$19,212
1979	5	2	0	0	$9,900

Lord Gallant
Own.—Appleton A I
Ch. c. 3, by My Gallant—Fleet Anita, by Ron's Babu
Br.—Diamond C Farm Inc (Fla)
Tr.—Goldfine Lou M
122

	Turf Record			St.	1st	2nd	3rd	Amt.
	1	0	0	1980	3	1	1	0	$13,877
				1979	1	0	0	0	$7,250

15Dec79—Run in Two Divisions 7th & 9th Races.

Spruce Needles
Own.—Lehmann Mrs V
B. c. 3, by Big Spruce—Knitted Gloves, by White Gloves II
Br.—Golden Chance Farm Inc (Ky)
Tr.—Adams William E
122

	Turf Record			St.	1st	2nd	3rd	Amt.
	2	1	1	0	1980	3	0	1	1	$6,313
				1979	9	3	1	2	$35,064

15Dec79—Run in Two Divisions 7th & 9th Races.
6Nov79—Placed first through disqualification

Prince Valiant
Own.—Greentree Stable
Ch. c. 3, by Stage Door Johnny—Royal Folly, by Tom Fool
Br.—Greentree Stud Inc (Ky)
Tr.—Gaver John M Jr
122

	St.	1st	2nd	3rd	Amt.
1980	4	3	1	0	$21,000
1979	0	M	0	0	

Koluctoo Bay

Own.—Lightning Stable

B. c. 3, by Creme Dela Creme—Incommunicado, by Double Jay
Br.—Chandler A H (Ky)
Tr.—Ferriola Peter

122

	St.	1st	2nd	3rd	Amt.
1980	1	0	1	0	$2,185
1979	8	2	1	2	$197,556

GR
19Feb80- 9Hia sly 1⅛ :47½ 1:12 1:42	Allowance	5 3 42½ 42 32 24½	Maple E	*101* 115	*1.60	88-17 PrinceValiant110⁴½KoluctooBy115½Two'sAPlenty115³ No excuse 8
3Nov79- 6Med gd 1⅛ :47½ 1:11¾ 1:43	Y'ng America	8 9 77½ 2½ 1hd	Velasquez J	*119* 112	10.30	96-17 Koluctoo Bay 112¹½ Gold Stage 119⁸ Joanie's Chief 122²½ Driving 15
14Oct79- 8Bel my 1 :46½ 1:12¾ 1:38½	Champagne	4 6 55½ 32 43½ 48	Velasquez J	112	14.50	63-24 Jonie's Chief122⅓OppenInlett... No excuse 8
30Sep79- 8Bel sly 7f :22½ :46½ 1:23¾	Cowdin	1 5 59½ 513 411 26	Velasquez J	115	38.70	78-24 Rockhill Native122² Koluctoo... Son A Dough12³½ Rallied 9
14Sep79- 6Bel fst 7f :22½ :45½ 1:24	Allowance	2 8 83¾ 75½ 46½ 33	Saumell L	b 120	8.00	79-17 Storm Wave 117ⁿᵈ Straight Strike 120³KoluctooBay120ⁿᵏ Rallied 9
3Sep79- 8Bel fst 6½f :23 :46½ 1:18¾	Md Sp Wt	5 10 74½ 1hd 1² 1²	Saumell L	b 118	3.40	84-17 KoluctooBay118²WarofWords118ⁿᵈRaiseACrown113⁷ Drew clear 13
11Aug79- 6Sar fst 6f :22½ 1:10½	Md Sp Wt	7 10 64½ 44 36 33¾	Saumell L	b 118	18.90	83-13 Attengur 118⅝ Speed To Spare 118³KoluctooBay118³½ No mishap 10
22Jly79- 6Bel fst 6f :22½ :45½ 1:11¾	Md Sp Wt	6 7 10½10½12 712 714	Saumell L	118	4.40	70-18 Fappiano 118⅓½ Buck Island 118⁶½ Rectory 118½ No factor 11
5Jly79- 6Bel fst 5½f :22½ :45½ 1:04	Md Sp Wt	10 8 75½ 56½ 46 45½	Saumell L	118	63.00	90-16 AfricanWater118³½SpeedToSpre118¹½Imromeo118⅓ Wide greenly 10

LATEST WORKOUTS   Mar 1 Hia 5f fst 1:01 h   Feb 16 Hia 4f fst :48½ b   ●Feb 8 Hia 3f fst :36 h   Feb 13 Hia 4f fst :48½ h

Hard held 28 5T (handwritten)

Rockhill Native ✻

Own.—Oak H A

Ch. g. 3, by Our Native—Beanery, by Cavan
Br.—Carolaine Farm & Thomas (Ky)
Tr.—Stevens Herbert K

122

	St.	1st	2nd	3rd	Amt.
1980	3	2	0	1	$42,535
1979	9	6	2	0	$267,112

GR
20Feb80- 9Hia fst 1⅛ :45½ 1:09¾ 1:49	Everglades	5 3 35 32 1½ 1½	Oldham J	*113*	3.30	87-16 Rockhill Native 122¹½ IrishTower114²⅓InlandVoyager112½ Driving 8
6Feb80- 9Hia fst 7f :23 :45½ 1:22¾	Bahamas	5 2 3½ 3½ 2½ 1¹½	Oldham J	*95*	*.10	78-20 IrishTwr711?ay'sWord117⁷ⁿᵏRockhillNtive122³ Brushed early 7
23Jan80- 5Hia fst 6f :22½ :46 1:11	Allowance	6 3 34 2hd 1² 1¹½	Oldham J	*106*	*.10	88-21 RockhillNtve122?yProspect122⁵½Silver Shears115¹ Easily 6
14Oct79- 8Bel fst 1 :46½ 1:12¾ 1:38½	Champagne	6 2 1½ 1² 11½ 1¹½	Oldham J	122	*.30	75-25 Joanie'sChief122⁴Oogoople122²½Gogoople122⁴½ Weakened 7
30Sep79- 8Bel sly 7f :22½ :46½ 1:23¾	Cowdin	5 4 45½ 21 1⁴ 16	Oldham J	122	*.30	84-24 RockhillNtive122⁶KoluctooBay122ⁿⁱSonOfADough122³ Ridden out 6
15Sep79- 8Bel fst 1⅛ :47½ 1:22	Futurity	7 1 1½ 1² 14 1⁴	Oldham J	122	*1.10	92-11 RockhillNtive122⁴GoldStage122? Bold State... Handily 8
25Aug79- 8Sar fst 6½f :22½ :44¾ 1:16½	Hopeful	2 9 22 2ⁿᵈ 1² 1⁶½	Oldham J	122	*1.10●	94-12 ⑩RockhillNative122⁶½J.P.Brother122?GoldStage122? Came over 12

25Aug79—Disqualified and placed sixth

11Aug79- 9Mth fst 6f :21½ 1:08¾	Sapling	7 2 32 2½ 1½ 1³	Oldham J	122	2.70	96-10 Rockhill Native122³ Antique Gold122⁷GoldStage122³ Ridden out 7
31Jly79- 9Mth fst 6f :22½ :45 1:03	Tyro	4 4 34 3²½ 1½ 1²	Oldham J	122	6.30	100-11 Antique Gold118² Rockhill Nati... 122⁴½IrishTower122ⁿᵏ 2nd best 4
30Jun79- 8CD fst 5½f :22½ :46½ 1:05½	Jeff Cup	2 6 44 3ⁿᵏ 1½ 1²	Oldham J	122	*.50	97-10 RockhillNative122²EarlOfOdessa122⁴Egg'sDynamite122½ Driving 9

LATEST WORKOUTS   Mar 2 Hia 5f sly 1:02½ h   ●Feb 27 Hia 7f fst 1:25 h   Feb 17 Hia 5f fst 1:00¾ h   Feb 13 Hia 1 fst 1:40 h

Stake Perfect Trip (handwritten)

Ray's Word

Own.—Johnston W E

B. c. 3, by Verbatim—Winable, by Etonian
Br.—Fourwyn Stable & Whitesell J & L (Ohio)
Tr.—Adams William E

122

Turf Record				St.	1st	2nd	3rd	Amt.
St.	1st	2nd	3rd	1980	4	0	2	1	$34,540
1	0	1	0	1979	11	5	5	0	$127,677

GR
20Feb80- 9Hia fst 1⅛ :45½ 1:09¾ 1:49	Everglades	7 5 54½ 47 58½ 68½	Brumfield D	*99*	13.60	85-16 RockhillNative122¹½IrishTower114²⅓InlandVoyager112½ Driving 8
6Feb80- 9Hia fst 7f :23 :45½ 1:22¾	Bahamas	2 6 52½ 4⁴ 43 43	Brumfield D	*115*	20.80	78-20 IrishTwr711?ay'sWord117⁷ⁿᵏRockhillNative122³ Up for place 7
14Jan80- 9Crc fst 1⅛ :48½ 1:12½ 1:45½	Trop Pk Dby	9 4 42 43 43 23	Marquez J	*105*	19.40	88-11 Irish Tower 121³ Ray's Word 121¹½ Gained place 11
1Jan80- 9Crc fst 1⁷⁰ :48½ 1:12½ 1:45	New Yr's Day	6 6 57 43 52½ 36	Marquez C	b	10.90	89-11 Irish Tower 121⁵Flashy Mac 117½ Ray's Word 122½ Weakened 9

1Jan80—Run in Two Divisions 7th & 9th Races.

| 15Dec79- 9Crc fm 1½ ⊕:49 1:13½ 1:45½ | Cty Of Miami | 3 3 2½ 3³ 2½ 22½ | Marquez C | b | 5.70 | 75-20 Angry Count 115²½ Ray's Word 120³ Prune Dew 115ⁿᵈ Gamely 7 |

15Dec79—Run in Two Divisions 7th & 9th Races.

| 27Oct79- 9Bel fst 1⅛ :47½ 1:12½ 1:45½ | ⑤Kindergarten | 6 4 34½ 32½ 1hd 2ⁿᵒ | Costa A J | b 124 | *.90e | 79-20 ⑩Bellbrook Boy 115ⁿᵒ Ray's Word 124ʰᵈ Sweet Audrey 121⁵½ 11 |

27Oct79—Placed first through disqualification

60ct79- 9Tdn gd 1 :47½ 1:13¾ 1:40½	⑤Juv Mile	3 4 3½ 1½ 1hd 1½	Costa A J	b 122	2.20e	75-24 Ray's Word 122½ Sweet Audrey 119½ Sir Gray 118⁴ Driving 12
15Sep79- 9Tdn fst 6f :22½ :46½ 1:11¾	Aspirant	4 8 45 44 3²½ 4²	Costa A J	b 124	*1.60	83-14 Lt. John 115²½ Ray's Word 124¹ Irish Escapade 117⁴ Rallied 11
2Sep79- 9RD fst 6f :22 :45½ 1:11¾	Cradle Stake	2 3 21 21½ 1hd	Costa A J	b 122	*1.20e	85-19 Ray's Word 122ⁿᵏ Going Magic 122¹ Etched In Gold 119⁵ 12

LATEST WORKOUTS   Feb 17 Hia 1 fst 1:12 h   Feb 3 Hia 5f fst 1:02 b   Jan 27 5f sly 1:04 b

+1 (handwritten)

Superbity

Own.—Frances A Genter Stable

Ch. c. 3, by Groshawk—My Dear Girl, by Rough'n Tumble
Br.—Frances A Genter Stable (Fla)
Tr.—Calvert Melvin

122

	St.	1st	2nd	3rd	Amt.
1980	3	2	0	0	$32,257
1979	2	2	0	0	$9,300

GR
20Feb80- 9Hia fst 1⅛ :45½ 1:09¾ 1:49	Everglades	3 2 2hd 2hd 34 42½	Vasquez J	*105* 119	*1.30	83-16 RockhillNative122¹½IrishTower122¹½InlandVoyger112½ Weakened 8
14Jan80- 9Crc fst 1⅛ :48½ 1:12½ 1:45½	Trop Pk Dby	10 1 1½ 1² 1² 13	Vasquez J	*118* 121	2.10	91-11 Superbity121³ Ray's Word121½IrishTower122? Handily 11
1Jan80- 7Crc fst 1⁷⁰ :48½ 1:12½ 1:45	New Yr's Day	4 1 1½ 1½ 14 1⁵	Vasquez J	*108* 114	*1.40	95-11 Superbity 114⁵ GarryOfThunderSpaceNewchargendily 5

1Jan80—Run in Two Divisions 7th & 9th Races.

| 21Dec79- 7Crc fst 6f :22½ :46½ 1:12¼ | Allowance | 5 4 11 1½ 11½ 13½ | Vasquez J | b 120 | *1.30 | 93-13 Superbity 120³½Hurricane Mercury117½HaddenHill113ⁿᵏ Ridden out 7 |
| 1Dec79- 4Crc fst 6f :23 :46½ 1:12¾ | Md Sp Wt | 5 5 3ⁿᵏ 11½ 1hd 1² | Vasquez J | b 120 | 4.30 | 88-15 Superbity 120² Fast Fast Freddie 120⁵ Orate 120ʰᵈ Driving 12 |

LATEST WORKOUTS   Feb 19 Hia 3f sly :35½ b   Feb 15 Hia 1 fst 1:37½ h   Feb 10 Hia 6f fst 1:14 h   Feb 6 Hia 4f fst :52 b

Rail nr. dust (handwritten)

The betting public made Rockhill Native the 7-to-5 favorite, Colonel Moran the surprisingly close second choice at 3 to 2, and Prince Valiant the third choice at 5 to 1. They were all different types of horses, but they had one thing in common: They had made their reputations with the aid of perfect trips. The odds on Prince Valiant were patently ridiculous. He had never even run in a stakes race, and his only big win in allowance company had come on a favorable rail against a rival, Koluctoo Bay, who wasn't even trying. Colonel Moran had not proved himself, either. In his one distance race before he came to Florida, he had been favored at 3 to 5 but had lost to a nonentity. Winning the Marion County Handicap with the aid of a track bias and a perfect trip hardly proved that he was ready to go 1⅛ miles against some of the best 3-year-olds in the country.

Of Rockhill Native I was not certain. He did have my top speed figure, but he had earned it under circumstances that he would probably never be lucky enough to see again. None of his three previous races had been particularly impressive. Rockhill Native certainly deserved a measure of respect, but he was a very beatable favorite.

If he were going to be beaten, there were two horses capable of doing it: Superbity and Koluctoo Bay. Superbity had done everything right until his loss in the Everglades. Sunshine Calvert blamed the defeat on his too-fast mile workout five days before the race, but even if a handicapper did not accept that rationalization (which I didn't), the fact remained that Superbity had run pretty well after engaging in that suicidal speed duel. Nothing in his previous past performances suggested that he was an uncontrollable front-running type, that he would have to get involved in a duel with the speedy Colonel Moran. I felt sure that he would run well in the Flamingo. And I thought that Koluctoo Bay would have to run well, too. His most recent race had been strictly a tune-up, and he had shown as a 2-year-old that he could run as well as any member of his generation.

In none of these judgments had my speed figures played an important part. The top three figures in the race belonged to the three horses I didn't especially like: Rockhill Native, Colonel Moran, and Prince Valiant. I was so unaccustomed to making decisions without them that I could not bring myself to make a massive plunge on the Flamingo, but I still made a reasonably healthy play in the exactas, combining Superbity, Koluctoo Bay, and (to a lesser extent) Rockhill Native.

TENTH RACE
Hialeah Park
MARCH 5, 1980

1 ⅛ MILES. (1.46⅗) 51st Running THE FLAMINGO STAKES (Grade I). $125,000 Added. 3-year-olds. By subscription of $250 each, which shall accompany the nomination, by Saturday, January 5, 1980, or by supplementary nomination of $5,000 each by Monday, March 3, 1980. $1,500 to pass the entry box, starters to pay $1,500 additional with $125,000 added. The added money and all fees to be divided 60% to the winner, 22% to second, 11% to third, 5% to fourth and 2% to fifth. weights 122 lbs. Flamingo Cup to winning owner. Closed Saturday, January 5, 1980 with 99 nominations. Supplementary nominations of $5,000 each may be made at closing time of entries. Value of race $179,750, value to winner $107,850, second $39,545, third $19,773, fourth $8,987, fifth $3,595. Mutuel pool $247,613. Perfecta Pool $147,298.

Last Raced	Horse	Eqt.	A.	Wt	PP	St	¼	½	¾	Str	Fin	Jockey	Odds $1
20Feb80 ^{9}Hia^4	Superbity	b	3	122	10	5	2^{3}	2^{6}	1^{hd}	1^{4}	1^{6}	Vasquez J	7.20
19Feb80 ^{9}Hia^2	Koluctoo Bay		3	122	7	8	$5^{\frac{1}{2}}$	$5^{1\frac{1}{2}}$	5^{4}	$3^{1\frac{1}{2}}$	2no	Maple E	15.70
20Feb80 ^{9}Hia^1	Rockhill Native		3	122	8	9	$4^{\frac{1}{2}}$	4^{4}	$4^{1\frac{1}{2}}$	$2^{1\frac{1}{2}}$	$3^{3\frac{1}{2}}$	Oldham J	1.40
20Feb80 ^{9}Hia^3	Inland Voyager		3	122	3	4	8^{hd}	9^{2}	8^{2}	6^{hd}	$4^{\frac{1}{2}}$	Cordero A Jr	15.60
15Feb80 ^{9}Hia^2	Lord Gallant	b	3	122	4	3	$3^{\frac{1}{2}}$	$3^{\frac{1}{2}}$	$3^{\frac{1}{2}}$	4^{2}	$5^{\frac{3}{4}}$	Thornburg B	164.00
20Feb80 ^{9}Hia^6	Ray's Word	b	3	122	9	10	9^{2}	8^{3}	$6^{1\frac{1}{2}}$	7^{3}	6^{3}	Brumfield D	103.90
15Feb80 ^{9}Hia^1	Colonel Moran		3	122	1	2	1^{2}	1^{3}	2^{3}	5^{1}	7^{nk}	Velasquez J	1.50
15Feb80 ^{9}Hia^5	Roar Of The Crowd	b	3	122	2	1	6^{hd}	6^{hd}	$7^{1\frac{1}{2}}$	8^{4}	8^{5}	Rivera M A	329.00
19Feb80 ^{9}Hia^1	Prince Valiant		3	122	6	6	7^{3}	7^{hd}	9^{2}	9^{2}	$9^{1\frac{1}{4}}$	Gonzalez M A	5.40
31Jan80 ^{9}Hia^2	Spruce Needles		3	122	5	7	10	10	10	10	10	Solomone M	200.20

OFF AT 5:48, EST. Start good, Won driving. Time, :23, :45⅘, 1:10⅘, 1:37, 1:51⅕ Track fast.

$2 Mutuel Prices:

10–SUPERBITY	16.40	7.20	4.20
7–KOLUCTOO BAY		15.80	5.20
8–ROCKHILL NATIVE			2.60

$2 PERFECTA 10–7 PAID $265.80.

Ch. c, by Groshawk—My Dear Girl, by Rough'n Tumble. Trainer Calvert Melvin. Bred by Frances A Genter Stable (Fla).

SUPERBITY broke in stride from his outside post, ducked in slightly soon after the start, was hustled along going into the first turn, tried to bear out going into the turn, settled leaving the first turn, while forcing the pace, began to advance leaving the backstretch, gained the advantage at the three-eighths marker and steadily increased the margin through the stretch run under steady left-handed pressure. KOLUCTOO BAY obtained a good position early, rallied midway the second turn, remained inside for the stretch run and prevailed over ROCKHILL NATIVE in the final stride. ROCKHILL NATIVE was forced to race wide into the first turn when caught outside of five rivals remained outside was three wide coming into the stretch, reached the attending position in early stretch, could not gain on the winner and just failed to hold the place. INLAND VOYAGER, unhurried early, rallied on the second turn and was improving his position at the finish. LORD GALLANT raced forwardly throughout, but lacked a closing rally. RAY'S WORD, slowest to begin, raced outside and failed to reach serious contention. COLONEL MORAN, away alertly, set the pace to midway the second turn, then steadily fell back when displaced. ROAR OF THE CROWD failed to respond to pressure. PRINCE VALIANT showed little. SPRUCE NEEDLES was always outrun.

Owners— 1, Frances A Genter Stable; 2, Lightning Stable; 3, Oak H A; 4, Darby Dan Farm; 5, Appleton A I; 6, Johnston W E; 7, Martin T B; 8, Edwards J F; 9, Greentree Stable; 10, Lehmann Mrs V.

Trainers— 1, Calvert Melvin; 2, Ferriola Peter; 3, Stevens Herbert K; 4, Rondinello Thomas L; 5, Goldfine Lou M; 6, Adams William E; 7, Kelly Thomas J; 8, Passarelli Michael; 9, Gaver John M Jr; 10, Adams William E.

The horses who had been winning with easy trips were finding life a bit more difficult in the Flamingo. Rockhill Native was parked in the 5-path around the first turn. Prince Valiant was being engulfed by superior rivals. Colonel Moran was leading, but he was being stalked by a high-quality speed horse, Superbity.

Approaching the final turn, Superbity moved up, challenged Colonel Moran, and pulled away from him after encountering only minimal resistance. He had taken a commanding lead by the time Rockhill Native started to rally in the 3-path. Koluctoo Bay, meanwhile, was beginning to move up on the inside, saving ground around the turn.

By midstretch, Superbity was on his way to an easy victory, and Koluctoo Bay was lumbering up the rail on those bad legs, trying to catch the tired Rockhill Native. This would prove to be the last stretch run of his career, but he may have been spurred on by a rising chorus of encouragement from me and trip handicappers like Jim Packer and Paul Cornman, who had also bet enthusiastically on the Superbity–Koluctoo Bay exacta.

After the photo finish disclosed that Koluctoo Bay had put his nose on the wire in front of Rockhill Native, the trip handicappers let out a new chorus of whoops and went to the windows to collect a $265.80 exacta. That payoff persuaded me for the last time that the art of trip handicapping was not so imprecise or limited as I had once thought.

But if the trip handicappers had fully comprehended the Flamingo, the majority of racetrackers were surprised by the failure of the three favorites. The trainers of the losers were quick to offer excuses, and they all fell back on Herb Stevens's old favorite, that the racing surface had been too deep and "cuppy." What exposes the falsity of this notion is the fact that "cuppiness" is used only as a rationalization for defeat. No trainer in the history of the game has ever said, "My horse loves a cuppy track." After the Flamingo, however, the trainers agreed that even the word *cuppy* was an inadequate description of the Hialeah track. "A plowed field" still suggested something earthly. The Flamingo horses might as well have been racing on moon dust or some other alien substance to which no member of the species had ever been exposed. "The minute I came out to the course I knew we weren't going to get anything," Stevens said. "I thought it was disgraceful to present an important race under such circumstances." *Daily Racing Form* columnist Joe Hirsch summarized the prevailing view of the track: "Some liked it. Some didn't. The result is that a true picture of the East's classic prospects [did not emerge] in the Flamingo."

But trip handicappers had thought that the results of the Flamingo were quite logical and consistent with the horses' previous performance, and history eventually proved them right. Rockhill Native was a decent horse but no champion; after the Flamingo he would win only one more stakes race in his career. Prince Valiant did not lose the Flamingo because of cuppiness, but because his reputation was spurious; a few weeks later, in the Blue Grass Stakes at Keeneland, he lost to Rockhill Native by 31 lengths. Colonel Moran tired badly in the Flamingo because he couldn't go 1⅛ miles, as the trip handicappers had suspected beforehand; the rest of his career would verify that he was nothing more than a miler. And the trip handicappers eventually got a confirmation of their opinion that the best racehorse in Florida in the winter of 1981 had been Irish Tower. After recovering from his injury, he went to New York the next winter and dominated the handicap races there.

While the speed handicappers had been perplexed and the trainers had been forced to resort to tired rationalizations, the trip handicappers had been able to comprehend the significance of just about everything that happened at Hialeah in the winter of 1980.

SIX

Speed Handicapping

ALMOST ALL successful trip handicappers look with skepticism or condescension on their brethren who espouse speed handicapping. Knowing that pace, track biases, loss of ground on the turns, and a hundred other variables can affect a horse's final time, they believe it is absurd to view this time as an absolute expression of a horse's ability. Bettors who are products of a harness-racing background are especially disdainful of the speed handicappers, because they know that only rank amateurs are mesmerized by fast final times in the standardbred sport. "It doesn't matter how fast they run," my friend Charlie has told me for years. "It's how they run fast that counts."

The speed handicappers, in turn, shrug off these attacks with the sublime confidence of people who know they possess Ultimate Truth. The central task in handicapping is to evaluate the ability that horses have shown in their previous races. Speed figures measure the ability of every horse in every race with precision, while the trip handicappers are forced to rely on subjective observations that may be utterly irrelevant. What does it matter if a horse was accelerating 5-wide on the turn if he was doing it in an extraordinarily slow race?

In the debates between these two intellectual camps, my loyalties still lie with the speed handicappers. Figures changed my life; they gave me an understanding of the game I had never thought possible; they transformed me into a winning horseplayer. They are the most formidable handicapping tool ever devised. If they have become somewhat less profitable than they used to be, it is only because so many bettors have discovered what a wonderful device they are and have thus cut the payoffs on standout figure horses.

Handicappers who set out to learn to make figures invariably experience the same sense of awe and wonderment that I once did; they are hypnotized by their own creations and follow them slavishly. Even after I had begun to appreciate the importance of trips, it was wrenchingly difficult for me to bet a horse with a figure of 70 and a tough trip against one with a 75 and a perfect trip. If I could do it over again, I would have planned my development as a horseplayer the other way around, and I would recommend this course to any newcomer who wants to get serious about handicapping: Learn about trips first. Learn that there are no absolutes in the game, that speed figures must necessarily have many limitations. Then learn to calculate and use the figures, because they are essential to a full understanding of the sport.

At the time when I wrote *Picking Winners,* there was such widespread skepticism about speed handicapping that I felt I had to justify the intellectual validity of my approach. I explained not only the mathematics but the philosophy that underlay every calculation. Now that speed handicapping has such broad acceptance, this ought not to be necessary. The following pages detail, step by step, my method of making figures; but this time I will ask readers to accept on faith my assurance that it is intellectually, mathematically, and philosophically sound, and that it works. Those who are interested in the underpinnings of the method are urged to refer to the earlier book.

The premise of speed handicapping is simple: The ability of horses is best measured by how fast they run. The techniques of speed handicapping exist to measure how fast they actually do run. There would be no difficulties if all races were contested at the same distance on a uniform artificial surface. Then a horse who ran six furlongs in 1:10 would obviously be two fifths of a second (or approximately two lengths) faster than a rival who ran in 1:10⅗. But races are, of course, run at many different distances, and a handicapper must know how to compare a horse who ran six furlongs in 1:10 with one who raced seven furlongs in 1:23. This is done by means of a chart that translates every time at every distance into a number, called a *speed rating,* for purposes of easy comparison. Six furlongs in 1:10 might have a rating of 106 and seven furlongs in 1:23 a rating of 103, thus suggesting that the horse who ran six furlongs in 1:10 is superior. (These numbers are arbitrary; another speed chart based on the same method might have assigned ratings of 906 and 903 respectively).

Besides comparing times at different distances, the other great difficulty in speed handicapping is comparing times run on different days. Because of the weather or the way the racing surface is maintained, the inherent speed of a track can change from day to day. A horse who runs six furlongs in 1:10 may run in 1:11 the next. A horse who ran in 1:10 may actually be slower than a rival who ran in 1:10⅗ over a deeper track.

A speed handicapper attempts to measure the inherent speed of a track analytically and precisely. He may conclude that a track one day is three fifths of a second slower than normal. Because he is working with figures, not actual times, he might express this by saying the track is seven points slower than normal. This is the *daily track variant,* an adjustment that is made to the time of every horse who ran that day to take into account the speed of the racing surface. When the daily track variant is added to a horse's speed rating, the result is his *speed figure.*

Compiling a set of speed figures for a track is neither so complex nor time-consuming as a glance at all the charts and numbers on the ensuing pages may suggest. It takes one afternoon to perform the necessary preliminary calculations, and then about ten minutes' work a day to compute each day's variant and figures. Some people may find the process boring; indeed, there is a certain amount of drudgery involved. But to me the process has always seemed exciting and a little bit magical, for it enables a horseplayer to take a jumble of data and turn it into a thorough understanding of what is happening at a track.

At the outset of 1983 I was going to make my first trip to the

West Coast for a serious assault on Santa Anita. I started my preparations for this venture a year in advance, compiling speed figures for the Santa Anita meeting that began on December 26, 1981. I had never seen the track, but those numbers would enable me to understand the nature of the racing surface, the quality of the competition, the differences between racing in the West and the East. Any horseplayer attempting to create a set of figures from scratch can do so by following the procedure I used for Santa Anita.

I knew, or at least thought I could safely assume, one thing about the track: the relationship of times at various sprint distances. If, for example, I wanted to compare the times of horses who had raced at six and seven furlongs, I had only to refer to the chart on the opposite page.

A handicapper attempting to compare a horse who had run six furlongs in 1:09⅗ with a rival who had run seven furlongs in 1:22 could glance at the chart and know that these performances were equivalent. Both times had a speed rating of 115. The principles on which this chart is based were taught to me by a Harvard classmate, Sheldon Kovitz, and they have withstood the test of years of practical experience. These ratings apply to all races that are run around one turn. (The one-mile chart here would be applicable only to tracks like Arlington and Aqueduct, where the mile races start out of a chute on the backstretch, and not to Santa Anita, where they start in front of the stands and are run around two turns.) I have found only a few minor deviations from the chart. At Calder Race Course I have to add a couple points to the seven-furlong ratings. At Hollywood Park I have to subtract a point for 6½ and 7 furlongs. At some tracks the 5- and 5½-furlong ratings seem a little suspect, but not enough races are run at these distances to provide an accurate gauge of their accuracy.

Just as there is a fixed relationship between times at sprint distances, there is also a fixed relationship between times in route races that are run around two turns.

ONE-TURN SPEED RATING CHART

5 fur.		5½ fur.		6 fur.		6½ fur.		7 fur.		1 mile	
:56	130	1:02	133	1:08	135	1:15	124	1:21	127	1:34	124
1	127	1	130	1	132	1	121	1	125	1	122
2	123	2	126	2	129	2	119	2	122	2	120
3	120	3	123	3	126	3	116	3	120	3	117
4	116	4	120	4	123	4	113	4	117	4	115
:57	113	1:03	117	1:09	121	1:16	111	1:22	115	1:35	113
1	109	1	114	1	118	1	108	1	113	1	111
2	106	2	110	2	115	2	106	2	110	2	109
3	102	3	107	3	112	3	103	3	108	3	107
4	99	4	104	4	109	4	100	4	105	4	105
:58	96	1:04	101	1:10	106	1:17	98	1:23	103	1:36	103
1	92	1	98	1	103	1	95	1	101	1	101
2	89	2	95	2	100	2	93	2	98	2	99
3	85	3	92	3	98	3	90	3	96	3	96
4	82	4	89	4	95	4	87	4	93	4	94
:59	79	1:05	86	1:11	92	1:18	85	1:24	91	1:37	92
1	75	1	83	1	89	1	82	1	89	1	90
2	72	2	79	2	86	2	80	2	86	2	88
3	68	3	76	3	84	3	77	3	84	3	86
4	65	4	73	4	81	4	74	4	81	4	84
1:00	62	1:06	70	1:12	78	1:19	72	1:25	79	1:38	82
1	59	1	67	1	75	1	69	1	77	1	80
2	55	2	64	2	72	2	67	2	74	2	78
3	52	3	61	3	70	3	64	3	72	3	76
4	49	4	58	4	67	4	62	4	70	4	74
1:01	45	1:07	55	1:13	64	1:20	59	1:26	68	1:39	72
1	42	1	52	1	61	1	57	1	65	1	70
2	39	2	49	2	59	2	54	2	63	2	68
3	36	3	46	3	56	3	52	3	61	3	66
4	32	4	43	4	53	4	49	4	58	4	64
1:02	29	1:08	41	1:14	51	1:21	47	1:27	56	1:40	62
				1	48	1	44	1	54	1	60
				2	45	2	42	2	51	2	58
				3	42	3	49	3	49	3	56
				4	40	4	37	4	47	4	54
				1:15	37	1:22	34	1:28	45	1:41	52

THEORETICAL TWO-TURN SPEED RATING CHART

1 mile		1 mile, 70 yds		1 1/16 miles		1 1/8 miles	
1:34	133	1:38	134	1:40	137	1:46	141
1	131	1	132	1	135	1	139
2	129	2	130	2	133	2	137
3	126	3	128	3	131	3	135
4	124	4	126	4	129	4	133
1:35	122	1:39	124	1:41	127	1:47	131
1	120	1	122	1	125	1	129
2	118	2	120	2	123	2	127
3	116	3	118	3	121	3	125
4	114	4	116	4	119	4	124
1:36	112	1:40	114	1:42	117	1:48	122
1	110	1	112	1	115	1	120
2	108	2	110	2	113	2	118
3	105	3	108	3	111	3	116
4	103	4	106	4	109	4	114
1:37	101	1:41	104	1:43	107	1:49	113
1	99	1	102	1	105	1	111
2	97	2	100	2	103	2	109
3	95	3	98	3	101	3	107
4	93	4	96	4	100	4	105
1:38	91	1:42	94	1:44	98	1:50	104
1	89	1	92	1	96	1	102
2	87	2	90	2	94	2	100
3	85	3	88	3	92	3	98
4	83	4	86	4	90	4	96
1:39	81	1:43	84	1:45	88	1:51	95
1	79	1	82	1	86	1	93
2	77	2	81	2	84	2	91
3	75	3	79	3	82	3	89
4	73	4	77	4	81	4	87
1:40	71	1:44	75	1:46	79	1:52	86
1	69	1	73	1	77	1	84
2	67	2	71	2	75	2	82
3	65	3	69	3	73	3	80
4	63	4	67	4	71	4	78
1:41	61	1:45	65	1:47	69	1:53	77

A horse who runs one mile in 1:37 earns a rating of 101; he is slightly superior to a rival who runs 1⅛ miles in 1:50⅖ and earns a rating of 100. These relationships have stood the test of time, too.

Unfortunately — and this is where the complexities in speed handicapping begin — this chart can't be employed in conjunction with the chart for sprint races. I can't use it to compare 1$\frac{1}{16}$-mile races at Santa Anita with those at six furlongs, which is something I obviously need to be able to do. There is no universal, fixed relationship between times in one-turn and two-turn races, because of the different contours of racetracks and many other factors.

I use the same chart for sprint races at every track; six furlongs in 1:10 has a rating of 106 everywhere I make figures. But at Keeneland all the routes have ratings 6 points higher than the theoretical chart. At Pimlico all the routes are 11 points slower. How could I determine what equals what at Santa Anita?

Speed handicappers discover these relationships by looking at the results of a number of races in the same class. If I took a large sampling of $10,000 claiming races and found that the average winning times were 1:11 at six furlongs and 1:45 at 1$\frac{1}{16}$ miles, that evidence would suggest that these two times should have the same value on a speed-rating chart. Compiling this data is a somewhat laborious process. In *Picking Winners* I suggested that a handicapper wait until a gloomy day to perform his calculations, and then sit down with two or three months of result charts, a large sheet of poster paper, and a bottle of Jack Daniels'. For a California track, a white wine spritzer might be more appropriate.

I used three months of old *Racing Forms* with Santa Anita charts as the basis for my research. Then on my sheet of poster paper I created a vertical column for each of the major classes of races that Santa Anita offers: claiming events for $10–12,000, for $14–16,000, all the way up to $50,000. I had a column for maiden-special-weight races, and one for each of the major categories of allowance races: "nonwinners of $2500 other maiden or claiming"; "nonwinners of $2500 twice . . ."; "nonwinners of $2500 three times . . ."; then a catch-all category for all other allowance races and another for stakes.

Next I drew a horizontal line across the middle of the poster paper, to use the top half for data on sprints and the bottom for routes. Now I started to burrow through all the results. Every time I came to a race for older male horses that was run over a fast track, I noted the time, referred to my basic speed-rating charts, and wrote down the rating for that time in the appropriate column on my poster board. If a $14–16,000 claimer at six furlongs was run in 1:10, I would note that time had a rating of 106, and then transcribe "106" into the portion of the $14–16,000 column reserved for sprint races. If a 1 1/16-mile maiden race went in 1:45, I would find its rating of 88 and put that number in the appropriate spot.

A few notes on this procedure: I use only fast-track data because the time of one race on an extraordinarily slow track can distort the averages I am trying to compile. I don't use races limited to 2-year-olds or 3-year-olds, because their capabilities change during the course of the year. Three-year-olds run a lot slower in January than they do in November, and these discrepancies would also distort the averages. I don't bother with maiden-claiming races because those horses are often so erratic. I will, however, use races for fillies and mares, especially if I am dealing with a limited amount of data and need a larger sampling of results to compile meaningful averages. I have found that races restricted to females are run, on the average, seven points slower than open races. So I add seven points to my speed rating if I use such a race in compiling my averages. If a filly race is run in 1:10 (a rating of 106) I will write down 113 in the appropriate column.

A portion of my data for Santa Anita looked like this:

	$10–12,000	$14–16,000	$18–20,000
	103	91	115
	118	109	115
	105	106	105
	92	116	112
	98	108	105
	118	102	106
SPRINTS	112	121	103
	112	112	116
	112	98	111
	95	127	average
	87	average	110
	110	109	
	88		
	average		
	104		

	$10–12,000	$14–16,000	$18–20,000
	93	109	108
	107	99	110
	107	103	113
	109	111	103
ROUTES	91	99	109
	98	106	108
	103	99	average
	89	average	109
	105	104	
	average		
	101		

In the $10–12,000 claiming bracket, the average speed rating for sprints was three points higher than for routes. Because I assume that $10,000 horses have the same level of ability regardless of what distance they are running, that piece of evidence suggested that I should add three points to the route ratings in my speed chart. In the $14–16,000 bracket, the sprint ratings averaged five points higher. At $18–20,000 they were one point higher. I performed the same calculations for all the other classes at Santa Anita, found the difference between routes and sprints in all of them, and then took the average of those differences. The sprint ratings were three points higher than the routes. To correct this discrepancy, I added three points to all the ratings on my theoretical speed chart for two-turn races. The chart on the next page expresses the relationship between times at every different distance at Santa Anita.

At this point I was almost ready to start calculating my daily track variants. To judge the inherent speed of a racing surface, handicappers don't analyze soil samples; we don't take a yardstick and measure the depth of the track. Instead, we study results and compare the way the horses ran with the way they theoretically should have run. If I know that the average $10,000 claiming race at a track is run in 1:11, and I see a $10,000 race won in 1:12, that piece of evidence suggests to me that the track may be one second slow. Expressed another way, if the average winning figure for a class is 92, and a race is run with a rating of 78, the track appears 14 points slow.

SANTA ANITA SPEED RATINGS

6f		6 1/2f		7f		1m		1 1/16		1 1/8	
1:08	135	1:15	124	1:21	127	1:34	136	1:40	140	1:46	144
1	132	1	121	1	125	1	134	1	138	1	142
2	129	2	119	2	122	2	132	2	136	2	140
3	126	3	116	3	120	3	129	3	134	3	138
4	123	4	113	4	117	4	127	4	132	4	136
1:09	121	1:16	111	1:22	115	1:35	125	1:41	130	1:47	134
1	118	1	108	1	113	1	123	1	128	1	132
2	115	2	106	2	110	2	121	2	126	2	130
3	112	3	103	3	108	3	119	3	124	3	128
4	109	4	100	4	105	4	117	4	122	4	127
1:10	106	1:17	98	1:23	103	1:36	115	1:42	120	1:48	125
1	103	1	95	1	101	1	113	1	118	1	123
2	100	2	93	2	98	2	111	2	116	2	121
3	98	3	90	3	95	3	108	3	114	3	119
4	95	4	87	4	93	4	106	4	112	4	117
1:11	92	1:18	85	1:24	91	1:37	104	1:43	110	1:49	116
1	89	1	82	1	89	1	102	1	108	1	114
2	86	2	80	2	85	2	100	2	106	2	112
3	84	3	77	3	84	3	98	3	104	3	110
4	81	4	74	4	81	4	96	4	103	4	108
1:12	78	1:19	72	1:25	79	1:38	94	1:44	101	1:50	107
1	75	1	69	1	77	1	92	1	99	1	105
2	72	2	67	2	74	2	90	2	97	2	103
3	70	3	64	3	72	3	88	3	95	3	101
4	67	4	62	4	70	4	86	4	93	4	99
1:13	64	1:20	59	1:26	68	1:39	84	1:45	91	1:51	98
1	61	1	57	1	65	1	82	1	89	1	96
2	59	2	54	2	63	2	80	2	87	2	94
3	56	3	52	3	61	3	78	3	85	3	92
4	53	4	49	4	58	4	76	4	84	4	90
1:14	51	1:21	47	1:27	56	1:40	74	1:46	82	1:52	89
						1	72	1	80	1	87
						2	70	2	78	2	85
						3	68	3	76	3	83
						4	66	4	74	4	81
						1:41	64	1:47	72	1:53	80

I found, to my initial surprise, that these average winning figures in claiming races are very much the same from track to track. The $20,000 claiming horses at Belmont will have the same degree of ability as the $20,000 horses at Keystone, despite the difference in purses for which they compete. So I felt safe in using the same set of average winning figures, or *par figures,* for Santa Anita.

Claiming Price	Par Figure
$4000	73
$5000	75
$6500	79
$7–8000	83
$10–12,000	85
$14–16,000	88
$18–20,000	91
$20–25,000	94
$25,000–35,000	96
$40,000–50,000	100

(Note: Par figures do not apply to races limited to 2-year-olds or 3-year-olds. For races limited to fillies and mares, subtract seven points.)

While claiming races are much the same from track to track, nonclaiming races vary considerably. The quality of allowance and maiden-special-weight horses at high-class tracks like those in New York and Southern California will naturally be higher than they are elsewhere. So I had to calculate par figures for these classes at Santa Anita.

I already had the basis for these calculations in my computation of average winning speed ratings. In the $10–12,000 claiming bracket, it will be recalled, I had found that the average sprint was won with a rating of 104. In routes the original number had been 101 before I had added three points to my entire speed-rating chart for two-turn races, making the average for the whole class 104. I proceeded to compare this average with my established par for $10–12,000 races as well as for other classes.

Class	Par	Santa Anita average	Difference
$10–12,000	85	104	19
$14–16,000	88	108	20
$18–20,000	91	111	20

These comparisons and those for the other claiming categories indicated that the races at Santa Anita were run 20 points faster, on the average, than my established pars. This is another way of saying that Santa Anita is 20 points faster than the average track.

In my earlier computation of results for all the classes at Santa Anita, I had found that the average maiden-special-weight race was won with a speed rating of 110. Now that I knew Santa Anita was 20 points faster than the norm, I could say that the par figure for the class was 90. The par for "nonwinners of $2500 other than maiden or claiming" was 98. Now I had a complete set of par figures for the track:

Class	Par Figure
$10–12,000	85
$14–16,000	88
$18–20,000	91
$20–25,000	94
$30–35,000	96
$40–50,000	100
Maiden special weight	90
Nonwinners of $2500 . . .	98
Nonwinners of $2500 twice . . .	101
Nonwinners of $2500 three times . . .	105
Other allowances	107
Stakes	114

With this chart, I had the basis for evaluating the inherent speed of the Santa Anita track on any day.

On opening day, December 26, 1981, the first race was a 1¹⁄₁₆-mile event for 3-year-olds and up with a claiming price of $18–20,000. The winner, Knight of Gold, was timed in 1:43, which gets a rating of 110 on my Santa Anita chart. The par figure for $18–20,000 claimers is 91. So this race was run 19 points faster than par. In such a manner did I analyze the entire card.

Race	Class	Distance	Time	Rating	Par	Difference
1	$18–20,000 clm	1 1/16	1:43	110	91	—19
2	$40,000 clm	6f	1:09	121	100	—21
3	2-year-olds	6f	1:09 2/5	115	—	—
4	2-year-olds	6f	1:10 4/5	95	—	—
5	turf					
6	NW $2500 twice	1 1/16	1:42	120	101	—19
7	turf					
8	stake	6f	1:08	135	114	—21
9	NW $2500	1 1/16	1:42 2/5	116	98	—18

The five races on which I had based my calculations had been faster than par by 19, 21, 19, 21, and 18 points. Averaging these numbers, I concluded that the Santa Anita track on December 26 was 20 points faster than par. The track variant was —20, meaning that I would subtract 20 points from the rating that every horse had earned running over it. Knight of Gold, who had won the first race in 1:43 — a rating of 110 — had earned a figure of 90. I entered the winning figure of each race into my notebook in this fashion:

Date	Variant	1	2	3	4	5	6	7	8	9
Dec 26	—20	90	101	95	75	T	100	T	115	96

I calculated the variant for January 8 in a similar way, although in actual practice I expend less ink, writing down only the par figure, the speed rating, and the difference.

Race	Par	Rating	Difference
1	78	72	+6
2	84	80	+6
3	—	69	—
4	—	77	—
5	—	100	—
6	—	81	—
7	101	109	—8
8	98	111	—13
9	98	101	—3

This day was somewhat more confusing, but after averaging +6, +6, −8, −13, and −3, I determined that the variant was −2, and again inscribed the results in my notebook.

Date	Variant	1	2	3	4	5	6	7	8	9
Jan 8	−2	70	78	67	75	98	79	107	109	99

With such calculations I was developing the means to compare horses who had raced over very different racing surfaces on different days at Santa Anita — such as Bond Rullah and Maxistar, who met each other in a six-furlong race on January 15.

Bond Rullah

Own.—Braun Katherine or R **115**

B. g. 5, by Exalted Rullah—Bond Clipper, by Poona II
Br.—Fallon T F (Cal) **1981 21 8 5 3 $109,175**
Tr.—Costello Arthur A **1980 8 1 0 1 $6,350**

26Dec81-2SA	6f	:213	:442	1:09 ft	*3	119	32	31½	1hd	15	Castaneda M6	40000	93	BondRullh,SupremGlow,BrPudding	9
13Dec81-6Hol	6f	:214	:444	1:101ft	4	116	2hd	31½	2½	1½	Castaneda M5	Alw	86	BondRullh,VictorySmpl,MdnghtMn	6
6Dec81-4Hol	6½f	:214	:443	1:163ft	4¼	116	1½	1½	12	3hd	Castaneda M1	40000	87	Giriama, Bold Khal, Bond Rullah	7
22Nov81-3Hol	1	:462	1:11	1:364ft	6	115	21½	2½	21	22	Castaneda M7	35000	80	Domineu,BondRullh,DefenseCounsl	7
7Nov81-1SA	6f	:213	:442	1:091ft	*2	117	1hd	2½	21	22½	Castaneda M5	32000	89	Bold Khal,BondRullah,BearPudding	8
1Nov81-1SA	6f	:22	:444	1:09 ft	3¼	117	1hd	3½	43	44¾	Castaneda M8	40000	88	Hacawind, He'saRing,BattenPocket	8
24Oct81-1SA	6f	:213	:443	1:092ft	3	117	2hd	1hd	1½	2¾	Malgarini T M2	32000	90	Bold Khal, Bond Rullah, Decoded	8
2Sep81-7Dmr	6f	:22	:45	1:10 ft	6¼	117	1hd	12	1½	31	Castaneda M2	Alw	87	Laughing Boy, Torso, Bond Rullah	6
21Aug81-7Dmr	6f	:221	:443	1:101ft	4	119	42	47½	36	33¼	Castaneda M5	Alw	84	BigPresenttion,BronzStr,BondRullh	7
10Aug81-3Dmr	6f	:222	:452	1:11 ft	2½	118	68	710	711	713	Castaneda M2	Alw	70	IrshPlyboy,‡LongLvthKng,BronzStr	7

Jan 9 SA 5f ft :59 h **Dec 3 Hol 3f ft :373 h** **Nov 17 Hol 5f ft 1:001 h**

Maxistar

Own.—The Hat Ranch **114**

B. c. 4, by Pia Star—General Store, by To Market
Br.—The Hat Ranch West (Cal) **1982 1 1 0 0 $12,100**
Tr.—Stute Melvin F **1981 9 1 0 1 $19,600**
Turf 2 0 0 0 $1,650

8Jan82-7SA	6f	:213	:443	1:094ft	3½	114	1½	11	12	11½	Lipham T4	Alw	89	Maxistar, Finitude, Sea Rullah Run	9
29Dec81-5SA	a6½f Ⓣ	:21	:433	1:142fm	19	114	11½	13	1½	41¾	Lipham T7	Alw	85	Cloonwlln,Mountbnk,Rostropovch	12
13Dec81-6Hol	6f	:214	:444	1:101ft	2¾	116	1hd	2hd	31½	54½	Delahoussaye E3	Alw	81	BondRullh,VictorySmpl,MdnghtMn	6
21Apr81-5SA	6f	:214	:45	1:103ft	5¼	120	2hd	31½	33½	47¼	Castaneda M2	Alw	79	Inception, Nevada Reality,Airroling	7
1Apr81-8SA	a6½f Ⓣ	:211	:433	1:143fm	25	115	1hd	2½	22	96	CastanedM10	Baldwin	80	Descaro, Motivity, Steelinctive	13
20Mar81-4SA	6½f	:222	:462	1:19 sl	2½	120	2½	2hd	46	313	Delahoussaye E2	Alw	62	Buen Chico, Descaro, Maxistar	4
11Mar81-9SA	1⅛	:452	1:101	1:49 ft	8	118	15	1hd	32½	67¾	McHrgDG3	Bradbury	76	Chiaroscuro,NativeTactics,Mehmet	9
11Mar81—Run in two divisions, 8th & 9th races.															
1Mar81-7SA	1 1/16	:462	1:13	1:474sy	*9-5	115	17	21½	310	531	Delahoussaye E3	Alw	31	SplendidSpruce,Prtez,GelicNvonod	6
11Feb81-8SA	7f	:223	:45	1:232gd	3	115	41	87¾	923	929	DlhoussyE8	Sn Vcnte	54	FlyingNashua,MinnesotChief,Torso	9
23Jan81-7SA	6f	:221	:454	1:102gd	*6-5	115	11½	12	11	12½	Delahoussaye E5	Alw	87	Maxistar,LongLivetheKing,Libanon	6

●Jan 4 SA tr.t 5f sl 1:00 h **Dec 23 SA 7f ft 1:271 h** **●Dec 18 SA 5f ft :581 h** **Dec 7 Hol 5f ft 1:01 h**

Bond Rullah had won his last start at six furlongs in 1:09. Maxistar had won at the distance in 1:09⅘. The typical horseplayer who picked up the *Racing Form* and looked at the naked times (or the *Form*'s own speed ratings) would conclude that Bond Rullah was vastly superior. A speed handicapper would know otherwise. Bond Rullah had run in the second race on opening day, and had earned a figure of 101. Maxistar had run in the seventh race on January 8, a considerably slower day, and had a figure of 107. Maxistar was clearly superior, but when he beat the favored Bond Rullah by 4½ lengths he paid $13.80. I was getting the impression that I might like California very much.

Sometimes the calculation of a daily track variant will produce a figure which seems to defy common sense. Suppose the data looks like this:

Race	Par	Rating	Difference
1	80	78	+2
2	83	77	+6
3	84	79	+5
4	73	100	−27
5	90	85	+5
6	89	88	+1
7	93	93	0
8	104	102	+2
9	78	77	+1

What happened in the fourth race? Either a horse or group of horses ran sensationally fast, or else something was wrong. Maybe there was a typographical error in the *Racing Form*. Maybe there was a malfunction by the electric timer. Maybe there was some strange, short-lived change in the condition of the racing strip. Taking this time at face value and including it in the calculations would make the track variant −1, a considerable distortion of the day's results. In this case, I would exclude the one aberrant time from my calculations, making the variant for the day +3 and the figure for the fourth race 103. I would put a large question mark next to this number and make a mental or written note to await a confirmation of the figure before I bet any money on the basis of it. I would look for one of the horses in that field to run again and see what kind of figure he earned. If he earned a giant figure I would believe that 103 — but not until then.

Situations like this are what make it so important for a handi-capper to calculate his own speed figures instead of buying or borrowing somebody else's. A horseplayer who does not know what has gone into the computation of the numbers is apt to accept and use them uncritically. He would probably bet blindly on the horse who had earned that spurious 103. A sound speed handicapper has to be able to say, sometimes, "This figure makes no sense; I don't believe it." Or he may say, "The figures were too tough this day; I'm not sure I trust them" — as in the following case.

Race	Par	Rating	Difference
1	76	72	+4
2	82	69	+13
3	87	84	+3
4	90	85	+5
5	90	87	+3
6	88	95	−7
7	93	96	−3
8	100	105	−5
9	86	92	−6

What happened here? Using normal calculations, the variant would be +1. But these results suggest that the speed of the track changed in the middle of the day. This would be especially plausible if there had been some dramatic change in the weather, but such a phenomenon occurs occasionally when there is not a cloud in the sky. The proper variant might be +6 (Races 1–5), −5 (Races 6–9). I am reluctant to split variants in this fashion unless the evidence is overwhelming, but however I deal with the day I will monitor closely the subsequent results of horses who ran on it.

Track-variant difficulties will sometimes take this form:

Race	Par	Rating	Difference	
1	62	71	−9	(sprint)
2	79	79	0	(sprint)
3	82	84	−2	(sprint)
4	88	90	−2	(sprint)
5	81	86	−5	(sprint)
6	87	70	+17	(route)
7	89	72	+17	(route)
8	101	106	−5	(sprint)
9	94	80	+14	(route)

There are days, and sometimes periods of days, when a speed handicapper is forced to calculate separate variants for sprints and routes. In this case, the proper variant would almost certainly be -6 (Sprints), $+16$ (Routes), although I would monitor the subsequent performances of the horses who raced on this day to verify that the routes were in fact so much slower than the sprints. If I see such a dichotomy between sprints and routes appear once or twice at the outset of a new racing season, I may suspect that there is a whole new relationship between one- and two-turn races at the track and that I will have to revise my speed-rating chart. In the fall of 1982 at Bowie, I discovered that the route ratings I had used for the better part of a decade had suddenly become nine points too fast. This was yet another situation where a horseplayer had better be making his own calculations instead of relying on someone else's. Anyone blindly using a prepackaged speed-rating chart could lose money very rapidly when a track changes in this fashion.

The figures I inscribe daily in my notebook are, of course, those for the winners of each race. To evaluate any other horse, I subtract from the winner's figure a number of points according to the margin by which the horse was beaten and the distance of the race. The beaten-lengths chart on the following page, which appeared originally in *Picking Winners,* takes into account the fact that the traditional equation of one length with one fifth of a second isn't quite right. It shows, for example, that if a horse loses a six-furlong race by five lengths, his figure is determined by subtracting 12 points from the winner's figure. If he loses a mile race by one length, two points are subtracted.

When I handicap a day's program, I begin by transcribing into my *Racing Form* the figures for the last two or three starts of each horse. I look at the date the horse ran, note the figure for the winner of that race, subtract the appropriate number of points according to the beaten-lengths chart, and write the resultant figure into the horse's past performances. This may sound like a very time-consuming process, but once a handicapper acquires some familiarity with the beaten-lengths chart he should be able to put down all his figures for the day in about 20 minutes. In the process he will have rendered unnecessary much of the research and analysis that consume the time of traditional handicappers. He will be able to evaluate and

BEATEN-LENGTHS ADJUSTMENT CHART

Margin	5 Fur.	6 Fur.	7 Fur.	Mile	1 1/16	1 1/8	1 1/2
neck	1	1	1	0	0	0	0
1/2	1	1	1	1	1	1	1
3/4	2	2	2	1	1	1	1
1	3	2	2	2	2	2	1
1 1/4	4	3	3	2	2	2	1
1 1/2	4	4	3	3	3	2	2
1 3/4	5	4	4	3	3	3	2
2	6	5	4	4	3	3	2
2 1/4	7	6	5	4	4	4	3
2 1/2	7	6	5	4	4	4	3
2 3/4	8	7	6	5	5	5	3
3	9	7	6	5	5	5	3
3 1/4	9	8	7	6	5	5	4
3 1/2	10	9	7	6	6	6	4
3 3/4	11	9	8	7	6	6	4
4	12	10	8	7	7	6	5
4 1/4	12	10	9	8	7	7	5
4 1/2	13	11	9	8	8	7	5
4 3/4	14	11	10	9	8	8	5
5	15	12	10	9	8	8	6
5 1/2	16	13	11	10	9	9	6
6	18	15	12	11	10	9	7
6 1/2	19	16	13	12	11	10	8
7	20	17	14	13	12	11	8
7 1/2	22	18	15	13	13	12	9
8	23	20	17	14	13	13	10
8 1/2	25	21	18	15	14	13	10
9	26	22	19	16	15	14	11
9 1/2	28	23	19	17	16	16	11
10	29	24	20	18	17	17	12
11	32	27	23	20	18	18	13
12	35	29	25	21	20	20	14
13	38	32	27	23	22	22	15
14	41	34	29	25	23	23	16
15	44	37	31	27	25	25	17

compare the previous performances of every horse with ease.

This is, essentially, the method that most contemporary speed handicappers use. Once I would have said that it was quite adequate for all but the most serious horseplayers, that having any kind of decent figures was vastly better than having none at all. Now that so many people are using figures I am not so sure. Anyone who hopes to beat the races has to be smarter than the great mass of bettors; a speed handicapper who hopes to beat the game needs figures that are superior to those of the masses.

When a handicapper calculates figures by comparing the results of races to his par figures, he is glossing over an obvious problem. If a horse dropping sharply in class wins a $10,000 claiming race by a dozen lengths, his figure might be closer to 100. An unusually weak group of $10,000 animals might run a 75. To assume that every $10,000 race should be run in the par figure of 85 is a patent error that can create great inaccuracies in the track variant.

I rely on par figures for only the first week or two of a new racing season. When I started making my Santa Anita numbers and was totally unfamiliar with the horses there, I had no other way to judge how fast they ought to run. But once the meeting was under way I could estimate how fast a race should have been run. If, for example, three $10,000 claimers had all earned figures of 79 in their previous starts and now wound up in a three-horse photo finish, I would think it more logical to use 79 as the projected figure for the race instead of the par figure of 85. This is the *projection method,* and while it requires a few minutes' extra effort a day, it produces track variants of considerably greater accuracy than the par-figure method. I look at horses' figures coming into a race, the way they finished, and the margins separating them, and then I try to make an educated guess: What figure was this race likely run in today? Here, for example, are my projections for Santa Anita on March 27, 1982.

FIRST RACE

FIRST RACE
Santa Anita
MARCH 27, 1982

1 1/16 MILES. (1.40⅘) CLAIMING. Purse $15,000. 4-year-olds and upward. Weight, 122 lbs. Non-winners of two races at one mile or over since December 25 allowed 2 lbs.; of such a race since then, 4 lbs.; since November 9, 6 lbs. Claiming price $16,000; for each $1,000 to $14,000, allowed 1 lb. (Races when entered for $12,500 or less not considered.) 68th DAY. WEATHER CLOUDY. TEMPERATURE 64 DEGREES.

Value of race $15,000, value to winner $8,250, second $3,000, third $2,250, fourth $1,125, fifth $375. Mutuel pool $313,847.

Last Raced	Horse	Eqt.A.Wt	PP	St	¼	½	¾	Str	Fin	Jockey	Cl'g Pr	Odds $1
17Mar82 ^{3}SA^1	Friendly Royalty	4 118	8	4	3^{hd}	4^2	3½	1^{hd}	1¾	McCarron C J	16000	6.10
6Mar82 ^{9}SA^5	Fleet Stone	6 116	2	3	4^2	3^{hd}	4^2	3^2	2 1½	Pierce D	16000	4.90
13Mar82 ^{2}SA^3	He Man Sam	5 116	4	8	6^1	6^4	5 1½	5^{hd}	3no	Asmussen C B	16000	2.30
17Mar82 ^{3}SA^2	In Triplicate	b 4 114	3	2	2 2½	2^2	2 1½	2^{hd}	4 1¾	Castaneda M	14000	29.60
17Mar82 ^{3}SA^4	Arcoville	8 116	7	5	7^3	7^1	8^{hd}	6 1½	5^{nk}	Hawley S	16000	8.60
13Mar82 ^{2}SA^4	The Big T.	6 115	5	9	8^{hd}	9	7^{hd}	7^1	6 1¼	Steiner J J^5	16000	11.70
12Mar82 ^{1}SA^1	Okie River	b 5 115	1	1	1^2	1 1½	1^{hd}	4^{hd}	7no	Valenzuela P A	15000	10.60
5Mar82 ^{9}SA^1	Apache Scout	7 116	6	7	9	8^{hd}	9	8 1½	8 6¾	Guerra W A	16000	7.00
20Mar82 ^{9}SA^4	Umaticca	b 4 120	9	6	5½	5^{hd}	6^{hd}	9	9	Pincay L Jr	16000	5.70

OFF AT 1:03. Start good. Won driving. Time, :23, :46⅕, 1:10⅗, 1:36⅕, 1:42⅖ Track fast.

Official Program Numbers↘

$2 Mutuel Prices:				
	8–FRIENDLY ROYALTY	14.20	6.80	4.00
	2–FLEET STONE		6.20	3.60
	4–HE MAN SAM			3.00

Ch. g, by Blood Royal—Your Friend, by Mustard Plaster. Trainer Truman Eddie. Bred by Gaylord Ann (Ky).

FRIENDLY ROYALTY, within easy striking distance while unhurried early, rallied outside the leaders entering the stretch and outfinished FLEET STONE. The latter raced alongside the winner most of the trip, responded in the drive but could not outfinish that one. HE MAN SAM rallied when roused leaving the backstretch, went to the middle of the track for the stretch drive and finished strongly. IN TRIPLICATE vied for the lead to the final furlong and weakened. THE BIG T. showed nothing. OKIE RIVER, used up making the early pace, tired in the stretch. UMATICCA was finished early.

Owners— 1, Budann Stable; 2, Sokolow L; 3, Chrys C S; 4, Pinero J & Yvonne; 5, Brinson-Buster-Grayson; 6, Hills Racing Stable; 7, Pitkin-Ritzer-Smiles Stables; 8, Teter & Wezelberg; 9, Barrera Carmen S.

Fleet Stone was claimed by Winning Ways Stable; trainer, Troeger Robert; He Man Sam was claimed by Keith-McCutcheon-Wilmot; trainer, McCutcheon James R; Arcoville was claimed by Eggers & Wilson; trainer, Truman Eddie.

Friendly Royalty *

Ch. g. 4, by Blood Royal—Your Friend, by Mustard Plaster
Br.—Gaylord Ann (Ky) — 1982 2 1 0 0 $6,950
Own.—Budann Stable **118** **Tr.—Truman Eddie** **$16,000** — 1981 9 2 2 1 $21,450
Lifetime 11 3 2 1 $28,400 — Turf 1 0 0 0

17Mar82-3SA	1 1/16	:48^2	1:13^4	1:46 sy	*9-5	117	3 1½	2½	1^{hd}	1 1½	McCarron [illegible]	c12500	71	FriendlyRoylty,InTriplict,Protctort	6
6Mar82-1SA	6f	:21^2	:44^2	1:09 ft	20	118	11^{14}	9 8¼	6^6	5 4¼	McCarron [illegible]	16000	89	CountCrlcio,ImFullofJoy,Unlkleet	12
11Dec81-3Hol	1 1/16	:46^3	1:11^4	1:45^{2}ft	2½	110^5	3 4½	2^{hd}	1^{hd}	1^1	Perez J^6	20000	68	FriendlyRoylty,SirK.Georg,JckthBr	7
21Nov81-2Hol	1 1/16	:47^2	1:12^1	1:44^{3}ft	4½	111^5	7 3¾	6 2½	4 6½	3^6	Perez J L^7	20000	66	HvGoodTm,Provdntl,FrndlyRoylty	12
22Oct81-1SA	6½f	:21^4	:44^2	1:15^{3}ft	31	117	11^{12}	11^{17}	11^{14}	9^{11}	Ramirez O^5	32000	81	Proud Duke,SoyRey,ImaTrackStar	12
12Oct81-1SA	6½f	:21^3	:44^3	1:16^{2}ft	20	117	7^{15}	7^{14}	7^{10}	6^{11}	McCarron C J^5	50000	77	BrightestRuler,ImportntMmo,I'vPt	8
13Aug81-8Dmr	1 1/16 Ⓣ	:49^1	1:13^4	1:44^{1}fm	4½	110	5 2½	7 3¾	8^{11}	8^{11}	McCarronCJ^8	Aw18000	77	Optimism, Chieffo, Midas Shadow	9
16Jly81-4Hol	7f	:21^3	:44^3	1:23^{2}ft	*3-2	116	5^4	4 2½	1½	1^2	McCarron C J^5	M40000	80	FrindlyRoylty,Dokimo,It'sthBrry's	11
2Jly81-6Hol	7f	:22^1	:45^1	1:23^{3}ft	*2½	116	5 1¾	3^2	2^3	2 1½	McCarron C J^7	M40000	77	Cnturus,FrindlyRoylty,Timbrsport	12
19Jun81-2Hol	6f	:22	:45^2	1:11 ft	6½	115	4 4½	3^3	3½	2 1½	McCarron C J^8	M50000	80	L'Oiseleur,FriendlyRoylty,GlicHour	9

●Feb 26 Hol tr.t 5f ft 1:03^4 h   Feb 20 Hol tr.t 4f ft :51^2 h   Feb 14 Hol tr.t 4f ft :51^4 h   Feb 9 Hol tr.t 4f ft :53 h

Fleet Stone — B. g. 6, by Fleet Advocate—Miss Redstone, by Sir Abbey

Own.—Sokolow L **116** Br.—Gilbert Mr-Mrs M (Colo) Tr.—Dorfman Leonard **$16,000**

1982	2	0	0	0	$400
1981	10	4	2	1	$49,420
Turf	1	0	0	0	$450

Lifetime 45 8 4 7 $82,193

6Mar82-9SA	1⅛	:463	1:103	1:491ft	14	1115	32½	2hd	32½	54¼	Steiner J J 85	20000	79	Mr.Reactor,OmahMike,Prodigious	12
12Feb82-9SA	1⅛	:473	1:124	1:513ft	5½	116	46½	74½	813	823	DelahoussyeE8	c16000	48	The Big T., PacificMorn,Umaticca	11
31May81-9Hol	1 1/16	:471	1:114	1:441ft	*8-5	119	42½	31	2½	22	McCarron C J9	12500	72	SuccessSeeker,FltSton,BndInthRod	9
14May81-9Hol	1 1/16	:471	1:112	1:43 ft	*9-5e	119	42	21½	32½	46¾	McCarron C J7	20000	73	Chrisrik,OfftoMont,Surrptitiously	10
26Apr81-1Hol	1 1/16	:471	1:123	1:444ft	*8-5e	119	34	2hd	2hd	1nk	McCarron C J6	20000	71	Fleet Stone, Arcoville, El Tiburon	9
21Mar81-2SA	1⅛	:463	1:12	1:522gd	*3-2	122	35½	22	1hd	1½	McCarron C J7	c16000	67	Fleet Stone, Rooney, Grandly	10
14Mar81-9SA	1 1/16	:462	1:111	1:43 ft	5½	120	45	73¾	32	12½	McCarron C J7	20000	86	FleetStone,ElTiburon,PlsticFntstic	9
22Feb81-2SA	1⅛	:463	1:102	1:492ft	5	117	41½	43½	45½	613	Pincay L Jr7	25000	69	FollowtheJudg,MistrBnjmin,Bndlir	8
8Feb81-9SA	1 1/16	:462	1:103	1:434sy	6¾	117	79	65¾	44½	47	Pincay L Jr3	25000	75	Surreptitiously, Owlwood, Teller	11
31Jan81-9SA	1⅛	:48	1:123	1:52 gd	2½	118	34	32	3½	32½	McCarron C J7	c20000	66	Gummo Joe, Public, Fleet Stone	7

Mar 23 SA 6f ft 1:142 h   Mar 1 SA 6f ft 1:132 h   Feb 22 SA 5f ft :59 h   Feb 9 SA 5f ft 1:03 h

He Man Sam — Gr. g. 5, by Olympiad King—Sweet Anastacia, by Isle of Greece

Own.—Chrys C S **116** Br.—Chrys C S (Cal) Tr.—Rettele Loren **$16,000**

1982	4	0	0	1	$2,250
1981	8	2	1	1	$29,700

Lifetime 19 3 3 2 $43,800

13Mar82-2SA	1⅛	:48	1:133	1:541gd	5	116	11	12½	1hd	34	Asmussen 85	16000	54	Pirata,Charlyn'Harrigan,HeMnSm	10
28Feb82-1SA	1⅛	:47	1:111	1:482ft	11	114	64½	98¼	1116	1115	Asmussen [77]	A25000	72	Pi'sPrinceAl,SoftMrkt,BoldDisply	11
17Feb82-5SA	6½f	:221	:45	1:163ft	9¼	115	72	74¼	75¾	79¼	AsmussenCB3	Aw22000	78	Bic's Gold,WickedHitter,Veschacho	7
4Feb82-6SA	6f	:22	:443	1:092ft	35	115	3nk	41	63	65¼	AsmussenCB6	Aw22000	86	Sea RullahRun,Torso,WickedHitter	7
2Sep81-9Dmr	1 1/16	:454	1:10	1:424ft	4¾	116	22½	22	23	1¾	Valenzuela P A3	16000	86	HeManSam,Prodigious,PirteFleet	12
23Aug81-9Dmr	1 1/16	:461	1:103	1:43 ft	5¼	116	54	65	75½	710	Chapman T4	32000	75	‡RuletheMrket,MsterCrmonis,Nino	8
26Jun81-7Hol	7f	:221	:45	1:224ft	27	122	—	—	—	—	Lipham T3	Aw22000	—	Disco Lark, MarkGuard,PokerPoint	9
26Jun81—Sulked															
15Apr81-9SA	1	:452	1:10	1:36 ft	*9-5	114	2hd	12	13½	1nk	ValenzuelPA6	Aw25000	89	He Man Sam,SummitRun,Optimism	8
1Apr81-9SA	1	:453	1:10	1:352ft	2½	114	53¾	42½	42¼	32¼	ValenzuelPA7	Aw23000	90	ChieftinsPrince,NowndThn,HMnSm	9
18Mar81-9SA	1	:45	1:091	1:35 ft	11	114	21	11	1½	22¼	ValenzuelPA8	Aw22000	92	NtiveProspctor,HMnSm,NowndThn	9

Mar 24 SA 4f ft :474 h   Jan 31 SA 5f ft 1:012 hg

Friendly Royalty, who ran an 88 in his last start, won narrowly over Fleet Stone, with an 85, and He Man Sam, also an 85. It makes perfect sense to assume that Friendly Royalty ran the same figure again. The time of the race, 1:42⅖ for a mile and one sixteenth, has a rating of 116. So I start my calculation of the March 27 variant in this fashion:

Race	Projection	Rating	Difference
1	88	116	—28

SECOND RACE

SECOND RACE
Santa Anita
MARCH 27, 1982

1 1/16 MILES. (1.40⅕) MAIDEN. Purse $18,000. Fillies. 3–year–olds. Weight, 117 lbs. (Non-starters for a claiming price of $25,000 or less preferred.)

Value of race $18,000, value to winner $9,900, second $3,600, third $2,700, fourth $1,350, fifth $450. Mutuel pool $406,590.

Last Raced	Horse	Eqt.A.Wt	PP	St	¼	½	¾	Str	Fin	Jockey	Odds $1
14Mar82 3SA11	Threat	3 117	7	5	2 1½	1hd	11½	11½	1½	Valenzuela P A	3.00
11Mar82 4SA6	Breezing Queen	b 3 117	8	4	51	52½	2hd	23½	22¾	Pincay L Jr	15.40
27Feb82 2SA8	Caro's Tune	b 3 117	4	10	9½	8½	71	4½	33½	Asmussen C B	7.60
26Feb82 6SA9	Vibrantly	3 117	2	9	71	71	51	5½	41¾	Toro F	35.00
11Mar82 4SA4	Weekend Time	3 117	1	1	4½	4hd	3hd	3hd	5¾	Castaneda M	7.50
13Mar82 3SA6	Baruna	b 3 117	12	11	111½	114	81½	74	64	Shoemaker W	9.80
21Feb82 4SA4	Happy Cali	3 117	10	6	3hd	3½	43	6hd	72½	Hawley S	2.50
27Feb82 2SA11	Royal Wench	b 3 112	11	7	6 1½	6 1	92	83	81	Steiner J J5	56.20
14Mar82 3SA9	Time Value	3 117	5	2	81	9½	10hd	10 1½	9¾	Pierce D	23.10
13Mar82 3SA7	Jennie's Image	b 3 117	3	12	12	12	12	12	10hd	Lipham T	59.10
9Mar82 6GG5	Surgeon's Johnnie	b 3 117	9	3	1hd	21	6hd	9hd	111½	Delahoussaye E	20.70
14Mar82 3SA7	Salute To Love	b 3 117	6	8	105	10hd	112	11 1½	12	Sibille R	8.00

OFF AT 1:40. Start good. Won driving. Time, :22⅘, :46⅖, 1:11⅘, 1:37⅖, 1:43⅘ Track fast.

$2 Mutuel Prices:	7–THREAT	8.00	4.80	3.60
	8–BREEZING QUEEN		12.60	8.00
	4–CARO'S TUNE			5.60

B. f, by Ack Ack—State, by Nijinsky II. Trainer Proctor Willard L. Bred by Claiborne Farm (Ky).

THREAT engaged for the lead soon after the start, drew clear on the far turn but was hard-pressed to hold BREEZING QUEEN safe near the end. The latter, in contention between horses from the outset, challenged inside the winner when set down in the drive but could not get up. CARO'S TURN lacked early speed but rallied willingly in the middle of the track through the stretch. VIBRANTLY did not reach contention with a mild late rally WEEKEND TIME, in contention and saving ground to the stretch, tired thereafter. HAPPY CALI was finished after six furlongs. SURGEON'S JOHNNIE tired after five furlongs.

Owners— 1, Claiborne Farm; 2, Howard & Whittingham; 3, Sturgis J R; 4, Gosden & Von Bleucher; 5, Breliant W; 6, Windblown Farm & Taylor; 7, Elmbrook Farms; 8, Novetzke R C; 9, Nrthwst Fm-El Rcho No Gota; 10, T 9 0 Ranch; 11, DiFiore Dr-Mrs F R; 12. Sack Dr R.

Threat

Own.—Claiborne Farm — **117**

B. f. 3, by Ack Ack—State, by Nijinsky II
Br.—Claiborne Farm (Ky)
Tr.—Proctor Willard L
Lifetime 5 0 0 1 $4,950

				1982	3 M 0 1		$2,700
				1981	2 M 0 0		$2,250

14Mar82-3SA	1 1/16 :472 1:132 1:47 sy	13 117	87¾ 1114 1116 1122	Lipham T9	ⓕMdn 44 Indianola, Grassy, GlamorousDaisz 11
27Feb82-2SA	1 1/16 :46 1:11 1:44 ft	29 117	32 31 33½ 34½	Lipham T	ⓕMdn 76 Far Song, Celinda, Threat 12
15Jan82-4SA	1 1/16 :462 1:111 1:44½ft	5 117	75 77½ 58 614	Valenzuela PA3	ⓕMdn 66 WhyZnthe,BronzeMrket,StreetLovr 9
27Dec81-3SA	6f :214 :443 1:102ft	15 117	63½ 57 57 49½	Valenzuela PA7	ⓕMdn 77 I'mFashionable,TangoDncer,Visto 12
9Dec81-6Hol	6f :22 :461 1:12 ft	23 117	64½ 63½ 45½ 47½	Valenzuela PA9	ⓕMdn 69 Melinda's Plum, Visto,CitizenKate 11

Mar 23 SA 4f ft :483 b   Mar 8 SA 6f ft 1:15 h   Feb 25 SA 4f ft :471 h   Feb 13 SA 6f ft 1:133 h

Breezing Queen

Own.—Whittingham H & C — **117**

Ch. f. 3, by Royal Derby II—Itsabreeze, by Nashville
Br.—Howard Mrs R S (Cal)
Tr.—Whittingham Michael
Lifetime 4 0 0 0 $2,050

				1982	3 M 0 0		$1,700
				1981	1 M 0 0		$350

11Mar82-4SA	6f :214 :444 1:092ft	65 117	95¾ 912 614 613	Olivares	ⒻⓈMdn 78 Hitwick, That Does It, Nanda Devi 12
26Feb82-6SA	7f :221 :452 1:23 ft	36 117	21 31½ 512 515	Olivares	ⒻⓈMdn 70 Elusive,ThatDoesIt,GlamorousDisz 11
27Jan82-4SA	6f :214 :45 1:101ft	24 117	84½ 86½ 77¾ 47½	Olivares	ⒻⓈMdn 79 Glddie'sRb,Mggi'sIntnt,RdintDwn 12
21Dec81-6Hol	6f :23 :464 1:112ft	5 117	2hd 31 511 521	Olivares F5	ⒻⓈMdn 59 CoffeeMaid,RoyaCurie,Agitatetress 6

Mar 22 SA 5f ft 1:014 h   Mar 17 SA tr.t 3f sy :40 h   Feb 22 SA 5f ft 1:02 h

Caro's Tune

Ch. f. 3, by Caro—Piper's Tune, by Princequillo
Br.—North Ridge Farm (Ky)   1982 3 M 0 0 $450

Own.—Sturgis J R   **117**   Tr.—Fulton John W   1981 0 M 0 0

Lifetime 3 0 0 0 $450

27Feb82-2SA	1$\frac{1}{16}$:46 1:11 1:44 ft	25	117	10^{12} 76$\frac{1}{2}$ 5^{10} 8^9	Asmuss	7 $\bullet$ ^{11}	ⓕMdn	72	Far Song, Celinda, Threat		12
13Feb82-4SA	1$\frac{1}{16}$:47^1 1:12^1 1:44^{4}ft	16	117	87$\frac{1}{2}$ 57 58$\frac{1}{2}$ 58$\frac{1}{2}$	Asmus	B^3	ⓕMdn	68	Permeability,HastyNijinsky,Celind	12
31Jan82-3SA	6f :21^4 :44^3 1:09^{3}ft	58	117	9^{12} 9^{11} 7^{14} 7^9	Asmussen C	B^6	ⓕMdn	81	SweetMystery,Celinda,HwiinShke	12

Mar 21 SA 5f ft 1:00 h   Feb 22 SA 5f ft 1:01^2 h   Feb 7 SA 5f ft 1:00^3 h

Threat was trounced by 22 lengths in the slop the last time she ran; that race was clearly untrue. Her next-to-last figure was a 78. The filly immediately behind her, Breezing Queen, was running in her first route race and had never earned a figure on which a meaningful projection could be based. The third-place finisher, Caro's Tune, had earned a 70 in her last start.

Caro's Tune finished 3¼ lengths behind the winner, and the beaten-lengths chart indicates that 3¼ lengths equals five points at this distance. Threat and Caro's Tune might have run, respectively, 78 and 73. They might have run 75 and 70. I choose to project a 78 for Threat, giving Caro's Tune credit for a little improvement since she is a lightly raced animal.

Race	Projection	Rating	Difference
2	78	103	—25

The third race was run on the grass.

FOURTH RACE

FOURTH RACE
Santa Anita
MARCH 27, 1982

6 FURLONGS. (1.07⅗) MAIDEN. Purse $17,000. Colts and geldings. 3–year–olds. Weight, 118 lbs. (Non–starters for a claiming price of $25,000 or less preferred.)

Value of race $17,000, value to winner $9,350, second $3,400, third $2,550, fourth $1,275, fifth $425. Mutuel pool $583,079.

Last Raced	Horse	Eqt.A.Wt PP St	¼	½	Str	Fin	Jockey	Odds $1
20Mar82 6SA[11]	Angelo G.	b 3 118 5 4	1½	11½	13½	11¾	Guerra W A	36.40
27Feb82 6SA[2]	Transamerica	3 118 3 6	3½	41½	2½	2[1]	Delahoussaye E	.70
14Mar82 4SA[3]	Senior Senator	3 118 7 2	5[2]	54	41½	3½	Valenzuela P A	4.90
17Mar82 2SA[3]	The Quilted Kid	3 118 4 5	4hd	3hd	3hd	4½	Ramirez O	40.70
7Mar82 4SA[9]	Mr. Lytle	b 3 118 2 8	8[3]	7[1]	6[1]	51¾	Castaneda M	15.30
	Alloy	3 118 6 7	6½	6hd	7hd	6nk	Sibille R	5.10
	Pleztobefirst	3 118 1 9	9	8[1]	8[3]	7½	Black K	28.40
	Aim Adhem	3 118 9 1	2[2]	2[2]	5[1]	8nk	Mena F	17.10
27Feb82 6SA[4]	Swift Bunny	3 118 8 3	7[1]	9	9	9	Lipham T	15.20

OFF AT 2:47. Start good. Won driving. Time, :21⅘, :44⅗, :57⅕, 1:10⅘ Track fast.

$2 Mutuel Prices:

5–ANGELO G.	74.80	14.20	5.60
3–TRANSAMERICA		2.80	2.40
7–SENIOR SENATOR			3.00

Ch. c, by Rainy Lake—Ask the Prince, by Princequillo. Trainer Barrera Lazaro S. Bred by Roebling J M (Ky).

ANGELO G. got the lead inside of AIM ADHEM in the opening quarter–mile, drew clear entering the stretch, then maintained a safe margin under pressure in the final sixteenth. TRANSAMERICA, shuffled back after the start, recovered and moved to contention early, rallied outside the leaders in the drive but could not overtake the winner. SENIOR SENATOR, never far back, responded in the drive but could not menace. THE QUILTED KID saved ground on the turn but lacked a strong rally. ALLOY was never dangerous. AIM ADHEM was finished after a half–mile.

Owners— 1, Green Dolly; 2, Saron Stable; 3, Koch-Abrhms-Katz-Zckr-Zckr; 4, Dillon Suzanne; 5, T 90 Ranch; 6, Katz & Semler; 7, Fowler Mr-Mrs S R; 8, Navarro E; 9, Turner F D.

Angelo G.
Own.—Green Dolly

Ch. c. 3, by Rainy Lake—Ask the Prince, by Princequillo
Br.—Roebling J M (Ky)   1982 1 M 0 0
118   Tr.—Barrera Lazaro S   1981 0 M 0 0
Lifetime   1 0 0 0

20Mar82-6SA	6½f :22	:45[1] 1:16[4]ft	12 118	84½ 74½11[12]1[20]	Hawley S[11]		Mdn 66 Ice Flow, Donbion, Prince OfNote 12

Mar 19 SA 3f m :37[3] h (d)   Mar 12 SA tr.t 5f sy 1:06[1] h   Mar 4 SA 5f ft 1:00[2] h   Feb 24 SA 6f ft 1:13[4] hg

Transamerica
Own.—Saron Stable

Ch. c. 3, by Full Pocket—Nashua's Pet, by Nashua
Br.—Thornton & Van Meter Jr (Ky)   1982 2 M 1 0 $3,400
118   Tr.—Drysdale Neil   1981 1 M 0 0 $1,275
Lifetime   3 0 1 0 $4,675

27Feb82-6SA	6f :21[3] :44[1] 1:09[4]ft	7½ 118	2hd 1hd 21½ 2[3]	Delahoussaye E[6]	Mdn 86 SilentMn,Trnsmeric,SeniorSentor 11
6Feb82-4SA	6f :21[3] :44 1:09[3]ft	9½ 118	10[9] 9[13] 7[16] 8[14]	Delahoussaye E[3]	Mdn 76 LeSmirk,PrinceOfNote,CelticSber 12
10Oct81-6SA	6½f :22 :45[1] 1:16[4]ft	2 118	2hd 2½ 45 4[14]	Delahoussaye E[9]	Mdn 72 BoldForli,LteSleeper,EbonyBronze 9

● Mar 21 SA tr.t 6f ft 1:13[2] h   Mar 15 SA 6f m 1:18[2] h   Mar 10 SA 5f ft 1:01[2] h   Mar 5 SA 4f ft :48[2] h

Senior Senator
Own.—Kch-Abrhms-Ktz-Zckr-Zckr

B. c. 3, by Senate Whip—Bet a Candy, by Candy Spots
Br.—Ellsworth Kim & R (La)   1982 2 M 0 2 $5,100
118   Tr.—Stute Melvin F   1981 0 M 0 0
Lifetime   2 0 0 2 $5,100

14Mar82-4SA	6f :22[1] :46 1:12[2]sy	3½ 118	21½ 31½ 22½ 3[6]	Valenzuela P A[8]	Mdn 70 Accoustical, Gaiters, SeniorSenator 8
27Feb82-6SA	6f :21[3] :44[1] 1:09[4]ft	9½ 118	45 33½ 35½ 3[6]	Valenzuela P A[8]	Mdn 83 SilentMn,Trnsmeric,SeniorSentor 11

● Mar 21 SA 4f ft :46 h   ● Mar 12 SA 4f m :48[3] h (d)   Mar 6 SA 5f ft 1:00[4] h   Feb 26 SA 3f ft :34[3] h

There is no way to project anything for Angelo G., who was annihilated in his racing debut, and so I try to base my projection on the runner-up, Transamerica, who ran an 86 in his last start. If he ran this 86 again, third-place Senior Sharp would have had to run an 84 to finish a length behind him, improving sharply upon his previous 74. The fourth- and finish-place finishers would have had to improve considerably, too. My guess is that Transamerica did not duplicate his 86. So now I base the projection on Senior Sharp. If he ran his 74 again, Transamerica would have run a 76. Angelo G. (who had won by 1¾ lengths, which equals four points at this distance) would therefore have run an 80. Projecting figures is no exact science, and this is the best I can do.

Race	Projection	Rating	Difference
4	80	95	—15

FIFTH RACE

FIFTH RACE
Santa Anita
MARCH 27, 1982

1 ⅛ MILES. (1.45⅘) ALLOWANCE. Purse $21,000. Colts and geldings. 3-year-olds, which have never won two races. Weight, 118 lbs. Non-winners other than claiming at one mile or over since December 25 allowed 4 lbs. (Winners preferred.)

Value of race $21,000, value to winner $11,550, second $4,200, third $3,150, fourth $1,575, fifths $262.50 each. Mutuel pool $365,307. Exacta Pool $573,982.

Last Raced	Horse	Eqt.	A.Wt	PP	St	¼	½	¾	Str	Fin	Jockey	Odds $1
28Feb82 ^{5}SA^2	Royal Captive		3 114	8	10	$9^{1\frac{1}{2}}$	7^1	4^2	$1^{2\frac{1}{2}}$	$1^{2\frac{3}{4}}$	Shoemaker W	1.40
15Feb82 ^{6}SA^1	Berbereau		3 118	1	1	$4^{\frac{1}{2}}$	6^1	5^{hd}	$3^{1\frac{1}{2}}$	$2^{\frac{3}{4}}$	Guerra W A	21.30
10Mar82 ^{8}SA^5	Fabulous Mystic		3 114	7	9	8^2	8^1	7^3	2^2	3^4	McCarron C J	5.10
7Mar82 ^{4}SA^1	Estoril		3 118	9	11	$10^{2\frac{1}{2}}$	9^{hd}	10^5	5^{hd}	$4^{1\frac{3}{4}}$	Delahoussaye E	2.90
13Mar82 ^{5}SA^2	DH Thunderhope		3 117	3	3	$5^{1\frac{1}{2}}$	$5^{\frac{1}{2}}$	$6^{\frac{1}{2}}$	7^2	5	Pincay L Jr	9.00
13Mar82 ^{5}SA^4	DH Reconfirm		3 118	6	6	$7^{\frac{1}{2}}$	10^5	9^2	$6^{2\frac{1}{2}}$	$5^{\frac{3}{4}}$	Castaneda M	24.60
3Mar82 ^{6}SA^2	French Commander		3 114	11	7	6^{hd}	4^{hd}	3^{hd}	4^{hd}	$7^{4\frac{1}{2}}$	Asmussen C B	11.50
18Mar82 ^{6}SA^1	Our Best Copy		3 109	2	2	1^{hd}	$3^{\frac{1}{2}}$	$8^{\frac{1}{2}}$	9^2	$8^{\frac{1}{2}}$	Steiner J J^5	71.50
13Mar82 ^{5}SA^7	West Coast Native	b	3 109	10	8	11	11	11	11	9^6	Blanco P J^5	85.80
13Mar82 ^{5}SA^5	Eruptive	b	3 115	4	4	2^1	1^{hd}	1^{hd}	8^3	10^2	Sibille R	38.70
13Mar82 ^{5}SA^8	Penngrove		3 118	5	5	$3^{\frac{1}{2}}$	2^1	2^{hd}	10^2	11	Lipham T	26.80

DH—Dead heat.

OFF AT 3:24. Start good. Won easily. Time, :22$\frac{3}{5}$, :46$\frac{2}{5}$, 1:11, 1:36$\frac{3}{5}$, 1:49 Track fast.

$2 Mutuel Prices:

8–ROYAL CAPTIVE	**4.80**	**3.00**	**2.60**
1–BERBEREAU		**12.00**	**6.00**
7–FABULOUS MYSTIC			**4.00**

$5 EXACTA 8–1 PAID $209.50.

Dk. b. or br. g, by Royal Ski—Bold Captive, by Boldnesian. Trainer Russell John W. Bred by Harcourt H (Fla).

ROYAL CAPTIVE, never far back, remained wide most of the trip, drove to a clear lead in the upper stretch and was not threatened thereafter. BERBEREAU, in good position and saving ground early, moved to contention inside horses at the far turn, awaited racing room around the final turn, then could not finish with the winner. FABULOUS MYSTIC, unhurried for six furlongs, rallied a bit wide between horses into the stretch and finished strongly. ESTORIL, shuffled back after the start, passed mostly tired horses with a mild late rally. THUNDERHOPE tired in the stretch. FRENCH COMMANDER was wide while prominent to the far turn. OUR BEST COPY was finished early. ERUPTIVE tired after six furlongs, as did PENNGROVE.

Owners— 1, Alsdorf-Russell-South Ridge St; 2, Winchell V H Jr; 3, Abatti-Blau-Morjoseph; 4, Seeligson A A Jr; 5, Frank-Selvin-Siegel; 6, Mamakos Jeanette & J L; 7, Ronketti Mrs R D; 8, Priestley P A; 9, Groves G P; 10, Round Tree Fms Ltd & Saikhon; 11, Christensen & Shapiro.

Overweight: Thunderhope 3 pounds; Eruptive 1.

Scratched—Frisky Purchase (13Mar82 ^{5}SA^6); Rockwall (27Dec81 ^{4}SA^4).

Royal Captive

Own.—Alsdorf-Russell-SouthridgSt **114**

Dk. b. or br. c. 3, by Royal Ski—Bold Captive, by Boldnesian
Br.—Harcourt H (Fla) **1982 1 0 1 0 $4,000**
Tr.—Russell John W **1981 3 1 1 0 $9,700**
Lifetime 4 1 2 0 $13,700

28Feb82-5SA	$1\frac{1}{16}$	:45^4	1:09^4	1:41^{1}ft	12	114	7^7	5^{12}	3^6	$2^{5\frac{3}{4}}$	ShoemkrW[illegible] 100	Aw20000	89	JourneyatSea,RoyalCptive,AskMe	12
8Nov81-6SA	1	:45^4	1:10^2	1:36^{2}ft	$6\frac{3}{4}$	115	4^4	$2^{\frac{1}{2}}$	3^4	2^1	ShoemkerW^5	Aw22000	86	BisonBay,RoyalCaptive,Prosperous	7
12Sep81-7Dmf	6f	:22^2	:46	1:10^{3}ft	$2\frac{3}{4}$	118	$3^{2\frac{1}{2}}$	2^{hd}	$1^{1\frac{1}{2}}$	1^6	Pincay L Jr^7	Mdn	85	RoyalCptive,SteelMsk,Suspenders	10
30Aug81-6Dmr	6f	:22^1	:45^1	1:10^{3}ft	30	118	$8^{8\frac{1}{4}}$	$6^{7\frac{1}{4}}$	6^5	$5^{9\frac{1}{4}}$	Gilligan L^9	Mdn	76	Eruptive, Prosperous, Suspenders	10

Mar 21 SA 7f ft 1:25^2 h **Mar 9 SA 6f ft 1:16^1 h** **Feb 24 SA 1 ft 1:41^3 h** **Feb 19 SA 7f ft 1:26^3 h**

Berbereau | B. g. 3, by Aloha Mood—Liking, by Viking Spirit
Br.—Winchell V H Jr (Ky) | 1982 4 1 2 0 $17,100
Own.—Winchell V H Jr | **118** | Tr.—Jolly Cecil | 1981 4 M 1 2 $9,075
Lifetime 8 1 3 2 $26,175

15Feb82-6SA	1$\frac{1}{16}$	:46^4	1:10^4	1:43^{1}ft	*9-5	118	5$4\frac{1}{2}$	4^3	3$1\frac{1}{2}$	1^{nk}	Delahoussa…	Mdn	85	Berbereau,Hatmoto,EnvoysIntrigue	8
31Jan82-6SA	1$\frac{1}{16}$	:46^3	1:12	1:44 ft	7$\frac{1}{4}$	118	4$2\frac{1}{2}$	2^{hd}	2^{hd}	2^1	Delahoussa…	Mdn	80	LordAdvocte,Berbereu,ChrgeBtwn	12
17Jan82-6SA	1$\frac{1}{16}$	:47^4	1:12	1:43^{1}ft	*2$\frac{1}{4}$	118	5$2\frac{1}{4}$	5$5\frac{1}{2}$	8^{11}	8^{16}	Delahoussaye E^7	Mdn	69	CrystlDrops,LordAdvocte,NtiveBllo	9
6Jan82-6SA	1	:48^2	1:15^2	1:43 hy	*7-5	118	2^4	2^2	2$2\frac{1}{2}$	2$5\frac{1}{4}$	Delahoussaye E^1	Mdn	49	Free Duty, Berbereau, Fleet Eric	7
26Dec81-4SA	6f	:21^3	:44^3	1:10^{4}ft	3	118	9$6\frac{3}{4}$	8^8	5$7\frac{1}{2}$	3$1\frac{1}{2}$	Delahoussaye E^3	Mdn	82	Fanjet, Supron, Berbereau	12
25Oct81-3SA	1	:45^4	1:11^1	1:38 ft	9-5	118	4^8	4$3\frac{1}{2}$	3^3	2^1	Delahoussaye E^1	Mdn	78	Bison Bay, Berbereau, Crystal Star	8
3Oct81-3SA	6$\frac{1}{2}$f	:22^1	:45^2	1:17 ft	12	118	8$6\frac{3}{4}$	6$6\frac{1}{2}$	3$5\frac{1}{2}$	3$4\frac{1}{2}$	Delahoussaye E^8	Mdn	80	Prosperous,FastReason,Berbereau	10
6Sep81-4Dmr	6f	:23	:46^2	1:10^{4}ft	7$\frac{3}{4}$	118	4^2	4^2	3^5	5$8\frac{1}{2}$	Delahoussaye E^7	Mdn	75	Raise the Tempo,Tular,LateSleeper	9

Mar 26 SA tr.t 3f gd :38 h   Mar 21 SA 1 ft 1:41^4 h   Mar 10 SA 4f ft :47^2 hg   Mar 3 SA 6f ft 1:12 h

Fabulous Mystic | Ch. c. 3, by Le Fabuleux—Irish Mystic, by Mystic II
Br.—Arnold G R (Ky) | 1982 3 1 0 1 $13,850
Own.—Abatti-Blau-Morjoseph | **114** | Tr.—Jones Gary | 1981 0 M 0 0
Lifetime 3 1 0 1 $13,850

10Mar82-8SA	1$\frac{1}{8}$	:45^4	1:10	1:47^{3}ft	10	118	3$3\frac{1}{2}$	3$2\frac{1}{2}$	2^6	5^{11}	McCrron C…	Bradbury	80	Journey at Sea, Ask Me, Algardi	11
14Feb82-2SA	1$\frac{1}{16}$	:47^1	1:11^3	1:43^{1}ft	*2	115	6$3\frac{1}{2}$	5^3	2^{hd}	3^{nk}	Asmus…	Aw20000	85	LordAdvocte,AskMe,FbulousMystic	8
30Jan82-6SA	6$\frac{1}{2}$f	:22	:44^4	1:16^{2}ft	27	118	1^{hd}	1^{hd}	1$3\frac{1}{2}$	1$4\frac{1}{2}$	Asmussen C B^1	Mdn	88	FbulousMystic,Htmoto,NtiveBello	12

Mar 20 SA 6f ft 1:13^4 hg   Mar 3 SA 7f ft 1:27 h   Feb 25 SA 4f ft :46^2 h   Feb 6 SA 7f ft 1:25^4 h

Royal Captive ran a 100 in his last start. If he ran it again today, Berbereau (86) and Fabulous Music (80, 88) would have had to improve sharply in order to finish close to him. But these are well-bred young horses who are quite eligible to improve. I consider it more likely for them to run better than for Royal Captive to go badly off form after such a promising race. I might arbitrarily project him a point or two below his last performance, but no more.

Race	Projection	Rating	Difference
5	99	116	—17

After continuing to analyze the card in this fashion, my entire day's calculations looked like this:

Race	Projection	Rating	Difference
1	88	116	—28
2	78	103	—25
3	turf		
4	80	95	—15
5	99	116	—17
6	76	103	—27
7	93	116	—23
8	turf		
9	92	114	—22
		Average	—22

The track variant is —22. When I apply it to the day's results I can look back and understand races that might have seemed perplexing at the time. In the fourth race, for example, the longshot Angelo G. earned a figure of 73. He won the race virtually by default, as all the contenders behind him went off form. In the fifth race, Royal Captive did decline more than I had anticipated, winning with a 94. But most of the horses' performances were in line with my projections.

The projection method produces extremely accurate figures, but it also causes one subtle problem — a problem I had once thought was due to my personal errors until I found that it troubles almost everyone who makes figures this way. When handicappers make their projections, they tend not to anticipate enough improvement for horses who win races. If the projections are lower than they should be, the resultant figures will be lower than they should be. And after a while the handicapper will notice that all his figures seem to be shrinking. He may find, for example, that over a period of time the average winning figure for $10,000 claiming races is 82 instead of 85, as it is supposed to be. When I first encountered this problem my figures were shrinking so fast that I could barely compare recent races to ones that had been run two months earlier. Fortunately, the remedy for this problem is a simple one. At the end of each month, I review all the results and compare the figure of each race with the par figure for that class. If I find that the races have been run, on the average, one point slower than par, I will retroactively add one point to all my variants and figures for the month.

Once I have accumulated a set of figures at a track, I have no problem maintaining them when the racing shifts to another track on the same circuit. When Santa Anita closed and Hollywood Park opened, I did have to create a speed-rating chart for Hollywood. But I could use my existing Santa Anita numbers as the basis for the projections at Hollywood without having to resort again to the crudity of the par-figure method. The numbers are perfectly interchangeable. A 90 at Santa Anita means the same thing as a 90 at Hollywood.

And, for that matter, it means the same thing as a 90 at Belmont Park or Boondock Downs. The method by which I initially calculated my Santa Anita numbers — by basing them on universal par figures — makes them interchangeable (or very nearly so) with the figures I make at other tracks. In an era when so many horseplayers have figures for their home track, the greatest edge a speed handicapper can have is the ability to evaluate shippers with precision. I have made money in Florida every winter by knowing how to compare the local horses with the invaders from New York, Kentucky, and elsewhere. As I prepared for Santa Anita I planned to develop figures for the Golden Gate Fields and Bay Meadows, so that I could assess shippers from those Northern California tracks.

To make sure that my figures at different racing circuits are properly aligned with each other, I look for consistent, reliable horses who ship from one track to another and I make note of the figures they run at each place. After I constructed my California figures, the horses who shipped from coast to coast seemed to be performing consistently. When It's the One earned a figure of 119 in the Hollywood Gold Cup, then went to Belmont for the Suburban Handicap and ran a 119 again, I felt confident that my figures for California and New York were comparable.

But when I developed a set of figures for Bay Meadows and Golden Gate Fields, I encountered problems. Horses who shipped to these tracks from Southern California tended to run bigger figures than they did at Santa Anita or Hollywood. After examining the performances of a number of them, I concluded that the average improvement was about three points.

What was happening? There was only one possible explanation. I had constructed my Northern California figures just as I had done at Santa Anita, starting with the assumption that my universal par figures were applicable and that the average $10,000 claiming race was run with a figure of 85. But the quality of competition at Bay Meadows and Golden Gate Fields was not this good; it was literally sub-par. So I redid my whole set of figures for these tracks, subtracting three points from everything; now the average $10,000 claiming race would be run in an 82. And now the figures at these tracks would be in line with Santa Anita and the rest of the world.

Having compiled all these figures, I knew that I would be able to walk into Santa Anita on opening day with an understanding of the ability of the horses and the nature of racing in the state, even though I had never set foot in Arcadia, California, before. I expected that the figures alone would generate at least a small profit for me. After two or three weeks of watching races and making notes, I would be able to relate each horse's figure to the trip with which he had earned it, and I would be in complete command of everything that was happening at Santa Anita.

SEVEN

Relating Trips to Figures

WHEN A HANDICAPPER HAS LEARNED how to make speed figures and to judge horses' trips, he will possess most of the important skills necessary to beat the races consistently. But as he attempts to employ them, he may feel that he has merely reached a more advanced state of confusion. What does he do with all this information? How does he relate something as objective as speed figures to something as subjective as his visual observations of races? How does he compare a horse who earned a figure of 90 with an easy trip to a rival who earned an 80 with a difficult trip? Typically, he may think that the answer is to translate aspects of horses' trips into numbers, too, so that they can be combined with speed figures to produce one ultimate mathematical evaluation of a horse's ability.

Old-time speed handicappers generally incorporated weight into their speed figures. Others make a numerical evaluation of the pace of a race and apply it to the figure. Len Ragozin and other modern speed handicappers adjust every horse's figure according to the ground he loses on the turns. All these methods are forced to gloss over some complexities, however. Ragozin's disciplines are apt to fare poorly when the inside part of a track is disadvantageous; their figures downgrade a horse who was running on the rail, saving ground, even if he was hindered by a strong bias. Mathematical methods that try to take too many complexities into account, however, tend to degenerate into exercises in Fun with Numbers. In *Winning Big at the Track with Money Management,* Don Passer details a wonderfully precise method of evaluating final time and ground loss on the turns, measuring horses' performance in hundredths of a second. Then he proceeds to throw the kitchen sink into his calculations, telling readers to upgrade a horse by 2½ lengths if he is being ridden by a hot jockey. Such approaches to the game strike me as being not terribly far removed from the crude systems that used to be advertised in pulpy racing magazines, that told you to give a horse five points for every in-the-money finish in the last month, a point for every pound he was dropping, and two points if the race was being run under the astrological sign of his birth.

I believe it is much more realistic to operate with naked, unadorned speed figures and to relate them to horses' trips in nonmathematical, nonrigid fashion. I ask myself: How was the figure earned? Does it fairly reflect a horse's ability? Does it overstate his ability because he earned it with an easy trip? Does it understate his ability because he had a tough trip?

Ideally, I prefer to bet on a horse who had a difficult trip in his last start, but still earned a figure superior to all the horses he is now facing, who seems likely to get an easier trip today, and whose virtues are so well-hidden that he will pay a big price. I also like to go out with women who look like Ursula Andress, who hold graduate degrees from Harvard, and who make a sensational pike mousse — but never attract any attention from other guys. It's hard to find perfection in any area of life.

Because of the scarcity of horses who represent an unequivocal combination of big figures, big trips, and big odds, the majority of my bets come on types that are more commonplace. For example:

- A horse who has earned a superior figure under honest circumstances, without the aid of an unusually favorable trip.
- A horse who had a difficult trip but still managed to earn a figure competitive with the rivals he is now facing.
- A horse whose last race can be ignored because of an impos-

sibly difficult trip but whose previous figures are competitive with or superior to those of the horses he is facing.

Conversely, I like to bet against these types:

- A short-priced horse who has no edge in the figures and who has been the beneficiary of easy trips.
- A short-priced horse who seemed to improve sharply in his most recent race, but whose improvement was due principally to a highly favorable trip.

Whenever I handicap a race, I first focus my attention on the horse who earned the best figure in his most recent start, although over the years I have learned to be wary of figures that seem almost too good. In *Picking Winners* I wrote, "Even if a horse has run a big figure in his last start . . . I will hesitate to bet him on the basis of just one exceptional performance." I wrote that if a horse ran figures of 70, 75, 69, 73, followed by a 90, I would view him skeptically and generally expect him to run in the 70s again.

What I did not understand then was that I had to evaluate the nature of that 90. Was it the result of a perfect trip? Or was it an honest effort that did indicate a legitimate improvement in the horse's ability? A handicapper must make this judgment of every superior figure. What, for example, would he make of one of the biggest figures ever run — General Assembly's in the Travers Stakes at Saratoga — when he came out of that race into the Marlboro Cup?

· · ·

General Assembly always had a lofty reputation. He bore a physical resemblance to his daddy, Secretariat, and had been expected to emulate him ever since he was a 2-year-old. He never did — until he won the Travers Stakes with an incredible figure of 134. Was this a one-time fluke?

Almost certainly. Only a slavish speed handicapper could have bet him on the basis of this performance. Over a track I labeled GR, S+, a favorable rail with a very strong speed bias, General Assembly had broken from the inside post position against a field in which there was no consequential speed. He had a two-length lead after a slow half mile, and the only rival chasing him was an undistinguished allowance horse. Under such circumstances, General Assembly almost had to run the race of his life. But two weeks later in the Marlboro Cup, where he was nominally the top-figure horse, Spectacular Bid blew him away. General Assembly ran a 119, which more accurately reflected his ability.

• • •

Geraldine's Store

B. f. 3, by Exclusive Native—Chain Store, by Nodouble
Br.—Whitney T P (Ky)
Tr.—Johnson Philip G

Own.—Whitney T P

116

Lifetime 1982 5 2 2 1 $31,720
5 2 2 1 1981 0 M 0 0
$31,720

27Jun82- 5Bel fst 1 :45¾ 1:10½ 1:36¾ 3+⑤Alw 20000 7 3 33 1hd 11 12½ Samyn J L 101 109 5.80 83–21 Geraldine'sStore109 Alzbell117 NicoleMonAmour109hd Driving 9
7Jun82- 6Bel gd 6f :23 :46 1:10¾ 3+⑥Md Sp Wt 10 7 42½ 3nk 1hd 12 Samyn J L 86 114 *1.80 88–13 Geraldine's... ...Time114½ Driving 10
3May82- 4Aqu fst 6f :22¾ :46 1:11¾ ⑥Md Sp Wt 9 3 42½ 34½ 38 27½ Samyn J L 77 121 3.50 76–24 Wimbledon... Gained place 11
22Apr82- 4Aqu fst 7f :24 :48¾ 1:27¾ ⑥Md Sp Wt 2 4 12 12½ 11 2nk Samyn J L 121 *.90 65–27 Saved Ground... Gabfest 121 2½ Sharp 7
14Apr82- 6Aqu fst 6f :22¾ :46¾ 1:12¾ ⑥Md Sp Wt 6 13 44 34½ 35 31½ Samyn J L 121 4.40 77–26 Steambath121... Geraldine'sStore121 6 Rallied 14

LATEST WORKOUTS   Jly 10 Bel tr.t 3f fst :35½ h   Jly 5 Bel 4f fst :48¾ b   ●Jun 21 Bel 6f fst 1:10½ h   Jun 16 Bel 4f fst :47⅖ h

Geraldine's Store is a somewhat more complicated case. She had improved from an 86 to a 101 in her last race, and a handicapper who encountered her when she ran at Belmont on July 13 would have to judge whether that big number was legitimate. Certainly, Geraldine's Store had every right to improve. She was a lightly campaigned, well-bred young filly, and her last start had been her first race at a distance. Maybe running a mile was her game.

Even so, I could not bet Geraldine's Store with any confidence. The trip notes for her last race read: "Stalk duel B, GP, 3T." On a day when the Belmont track was very slow, two fillies had engaged in an all-out head-and-head battle for the lead, running the first half mile in a lightning 45⅖ seconds. Geraldine's Store was sitting in an ideal position three lengths behind them, with no other horse near her. As the leaders weakened, she moved in the 3-path around them — a perfect trip.

If she had run a 101 under these optimal circumstances, what would she do under more normal conditions? I had no idea, but I knew I could never bet her on the basis of that single good figure. Geraldine's Store finished second in her next start, with a figure of 88.

• • •

Frank Gomez — Own.—Schoninger B

Ch. c. 3, by Rainy Lake—Keen Observer, by Smart
Br.—Brewer Katherine A (Ky)
Tr.—Gomez Frank

116

	St.	1st	2nd	3rd	Amt.
1982	2	0	2	0	\$4,140
1981	2	1	0	0	\$4,890

23Jan82- 5Hia	fst	6f	:21⅘	:44⅗	1:10	Allowance	9	3	4^{2}	3½	$1^{1\frac{1}{2}}$	2½	Maple E	109	116	9.50	92-19	Cut Away 116½ Frank Gomez 116^{5} Star Choice 120^{2}	Gamely 12
1Jan82- 8Crc	fst	7f	:22⅘	:45⅗	1:24	Allowance	10	2	$3^{1\frac{1}{2}}$	2^{3}	2^{5}	2^{7}	Vasquez J	91	115	4.70	89-13	Rex's Profile 115^{7}FrankGomez115^{2}Dale'sGros117^{3}	Best of others 12
18Dec81- 5Crc	fst	6f	:22⅘	:47	1:12⅘	Md 35000	11	1	2½	2^{hd}	$1^{2\frac{1}{2}}$	1^{7}	Vasquez J	87	119	5.80	88-16	FrnkGomez119^{7}Mrlowe'sMdness119^{nk}Ann'sDrling119¾	Drew clear 1
2Dec81- 8Crc	fst	6f	:22⅘	:47	1:13⅘	Md 50000	11	2	1½	4^{5}	7^{13}	7^{17}	Vasquez J		119	2.80	66-22	Really Funny $119^{1\frac{1}{2}}$ Catch Villa $119^{1\frac{1}{2}}$ Anne's Darling $119^{1\frac{1}{4}}$	Tired 1

LATEST WORKOUTS ●Jan 14 Crc 5f fst 1:01⅗ b Dec 27 Crc 6f fst 1:15⅗ h Dec 14 Crc 5f fst 1:02 h

Frank Gomez had improved dramatically in his last race, running an extraordinary figure of 109. If he approximated that performance, he would win his next start, at Hialeah on February 7, even though the field included one colt, Lejoli, who was being trumpeted as a Kentucky Derby contender. But if that last figure was not legitimate, his others — 91 and 87 — would probably not be sufficient to win.

My trip notes for Frank Gomez's last race said only "3T." He had rushed up to challenge a hot pace, battling in the 3-path with leaders who were running a half mile in :44⅗, and took the lead, only to be caught in the stretch. This was not an extraordinary trip, but there was certainly nothing easy about it. The other horses who had been vying for the lead had all collapsed and finished out of the money. Frank Gomez's last race looked like a legitimate performance by a good, improving young horse, and it gave him an edge of seven lengths over his nearest competition. Under the circumstances I did what any rational man would. I bet all I could. Frank Gomez won by 6½ lengths and paid \$7.20.

It is relatively easy to judge the legitimacy of a single horse's figure. And it is comforting to be able to bet on a horse like Frank Gomez, knowing that if the figure is true he is virtually certain to win. More often, though, a handicapper will be forced to deal with those comparisons involving an easy trip/good figure and a tough trip/poor figure. Sometimes he will be forced to conclude that the ambiguities are irresolvable. But there are many times when he will be able to identify the superior horse confidently, and those situations are almost always lucrative.

Cold Coin
Own.—Aronow Stable

B. g. 5, by Key to the Kingdom—Triple Jayleen, by Sailor
Br.—Jones & Owens N & P (Ky)
Tr.—Green Newcomb
$16,000

Turf Record — St. 1st 2nd 3rd — Amt.
St. 1st 2nd 3rd 1982 1 0 1 0 $1,260
3 0 0 1 1981 23 2 2 5 $12,907

1115

89-13 Kcaj 112¹ Cold Coin 109³ Northern Effort 109² Rallied 12
85-17 Mr.Excavator 111³ Mmmy'sJoe118ⁿᵏ NorthenWheys 116³ No factor 12
71-20 Lawson Isles He's Right 116¹⅓ El Oliver 115¹ Tired 9
82-20 Maryv 116² Freels Hed 115¹³ Happy Relic 116² Pinched back 12
83-21 Cold Coin 116² Edan One 106ⁿᵒ Erin's Dancer 111ⁿᵏ Driving 7
83-15 M. J.'s Glory 116⁴ Lawson Isles 120¹ Cold Coin 114¹⅓ Evenly 8
78-19 Lawson Isles 122¹ Northen Wheys 116⁶ Cold Coin 114⁵⅓ Bumped 10
76-17 He's Just Right 120ⁿᵏ El Oliver1071⅓ColdCoin114³ Blocked, hung 11
84-21 Salinity 112ⁿᵏ A. J.'s Chap 116³ Cold Coin 115³ Evenly 8
71-20 The Big H. 114¹ Gait La Rue 114³ For Fun 122² Outrun 9

LATEST WORKOUTS Nov 14 Crc 4f fst :49 h

Mr. Kapacity ✳
Own.—Sefa F

Ch. g. 6, by Nice Dancer—Sleep Lonely, by Pia Star
Br.—Kapchinsky H D (Can)
Tr.—Edwards Larry D
$15,000

Turf Record — St. 1st 2nd 3rd — Amt.
St. 1st 2nd 3rd 1981 20 2 2 1 $21,538
4 0 0 0 1980 16 3 2 0 $32,281

1095

80-17 Mr.Excavator111³Mmmy'sJoe118ⁿᵏ NorthenWheys116³ Brief foot 12
74-22 Hattab Al 113ⁿᵒ Indian Recall 111⁴ᵏ Kapacity 107³ 9
63-22 Torsions Lad He's J... gdp 117¹⅓ Jungle Hemp 113⁵ 10
78-19 Not On My Three ⁴⅓ Mr. Kapacity 114² Turnbuckle 112¹⅓ 12
66-27 Rattle the Keys 115⅓ Big Richard 115² Puffin 115¹⅓ 6
— — Hudson 120⁴⅓ Frederick Town 113² Rich and Ready 119⁶ Eased 7
59-22 Baca County Kid 110² K.C. Clinch 115ⁿᵏ Goal Pen 117³ 6
47-23 Mocha Mousse 122²⅓ Bet On Brad 117¹⅓ Garrotero 117ʰᵈ 7
56-13 Hudson 114²⅓ Hotfoot 113²⅓ Noble Irishman 117ⁿᵒ 9
72-20 Swift Spruce 110¹⅓ Fastway Home 115² Goal Pen 117³ 7

LATEST WORKOUTS Nov 11 CD 4f fst :50 b

I had prepared for the 1982 Hialeah season by spending some time at Calder, watching the trips of horses over that rail-biased track. I did not have to wait long for my work to pay dividends, for I encountered Cold Coin and Mr. Kapacity in a seven-furlong race on opening day.

Cold Coin had the top figure in the race. But my notes on his performance read, "Rail B, T, 2S." He had run on the favorable rail almost all the way, until he eased out into the 2-path in the stretch. My notes for Mr. Kapacity said, "3B, 4T." After breaking from post position 11, he had raced in the 3-path down the backstretch and even wider thereafter — the kind of trip with which no horse could win at Calder. His prior figure, the 90 that he earned at Churchill Downs, was good enough to beat Cold Coin and the rest of the horses in the field. But the betting public scarcely appreciated the relative merits of the two horses. Cold Coin finished fourth as the 5-to-2 favorite, as Mr. Kapacity won by five lengths and paid $46.40.

Flaming Royal
Own.—Rosen C

B. g. 5, by Personality—Flighty Duchess, by Sunrise Flight
Br.—O'Neal Mr—Mrs D D (Ky)
Tr.—Lotti Gene Jr
$10,000

Turf Record — St. 1st 2nd 3rd — Amt.
St. 1st 2nd 3rd 1982 3 1 0 1 $4,975
7 0 0 1 1981 17 1 0 3 $8,120

1115

89-22 Flaming Royal 111⁷ Racquet Ball116⁴PrinceofAce's111ʰᵈ Handily 12
80-19 Skeet Shooter 106¹ logol'sbean 116²Flamingoroyal11½ᵏ Weakened 12
80-18 NoctrnalTechngForLbor121³ᵏ... ᵏ... Nels 12
74-14 Benninoᵏ ⅓ Quite A Stellar 116¹⅓ Rifleman 116¹ No factor 12
84-16 SndfordBoy111²⁴ᵏAmbtos(Conter)16²GoeRvs... 12
74-10 Len Warren Sagmind... What A star... Tired 6
83-14 Rifleman 118¹⅓ Lectric Luck 116³ Spirit of Fun 109¹ Tired 7
73-20 Star Encounter 106ⁿᵒ Catiline 114⅓ Special Flair 115¹ Tired 11
65-25 New Look 116ⁿᵒ Mister Blades 116⁵ Anoint 109² Tired 11
80-22 Nice Sailing 119⅓ Lambidextrous 116² Flaming Royal 119ⁿᵏ Tired 12

12Sep81—Evening Program

LATEST WORKOUTS Jan 21 GP 5f fst 1:01¾ h Jan 9 GP 3f fst :38 b

Sean Christopher		Dk. b. or br. g. 5, by Lothario—Virnislee, by Porterhouse									

Sean Christopher
Own.—Zimbisky R $10,000

Dk. b. or br. g. 5, by Lothario—Virnislee, by Porterhouse
Br.—Walker L V (Ky)
Tr.—Zimbisky Robert

116

	Turf Record	St.	1st	2nd	3rd	Amt.
	St. 1st 2nd 3rd	1982	4	0	1	2	$2,980
	2 0 0 0	1981	13	0	4	1	$7,420

10Feb82-10Hia sly 1⅛ :46⅘ 1:11¾ 1:51¾ Clm c-8000 2 3 2½ 1hd 2hd 3½ Hernande **87** b 109 4.90 74-16 ToHisCredit112nk PortVncouver116¹SnChristophr109²½ Weakened 11

1Feb82-4Hia fst 1⅛ :47⅘ 1:13 1:52⅘ Clm 8000 9 2 2hd 11 1² 3²¾ Perret C **78** b 116 7.40 65-25 J.R.C.AndMe111nk LeLorrain162½SeanChristopher116⁴ Weakened 9

27Jan82-2Hia fst 6f :22⅘ :46⅕ 1:12 Clm 8000 10 8 118½ 910 5² 5³ Velasquez J b 116 6.20 80-19 Skeet Shoot... Royal111nk Late bid 12

20Jan82-4Hia fst 7f :22⅘ :45½ 1:25½ Clm 8000 2 10 45½ 412 44 23 Perret C b 116 43.10 74-23 Pollster112... istoph 161... DistinctivII1111² Best of others 11

20Jly81-9AP fm 1⅛ T :48¾ 1:13⅗ 1:47¾ 3+Clm 9000 5 7 67½101110141028 Hirdes R J Jr b 115 31.00 36-35 Miessen's Mission 115nk Gem's Top 113¾¼ Astral Plane 117¾¼ 10

1Jly81-9AP fst 1 :47⅕ 1:13¾ 1:39¾ 3+Clm 9500 7 5 52 51¾ 63¾ 79¾ Lively J b 117 7.80 52-29 Iron Ring 110²½ Bar Ja 117²¾ Gem's Top 113¹¼ 9

15Jun81-9AP fst 1 :46½ 1:11¾ 1:38⅝ Clm 8500 5 4 42 44½ 31½ 23 Lively J b 117 6.40 65-25 Sly Shadow 119³ Sean Christopher 117¹ Whywouldnthe 113⁶ 8

4Jun81-6AP fm 1⅛ T :47¾ 1:12½ 1:46¾ Clm 9500 2 5 74 98¾ 78½ 65½ Lively J b 117 13.70 65-30 Fleeting Fury 117²¾ Self Pruner 117³ Chuckie Sue 112¹ 9

28May81-4AP fst 1 :46⅘ 1:11¾ 1:38⅞ Clm 10000 1 4 56 57½ 65½ 75¾ Gallitano G b 117 4.70 63-16 Parmetti 117hd Master of Malice 113¹ Takeoff N'Turn 117¹ 9

18May81-2AP fst 7f :23 :47 1:25¾ Clm 12500 11 2 86½ 85½ 54½ 64¾ Gallitano G b 117 23.80 68-19 Can't Hear Me 117hd Arctic Challenge 111nk Blanket Finish 122¾ 11

LATEST WORKOUTS Feb 7 GP 3f fst :36⅖ h   Jan 26 GP 3f fst :37⅖ b   Jan 19 GP 3f fst :36 h   Jan 15 GP 5f fst 1:02 bg

The comparison of Flaming Royal and Sean Christopher, who faced each other in a seven-furlong race at Hialeah on February 20, 1982, was a textbook case that could have come straight out of *Picking Winners*. Flaming Royal was the type of horse I always loved to bet: He had a superior figure; he had an ace trainer; he was in sharp condition and was stepping up in class. The number he had earned in his last start, a 93, gave him a three-length edge over Sean Christopher, who was his closest rival. Not only did Sean Christopher have inferior figures, but he had just been claimed by an unknown trainer and he was a chronic "sucker horse." With zero victories, five seconds, and three thirds over the last two years, he did not seem to know how to win.

I loved him. And when I went to the window to bet on Sean Christopher enthusiastically, my figure-oriented friend Mark Hopkins said, "I hope nobody who read your book sees you. They'll think you lost your mind."

Flaming Royal's big figure, I thought, was strictly the product of his trip. In that race, three speedballs had been battling for the lead in fractions of :22⅕ and :45⅖, extraordinary times for an $8000 claiming race. Flaming Royal lurked behind them, and when the leaders fanned out into the stretch he shot through the opening on the rail and surged to the lead. My notes read, "Rail T, got thru, perfect trip."

Sean Christopher, on the other hand, was better than his figures indicated. And despite that dreadful 0-for-17 record, he was certainly no sucker horse. His performance on February 1 had been the gamest I had seen all season, and it left me writing notes feverishly: "Pushed from G, couldn't clear, 3B, hard duel, to rail, held well." Breaking from the outside post, Sean Christopher had raced three-wide in a speed duel around the first turn and into the backstretch. He disposed of those horses (they both wound up losing by more than 20 lengths) and took a momentary lead, but when he did the eventual winner rushed outside him as if he were going to blow past. But Sean Christopher fought back and held on till mid-stretch before he faded to finish third.

The next time he ran he got into another all-out duel for the lead, running head-and-head in :46⅘ and 1:11⅖. (Earlier in the week, on a comparably fast track, the fractions in the $50,000 Seminole Handicap had been :47⅖ and 1:11⅖.) But even after this exertion, Sean Christopher had held on well and lost by little more than a length.

Sean Christopher came back to win, while Flaming Royal finished ninth. But I went to collect the $19.60 payoff discreetly, just in case any readers of *Picking Winners* were in the vicinity.

• • •

Nivernay Dk. b. or br. c. 2, by L'Enjoleur—Let Me Linger, by What A Pleasure — Lifetime 3 0 1 0 $3,360 — 1982 3 M 1 0 $3,360
Br.—Willcox Mrs & A A (Fla) — 118
Own.—Willcox Mrs & A A — Tr.—Jackson Evan S

1Sep82- 6Bel fst 7f :23⅘ :47 1:24⅕ Md Sp Wt 1 5 7³½ 8⁵½ 6⁶ 4⁵¾ Fell J 72 118 11.00 75-13 Ski's Heart 118³½ Torpedo Los 118²Countertrade118½ Raced wide 8
11Jun82- 3Mth fst 5f :22⅕ :45⅗ :58 Md Sp Wt 3 5 6⁶ 6⁹½ 4⁹ 4⁸ Brumfield D 73 118 2.50e 88-18 Truby 11 ... Dashing Duke 118³ No menace 9
1Jun82- 3Mth fst 5f :22⅗ :45⅖ :57⅗ Md Sp Wt 3 3 2⁴ 2³ 2⁵ 2⁶¾ Perret C 118 4.90 91-15 Laus' Cause 118⁶¾ Nivernay 118¹¹ Dr. Gaston 118²½ Held place 7
LATEST WORKOUTS Sep 10 Bel 3f fst :38 b — Jly 24 Bel 5f fst 1:01 h — Jly 19 Bel 4f fst :49⅘ b — Jly 14 Bel 4f fst :48 h

NPG, 5E

White Birch Gr. c. 2, by Nijinsky II—Snow Peak, by Sword Dancer — Lifetime 2 0 2 0 $7,480 — 1982 2 M 2 0 $7,480
Br.—Brant P M (Ky) — 118
Own.—Brant P M — Tr.—Jolley Leroy

BR 21Aug82- 4Sar fst 6f :22⅗ :46 1:10⅗ Md Sp Wt 3 3 2hd 2hd 2½ 2¹½ Cordero A Jr 92 118 *.50e 85-14 Raise One 118¹½ White Birch 118hd Ski's Heart 118½ Rallied 9
7Aug82- 6Sar fst 6f :22 :45⅘ 1:11 Md Sp Wt 2 6 4³½ 3½ 1hd 2¹½ Cordero A Jr 80 118 2.20 83-14 Savour 118¹½ White Birch 118¹½ Seligman 118⁴ Gamely 12
LATEST WORKOUTS Sep 5 Bel 7f fst 1:25 h — ●Aug 29 Sar 1 fst 1:40 h — ●Aug 15 Sar 5f fst :58⅕ h — Aug 4 Sar 4f fst :46⅖ h

2T, 23

I was excited when I saw Nivernay's name in the Belmont entries for September 12, 1982, because his previous performance had been a memorable one. Money had poured onto him the last few minutes before post time, cutting his probable quinella payoffs in half, but if he was supposed to win that day jockey Jeffrey Fell didn't seem to know it. There was no speed in the race, and Nivernay looked as if he might be able to take the lead, but after breaking from the inside post Fell displayed his characteristic reluctance to ride on the rail. He put his mount under restraint and dropped back into last place while the leaders were setting a very slow pace. Fell swung Nivernay into the 5-path on the turn, and the colt closed about as well as could be expected under the circumstances.

If I didn't use figures, I would have made a big bet on Nivernay at 13 to 1. But as I looked at the numbers I was confused. The favorite, White Birch, had earned an excellent figure of 92 in his last start. He had done so with a relatively easy trip in the 2-path,

but the figure gave him an edge of 20 points — or eight lengths —
over Nivernay. Would Nivernay be able to run that much better?

There was no correct answer to this handicapping riddle. The
situation was ambiguous. I made a small bet on Nivernay, because
I do not want to watch empty-handed when a horse I like wins at
13 to 1, but I do not care to lose much on horses who have such a
disadvantage in the figures.

The outcome of the race was a bit ambiguous, too. White Birch
won at 3 to 2. Nivernay finished fourth, 2½ lengths back, after being blocked in the stretch, and was moved up to third place after a
disqualification.

Once a handicapper has evaluated the significance of horses's figures and their previous trips, he must look ahead and try to anticipate what will happen today, whether any of the contenders seems
likely to have an eventful trip that will notably help or hurt his
chances. Of course, no one can plot, step by step, the way a race is
going to develop. But when a bias exists, a handicapper must attempt to judge which horses will be helped and which hindered by
it. If a field is full of habitual front-runners or else devoid of speed,
he must anticipate how horses will be affected by the pace. He must
always try to judge whether any horse is likely to take the lead without difficulty. Sometimes it may even be possible for a handicapper
to anticipate specific details of horses' trips. If, for example, there
are five speed horses in a race with a short run to the first turn, the
one in the outermost post position is likely to have a troublesome
journey.

For someone who attempts to make all these difficult judgments,
handicapping is infinitely more complex and ambiguous than for
the mathematicians who use neat systems and arrive at a neat solution to each race. But every once in a while a serious handicapper,
too, will find a race where everything seems to fall into place —
trips, figures, the likely development of the race. All the factors fell
into place for me at Saratoga in 1982, at a time when I desperately
needed them to.

After my spectacularly successful meeting there the year before,
I felt I had made a great intellectual breakthrough and had finally
learned how to relate trips to figures. I had been enjoying largely

unbroken success since then, and so I returned to Saratoga brimming with confidence. But I started losing. And losing. Losing more money than I had ever lost before at a single race meeting. Midway through the season I sat down with all the results, analyzed all my wagers, and tried to determine whether I had been doing anything wrong. I concluded that I was not making any perceptible mistakes, that this was only a random distribution of bad events. But that was small consolation. I was losing more than $14,000 for the meeting when I sat down to contemplate the past performances for the fourth race on August 23.

③ SARATOGA — 7 FURLONGS — SARATOGA

7 FURLONGS. (1.20⅔) ALLOWANCE. Purse $19,000. 3-year-olds and upward which have never won a race other than maiden, claiming or starter. Weights, 3-year-olds, 117 lbs.; older, 122 lbs. Non-winners of a race other than claiming since August 1 allowed 3 lbs.; such a race since July 15, 5 lbs.

Gust of Reason — B. c. 3, by Limit to Reason—Gustoletti, by Gustav. Br.—Griffith & Humphrey (Va). Tr.—Pierce Joseph H Jr. Own.—Kligman H — 117

Dave The Dude — B. c. 3, by His Majesty—Electrifying, by Reviewer. Br.—Allen J (Ky). Tr.—Tesher Howard M. Own.—Allen J — 112

North Coast — Dk. b. or br. g. 4, by North Sea—Velocity Ann, by Veloz II. Br.—Brissenden Mary Rose (Md). Tr.—Bruce R R. Own.—Bruce Mary Rose — 117

El Bombay — B. c. 4, by Bombay Duck—Maria L, by Mystic II. Br.—Luca S (Fla). Tr.—Luca Santo. Own.—Luca S — 1107

Cintula — B. c. 3, by Ramsinga—Thill, by Iron Ruler
Br.—Tartan Farms (Fla)
Own.—Tartan Stable — Tr.—Nerud Jan H
10410 — Lifetime 4 1 1 0 $15,560 — 1982 4 1 1 0 $15,560 — 1981 0 M 0 0

21Jun82- 6Bel fst 1 :47 1/5 1:11 4/5 1:36 4/5 3↑Md Sp Wt 8 5 52 3/4 3 1/2 21 1/2 1 1/2 Cordero A J [93] 114 3.50 82-14 Cintula 114 1/2 Trenchant 114 1/2 Fulton 1145 1/2 Driving 10
2Jun82- 3Bel fst 6f :23 1/5 :46 2/5 1:09 4/5 3↑Md Sp Wt 6 5 32 1/2 2hd 2 1/2 43 Rogers K L [95] 114 4.60 90-11 MuskokWyck114noExclusivOn1142 3/4LWshingtonin114nk Weakened 7
8May82- 4Aqu fst 7f :23 :46 3/5 1:24 4/5 3↑Md Sp Wt 4 4 57 58 33 2no Rogers K L 113 10.00 77-19 Puritan Chief 119no Cintula 1137 Governorship 1131 3/4 Sharp 6
21Apr82- 6Aqu fst 7f :23 :46 1/5 1:24 1/5 3↑Md Sp Wt 7 5 64 3/4 710 611 510 Rogers K L 112 2.30e 70-24 Faces Up 1141 Roulette Wheel 112hd Fulton 1145 1/2 Outrun 7
LATEST WORKOUTS Aug 16 Sar 5f fst 1:00 1/5 h — Aug 11 Sar 5f fst 1:02 b — Aug 6 Sar tr.t 4f fst :49 2/5 b — Aug 1 Bel tr.t 4f fst :51 4/5 b

Mr. Peruser — B. c. 3, by Mr Prospector—Speak Softly, by The Pruner
Br.—Happy Valley Farm & Peskoff S (Fla)
Own.—Cruguet Denise — Tr.—Cruguet Denise
112 — Lifetime 7 1 0 1 $3,013 — 1982 1 0 0 0 — 1981 6 1 0 1 $3,013 — Turf 7 1 0 1 $3,013
Entered 22Aug82- 7 SAR

6Aug82- 9Sar fm 1 3/16 ①:49 1:12 4/5 1:55 4/5 3↑Alw 20000 12 12 1210 106 1211 1215 Cruguet J 112 17.10 72-20 Eyepleaser 1122 1/2 Silver Tom 117nk Condition Red 1122 1/2 Outrun 12
9Sep81♦6Doncaster(Eng) gd 6f 1:14 4/5 ① Rouse Nursery Hcp 68 1/4 Hide E 130 20.00 — — BsilBoy111 3/4 ComeOnTheBlues1272 1/2 MummysGm1241 1/2 No threat 14
1Sep81♦4Ripon(Eng) fm 6f 1:12 2/5 ① Wensley Stakes 31 3/4 Hide E 129 20.00 — — Pomegranate 121nk Rosier 1301 1/2 Mr Peruser 1293 Bid, blocked 8
20Aug81♦3Yarmouth(Eng) gd 7f 1:25 2/5 ① MillsAheadNurseryHcp 615 Reid J 128 7.00 — — Starters Image 1002 Bancario 1218 Major Irish 121hd No factor 6
10Jly81♦2York(Eng) gd 6f 1:16 ① Black Duck Stakes 42 Piggott L 128 4.00 — — Full Extent 1281 1/2 Tachyaun128hd ComeOnTheBlues128 1/2 Fin. well 4
26Jun81♦2Doncaster(Eng) fm 6f 1:13 1/5 ① Grimthorpe Stakes 52 Hide E 123 7.00 — — LinusGinseng1231 1/2 MjorsAffir123hd Wstonbirt120no Well up, led 11
9Jun81♦1Yarmouth(Eng) gd*5f 1:03 4/5 ① JohnHoldrichStks(Mdn) 1 3/4 Hide E 126 16.00 — — MrPrusr126 3/4 ComOnThBlus1261 1/2 ChildownBlu1265 Well up, drvg 12
LATEST WORKOUTS ●Aug 13 Sar 5f fst 1:00 1/5 h — ●Jly 30 Sar ① 7f fm 1:25 h — Jly 16 Sar ① 6f hd 1:16 3/5 b

Straight Main — B. rig. 3, by Accipiter—Cutting Straight, by Dr Fager
Br.—Evans T M (Va)
Own.—Buckland Farm — Tr.—Campo John P
112 — Lifetime 11 1 2 0 $18,085 — 1982 7 0 1 0 $5,320 — 1981 4 1 1 0 $12,765 — Turf 1 0 0 0

7Aug82- 2Sar fst 7f :22 4/5 :45 2/5 1:22 2/5 3↑Alw 19000 6 8 65 56 1/4 67 69 1/4 Bailey J D [83] b 112 12.60 81-14 TheTimeIsNow1122Tarntr1141 1/2KingNskr1051 1/2 Lacked a response 11
8Jly82- 7Bel fst 7f :23 1/5 :46 1/5 1:24 3↑Alw 19000 6 12 108 3/4 99 1/4 76 1/4 45 1/4 Beitia E [87] 111 50.90 77-23 Le Washingtonian 116hd Fortuis 1132 1/2 King Naskra 1112 3/4 Rallied 13
20Jun82- 9Bel fst 7f :23 1/5 :46 1/5 1:22 3/5 3↑Alw 19000 11 8 86 1/4 107 3/4 1110 1012 Beitia E 110 12.10 77-10 Exclusive One 1141 1/2 Nathan Detroit 1131 1/2 Fortuis 112no Outrun 11
5Jun82- 2Bel gd 7f :22 4/5 :45 2/5 1:23 3↑Alw 19000 6 7 96 1/4 97 1/2 74 1/4 2 1/2 Beitia E 110 21.40e 86-11 Faces Up 113 1/2 Straight Main 110hd Hardy Hawk 110no Rallied 10
17May82- 7Aqu fm 1 1/8 ①:49 1:13 1:51 1/5 Alw 20000 4 9 810 87 1/2 89 1/4 88 1/4 Lovato F Jr b 117 13.90e 79-14 Four Bases 117hd Victory Zone 1173 TheYoungSquire117 3/4 Outrun 12
25Mar82- 8Aqu fst 1 1/8 :49 4/5 1:14 1/5 1:52 4/5 Alw 17000 2 5 61 3/4 76 1/4 66 1/4 64 1/4 Skinner K b 117 8.80 66-27 HeroicSpirit117noHelloFederal1121 1/4ReservtionAgent1172 1/4 Outrun 7
12Feb82- 8Aqu fst 1 1/16 ⊡:47 4/5 1:12 3/5 1:44 1/5 Whirlaway 7 6 66 3/4 65 1/4 69 511 MacBeth D b 117 13.40 81-17 Ask Muhammad 1191Wolfie'sRascal1192 1/4FastGold117 3/4 No threat 7
31Dec81- 3Aqu fst 1 1/8 ⊡:48 3/5 1:13 2/5 1:52 3/5 Md Sp Wt 2 3 32 1/2 31 1/2 1hd 1 3/4 MacBeth D b 118 *2.00e 83-12 Straight Main 118 3/4 A Real Leader 1132 Private Sun 118no Driving 8
5Dec81- 8Key my 1 1/16 :46 4/5 1:13 1:46 2/5 Allegheny 6 9 811 89 77 1/2 59 1/4 Saumell L 114 9.00 63-22 House Speaker 112 1/2 Uno Roberto1126SharpCorynth1122 1/4 Outrun 9
5Dec81-Run in Two Divisions: 7th & 8th Races.
29Nov81- 6Aqu fst 7f :23 3/5 :48 2/5 1:28 2/5 Md Sp Wt 5 6 77 1/2 87 1/2 57 1/2 25 3/4 Saumell L 118 6.90 53-33 Katana 1185 3/4 Straight Main 118nk Fort Monroe 1131 Angled out 9
LATEST WORKOUTS Aug 19 Sar tr.t 5f fst 1:03 b — Aug 14 Sar tr.t 4f fst :50 1/5 b — Aug 1 Sar tr.t 5f fst 1:02 3/5 b — Jly 22 Bel tr.t 5f fst 1:01 h

Chapter One — B. c. 3, by Nostrum—Empormila, by Emporium
Br.—Twin Eagles Farm Inc (Ky)
Own.—Sommer Viola — Tr.—Martin Frank
112 — Lifetime 21 3 7 3 $69,590 — 1982 15 3 5 2 $62,080 — 1981 6 M 2 1 $7,510 — Turf 3 0 0 0

19Aug82- 2Sar fm 1 1/2 ①:49 2/5 2:04 3/5 2:30 1/5 3↑Alw 20000 3 2 3 1/2 56 614 721 Velasquez J b 112 6.40 70-10 London Times 1175 Kanduit 1123 1/2 Strivor 1122 1/4 Stopped 7
30Jly82- 5Bel fst 1 :46 1:10 2/5 1:36 3/5 Clm 90000 10 6 51 3/4 3 1/2 32 1nk Bailey J D [93] b 118 3.10 83-16 Chapter One 118nk Speeding Holme 116 1/2 Brae Axe 1141 1/2 Driving 11
9Jly82- 7Bel fst 1 1/4 :49 4/5 1:38 4/5 2:04 1/5 3↑Alw 20000 3 1 12 1 1/2 1 1/2 2 3/4 Bailey J D [97] b 113 3.00 78-22 Sever 112 3/4 Chapter One 113 3/4 A Real Leader 1115 3/4 Drifted out 6
20Jun82- 3Bel fst 1 :46 3/5 1:11 2/5 1:36 2/5 Clm 50000 1 5 21 21 1/2 11 1/2 16 1/2 Bailey J D b 117 *1.50 84-10 Chapter One 1176 1/2 Katana 1171 Gauley 1175 3/4 Drew clear 8
31May82- 7Bel sf 1 ①:48 1:14 2/5 1:41 Clm 80000 2 7 67 87 1/2 109 3/4 1011 Cordero A Jr b 114 6.70 49-39 Whippin 112nk Full Concert 1142 1/2 Class Hero 117nk No excuse 10
17May82- 7Aqu fm 1 1/8 ①:49 1:13 1:51 1/5 Alw 20000 3 1 11 11 33 1/2 64 3/4 Fell J b 117 4.50 83-14 Four Bases 117hd Victory Zone1173TheYoungSquire117 3/4 Used up 12
10May82- 4Aqu fst 1 1/8 :50 1/5 1:15 4/5 1:53 Alw 20000 6 6 43 1/2 3 1/2 2 1/2 2 3/4 Vergara O b 117 3.10 69-29 Cosmic Reason 117 3/4 Chapter One 1173 Shy Groom 1174 1/2 Gamely 7
14Apr82- 7Aqu fst 1 :47 1:12 2/5 1:37 4/5 Alw 20000 5 7 75 1/2 42 1/2 42 1/4 21 1/2 Vergara O b 117 2.70 75-26 Illuminate 1171 1/2 Chapter One 1172 3/4 What A Charger 1172 Rallied 7
3Apr82- 1Aqu fst 1 :46 4/5 1:11 1/5 1:37 2/5 Clm 80000 2 3 41 1/2 21 1/2 2 1/2 2nk Vergara O b 114 3.50 79-25 Class Hero114nkChapterOne1147JasonTheRacer118no Ducked out 6
27Mar82- 3Aqu fst 6f :23 :47 2/5 1:13 Clm c-50000 5 4 64 1/2 55 36 1/2 23 1/2 Venezia M b 119 4.50 72-31 Stone Ness 1133 1/2ChapterOne119nkMajorFrank1175 1/2 Gained place 8
LATEST WORKOUTS Aug 12 Sar 5f fst 1:01 h — Aug 6 Sar 4f fst :48 h — Jly 29 Bel tr.t 4f my :49 2/5 h — Jly 23 Bel tr.t 3f fst :37 b

The horse with the best figure in this field, El Bombay, had a record that was fraught with ambiguities. He had earned that 104 in his next-to-last race under conditions that some trip handicappers thought were highly favorable. August 5 was the day that all five races had been won by speed horses on the rail; El Bombay had been one of them. But the subsequent performances of horses who ran on that day suggested that no bias had existed. Other front-running winners came back to run just as well. Stretch-runners on August 5 had not come back to improve. I had scratched the notation "GR, S+" from my notebook and concluded that the track had been normal that day. And that made El Bombay's performance a very impressive one. Although handicappers rightly look with skepticism on victories by horses who get loose on the lead, El Bombay did not get loose by default. My one note on his performance was "Big speed." He had outsprinted a field full of tough front-runners and held them safe. He had run his fractions of :22⅖ and :45⅗ on the same day that the stakes-quality speedball Maudlin ran in :22⅘ and :45⅗.

The next time El Bombay ran, from post position one, I thought the rail might have been bad, but there wasn't enough evidence to support that conclusion. Even so, the colt encountered insurmountable difficulties. He was entered against a field of bullets who proceeded to run the first quarter in :21⅕, the fastest early fraction of the entire Saratoga meeting. He chased the leaders for a while before tiring to lose by 7½ lengths, but his figure of 85 was no disgrace.

In this seven-furlong race, El Bombay was not going to be subjected to any such early pressure. The only other horse in the field with speed, Dave the Dude, had run dismally in his only recent race, with no excuses. El Bombay figured to be able to dust him off at will.

As for the others, Gust of Reason had been visually impressive in his previous start — my comment was "3T move" — but his figure suggested he was somewhat overmatched here. Cintula and Chapter One both had good figures in the mid-90s, but both had strikes against them. Cintula was being ridden by a woeful 10-pound apprentice, Eddie Bernhardt. Chapter One looked as if he wanted more distance than seven furlongs. Both were going to be coming from well off the pace in a field with little speed. And their best races would not be good enough, anyway, if El Bombay ran anywhere near that figure of 104.

I had hoped that El Bombay's virtues were hidden well enough for his odds to be 4 to 1 or so. When he went off at the astonishing price of 11 to 1, I saw hope for salvation for the Saratoga season and bet $1000 to win.

While El Bombay was stalking Dave the Dude, Cintula found himself in tight quarters on the backstretch. Bernhardt looked around helplessly, checked his mount sharply, and dropped back. Then as El Bombay was taking the lead, Cintula started to accelerate again, but lost momentum as the apprentice steered him into the 6-path on the turn. Even after all this, Cintula rushed up and

THIRD RACE
Saratoga
AUGUST 23, 1982

7 FURLONGS. (1.20⅖) ALLOWANCE. Purse $19,000. 3-year-olds and upward which have never won a race other than maiden, claiming or starter. Weights, 3-year-olds, 117 lbs.; older, 122 lbs. Non-winners of a race other than claiming since August 1 allowed 3 lbs.; such a race since July 15, 5 lbs.

Value of race $19,000, value to winner $11,400, second $4,180, third $2,280, fourth $1,140. Mutuel pool $114,873, OTB pool $134,226. Exacta Pool $134,818. OTB Exacta Pool $203,793.

Last Raced	Horse	Eqt.A.Wt	PP	St	¼	½	Str	Fin	Jockey	Odds $1
15Aug82 9Sar8	El Bombay	4 110	4	3	2hd	11	1½	1no	Alvarado R Jr7	11.50
21Jun82 6Bel1	Cintula	3 107	5	8	6hd	61	31½	2½	Bernhardt E J Jr10	2.70
19Aug82 2Sar7	Chapter One	b 3 113	8	1	51½	43	21	32¾	Bailey J D	2.20
7Aug82 2Sar6	Straight Main	b 3 112	7	2	8	76	718	42½	Beitia E	17.20
17Jly82 9Bel6	Dave The Dude	3 112	2	6	1hd	2½	41	51½	Velasquez J	4.50
6Aug82 9Sar12	Mr. Peruser	3 112	6	4	41	3hd	6½	61¾	Cruguet J	4.90
12Aug82 2Sar1	Gust of Reason	3 112	1	7	71	5hd	5½	722	Cordero A Jr	8.80
5Mar82 9Aqu8	North Coast	b 4 117	3	5	3½	8	8	8	Rogers K L	55.40

OFF AT 2:35 Start good, Won driving. Time, :22⅗, :45⅘, 1:10⅕, 1:23 Track fast.

$2 Mutuel Prices:				
	4-(D)-EL BOMBAY	25.00	9.60	4.40
	5-(E)-CINTULA		5.60	3.60
	8-(H)-CHAPTER ONE			3.00
	$2 EXACTA 4-5 PAID $121.40.			

B. c, by Bombay Duck—Marla L, by Mystic II. Trainer Luca Santo. Bred by Luca S (Fla).

EL BOMBAY had speed from the outset, made the pace into the stretch while racing well out in the track and lasted in a long drive. A foul claim against the winner by the rider of CINTULA, for alleged interference through the stretch, was not allowed. CINTULA, off slowly, was checked between horses racing into the turn, drifted very wide while moving entering the stretch and finished with good courage, just missing. CHAPTER ONE rallied while racing wide approaching the stretch, moved to the inside of EL BOMBAY to loom a threat a furlong out but wasn't good enough. STRAIGHT MAIN raced very wide. DAVE THE DUDE tired. MR. PERUSER, a factor to the stretch gave way. GUST OF REASON had no apparent excuse. NORTH COAST was finished early.

Owners— 1, Luca S; 2, Tartan Stable; 3, Sommer Viola; 4, Buckland Farm; 5, Allen J; 6, Cruguet Denise; 7, Kligman H; 8, Bruce Mary Rose

Trainers— 1, Luca Santo; 2, Nerud Jan H; 3, Martin Frank; 4, Campo John P; 5, Tesher Howard M; 6, Cruguet Denise; 7, Pierce Joseph H Jr; 8, Bruce R R.

Corrected weight: Gust of Reason 112 pounds. **Overweight:** Cintula 3 pounds; Chapter One 1.

drew abreast of El Bombay in the stretch, looking as if he were about to blow past him. In my mind I had torn up my tickets already. But every time Bernhardt attempted to whip the horse, he virtually fell back in the saddle and retarded Cintula's momentum. The two horses reached the finish line almost simultaneously, but the photo-finish camera disclosed that El Bombay had won by a nostril.

After I collected the $12,500 payoff that launched my comeback at Saratoga, some of my churlish friends attempted to tell me that I had been lucky. I responded that I had analyzed the horses' trips and figures with a sophistication that was beyond their comprehension, anticipated the way the race was going to develop, figured that Cintula was going to get into about six lengths' worth of trouble, and that El Bombay was going to win by about an inch. It's an easy game.

EIGHT

Modern Betting Strategy

IN THE HISTORY of thoroughbred racing, there have been two great revolutions in the way horseplayers bet. One occurred in the early part of this century, when parimutuel machines began displacing on-course bookmakers and necessitated changes in the strategy of every gambler. The other reached full flower in the late 1970s, as tracks offered increasing numbers of what are called multiple or gimmick or exotic bets — wagers that involve more than one horse. The proliferation of bets like the exacta and the triple has fundamentally altered the nature of the game.

In every revolution there is an old guard that deplores and denounces the changes. When New York abolished legal bookies, journalist Toney Betts wrote, "I thought the professionals would swear off and start an organization named Horse Players Anonymous." Many modern experts similarly decried the coming of exotic bets. "The daily double, exacta, perfecta, quinella, trifecta, and similar parimutuel attractions are gambling, impure and simple," Tom Ainslie wrote. "Moreover, they are forms of gambling without the slightest incentive for a competent player of horses. They are strictly sucker bait." In the view of the traditionalists, there had always been and would always be only one proper way to play the game: to identify the superior horse in a field and bet him to win.

But the exotics have completely altered the definition of a sound wager. They have created opportunities that once did not exist. Every horseplayer has encountered races where he knows a 3-to-5 favorite is clearly superior, but perceives some hidden virtues in a 20-to-1 shot who may be second best. What does he do? In the old days, all his choices were bad ones. He could bet the favorite to win and hope for a small payoff; bet the longshot to place and hope for a modest payoff; bet the longshot to win and expect to be frustrated if he ran second. The most rational course of action was not to bet at all. But if exotic wagering is offered on such a race, it may create a great opportunity. An exacta combining the favorite with the longshot might pay 15 to 1. How often in their lives did the old-timers get to collect 15 to 1 on what they considered the most probable outcome of a race?

In the pre-exotic era, a bettor with moderate capital could not realistically hope to make great killings — not by betting 3-to-1 shots to win. He had to hope to grind out moderate profits consistently. But even though the exotics have made the game so much more potentially profitable, most books that touch on betting strategy continue to extol the old grind-it-out philosophy. In *Winning Big at the Track with Money Management,* Don Passer tells his readers that they should strive to make $100 per day, and recommends a money-management plan that "enables you to realize a predetermined income with very minimal risks." He makes playing the horses sound only slightly less dependable as a source of income than clipping the coupons from one's bonds and mailing them to the bank.

In no area of the game does published theory conflict so sharply with reality. I know few if any professional horseplayers who would claim that they beat the game with a slow, steady accumulation of profits. They win with occasional windfalls. When a gambler looks back on a successful year he will probably be able to identify a handful of big scores that were the source of all his profits. This fact of life may make the game sound frightfully chancy to a newcomer — and it is chancy! I had originally planned to conclude this book with a chapter chronicling my season at Saratoga in 1982.

My results there — a profit of $21,000 in 27 days of racing — would have justified it. But to reach this final figure, I lost a frightening $22,000 in the first 10 days of the meeting. I recovered slowly and got almost even when El Bombay won his desperate photo finish at 11 to 1. The next day I hit the triple for $21,000. The day after that I hit the triple for $9000. And the next day I hit the triple for $3000. When the roller coaster had come to a halt, I was a $21,000 winner. While it may not have been quite the archetypal gambling experience that I would want to put in a book, this is the way the game is played.

The best summation of the proper philosophy of playing the horses appears not in any handicapping book, but in a classic work on the stock market, Gerald Loeb's *The Battle for Investment Survival.* "I am personally convinced of the inevitability of loss when attempting to secure a safe income of small return," Loeb wrote. "I constantly suggest speculation rather than investment as the policy less apt to show a loss and more apt to show a profit."

The horseplayers surest to lose are the ones who attempt to secure that "safe income of small return," who go to the track with modest aims: "I'll be happy to grind out a hundred bucks today." "I'll just find a couple of solid favorites and bet them to place." The people who beat this game are the ones who recognize that they will probably have to do it with occasional big wins that will usually come from exotic wagers. Just as Baltimore's Earl Weaver challenged the orthodox baseball view that the way to win games is with finesse, and proclaimed that his favorite offensive weapon was the three-run homer, a horseplayer should stop trying to bunt for singles and start swinging for the fences.

I arrived at this philosophy, and developed a strategy for implementing it, only after many years of the sort of erratic, costly money management with which most horseplayers are all too familiar. I would have days when I picked six winners in nine races and somehow managed to go home a loser; I would sometimes find myself betting more on races where I had no cogent opinion than on horses I loved. So I kept thorough records of all my wagers, analyzed what I had been doing, and tried to determine which bets were productive for me and which were not. The answer was a revelation. I found that the types of plays that are supposedly the foundation of success at the track — win wagers on solid, if conservative, selections — were not particularly profitable for me. I was winning with my more venturesome exotic bets. But if I had been putting $400 on those solid, conservative horses, I might be risking only $100 on a typical play in the exotics. It seemed only logical to shift the emphasis, to bet less on the supposedly "safe" races and more on the "risky" ones that had been providing me my profits.

I set forth these conclusions with some trepidation, because I know there are no absolute rights and wrongs in betting. Horseplayers with differing temperaments, expectations, and bankrolls can reasonably be expected to employ different styles of wagering. Nevertheless, I advocate my philosophy because I know it is at least superior to that held by the majority of horseplayers — which is to say, none at all. If the typical handicapper has one fatal flaw, it is that he has no consistent betting strategy and makes no effort to formulate one. He may devote 98 percent of his mental energy to making his selections and expend the remaining two percent on deciding how to bet them. The emphasis should be 50–50; knowing how to bet is every bit as important as knowing how to handicap. Pittsburgh Phil declared that "the financing of your money is the high road to success," and that was in the pre-exotic era when there were relatively few betting decisions to be made. The modern game offers many more complexities and many more opportunities to go awry. The most complete handicapper I know — a man who is a competent speed handicapper, an astute race-watcher, and a brilliant judge of horses' physical appearance — is not rich and is never going to be rich because his betting habits are so undisciplined. Conversely, I know one man who makes no pretense of being a great handicapper but earns his living as a professional gambler because he knows how to bet, and because he recognizes that tremendous opportunities lie hidden in the exotic-wagering pools.

Doc had finished medical school and passed his exams in 1976, and decided to go to Saratoga for a month's diversion before entering the profession for which he had so long prepared. "That month," he recalled, "I really cleaned up." So he postponed the start of his medical career until after the fall meeting at Belmont. "I cleaned up at Belmont, too," he said, and the career was postponed until after the winter Aqueduct meeting. Doc still has not hung up his shingle.

Instead he has established himself as one of the most consistent and durable professional horse bettors in New York.

Doc's betting tactics were molded by his experiences as a casual racing fan in the early 1970s. He had observed a number of horse-players wielding clipboards, standing in front of television monitors, charting the fluctuations of exacta and daily-double prices, and he began to emulate the methods of these so-called "chartists." Much of the money wagered on races in New York came from the un-sophisticated clientele at Off-Track Betting establishments, and the chartists looked for horses who were getting relatively heavy play from the smarter bettors at the track. "It was amazing," Doc said. "If a horse was dead on the board [i.e., if he were not getting on-track support] he almost never won. You didn't have to handicap. You just kept raking it in. I'd spread out all my bets over all the live combinations in exactas and doubles so that I would play a lot of numbers; I might play 10 out of 50 possible combinations. That wasn't too sophisticated, but if you win, why argue? It was scary how easy it used to be. There was one streak where I hit 29 daily doubles in a row."

Those easy pickings gradually disappeared. OTB players started getting smarter; more important, they got odds boards in the bet-ting shops to help guide them. But while the game has changed, Doc has maintained the philosophy that the way to win is to look for values in the different wagering pools and to spread his bets broadly. Clipboard in hand, he spends every racing day standing in front of a television monitor that shows exacta, quinella, or daily-double prices. His concentration is legendary. (Once, it is said, a horse-player near him keeled over and somebody shouted, "Is there a doctor here? This man's had a heart attack!" Doc's eyes left the television monitor only for the split second he needed to make a diagnosis. "It's epilepsy," he said, shoved a stick in the victim's mouth, and returned to his charting.) What Doc looks for, most of all, are betting mistakes by the public. "I don't have strong opin-ions very often," Doc said. "I'll very rarely key on one horse. I much prefer to have a negative opinion on one or two of the favor-ites. If I don't like a particular horse, I'll try to construct a situa-tion where I'm sure to win if I'm right."

The idea of "constructing a situation" — as opposed to betting a horse straightforwardly to win — would be alien to most traditional racetrackers, but Doc does it every day. On August 10, 1982, for example, he encountered this race at Saratoga:

7 SARATOGA INNER TURF COURSE 1 MILE SARATOGA START FINISH

1 MILE. (INNER-TURF). (1.35⅕) ALLOWANCE. Purse $27,000. Fillies and Mares, 3-year-olds and upward which have never won four races other than Maiden, Claiming or Starter. Weight, 3-year-olds, 117 lbs. Older 122 lbs. Non-winners of two races other than maiden or claiming at a mile or over since July 1 allowed 3 lbs. Of such a race since July 15 5 lbs.

Chilling Thought Gr. f. 3, by Icecapade—Ribot's Fantasy, by Ribot
Own.—Firestone Mrs B R Br.—Poe Mrs P (Ky) Tr.—Hough Stanley M
112 Lifetime 15 4 4 4 $146,683 1982 7 2 2 2 $33,860 1981 8 2 2 2 $112,823
18Jly82- 6Bel fst 7f :23⅗ :46⅘ 1:23⅗ 3↑ⒻAlw 23000 5 3 2½ 2hd 1hd 1nk Bailey J D 112 3.30 84-21 Chilling Thought 112nk Number 1125 Esplanade 11310 Driving 6
30Jun82- 7Bel gd 7f :23⅕ :45⅗ 1:22⅕ 3↑ⒻAlw 23000 4 3 43 44 57 36½ Russ M L 109 8.90 85-11 Bravest Miss 1123½ GildedLilly1122¾ChillingThought109hd Rallied 7
7Jun82- 1Bel my 7f :22⅘ :46 1:23⅗ 3↑ⒻAlw 23000 2 3 32 33 41¾ 31½ Fell J 114 2.60 82-13 MchllMonAmor109hdGlddLlly1131½ChllngThoght1143½ Weakened 6
26Apr82- 6CD sly 7f :23⅖ :47 1:26⅕ ⒻLa Troienne 6 7 53½ 41½ 911 915 Brumfield D 121 3.30 61-22 Betty Money 1211¾ Avadewan 112½ All Sold Out 1121 Tired 9
26Apr82-Run in Two Divisions 6th & 8th Races.
16Apr82- 6Kee fst 6½f :23 :46⅘ 1:18⅕ ⒻAlw 18100 2 8 1hd 2hd 21 22 Brumfield D 121 *.90 84-17 Hoist Emy's Flag 1152 Chilling Thought 1214 Sultry Lady 1151½ 9
3Feb82- 8Hia fst 7f :23⅖ :46⅕ 1:24 ⒻAlw 14000 4 7 1½ 1½ 12½ 14 Brumfield D 116 *.60 83-24 Chilling Thought 1164 PricelessHero1162½OurDarling1162 Handily 9
11Jan82- 8Hia fst 6f :22⅗ :46⅗ 1:11⅖ ⒻAlw 14000 3 7 55 63¼ 34 22¼ Brumfield D 116 *1.30 84-25 BrvestMiss1182¼ChillingThought1161¼Attrctiv1181 Best of others 11
31Oct81- 8Lrl fst 1 1/16 :46⅘ 1:13⅕ 1:46⅕ ⒻSelima 5 3 310 36 31½ 33¼ Turcotte R L 119 4.80 74-24 SnowPlow1192¼AmbssdorofLck1191ChllngThoght1196 Weakened 6
17Oct81- 7Kee fst 1 1/16 :47⅗ 1:13 1:45⅕ ⒻAlcibiades 6 8 87½ 61¾ 21 2¾ McHargue D G 118 5.40 79-19 Apalachee Honey 118¾ Chilling Thought1184¾Casual1183 2nd best 10
4Oct81- 8Bel fst 1 :47 1:12⅖ 1:38⅘ ⒻFrizette 9 4 54 42½ 24 34¾ McHargue D G 119 7.50 69-25 ProudLou1194¼MystclMood119½ChllngThoght1193 Bid, weakened 12
LATEST WORKOUTS Jly 29 Bel tr.t 5f my 1:02 b Jly 16 Bel 4f fst :49 b Jly 10 Bel 5f fst 1:02⅖ b ●Jun 24 Bel 6f fst 1:11⅘ h

Wittles Lane Blk. m. 5, by Shasta Lane—Wittle, by Woodchuck
Own.—Tantalo N F Br.—Spencer-Hill Farm Inc (NY) Tr.—Tantalo Nicholas
117 Lifetime 47 4 4 5 $46,554 1982 6 0 0 1 $2,040 1981 17 1 2 1 $19,260
1Aug82- 7FL fst 6f :22 :45⅖ 1:11⅖ 3↑Ⓕ[S]VandySueH 1 10 1115 1113 98¾ 77¼ Burns C W 112 108.50 85-15 Bong Shik 126½ Cassie's Birthday1252½BelwoodKate110nk Outrun 11
18Jly82- 9FL fst 6f :22⅖ :46 1:11⅘ 3↑Ⓕ[S]Steuben H 12 1 96¾ 109½ 87¼ 89½ Cook R W 108 94.80 80-20 Bong Shik 1191 Cassie's Birthday 1241 Foudroyant 1265 Outrun 14
10Jly82- 8FL fst 6f :22⅕ :45⅘ 1:12⅖ 3↑Ⓕ[S]Alw 11100 2 7 813 816 69 38 Whitley K 113 4.60e 79-23 Amazing Maj 1136½ Rootabebin 1131½ Wittles Lane 1132 Rallied 9
5Jly82- 9FL fst 6f :22⅖ :46⅖ 1:12⅗ 3↑ⒻSonnenbergH 2 9 99½ 1012 912 912 Giraldo A J 114 88.00 74-21 Bong Shik 114¾ Final Decision 121½ Cassie's Birthday126½ Outrun 10
8Jun82- 8FL fst 6f :22⅕ :46 1:12 3↑Ⓕ[S]Alw 11800 5 4 68½ 611 47 413 Drury G E 113 31.90 76-23 Key Kat 1132 Amazing Maj 113½ Talented Jet 11910 Wide 6
29May82- 7FL fst 170 :48 1:13⅘ 1:44⅗ 3↑[S]Alw 11800 2 4 77½ 68 712 721 Drury G E 108 7.40e 57-20 All Guns 11312 Lovers Fling 1123 Johnel 108½ No factor 7
19Dec81- 2Aqu fst 6f [•]:23⅕ :47⅗ 1:12⅕ 3↑[S]Clm 45000 1 3 21½ 75¾ 710 713 Whitley K 110 30.10 70-17 Edge Of Wisdom 1152¼ Slip 1122 Quiche 119no Stopped 7
13Dec81- 7Pen fst 6f :22⅗ :45⅘ 1:11⅖ 3↑ⒻAlw 6900 6 5 69½ 613 611 614 Masia A 113 18.10 73-20 Sprouted Rye 1161 Carlisle Jim 1134 Brazen Love 1133½ Outrun 6
14Nov81- 7FL fst 6f :23⅕ :47 1:13 3↑[S]Clm 30000 7 3 97½ 99¾ 89 87 Fussell W 119 5.00e 77-20 Native Target 113no Eddie Meath 1121 Andy's Sister112hd Outrun 9
1Nov81- 8FL fst 170 :48 1:13⅕ 1:44⅖ 3↑ⒻAlw 6300 5 5 56 34 21½ 22½ Hulet L 114 8.00 76-23 Bong Shik 1162½ Wittles Lane 1142 Lovers Fling 114¾ 2nd Best 6

Vocal B. f. 3, by Tell—Conella, by Cohoes
Own.—Stark M D Br.—Kaufman & Stark (Ky) Tr.—Maloney James W
112 Lifetime 6 3 0 1 $42,120 1982 5 2 0 1 $30,120 1981 1 1 0 0 $12,000 Turf 5 3 0 0 $39,600
11Jly82- 8Bel fm 1¼ [T]:50⅖ 1:39 2:02⅘ ⒻGarden City 6 6 32½ 42 85¼ 96¼ Hernandez R 114 5.40 74-17 Smart Heiress 118¾ Larida 121¾ Dearly Too 118nk Tired 10
25Jun82- 8Bel fm 1 Ⓣ:46 1:09⅘ 1:34 3↑Alw 27000 10 10 105¼ 96½ 811 810 Hernandez R 112 13.10 85-11 Hrmonizer1171¾HollywoodHendrson1141¾Erin'sTiger1193½ Outrun 11
15May82- 1Aqu fm 1⅛ Ⓣ:48⅖ 1:12⅖ 1:50⅗ 3↑ⒻAlw 25000 2 5 45 32½ 32½ 21¼ Hernandez R 112 3.20 90-13 [D]So Pleasantly 1211¼ Vocal 112nk Valid Offer 1193¾ Game try 6
15May82-Placed first through disqualification
5May82- 4Aqu fm 1⅛ Ⓣ:50⅕ 1:14⅖ 1:51 3↑ⒻAlw 21000 3 4 33½ 21 2½ 11 Hernandez R 113 *.70 89-10 Vocal 1131 Partridgeberry 119hd Charge MyAccount1121¼ Driving 5
24Apr82- 6Aqu fst 1 :47⅖ 1:12 1:38 3↑ⒻAlw 21000 4 2 4nk 41¼ 43½ 35¾ Hernandez R 113 2.10 70-21 Foolish Spin 1072¾ Liz Matizz 1243 Vocal 1131¾ Wide 6
10Oct81- 3Bel fm 1 1/16 [T]:47⅘ 1:12⅖ 1:44 ⒻAlw 20000 1 8 75 31½ 1hd 13½ Hernandez R 116 4.10 81-15 Vocal 1163½ Suspicious 121hd Gulf 1162½ Drew clear 8
LATEST WORKOUTS Aug 5 Sar tr.t 5f fst 1:03⅖ b ●Jly 29 Bel [T] 6f yl 1:16⅗ b (d) Jly 25 Bel 3f fst :35⅗ h Jly 3 Bel 5f fst 1:00⅖ h

Glad Heart B. f. 4, by Hearts Of Lettuce—Cheery Wind, by Crimson Satan
Own.—Michael R Jr Br.—Crimson King Farm (Ky) Tr.—Warren Ronnie
117 Lifetime 18 4 1 3 $41,545 1982 5 1 0 0 $10,155 1981 13 3 1 3 $31,390 Turf 1 0 0 0
31May82- 8CD gd 1 :46⅘ 1:11⅕ 1:37⅕ 3↑ⒻLocust Grove 7 9 911 812 811 — Gavidia W 114 23.70 — — ExcitableLdy1207Dwn'sBeginning111nkSweetestFntsy1111½ Eased 9
8May82- 8CD fst 7f :23⅕ :46⅖ 1:25⅕ ⒻMint Julep 1 8 87½ 813 66¾ 44 Gavidia W 112 15.10e 77-26 Kate'sCabin1153½MeanMartha112½ForeverCordial112hd Mild rally 8
22Feb82- 9FG fm *1⅛ Ⓣ 1:50⅕ ⒻAlw 15000 11 11 1119 1114 85½ 97 Imparato J 115 25.30 — — Lady Offshore 118nk Roman Starlet 116¾ Really Royal 117¾ 11
23Jan82- 9FG fst 1⅛ :47⅕ 1:11⅘ 1:50⅖ ⒻFurl Sail H 6 12 1121 1018 79¾ 48¼ Imparato J 114 4.70e 84-15 Roman Starlet 1132 Knights Beauty 1226 VibroVibes115nk Rallied 12
1Jan82- 7FG fst 140 :47⅗ 1:13 1:41⅗ ⒻAlw 10700 2 10 99 64½ 11 13½ Imparato J 116 *3.30 85-19 Glad Heart 1163½ DewanDiddy113¾Tyson'sCreamPuff1143 Driving 10
11Dec81- 6FG fst 140 :48⅗ 1:14⅘ 1:44 ⒻAlw 10000 5 10 1012 94¼ 55½ 21½ Melancon L 116 1.70 71-26 Apple Haven 1201½ Glad Heart 116nk Dewan Diddy 1136 10
27Nov81- 8CD fst 1 1/16 :48⅖ 1:13⅕ 1:46⅕ 3↑ⒻFalls City H 13 13 1311 1312 88 77¾ Whited D W 114 23.10e 69-26 Safe Play 1231½ Sweetest Chant 118noFriendlyFrolic1121½ Outrun 13
14Nov81- 8CD fst 7f :23⅖ :46⅖ 1:24⅕ 3↑ⒻKy Cardnal H 8 9 1014 1012 86¼ 45 Melancon L 112 44.90 81-16 Safe Play 1221 Lillian Russell 1221 La Vue 1193 Mild rally 10
14Nov81-2nd Div
2Nov81- 4CD fst 7f :24⅖ :48⅗ 1:26⅖ ⒻAlw 14700 3 6 611 58 31 14 Melancon L 115 3.00 75-22 Glad Heart 1154 Baba Au Rum 1181¼ Fear Itself 1152 Driving 6
10Oct81- 8Kee fst 1 1/16 :47 1:11⅕ 1:43 3↑ⒻAlw 18100 5 12 1217 1213 75¾ 68¾ Sayler B 114 28.00 82-16 Whitesburg Lass 1122½ Silver Oaks 1181¼ Workaday 1092 12

Norsan Ch. f. 3, by Norcliffe—Nursandy, by Dust Commander
Own.—Ring G Br.—Fairmount Farm (Fla) Tr.—Garcia Carlos A
112 Lifetime 14 4 4 2 $56,595 1982 9 3 3 1 $44,515 1981 5 1 1 1 $12,080 Turf 4 2 1 0 $17,960
31Jly82- 5Mth fm *1 1/16 Ⓣ:48⅘ 1:13⅕ 1:46 3↑ⒻAlw 15000 2 3 35 32½ 33½ 23 Saumell L 114 2.50 86-14 Ever Alone 1153 Norsan 114nk Slady CastleGirl1173 Gained Place 8
27Jun82- 9Del fst 1 1/16 :45⅗ 1:09⅘ 1:42⅗ ⒻKiss Me Kate 1 4 32 31½ 1hd 22½ Miller D A Jr 112 *1.10 92-12 Immense 1142½ Norsan 1121 Suspicious 1199 Tired 7
11Jun82- 5Del fm 1 1/16 Ⓣ:48⅕ 1:13⅕ 1:44⅖ 3↑ⒻAlw 10000 5 5 32 1½ 1½ 1½ Miller D A Jr 112 2.40 82-15 Norsan 112½ Party Bonnet1192BeringSea110nk Bothered st., drvg 7
12May82- 7Aqu fst 1 :47 1:11⅘ 1:37⅗ 3↑ⒻAlw 25000 6 4 43½ 53½ 45 69 McCarron G 113 2.70 69-19 Penny's Chelly 1194½ Good Musical 1191¾GallantRuby1191½ Tired 8
24Mar82- 9GP fst 1 1/16 :47⅘ 1:11⅘ 1:44⅕ ⒻBonnie Miss 3 2 31½ 42½ 42 23 Saumell L 113 3.60 77-22 Christmas Past 1213 Norsan 1131 OurDarling1121½ Best of others 6
4Mar82- 5Hia fst 1 1/16 :47 1:11⅖ 1:44⅗ ⒻAlw 15000 2 2 21 11½ 13 18½ Saumell L 120 1.60 80-23 Norsn1208½ChrgMyAccount1162½ShCommndum116nk Ridden out 7
9Feb82- 8Hia fm *1⅛ Ⓣ 1:50⅖ ⒻAlw 14000 7 3 41 22 12½ 11½ Saumell L 116 3.80 80-21 Norsan 1161½ All In Mist 1163½ Cagey Colleen 1162½ Driving 11
23Jan82- 6Hia fm 1 1/16 Ⓣ 1:43 ⒻAlw 14000 8 3 2½ 2½ 41 46½ Saumell L 116 11.10 76-11 Regal Actress 1165 Dearly Too 1131 Solo G.String116½ Weakened 12
8Jan82- 8Hia fst 7f :23⅕ :46 1:24⅘ ⒻAlw 13000 9 4 51¼ 32½ 3½ 31½ Saumell L 116 18.50 77-15 Smart Heiress 1161½ Dearly Too 113hd Norsan 116no Evenly 10
16Nov81- 2Aqu fst 7f :23⅕ :46⅘ 1:24⅘ ⒻMd 50000 6 2 3½ 2hd 12 14¾ McCarron G 117 *2.10 77-21 Norsan 1174¾ Asamara Fact 114¾ Yearofthechild117no Ridden out 8
LATEST WORKOUTS Jly 29 Bel [T] 4f yl :50 b (d) Jly 24 Bel 5f fst 1:00⅗ h Jly 19 Bel 5f fst 1:01⅘ h Jly 14 Bel 4f fst :48 h

Michelle Mon Amour — B. f. 3, by Best Turn—Coxswain's Meg, by Sailor
Br.—Rose Hill Farm (Ky)
Own.—de Kwiatkowski H — Tr.—Stephens Woodford C — **112**

Lifetime							
15 4 3 1	1982	8	2	1	1	$28,381
$73,353	1981	7	2	2	0	$44,972
	Turf	1	0	0	0	

27Jun82- 7Bel	fm	1 1/16	[T]:47 1:09⅘ 1:41⅘	3↑ⒻAlw 35000	7 6 65¼ 77 89 812	Venezia M	b 108	9.50	80-08	Memory'sBest115nk IfWinterComs115nk Mrs.Robrts1155	No factor	8
7Jun82- 1Bel	my	7f	:22⅘ :46 1:23⅗	3↑ⒻAlw 23000	4 5 53 43 31½ 1hd	Venezia M	b 109	5.60	84-13	MichllMonAmour109hd GilddLlly1131½ ChllngThought1143½	Driving	6
29Apr82- 8Aqu	fst	7f	:23⅗ :47⅖ 1:23⅗	3↑ⒻAlw 23000	2 9 32½ 52½ 66½ 66½	Maple E	b 113	6.50	76-22	Vestris 1094½ Stunning Native 1211¼ Beau Cougar 114½	Tired	9
10Apr82- 7GP	fst	7f	:22⅖ :45⅕ 1:24⅖	ⒻAlw 13000	1 7 43¼ 43¼ 12½ 15	Saumell L	b 116	*.90	82-18	MichelleMonAmour1165 ReinsttHr1212 CornishTx116hd	Drew clear	7
24Mar82- 9GP	fst	1 1/16	:47⅘ 1:11⅘ 1:44⅕	ⒻBonnie Miss	1 5 63¼ 53½ 65¼ 55½	Maple E	b 112	11.90	74-22	Christmas Past 1213 Norsan 1131 Our Darling 1121½	No factor	6
2Mar82- 9Hia	fst	6f	:23 :45⅘ 1:10⅖	ⒻAlw 14000	1 7 31 33 35½ 37½	Maple E	b 116	1.80	84-21	Dearly Too1177 Wendy'sTen120nk MichelleMonAmour1167½	Evenly	8
11Feb82- 5Hia	fst	7f	:23⅕ :45⅘ 1:23⅗	ⒻAlw 14000	7 5 31 2hd 2hd 2no	Maple E	b 116	*.80	85-15	OurDarling116no MichelleMonAmour1166 LdyAmber116½	Game Try	8
3Feb82- 8Hia	fst	7f	:23⅖ :46⅕ 1:24	ⒻAlw 14000	6 9 73 74½ 55½ 48½	Maple E	b 116	3.50	74-24	ChillingThought1164 PricelessHero1162½ OurDarling1162	No factor	9
15Nov81- 8Aqu	fst	1⅛	:49⅘ 1:15⅖ 1:53	ⒻDemoiselle	8 6 53½ 53 77¾ 65¼	Velasquez J	b 113	*1.50e	65-23	Snow Plow 1211¼ Larida 1131¼ Vain Gold 121½	No factor	8
2Nov81- 8Aqu	fst	1	:47⅖ 1:12⅖ 1:38	ⒻTempted	4 4 43½ 42 22½ 21	Maple E	b 114	2.50	75-26	ChorlGroup1211 MichelleMonAmour1144 MiddlStg113¾	Lost Whip	7

LATEST WORKOUTS Aug 4 Sar 5f fst 1:00⅘ h — Jly 28 Bel 5f sly 1:00⅘ h — Jly 22 Bel 6f fst 1:13⅘ h — Jly 16 Bel 5f fst 1:02⅖ h

Debonair Dancer — B. f. 4, by Staff Writer—In The Bag, by Lucky Debonair
Br.—Marablue Farm & Training Center (Fla)
Own.—Marablue Farm — Tr.—Schulhofer Flint S — **117**

Lifetime							
16 5 2 3	1982	3	0	0	1	$10,356
$85,574	1981	9	3	0	2	$49,058
	Turf	1	0	0	0	

14Jly82- 8Bel	fst	1 1/16	:45⅗ 1:10⅕ 1:43	3↑ⒻImp	4 3 21 22 23½ 34¾	Samyn J L	116	25.40	82-20	Love Sign 1252 Hitting Irish1162¾ DebonairDancer1161	Weakened	5
28Jun82- 7Bel	fst	7f	:23⅗ :46 1:23⅕	3↑ⒻAlw 32000	7 2 21½ 32½ 46½ 47¾	Samyn J L	117	13.60	78-17	Tell A Secret 117¾ Penny's Chelly 1192½ Tonalist1174½	Early foot	7
11Jun82- 8Bel	fst	6f	:22⅕ :45⅖ 1:10⅖	3↑ⒻAlw 32000	1 1 32½ 43 42 46½	Samyn J L	115	34.40	83-15	Prime Prospect 1151¼ Tell A Secret 1154¼ Tonalist1151	Weakened	8
11Oct81- 9Suf	fst	1 1/16	:47⅖ 1:12 1:44⅖	3↑ⒻH. Dustin H	4 5 74½ 65½ 69½ 513	Lovato F Jr	116	10.20	74-26	Weber City Miss 1266 Ange Gal 114½ WaterDance1162½	No factor	8
26Sep81- 8Key	fst	1 1/16	:47⅘ 1:11⅖ 1:42⅘	ⒻCotillion	2 2 21½ 21½ 23½ 34¾	Samyn J L	118	30.40	85-20	TrulyBound1214½ PukkPrincess118nk DebonirDncr1181	Angled out	8
3Sep81- 7Bel	gd	1	Ⓣ:47 1:11⅗ 1:37	3↑ⒻAlw 27000	7 5 55¾ 511 620 623	Samyn J L	113	13.10	57-27	Shark Song 1147 Andover Way 1157½ Idiomatic 1173½	Outrun	8
29Jly81- 3Sar	sly	1⅛	:48 1:12⅖ 1:51	3↑ⒻAlw 25000	4 2 21 1hd 1½ 1¾	Samyn J L	113	5.20	80-18	Debonair Dancer 113¾ Kyra'sSlipper1177¾ KujaHappa1162¾	Driving	6
15Jly81- 5Bel	fst	1 1/16	:45⅘ 1:10⅘ 1:44	3↑ⒻAlw 21000	7 4 25 21 12 14	Samyn J L	111	6.30	82-20	DebonairDancer1114 HappyOne1149 FbulousMusic114½	Ridden out	7
7Jun81- 2Bel	fst	7f	:22⅘ :46 1:24	3↑ⒻAlw 20000	5 7 712 67½ 68½ 512	Arellano J	114	11.90	70-20	Discorama 1142 B'Lori Ann 1147½ Thanks Eddie 1121¼	Outrun	7
25May81- 7Bel	fst	7f	:22⅘ :46⅕ 1:25⅗	3↑ⒻAlw 19000	5 4 66½ 53¼ 14 11¼	Arellano J	108	4.00	74-22	DebonairDancer1081¼ GottaBeu1098½ NobleDmsel108nk	Ridden out	7

LATEST WORKOUTS ●Aug 1 Bel 6f fst 1:13 b — Jly 22 Bel 4f fst :48⅗ h — Jly 12 Bel 4f fst :49 b — Jun 19 Bel 4f fst :49⅘ b

Morning rain had forced the transfer of races from the grass to the dirt. The seventh race, originally scheduled for one mile on the turf, was now being run at seven furlongs on the main track. But public handicappers who had made their selections for a grass race were still influencing many bettors, and some benighted OTB customers had put their money down on the assumption that the race was on the turf. As soon as the probable exacta payoffs started to flash on the television monitors, Doc saw an opportunity. "I don't think Vocal has a chance," he said, and few handicappers could quarrel with that opinion. The filly was a turf specialist; she had finished a poor third in a weak six-horse field the only time she had run on dirt; she didn't appear to be suited for seven furlongs. But when the betting opened, the exacta combination with Chilling Thought on top of Vocal was the favorite at $21. The reverse combination was worth $30. "Vocal has maybe 25 percent of the money in the exacta pool," Doc said. "If the takeout is 17 percent, you've already got an edge. Whoever else you like — even if you pick numbers blindly — you've got to win."

Eliminating two other horses who obviously didn't have a chance, Wittles Lane and Glad Heart, Doc "constructed a situation" around the four remaining contenders — Chilling Thought (No. 1), Norsan (8), Michelle Mon Amour (10), and Debonair Dancer (11). He preferred Chilling Thought, and liked Norsan least of the four ("she was kind of dead on the board") and so bet exactas in the following fashion:

1–8	**$60**	**10–11**	**$15**
1–10	**$60**	**11–10**	**$15**
1–11	**$60**	**8–10**	**$10**
8–1	**$30**	**10–8**	**$10**
10–1	**$30**	**8–11**	**$10**
11–1	**$30**	**11–8**	**$10**

SEVENTH RACE
Saratoga
AUGUST 10, 1982

7 FURLONGS. (1.20⅘) ALLOWANCE. Purse $27,000. Fillies and Mares, 3–year–olds and upward which have never won four races other than Maiden, Claiming or Starter. Weight, 3–year–olds, 117 lbs. Older 122 lbs. Non–winners of two races other than maiden or claiming at a mile or over since July 1 allowed 3 lbs. Of such a race since July 15 5 lbs. (Originally carded to be run at 1 mile inner turf course).

Value of race $27,000, value to winner $16,200, second $5,940, third $3,240, fourth $1,620. Mutuel pool $128,990, OTB pool $108,499. Exacta Pool $142,169; OTB Exacta Pool $154,838.

Last Raced	Horse	Eqt.A.Wt	PP	St	¼	½	Str	Fin	Jockey	Odds $1
18Jly82 ^{6}Bel^{1}	Chilling Thought	3 112	1	4	$1^{\frac{1}{2}}$	$1^{\frac{1}{2}}$	$1^{1\frac{1}{2}}$	$1^{2\frac{1}{2}}$	Bailey J D	2.40
27Jun82 ^{7}Bel^{8}	Michelle Mon Amour b	3 112	6	3	2^{1}	2^{2}	$2^{1\frac{1}{2}}$	$2^{\frac{3}{4}}$	Maple E	2.80
31Jly82 ^{5}Mth^{2}	Norsan	3 112	5	2	4^{3}	4^{4}	3^{3}	3^{4}	Velasquez J	5.30
11Jly82 ^{8}Bel^{9}	Vocal	3 112	3	6	$5^{1\frac{1}{2}}$	5^{6}	5^{7}	$4^{1\frac{1}{2}}$	Hernandez R	6.70
14Jly82 ^{8}Bel^{3}	Debonair Dancer	4 117	7	1	3^{2}	$3^{\frac{1}{2}}$	4^{hd}	5^{10}	Samyn J L	2.40
1Aug82 ^{7}FL^{7}	Wittles Lane	5 117	2	5	6^{4}	7	6^{2}	$6^{\frac{1}{2}}$	Lovato F Jr	40.90
31May82 ^{8}CD	Glad Heart	4 117	4	7	7	6^{3}	7	7	McCarron G	33.50

OFF AT 4:44 Start good, Won driving. Time, :22⅘, :45, 1:09⅖, 1:22⅕ Track good.

$2 Mutuel Prices:			
1–(A)–CHILLING THOUGHT	**6.80**	**3.60**	**2.60**
10–(J)–MICHELLE MON AMOUR		**3.80**	**3.20**
8–(H)–NORSAN			**3.60**

$2 EXACTA 1–10 PAID $24.40.

Gr. f, by Icecapade—Ribot's Fantasy, by Ribot. Trainer Hough Stanley M. Bred by Poe Mrs P (Ky).

CHILLING THOUGHT saved ground while making the pace to the stretch and drew away under brisk urging. MICHELLE MON AMOUR raced outside CHILLING THOUGHT while prompting the pace into the stretch but was no match for the winner. NORSAN came out while rallying leaving the turn but lacked the needed late response. VOCAL failed to seriously menace. DEBONAIR DANCER tired.

Owners— 1, Firestone Mrs B R; 2, de Kwiatkowski H; 3, Ring G; 4, Stark M D; 5, Marablue Farm; 6, Tantalo N F; 7, Michael R Jr.

Trainers— 1, Hough Stanley M; 2, Stephens Woodford C; 3, Garcia Carlos A; 4, Maloney James W; 5, Schulhofer Flint S; 6, Tantalo Nicholas; 7, Warren Ronnie.

Scratched—Lyfessa (3Jly82 ^{6}Lrl^{7}); If Winter Comes (24Jly82 ^{8}Bel^{2}); Leap Lively. (13Sep81 ^{5}Fra^{8}); Coussika (1Aug82 ^{8}Del^{4}).

Having invested $340 in the race, Doc collected $732 when Chilling Thought and Michelle Mon Amour ran one–two. Had the order of finish been reversed, his return would have been $465. If Norsan had beaten Michelle Mon Amour for the place, Doc would have collected $900. He was covered, and he had fashioned this play simply by throwing out a 6-to-1 shot whose deficiencies should have been apparent to any handicapper.

Doc understands and employs many other techniques for capitalizing on opportunities created by the betting pools. He devised a show-betting strategy that arises only a few times a year and offers perhaps the only true sure thing in racing; he can spread his bets in such a way that he is guaranteed about a three percent profit no matter what the result. Few of us possess the discipline and concentration that Doc needs to make a living the way he does, but his success demonstrates the unprecedented opportunities that are being offered by modern-day forms of betting.

When a handicapper has formulated his opinion of a race, he must first choose the betting pool into which he should put his money: win, place, show, or exotic. Part of the answer is easy: Place and show wagering are almost always losing propositions. The mathematics of the game is such that place and show bets always return less than win bets over the long run. They offer only the illusion of safety, not real safety or value. But the choice between betting to win and betting an exotic is a difficult and crucial one.

Sometimes my choice will be influenced by the fact that a horse is more or less heavily bet in the exotic pool than in the win pool, as in the case of the horse Doc didn't like, Vocal. These disparities exist most often in the case of a "hot horse," such as a first-time starter, who takes late betting action. Such animals usually offer better values in the exotics than the straight pool.

If a horse's odds are 7 to 2, and the exactas coupling him with the other horses in the field are returning $40, $50, $56, $80, $100, $100, and $225, is he a better value in the win pool or the exacta pool? The answer can be calculated rather easily. To do so, I jot down the exacta payoffs and, next to them, the amount of money that would have to be bet on each to produce a return of $1000. In the case of the exacta combination returning $40, it would take 25 $2 tickets — an investment of $50 — to get back $1000. The compilation for the whole field would look like this:

Exacta Price	Investment needed to return $1000
$40	$50
50	40
56	36
80	25
100	20
100	20
225	9
	Total $200

A bettor could invest $200 in such a way as to achieve a $1000 return if this horse wins. Thus the horse is a 4-to-1 shot in the exacta pool. (A $200 bet at 4 to 1 yields an $800 profit, plus the original wager, to equal $1000.) Betting the horse to win at 7–2 would therefore be an error.

When I am studying a race, however, I am looking for more than a slim mathematical edge. I am looking to see if there is a good opportunity to make a big score, and my conclusion will largely determine whether I bet in the win pool or in the exotics.

If a horse I consider a standout is a big price, I will usually not get too involved in the exotics. I don't want to risk missing a sizable win payoff. When I fell in love with El Bombay at Saratoga, I thought I had correctly identified the other contenders and might reasonably have put all my money in exactas, but with his odds at 11 to 1 I did not want to fool around. If El Bombay had been 3 to 1, however, my approach to the race would have been altogether different. Now I would put some or all of my money into exactas in an effort to make a killing — assuming that I had some intelligent opinion about who was likely to run second. If a horse I love is a very short price, 6 to 5 or less, I would never bet him to win and would play the race only if I saw opportunity in the exotics.

When I think I have doped out the probable winner of a race, I always take a further look at his competition to see if I can identify the horse or horses likely to run second. If not, I bet to win. If so, I look to make a big score in the exacta. But I also analyze the race (in the manner of Doc) to determine if I can play it in a way that will keep my risks to a minimum. The two objectives are not as contradictory as they may sound.

Typically, I will play one or two prime combinations that will yield a large return, and then make smaller plays on peripheral combinations to produce a small profit or at least enable me to break even. I might put 50 to 60 percent of my total investment into the go-for-the-kill combinations, and use the remainder for hedging. If I love No. 1, think No. 2 is clearly the second-best horse in the field, and consider No. 3 third best, my prototypical $100 exacta play might look like this:

1–2	$60
1–3	$20
2–1	$20

In this fashion I have simultaneously taken a shot for a big win and protected myself against the most likely adverse results.

While committing myself to such an aggressive betting strategy, I recognize that I cannot realistically expect to hit my crusher combinations with great frequency. And no horseplayer can afford (either financially or psychologically) too long a dry spell between trips to the cashier's window. For this reason the crucial part of the whole approach is to plan the peripheral bets, the savers. I want to hit a lot of them. If my analysis of a race is generally correct, but not quite perfect, I still want to make money; at the very least I don't want to get hurt. Even when I have ironclad opinions about a race, when I am shouting that a particular bet is a three-star, can't-lose, mortal-lock proposition, I try to protect myself against the most likely scenario for defeat. I usually wind up regretting my occasional lapses into obstinacy. One day at Gulfstream Park I bet $400 on a cold exacta, watched my horses finish in the wrong order, and lost everything when a mere $20 saver would have covered me. I was preparing to bang my head against the wall when Sam Engelberg, the sagacious handicapper for the *Miami News,* observed my frustration and promptly related a tale with an obvious moral. It will forever be emblazoned on my memory.

Early in 1948, Engelberg told me, a friend of his named Harvey made a number of substantial wagers on Thomas E. Dewey to win the presidential election. He stood to win $100,000 if he were right, and as election day approached the outcome seemed to be a foregone conclusion. In gambling circles the odds had skyrocketed to 10 to 1, and even at that price almost nobody was willing to bet on Harry Truman. A respected New York bookmaker knew of Harvey's enviable position, and on election day he approached the gambler with a proposition. "Tell you what I'll do," he said to Harvey. "I'll let you bet me $15,000 on Truman at 7 to 1. That way you've got a sure thing. If Dewey wins you make $85,000 and if Truman wins you don't lose anything."

"You're trying to rob me!" Harvey shot back. "You know the price ought to be at least 10 to 1."

"I know it," the bookmaker conceded, "but tell me where else you can bet $15,000 and know you're going to get paid. I'll post the cash in advance."

Harvey was unmoved. "You're not going to cheat me," he said flatly. The next morning, of course, he woke up to find out that Harry Truman had won the election.

"I saw him that day," Engelberg recalled, "and he looked as if losing the bet had made him seriously, physically ill. But he told me he was going to go to Vegas to try to recoup. Well, he went there, and he lost $50,000 — just about everything he had left in the world. On the plane flight back to New York he dropped over in his seat, dead of a heart attack."

The moral was not lost on me. A gambler has to anticipate results that will cause him to bang his head against the wall (or worse) and protect himself against them if he can do it cheaply enough.

Consider again the hypothetical race in which I bet the 1–2, 1–3, and 2–1 exactas. If, in that race, No. 1 was 5 to 1 and my other two horses were both 10-to-1 shots, I would be very annoyed if my top selection won and I lost everything. I would also feel rather foolish if the 2–3 or 3–2 exacta combinations produced a giant payoff that I didn't collect. So I might rework my play in this fashion:

1–2	$50	2–3	$2
1–3	$20	3–2	$2
2–1	$12	1–4	$5
3–1	$5	1–5	$4

Now I have broadened my wager. I have protected myself further against the possibility that No. 1 would win and I wouldn't collect anything. I have guarded against other bang-your-head-against-the-wall results. But I still have not strayed from the basic plan of going for the big score.

I attempt to employ the same aggressive-yet-cautious strategy in every form of exotic wagering. In the daily double, where No. 1 was my top choice in each race and No. 2 my second choice, I might play:

1–1	$60
1–2	$20
2–1	$20

Betting triples is a lot more complex, of course. Because hitting a triple cold is about as easy as making a hole-in-one in golf, it is necessary to do a lot of hedging. Marginal horses can sneak into third place on a triple ticket very easily. But most handicappers, when they play a multiplicity of triple combinations, make little or no distinction between their top horses and their marginal ones. A bettor who makes a four-horse box (i.e., plays all possible combinations involving four numbers) is making no distinction whatsoever. I still like to swing for the home run. In a race where my top choices in order of preference were Nos. 1, 2, 3, 4, and 5, I might invest $100 like this:

1–2–3	$20	1–4–3	$4
1–3–2	$20	1–5–2	$4
1–2–4	$8	1–5–3	$4
1–2–5	$8	2–1–3	$4
1–3–4	$8	3–1–2	$4
1–3–5	$8	2–3–1	$2
1–4–2	$4	3–2–1	$2

Betting triples in such volume sometimes causes problems at the mutuel windows. Once, when Hialeah was still operating with the old-fashioned, one-ticket-at-a-time machines, I went to a seller and told her gently, "I want the 3 over the 1-7-8-9-11 sixteen times and second with the 1-7-8-9-11 nine times." This was a $1000 investment — 500 $2 tickets. The seller stared dumbstruck for a pregnant half minute, then very tentatively punched the keys on her machine. Three. One. Seven. The first ticket came out. "How am I doing?" she asked. Now that most tracks have installed computerized equipment, that same transaction could be put on two tickets, assuming that the seller knows all the functions of his own machine, which many of them don't. So a player should make an effort to learn the capabilities of the equipment and to ask for his combinations properly. If I had been betting with the modern American Totalizator machines, the magic words would have been: "Thirty-two dollar triple key entry: 3–1–7–8–9–11. Eighteen dollar triple part wheel: 1–7–8–9–11 with 3 with 1–7–8–9–11."

I have cited these hypothetical examples to demonstrate that it is easily possible to combine aggressiveness and conservatism in the same wager. But, of course, there are no neat formulas that can be applied to actual betting. In order for a horseplayer to bet intelligently, he must formulate his handicapping opinion of a race and then translate it into a wager that perfectly expresses all the nuances of that opinion. This is an art every bit as important and challenging as the handicapping process. Any horseplayer gets satisfaction from declaring, "I've found a cinch in the next race." I get equal satisfaction from saying, "I've bet the next race so that I'll make a profit from any plausible result."

After I had made a windfall profit on the ninth race at Hialeah on February 20, 1982, my friend Pete Axthelm gibed, "That's a typical Beyer hit — a bet that a 10-year-old could have come up with." Pete meant this as a good-natured insult; I took it as a compliment. I had been able to take a fairly obvious set of handicapping observations and turn them into one of the scores that makes a horseplayer's year.

9 HIALEAH START ▾ 6 FURLONGS HIALEAH ▴FINISH

6 FURLONGS. (1.08⅗) ALLOWANCE. Purse $20,000. 4-year-olds and upward, which have not won $7,205 twice since August 15 other than Maiden, Claiming or Starter. Weight, 122 lbs. Non-winners of $15,000 since December 1 allowed 3 lbs. $9,600 since November 1 5 lbs. $7,200 twice since July 15 7 lbs. (Maiden, Claiming and Starter races not considered in allowances.)

Band Practice — **B. c. 4, by Stop the Music—Fleet Empress, by Young Emperor**
Own.—Minttree Stable — **Br.—Kercheval R G (Ky)** — **Tr.—Laurin Roger** — **117**
Turf Record: St. 1st 2nd 3rd — 5 1 2 0
St. 1st 2nd 3rd Amt. — 1982 2 0 1 0 $4,800 — 1981 7 3 0 0 $43,290

11Feb82- 9Hia fst 6f :22 :44⅖ 1:08⅘ Allowance 2 3 21 22 23 25½ Perret C 108 b 115 6.20 93-15 King'sFshion1225½BndPrctic1152½ImprilDlmm112½ Best of others 8
2Feb82- 9Hia fst 6f :22⅕ :44⅗ 1:09⅖ Allowance 5 7 42 44½ 44 44½ Migliore 108 b 117 3.00 91-20 Foolish Crisis 115no Done Well 1224 Gratification 115½ Evenly 8
3Nov81- 7Aqu fst 6f :22⅖ :45 1:09⅖ 3↑ Allowance 5 5 3½ 33 46 47 Cordero 104 b 117 1.60 87-21 Rare Performer 1152 Millbank 1101½ Stiff Sentence 1153½ Wide 6
24Oct81- 6Aqu my 6f :22⅘ :45⅖ 1:09⅖ 3↑ Allowance 4 1 21 1hd 1½ 13 Cordero 115 b 114 4.50 94-16 Band Practice 1143 DelayofGame115½Mr.Wilford1141¼ Drew clear 6
17Oct81- 3Med fst 6f :22⅖ :45⅖ 1:09⅘ 3↑ Allowance 2 6 66 612 69½ 58¾ Cordero A Jr b 114 4.10 85-12 ThirtyEightPaces1194½BoldEgo1193½TravellingMusic116hd Outrun 6
27Aug81- 8Bel fm 6f Ⓣ:22 :45⅕ 1:09⅘ 3↑ C Hatton 12 8 32½ 86½ 1215 1217 Cordero A Jr b 112 6.20 82-15 Miswaki 1142 Dr. Blum 121¾ Restless Thief 117½ Wide 12
12Aug81- 7Sar gd 6f :22⅕ :45 1:09⅗ 3↑ Allowance 4 4 1½ 11½ 12½ 13¾ Cordero A Jr b 113 3.90 92-12 BandPractice1133¾GallantDnce1174¾CopperMine112¾ Ridden Out 7
23Apr81- 5Aqu fst 6f :22⅕ :45 1:09⅘ Allowance 1 4 33 33½ 36½ 512 Cordero A Jr b 122 3.20 80-22 Engine One 1176 Double Leader 1171½ Silver Express 1122½ Tired 6
11Apr81- 5Aqu fst 6f :22⅖ :45⅘ 1:11⅕ Allowance 7 8 31 1½ 13 1nk Cordero A Jr b 117 *1.00 85-22 Band Practice 117nk Was He Fuzzy 112½ Ever Noble1172¾ Driving 8
2Oct80 ♦3Newmarket(Eng) gd 6f 1:11⅕ Ⓣ Middle Park Stakes(Gr.1) 44½ Swinburn W 126 5.50 — — Mattaboy 126½ Bel Bolide 1262 Poldhu 1262 Raced evenly 9
LATEST WORKOUTS ●Jan 28 GP 5f fst :59 h Jan 21 GP 3f fst :37⅖ b ●Jan 16 GP 5f fst :59⅗ h ●Jan 12 GP 4f fst :46⅖ h

Go With the Times — **Ch. g. 6, by Blade—Trying Times, by He's A Pistol**
Own.—R L Reineman Stable Inc — **Br.—Nuckols Bros (Ky)** — **Tr.—Bollero Joseph M** — **115**
Turf Record: St. 1st 2nd 3rd — 1 0 0 0
St. 1st 2nd 3rd Amt. — 1981 11 1 1 1 $31,435 — 1980 16 4 3 4 $83,438

24Jun81- 8AP sly 7f :22⅗ :45⅗ 1:25⅖ 3↑ Allowance 5 5 75 85¼ 86¼ 88¼ McKnight J 122 3.30 67-26 Star Balou 122nk Lord Gallant 1152 Silver Shears 1221¾ 8
6Jun81- 8AP fst 1 :46 1:10⅘ 1:35⅘ 3↑ Equipoise H 3 1 1hd 1hd 3½ 76 McKnight J 112 17.40 76-24 J.Burns115nkSummerAdvocte1152¼Brnt'sTrnsAm1141¾ Used early 11
20May81- 8AP fst 6f :22 :44⅘ 1:09⅘ Allowance 2 6 88¼ 88¼ 63¾ 62½ McKnight J 117 3.70 90-12 Wolf Creek Pass 115¾ Bold Kabota 115no Feisty Fighter 115no 9
9May81- 8AP fst 7f :22⅖ :45 1:22⅘ 3↑ Shecky Gr H 2 6 63¾ 88½ 93 53½ Day P 116 8.00 84-15 It's a Rerun 111¾ Prince Majestic 119¾ J. Burns 116½ Outrun 10
21Apr81- 7Kee fst 6½f :23 :45⅘ 1:16⅖ Allowance 2 4 21½ 43 36 37½ Brumfield D 99 120 2.70 87-19 Zupprdo'sPrince1203Lsserre1204½GoWiththeTims1201 Weakened 4
4Apr81- 7Kee fst 6f :22⅖ :45⅕ 1:09⅖ 3↑ Phoenix H 5 3 42½ 54¼ 68 47¼ Gallitano G 95 119 *1.30 88-18 Turbulence115½FinalTribute1145½It'sRerun1141¼ Lacked response 9
4Apr81-Run in two divisions 7th & 8th races.
6Mar81- 7GP fst 7f :22⅕ :44⅖ 1:22⅕ Allowance 8 3 35 44¼ 43¼ 1hd Gallitano G 117 2.30e 93-17 GoWiththeTimes117hdDurhmRngr110nkIntrcontinnt1102½ Driving 11
14Feb81- 6GP fst 7f :22 :44⅘ 1:23 Allowance 2 7 73¼ 73¾ 86¼ 44¾ Gallitano G 117 *1.90 84-20 Speedy Prospect 119¾ Two'sAPlenty1191MyOnlyLove1193 Rallied 9
31Jan81- 8GP fst 7f :22 :45 1:22⅘ Allowance 4 3 33 63½ 31½ 2½ Cordero A Jr 119 2.40 89-22 Hot Words 117½ Go With the Times 1192½AllaBreva119¾ Checked 9
24Jan81- 9GP sly 7f :22⅕ :44⅘ 1:22⅗ 3↑ Sprint Chp H 1 5 2hd 44¼ 46 57¼ Gallitano G 116 30.70 84-20 King's Fashion1222½JaklinKlugman1241½Joanie'sChief1081¼ Tired 7
LATEST WORKOUTS Feb 17 GP 4f fst :48 b ●Feb 10 GP 5f fst 1:00 h Jan 27 GP 5f fst 1:01⅗ b Jan 20 GP 5f fst 1:01 b

Satan's Parade — **Ch. c. 4, by Whitsburg—Penny Parade, by Prince Dare**
Own.—Ostrow Ruth — **Br.—Hooper D E (Ky)** — **Tr.—Draper Manley** — **115**
St. 1st 2nd 3rd Amt. — 1981 4 3 0 0 $11,700 — 1980 0 M 0 0

17Oct81- 6Kee fst 6f :22⅗ :46 1:10⅘ Allowance 7 3 1hd 2½ 77 812 Haire D 68 115 *2.00 76-19 Diverse Dude 118no Glass Star 1162 Top of List 1132¾ 9
29Aug81- 7Det fst 6f :22⅗ :45⅘ 1:11⅘ 3↑ Allowance 1 6 12 13 14 15 Low S 117 1.70 81-22 Satan's Parade 1175 Solo Ride 1184 Deserve the Crown 1052 7
21Aug81- 9Det fst 6f :22⅗ :46 1:11⅘ 3↑ Spec'l Wt 8 3 12 11 12 1½ Low S 112 *1.00 81-30 Satan's Parade 112½ Deserve the Crown 1026 Bunkie B. B. 113½ 10
8Aug81- 1Det fst 6f :22⅖ :45⅘ 1:11⅗ 3↑ Md Sp Wt 3 6 31½ 11½ 13 18 Low S 112 *1.40 82-22 Satan's Parade 1128 Atomic Win 1144½ Root Beer Brown 1121 8
LATEST WORKOUTS Feb 15 GP 4f fst :48 hg ●Feb 9 GP 6f fst 1:13⅗ h Feb 3 GP 5f fst 1:01 h ●Jan 29 GP 5f fst 1:00 h

The Payoff

Dk. b. or br. g. 4, by Daryl's Joy—Miss Rossean, by Intentionally
Br.—Hooper F W (Fla)
Tr.—Newman James L

Own.—Hooper F W

Turf Record — St. 1st 2nd 3rd — 1982 3 0 0 0 — Amt. $570
1982 2 0 0 0 — 1981 19 2 5 0 — $55,251

105 10

11Feb82- 9Hia fst 6f	:22¾ :44⅘ 1:08⅘	Allowance	8 6 5⁵ 56½ 66½ 820	Rivera M A	b 115	87.40	79-15 King'sFashion122⅛BndPrctice115²¼ImperiiDilemm112½ No factor 8
4Feb82- 5Hia fst 6f	:22½ :46⅖ 1:10⅘ 1:43¾	Allowance	2 3 1¼ 46½ 615 623	Velasquez J	b 116	7.00	62-21 Grey Tiger 116¼ King Of Mardi Gras116⁵AugustManner116³ Tired 6
16Jan82- 5Hia fst 6f	:22½ :45 1:09⅞	Allowance	6 9 65½ 55½ 57	Fell J	b 115	35.50	85-15 Done Well 119⁶ Special Tiger 117²½ Hot Words 110ⁿᵒ Third 11
26Dec81- 8Crc fst 7f	:22¾ :46 1:24⅘	3+Allowance	2 7 42 32 3²	Castaneda K	b 120	9.60	88-12 Priority 114² Sailor Talk 113²½ Incredible John 117¹ Weakened 10
24Nov81- 9Crc fst 7f	:23 :46⅖ 1:26	3+Allowance	5 1 53½ 41½ 6¹¹	Castaneda K	b 115	10.90	69-20 Wooster Sq. 116⁴ Hypnotized 116ⁿᵏ Timeless Ride 117¹ Tired 6
14Nov81- 9Crc fst 7f	:22½ :45⅘ 1:13½	3+Allowance	7 1 2ʰᵈ 2ⁿᵈ 63½ 7¹⁴	Puckett H⁵	113	5.70	80-16 Jayme G. 119³ Penn Station 117½ Speedy Prospect 1171½ Tired 7
17Oct81- 7Crc fst 6½f	:22⅘ :45⅘ 1:17⅘	3+Allowance	1 4 41¼ 31½ 2² 2⁴	Prosper G	b 111	8.60	92-17 Lake Intrepid 119⁴ The Payoff 111¹¼ PennStation117¹ Bid, hung 5
10Oct81- 7Crc fst 6½f	:22⅘ :45⅘ 1:17¾	3+Allowance	4 5 3¹ 2² 2² 2ⁿᵏ	Puckett H⁵	b 109	2.00	91-16 Cowboy Cadillac 1193¼ The Payoff 109⁴Marzapan 1151½ 2nd best 6
30Sep81- 9Crc fst 6f	:22½ :45⅘ 1:11⅘	3+Allowance	1 2 1ʰᵈ 1ʰᵈ 11½ 2ⁿᵒ	St Leon G	b 114	4.50	89-20 SpeedyProspect117ⁿᵒThePayoff114¹CtchThtPss116⅃ Just missed 9
22Sep81- 9Crc fst 6f	:22⅘ :45⅘ 1:13¼	3+Allowance	1 6 35½ 34 43½ 45½	Londono O J	b 119	*1.60	80-28 Hot Words 1122½ Incredible John 116¹½ Takedown 1171½ No rally 6

LATEST WORKOUTS   Jan 13 Hia 4f fst :48½ h

Glare Ice

Gr. h. 5, by Icecapade—Misty Bride, by Hethersett
Br.—Meadowhill (Ky)
Tr.—Cabrera Efrain L

Own.—Cabrera's Stable

115

Turf Record — St. 1st 2nd 3rd — 1982 2 0 0 0 — Amt. $2,400
7 0 0 0 — 1981 23 2 3 1 — $28,480

88 89 — 28 vs little speed

6Feb82- 8Hia fst 7f	:23½ :46¾ 1:22¾	Allowance	9 7 22½ 24 71² 71²	Lopez R D	b 115	41.10	82-13 Flag Stone 115½ Tent Pole 117ʰᵈ Her Pal 110ⁿᵏ Gave way 9
30Jan82- 8Hia fst 7f	:23½ :46¾ 1:22⅘	Allowance	3 8 77½ 97½ 95½	Soto S B	b 115	96.30	82-12 Special Tiger 119½ Flag Stone 115¹ Herb Water 115¹ Outrun 12
23Nov81- 4Lrl fst 6f	:49¾ 1:13⅘ 1:45⅘	3+Thnksg Day H	3 6 67 71⁰ 71² 713	Russ M L	b 115	53.30	77-15 Pairof'Ces112⅃Two'sAPair113ⁿᵏStutzBlackhaw112⅃ In Jose 9
17Nov81- 7Crc fst 6f	:22½ :45⅘ 1:11⅘	3+Allowance	5 3 3³ 55½ 67½ 6⁹³	Russ M L	b 115	6.50	73-21 Ells Run 112ⁿᵏ Explosive Bid 115½ Wooster Sq 112⅃ In nose 8
7Nov81- 7Crc fst 6f	:22⅘ :45⅘ 1:11⅘	3+Allowance	4 4 33½ 43½ 5⁷ 6¹¹	Velez J A Jr⁵	b 107	6.50	74-15 CourtAppeal 112½ PairofDeuces 115ⁿᵏLittleBaby112⅃ Checked 8
29Oct81- 9Crc fst 7f	:23 :46⅘ 1:24¾	3+Allowance	4 2 22½ 2ʰᵈ 2½ 2⁵	Sanchez J A	b 114	22.20	79-23 Never Lark 114½ Glare Ice 114¹ Allan Blue 117ⁿᵒ Hung 7
17Oct81- 7Crc fst 7f	:23½ :46¾ 1:25	3+Allowance	6 3 65½ 55½ 66 46½	Sanchez J A	b 114	9.70	89-17 Lake Intrepid 119⁴ The Payoff 111¹½ PennStation117⅃ No Factor 7
10Oct81- 7Crc fst 6f	:22¾ :45¾ 1:11⅘	3+Allowance	3 6 65½ 57 49 46½	Sanchez J A	b 113	3.60	85-16 Cowboy Cadillac 1193¼ The Payoff 109⁴½ Marzapan 115½ Rallied 6
28Sep81- 9Crc fst 6f	:22⅘ :45⅘ 1:13⅘	3+Allowance	9 4 3¹ 36 42½ 46½	Prosper G	b 113	8.00	85-19 Robsphere 118½ Littlebitababy 115³¼ Court Of Flags 1082¼ Tired 9
19Sep81- 9Crc fst 7f	:22⅘ :45⅘ 1:24⅘	3+Allowance	4 2 1ʰᵈ 2ʰᵈ 41½ 6¹¹	Prosper G	b 113	3.80	77-17 King's Fashion 112½ Poking 124¹ Penn Station 115¹½ Outrun 9

LATEST WORKOUTS   ● Jan 29 Crc 4f fst :48 h   Jan 23 Crc 1 fst 1:43 h   Jan 14 Crc 3f fst :36⅖ b

Monetary Gift

Ro. c. 4, by Gold And Myrrh—Swan, by Dancing Dervish
Br.—Miller Delphine & R M (Mich)
Tr.—Miller Robert M

Own.—Del Rob Farm

112 5

Turf Record — St. 1st 2nd 3rd — 1982 2 0 0 1 — Amt. $4,483
1 0 0 0 — 1981 19 4 3 5 — $43,458

97 105

30Jan82- 7Hia fst 6f	:22⅘ :44¾ 1:22¼	3+Sprint Chmp	6 4 66½ 65½ 66	Perret C	114	38.20	85-12 Pentaquod112¹½Dsh0'Plesure114½ExplosiveBid114ⁿᵏ Lacked rally 7
8Jan82- 9Crc fst 6f	:21⅘ :44½ 1:08⅘	3+Tallaha'e H	13 4 62½ 59½ 48 37	St Leon G	113	124.90f	93-15 King's Fashion 121² Pentaquod 112⁵ Monetary Gift 113ⁿᵒ Rallied 13
26Dec81- 9Crc fst 6f	:21⅘ :44½ 1:11⅘	3+Sunny Isle H	5 3 2ʰᵈ 31½ 77½ 71⁰	St Leon G	113	13.40	86-12 ⓓExplosive Bid 112½ Speedy Prospect 114¹WoosterSq.112⅃ Tired 9
18Dec81- 9Crc fst 6f	:22⅘ :46⅘ 1:11⅘	3+Allowance	4 4 52 42 43½ 43½	Fires E.	118	3.60	90-14 Sandbagger 118½ Speedy Prospect 114¹ Buckn'Shoe117¹ Evenly 6
2Dec81- 9Crc fm 1ₘ ①	:22 :45⅘ 1:13⅘	3+Allowance	1 1 1ʰᵈ 6¹³ 61⁶ 72⁰	Lee M A	120	7.50	61-23 Nar 117⁵½ Banjo 114½ Houdini 122⅃ Gave way 8
29Oct81- 6Med fst 6f	:22 :45⅘ 1:11¾	3+Allowance	5 2 1ʰᵈ 1½ 31½ 31½	Campbell R J	113	22.80	84-22 Khartoum 113½ Explosive Bid 114½ Monetary Gift115¹ Weakened 10
26Sep81- 5Haw fst 6f	:22⅘ :45⅘ 1:17⅘	3+Oil Capitol	1 3 1½ 1ʰᵈ 2ʰᵈ 11½	Morgan M R	118	*1.40	95-21 Monetary Gift 118⁴½ Fleatune 114½ Suntrana112¹¼ Drew clear 7

26Sep81-Run in Two Divisions: 5th & 7th Races.

6Sep81- 9Det fst 1₁	:47½ 1:13½ 1:47½	⑤Dowling H	6 1 14 11 11½ 44½	Kunitake J	119	*1.10e	63-27 King Quail 114³ Star Tracer 120ⁿᵏ Three Kisses 112¹ Weakened 6
15Aug81- 2Det fst 6f	:21⅘ :45⅘ 1:11⅘	Marigold	2 4 12 13 1ⁿᵒ 1¹¼	Kunitake J	119	*.20	84-16 Monetary Gift 119⁷ StarTracer115³LegendHeiress111½ Drew clear 6
7Aug81- 8Det fst 6f	:22 :45⅘ 1:12⅘	Spec'l Wt	5 6 56½ 58 33½ 1¹½	Campbell R J	119	*.40e	83-26 Monetary Gift 119¹½ Hurricane Caesar 120² King Quail 119ⁿᵏ Driving 6

LATEST WORKOUTS   Feb 18 Crc 3f sly :36⅘ h   Jan 28 Crc 4f fst :48½ b   Jan 21 Crc 3f fst :35⅘ b   Jan 16 Crc 5f fst 1:01⅘ hg

North Course

Gr. g. 7, by Northern Jove—Irish Course, by Irish Lancer
Br.—Helmore Farm (Md)
Tr.—Sanborn Charles P

Own.—Helmore Farm

115

Turf Record — St. 1st 2nd 3rd — 1981 4 1 0 0 — Amt. $24,871
33 4 2 2 — 1980 11 2 2 1 — $55,664

6Mar81- 8GP fm 1₁ ① :45¾ 1:09⅘ 1:40⅘		Allowance	9 8 51⁴ 75 66½ 64½	Thornburg	b 122	3.50	93-05 Foretake122²SomeOneFrisky115ʰᵈHonestMoment115²½ No factor 10
31Jan81- 8GP fm 1₁ ① :46⅘ 1:10½ 1:41		3+Canadian H	6 8 84 74³ 64½ Thornburg	b 115	11.80	92-06 Proctor 119ⁿᵈ Imperial Dilemma 117ʰᵈ Foretake115ⁿᵒ No menace 9
17Jan81- 9GP fm 1₁ ① :46⅘ 1:10¾ 1:41¾		3+Appleton H	5 8 86 74½ 71½ 64½	Thornburg	b 115	3.20	96-05 North Course 115½ Proctor 120² Royal Centurion 113ⁿᵒ Driving 11

17Jan81-Run in Two Divisions: 8th & 9th Races.

10Jan81- 9GP fst 7f	:22¾ :45⅘ 1:24	3+Renais'nce H	7 8 85½ 76½ 44½ 64½	Thornburg	b 122	36.70	87-17 King'sFshion122²½MyOnlyLove115ʰᵈJonie'sChif109ʰᵈ No menace 10
20Sep80- 7Med fst 1½	:47⅘ 1:12⅘ 1:44½	3+Allowance	4 5 33½ 32½ 4⁴ 5⁷	Thornburg	b 122	3.20	80-23 Corre Pronto 115³ Do TellGeorge115ⁿᵏStutzBlackhawk114½ Tired 5
8Sep80- 6Med fm 1₁ ① :47⅘ 1:11¾ 1:42⅘		3+Allowance	5 6 41½ 32½ 31½ 1ʰᵈ	Thornburg	b 122	9.10	89-11 North Course117²CommodoreC.117ⁿᵒAudciousFool112⅃ Drew clear 7
1Sep80- 8Atl fst 7f	:22 :45½ 1:21	3+Atl City H	5 6 52½ 43 63½ 46½	Vasquez J	b 122	2.10	90-18 Cabin's Pride 116²½ No House Call 120³ Steelwood 112¹ Bore in 7
12Jly80- 9Mth fm 1₁ ① :47¾ 1:12½ 1:42⅘		3+Oceanport H	4 6 46½ 54 41½ 4¹½	Thornburg	b 117	*1.50	85-14 Subordinate 115³ London Bell113½ SpyCharger115ⁿᵒ No factor 7
4Jly80- 7Bel fst 7f	:22⅘ :45⅘ 1:22	3+Allowance	3 3 41½ 43 45 48½	Vasquez J	b 115	*1.50	80-20 Horatius 111½ Pipedreamer 116³ North Course 115⁴ No menace 11
21Jun80- 8Mth fm 1₁ ① :46½ 1:10½ 1:35		3+Red Bank H	4 5 52½ 41½ 33½ 34	McCauley W H	b 114	7.40	85-14 Horatius 117¹ Pipedreamer 116³ North Course 115⁴ No menace 11

LATEST WORKOUTS   ● Feb 15 GP 5f fst 1:23½ h   Feb 10 GP 5f fst 1:02 h   Feb 6 GP 4f fst :49 b   Jan 30 GP 5f fst 1:02 b

Tent Pole

B. h. 5, by Tentam—Monolith, by Ribot
Br.—Sharp Bayard (Md)
Tr.—Peoples Charles

Own.—Sharp B

117

Turf Record — St. 1st 2nd 3rd — 1982 2 0 1 0 — Amt. $3,600
4 0 0 1 — 1981 16 3 3 3 — $54,468

103 91 — Loose vs little speed

6Feb82- 6Hia fst 7f	:23½ :45⅘ 1:22½	Allowance	3 3 41½ 45 77½ 89	Gonzalez B	b 117	6.40	89-13 Flag Stone 115½ Tent Pole 117ʰᵈ Her Pal 110ⁿᵏ Weakened 9
30Jan82- 7Hia fst 7f	:23½ :46¾ 1:22⅘	3+Sprint Chmp	8 3 31½ 43 77½ 89	Gonzalez B	b 117	36.70	82-12 SpecialTiger 119½ FlagStone 115¹ ExplosiveBid114ⁿᵏ Weakened 8
18Nov81- 8Lrl fst 1₁	:47 1:12⅘ 1:46¾	3+⑤Allowance	5 4 58 64 65 61⁰	Miller D A J⁵	b 114	27.00	76-26 Her Pal 116ⁿᵏ Lordly Love 121¹½ AllaBreva117¹ Weakened 9
7Nov81- 6Lrl fst 1₁	:46 1:11½ 1:43½	3+Handicap	1 1 11½ 11½ 41⁴	Agnello A	b 114	7.50	88-18 Reef 5⁴ Cher Flot Sunny Winters105ⁿᵏAllaBreva117½ Weakened 8
20Oct81- 8Bow fst 1₁	:48½ 1:13 1:45⅘	3+Allowance	1 1 1½ 11½ 13 14	Smith G P⁵	b 112	*1.00	83-24 Tent Pole 112⁴ Torsionaire 1169 Her Pal 114¹ Ridden out 6
23Sep81- 5Bow fst 1₁	:47¾ 1:12 1:44⅘	3+Allowance	2 1 12 2ʰᵈ 2²	Black K	b 117	*.60	81-23 Red Plume 117¹ Tent Pole 117⁵ Clarinet King 117¹⁵ Failed 4
12Sep81- 8Bow fst 1₁	:47⅘ 1:12⅘ 1:44½	3+Allowance	3 3 31 76½ 53½ 52½	Passmore W J	b 115	8.00	80-21 Boston Tea 111ⁿᵏ Southern Rogue 116½ Bold Josh 117ⁿᵏ Bumped 7
12Aug81- 8Tim sly 1₁	:47⅘ 1:13 1:39⅘	3+Allowance	1 2 23½ 21½ 21½	Grove P	b 112	4.20	84-17 Torsionaire 1162¼ Tent Pole 11²ⁿᵏ Michael's Lead 1121⅃ Gamely 7
20Jly81- 7Pim fst 6f	:22 :45⅘ 1:11½	3+Allowance	5 3 2ⁿᵏ 62½ 53½	Byrnes D	b 117	7.50	94-17 Tent Pole 1199 Lord Louis 1129¼ Same Play 112¹ Easily 6
12Jly81- 8Del fst 6f	:22 :45⅘ 1:09⅘	3+Allowance	2 3 3ⁿᵏ 42½ 4⁹	Byrnes D	b 117	4.10	87-12 Suliman 117³¼ Lordly Love 111½ Silent Basis 105ⁿᵏ Tired 7

LATEST WORKOUTS   ● Feb 5 Hia 3f fst :35 h   ● Jan 27 Hia 4f fst :59½ h   Jan 16 Hia 5f fst :59 h

West On Broad

B. c. 4, by Banquet Circuit—Stealaway, by Olympia
Br.—Galbreath J W (Ohio)
Tr.—Rondinello Thomas L

Own.—Darby Dan Farm

BR

115

St. 1st 2nd 3rd — 1982 2 0 0 0 — Amt. $400
1981 13 2 0 3 — $47,346

101 86 95 — A vs T's

23Jan82- 7Hia fst 6f	:21½ :44⅘ 1:10½	Allowance	1 10 54 65½ 63½ 52½	Rivera M A	b 115	11.10	89-15 Lord Darnley 112½ Grey Tiger 115½ Explosive Bid 115¹ In tight 10
9Jan82- 2Crc fst 6f	:22⅘ :47⅞ 1:12¾	Allowance	2 8 42 44½ 63½ 63½	Rivera M A	b 115	6.70	84-21 Cherokee Sky 117¹ Explosive Bid 115¹½ Miroman 115ⁿᵏ Tired 12
4Dec81- 9Hia fst 6f	:22⅘ :46⅘ 1:13⅘	3+Allowance	4 5 68½ 65 55½ 44½	MacBeth D	b 115	5.20	91-15 King's Wish 112½ JiggsAlarm117ⁿᵏ Verontas 115¹ No factor 7
23Nov81- 2Crc fst 6f	:22½ :46 1:24	3+Allowance	8 5 43½ 44½ 42	MacBeth D	112	5.20	75-17 InFromDemise115³¼ PoinerEspionge115ⁿᵏ Weakened 9
26Oct81- 7Aqu fst 1₁	:48⅘ 1:13½ 1:46½	3+Allowance	3 4 36 36 5¹⁰	MacBeth D	112	*2.10e	75-17 ⓓJiggs Alarm 113½ Contare 110¹½ Alla Breva 117³ Impeded 6

26Oct81-Placed fourth through disqualification

9Aug81- 6Sar fst 7f	:22⅘ :45⅘ 1:21½	3+Allowance	4 5 68½ 68 46 49	Velasquez J	112	5.70	87-13 Far Out East 117² PassTheTab114⁵⁴WildMoment106¹½ Lugged In 6
10Jly81- 8Bel fst 6f	:22⅘ :45⅘ 1:10	3+Allowance	5 4 1½ 1¹ 41½	Velasquez J	112	7.90	72-Tax Holiday 112³¼ West On Broad 109¹¼ JiggsAlarm109ⁿᵏ Rallied 5
18Jun81- 7Bel fst 7f	:23 :45⅘ 1:22½	3+Allowance	5 4 51½ 46 34½	Velasquez J	111¼	7.50	89-12 NobleNashua112ʰᵈFiveStarFlight112⅃ⓓ⁴WestOnBrod111⅃ Rallied 9

18Jun81-Dead heat

24May81- 8Bel fst 1₁	:48 1:11⅘ 1:48½	Peter Pan	7 3 51½ 33½ 38 3¹¹	Velasquez J	120	3.90e	74-24 Tap Shoes 126ⁿᵏ Willow Hour 117¹¹ West On Broad 120¹½ Tired 7
6May81- 1Bel fst 1₁	:48 1:13⅘ 1:44⅘	Allowance	3 3 34½ 3¹ 2ᵒ 1ʰᵈ	Venezia M	109	*1.60	91-20 West On Broad 109ʰᵈ King's Wish 119² French Cut 119³ Driving 7

LATEST WORKOUTS   Feb 18 Hia 4f fst :50 b   Feb 13 Hia 5f fst 1:03½ b   Feb 4 Hia 4f fst :51 b   Jan 30 Hia 4f fst :52¾ b

Speed To Spare — Ch. g. 5, by Executioner—Lady Attica, by Spy Song
Br.—General Agricultural Services Ltd (Ky)
Own.—Ring G — Tr.—Garcia Carlos A — **115**

	St.	1st	2nd	3rd	Amt.
1982	2	0	0	0	$1,200
1981	11	4	1	1	$72,380

23Jan82- 7Hia	fst	6f	:21⅘	:44⅖	1:10⅕	Allowance	9	7	64	44	95¼	84½	Saumell L	115	3.20e	87–19 Lord Darnley 1121¼ Grey Tiger 115nk Dash O'Pleasure1151¼	Tried 10
16Jan82- 5Hia	fst	6f	:22⅕	:45	1:09⅗	Allowance	4	5	22½	22	24	48½	Saumell L	117	6.50	87–15 Done Well 1196 Special Tiger 1172½ Hot Words 110hd	Weakened 11
7Dec81- 3Aqu	fst	6f	⊡:22⅗	:45⅗	1:10⅖	3↑Clm 75000	2	6	11	2hd	21½	53¾	McCarron G	117	*2.40	88–16 Gallant Dance 1131¼ Mighty Nasty 108½ Southerner 115½	Tired 9
22Aug81- 7Sar	fst	6½f	:22⅖	:45	1:15⅘	3↑Allowance	2	4	41	31½	3½	46½	McCarron G	122	*2.20	86–11 Starbinia 117¾ LordDarnley1123¾ShekelsandPesos1152	Weakened 6
13Aug81- 8Sar	fst	6f	:21⅘	:45	1:10⅖	3↑Allowance	6	2	34	22	1hd	1¾	McCarron G	115	2.60	88–24 SpeedToSpare115¾CharmingNtive1151¼ExplosiveBid1103¾	Driving 7
2Aug81- 1Sar	fst	6½f	:22⅖	:45⅕	1:16	3↑Clm 75000	7	2	22	21½	1hd	1½	McCarron G	117	2.30e	92–11 Speed To Spare 117½ Subordinate 1131¼Hotspur1171¼	Ridden out 8
16Jly81- 8Bel	fst	6f	:22⅕	:45⅖	1:10⅖	3↑Allowance	4	2	3½	3½	2hd	2nk	McCarron G	115	13.70	90–23 FacetheMoment108nkSpeedToSpare1151¼Bolductive1191½	Bore in 6
1Jun81- 8Bel	fst	6f	:22⅕	:45⅖	1:10⅕	3↑Allowance	6	6	21½	42½	59	415	McCarron G	117	5.20	76–16 Bolductive 1154 Dr. McGuire 1128 Ribosom 1022¾	Weakened 6
23May81- 7Bel	fst	6f	:22⅗	:45⅗	1:10⅗	3↑Allowance	1	1	1hd	2hd	2hd	41	McCarron G	124	4.40	88–13 Rectory 119hd Shekels and Pesos 119½Dr.McGuire121½	Weakened 7
27Apr81- 8Aqu	fst	6f	:22⅗	:45⅘	1:10⅕	3↑Allowance	1	3	1hd	1½	11½	1¾	McCarron G	121	6.00	90–18 Speed To Spare 121¾ Dr. McGuire121nkWestOnBroad1094	Driving 5

LATEST WORKOUTS Feb 17 Hia 5f fst 1:01⅗ h ●Feb 13 Hia 3f fst :35 h Feb 3 Hia 4f fst :48⅗ h Jan 12 Hia 3f fst :36⅕ b

Quick Rotation — B. c. 4, by Best Turn—Speedy Lois, by Gallant Romeo
Br.—Walden B P (Ky)
Own.—Due Process Stable — Tr.—Nobles Reynaldo H — **110⁵**

	Turf Record St.	1st	2nd	3rd		St.	1st	2nd	3rd	Amt.
	1	0	0	0	1982	2	1	0	0	$8,800
					1981	14	3	1	0	$54,032

19Jan82- 8BM	sly	6f	:23⅕	:45⅘	1:10⅗	Allowance	5	2	31½	1hd	2½	1nk	Campas R	b 117	8.90	87–26 Quick Rotation 117nk Kobuk Country 1213½ Head Hawk 121½	6
7Jan82- 8SA	sl	6½f	:22⅗	:46	1:18	Allowance	7	3	76½	711	711	77¾	McHargue D G	116	39.10	72–25 No No 117¾ Foyt's Ack 114nk Pirate Law 1141¾	7
9Nov81-10LA	fst	1 1/16	:45	1:11	1:42⅖	Irvine Hcp	9	8	98¼	98¾	917	923	Mena F	b 114	47.60	74–15 Rock Softly 115¾ Damas 1162 Table Torch 1167½	9
17Oct81- 3Med	fst	6f	:22⅖	:45⅖	1:09⅘	3↑Allowance	3	4	53½	55½	56½	69	Gonzalez B	b 112	23.80	85–12 ThirtyEightPaces1194½BoldEgo1193½TravellingMusic116hd	Outrun 6
8Oct81- 6Med	fst	6f	:22⅗	:46	1:10⅗	3↑Allowance	2	2	1½	2½	23	410	Nemeti W	b 119	12.40	80–18 Gold's Up 1124½ Miroman 1225 Pace Jean 116¾	Tired 6
20Sep81- 8Key	fst	6f	:22⅕	:45⅗	1:12	Allowance	5	4	77	79¼	59½	54¼	Ashcroft D C	b 119	*1.70	78–24 With Caution116noSicilianJet1163½SilverDollarBoy112¾	No threat 8
17Aug81- 8Wat	fst	1⅛	:46	1:10⅕	1:49⅗	W.va. Derby	7	2	31½	32	3½	42	Nemeti W	b 115	10.50	87–15 Park's Policy 1151½ Diverse Dude 115nk Iron Gem 115nk	Tired 9
17Aug81-Run in Two Divisions: 8th & 10th Races.																	
7Aug81- 7Atl	fst	6f	:22⅖	:45⅗	1:10	3↑Allowance	3	3	2½	2hd	3nk	2¾	Nemeti W	b 117	2.40	91–20 Prince Crimson 122¾ Quick Rotation 117nk Prunay 11712	Gamely 6
4Jly81- 5Atl	sly	7f	:22⅕	:44⅗	1:22	Allowance	3	1	3½	44	47½	48½	Brumfield D	b 120	1.70	83–18 Wild Moment 1133 Standpoint 1135 Big Bay Cat 108½	Tired 4
25May81- 9Key	fst	1⅛	:46⅗	1:10⅖	1:49	Penn Derby	6	3	57	610	617	621	Edwards J W	b 122	7.60e	69–16 Summing 1221½ Sportin' Life 1221½ Classic Go Go 1221¾	Tired 9

LATEST WORKOUTS Feb 17 Hia 5f fst 1:02 b

Pitch Game — B. h. 5, by Proudest Roman—True Pitch, by In Reality
Br.—Frances A Genter Stable (Fla)
Own.—Frances A Genter Stable — Tr.—Calvert Melvin — **115**

	Turf Record St.	1st	2nd	3rd		St.	1st	2nd	3rd	Amt.
	1	0	0	0	1981	13	5	2	3	$75,741
					1980	14	6	5	1	$58,635

28Oct81- 8Lrl	my	6f	:22⅗	:47	1:12⅘	3↑Allowance	3	1	33	31	21	33¾	Pino M G	122	*2.50	75–33 Mr. Baggins 1091 Lordly Love 1162¾ Pitch Game 122no	Weakened 6
29Aug81- 8Mth	fst	6f	:22⅗	:45⅗	1:10	3↑Allowance	6	1	2hd	2hd	2hd	1hd	Thomas D B	119	2.00	90–19 Pitch Game 119hd Feathers Lad 119nk Bill Wheeler 119no	Driving 7
19Aug81- 9Mth	fm	5f	Ⓣ:22⅕	:45	:57	3↑Allowance	8	2	54¼	67½	611	611	Gomez E R5	117	3.30	87–13 FethersLd1151Mri'sBook1101¼Georgendthedrgon1223½	No threat 8
18Jly81- 5Atl	fst	7f	:21⅘	:44⅖	1:22⅕	3↑Sprin Cham H	8	1	32½	31	1hd	23	Thomas D B	119	3.00	88–22 Wild Moment 1103 Pitch Game 119no Fast Today 1151¼	Gamely 8
18Jly81-Run in Two Divisions: 4th & 5th Races.																	
20Jun81- 8Pim	gd	6f	:22⅘	:46	1:10⅕	3↑Terrapin H	6	6	43½	54¼	45	37	Thomas D B	117	*1.90	88–19 Piedmont Pete 113no Gasp 1157 Pitch Game 1172½	Lacked rally 6
6Jun81- 5Mth	fst	6f	:22⅘	:46⅖	1:11⅖	3↑Allowance	6	4	42	32	11	12½	Thomas D B	122	*.60	83–24 Pitch Game 1222½ Sneaky Feats 117½ Spunky 1101	Driving 7
9May81- 8Mth	fst	6f	:21⅘	:44⅖	1:08⅘	3↑Sea Bright H	3	4	3nk	2hd	1½	12¾	Thomas D B	113	2.40e	96–16 Pitch Game 1132¾ Piedmont Pete 1122½ Convenient 1172	Driving 8
15Apr81- 9Hia	fst	7f	:22⅖	:44⅗	1:21⅘	3↑Sprint Champ	1	6	33	33½	55	55¾	Fires E	117	*.50e	88–20 CommadoreC.1121¼LaddieDancer112nkDistntMemories116¾	Tired 8
27Mar81- 9Hia	fst	7f	:22⅗	:44⅘	1:22	3↑Ⓢ Roman Bro H	6	2	44	55¼	56¾	36	Fires E	118	1.60e	87–20 Distant Memories 1133 Poverty Boy 1153PitchGame118¾	Mild bid 7
18Mar81- 8Hia	fst	7f	:22⅗	:45⅕	1:21⅘	Allowance	1	4	1½	1hd	2hd	1½	Fires E	116	*2.00	94–17 Pitch Game 116½ Super Hit 1163¼ Dynamic Move 113½	Driving 8

LATEST WORKOUTS Feb 13 Hia 5f fst 1:02⅖ b Feb 7 Hia 6f fst 1:15 b Feb 2 Hia 5f fst 1:02 b Jan 28 Hia 4f fst :51 b

Even a 10-year-old should have been able to identify Band Practice as the superior horse in this field. His speed figures were all superior: the 108s he had earned in his last two starts were good enough to overpower every horse in this field, unless Pitch Game happened to duplicate his best performances from the previous year. Band Practice had earned his figure chasing King's Fashion, the best sprinter in Florida, through swift fractions of :22 and :44⅘. If this had been the old win-place-show era, I would have planned to make a sizable win bet on Band Practice. But because Hialeah was civilized enough to offer both exacta and triple wagering on the race, I scrutinized every horse in the field to assess the possibilities.

I saw three horses — and only three horses — who looked like contenders. West on Broad had earned the second-best figure in the field while running all the way on a bad rail in his last start. Pitch Game had to be respected on the basis of his 1981 form; his trainer, Sunshine Calvert, is especially astute at bringing horses back from a layoff. Monetary Gift's next-to-last start had been sensational; he had run a 105 with a very eventful trip. His last race was not great but it was nevertheless respectable, and it was possible that Monetary Gift had not been suited to the seven-furlong distance.

There was nothing esoteric about any of these opinions. But for the purpose of playing exactas or triples, I had to determine: Can anybody else bust me out? I looked hard at Tent Pole, who was the consensus choice of the *Daily Racing Form* handicappers. He had earned a good figure in his last start, but my trip notes said, "Loose vs. little speed." He had found himself four lengths on top after running a half mile in 45⅕ seconds. The only good races in his past performances had been those in which he got loose on the lead. When he was outrun early he always performed dismally. And he was certainly going to be outrun by Band Practice. I looked hard at Speed to Spare, but concluded that if he could not beat West on Broad while that rival had been on a bad rail he could not do it today. I was convinced that only three horses could finish in the money behind Band Practice. The public was betting the contenders this way:

Band Practice (No. 1)	8–5
Tent Pole (No. 8)	5–2
West on Broad (No. 9)	6–1
Monetary Gift (No. 6)	7–1
Pitch Game (No. 12)	7–1

Band Practice was a generous price at 8 to 5, and would have merited a win bet if there had been no other alternatives. But I was just as confident in my negative assessment of Tent Pole. He was being so overbet that he was creating great values in the other pools. The exactas coupling Band Practice with Monetary Gift and West on Broad were paying about $35 each; the exacta of Band Practice and Pitch Game was worth $60. If I had been investing $100 in exactas, I might have done it in this fashion.

Band Practice–Monetary Gift	$30
Band Practice–West on Broad	$30
Band Practice–Pitch Game	$30
Band Practice–Speed to Spare	$5
Pitch Game–Band Practice	$5

But the existence of triple wagering made the opportunities here even richer. I swung for the fences, betting in this way (per $100).

1–6–9	**$14**	**1–6–8**	**$2**
1–6–12	**$14**	**1–6–10**	**$2**
1–9–6	**$14**	**1–9–8**	**$2**
1–9–12	**$14**	**1–9–10**	**$2**
1–12–6	**$14**	**1–12–8**	**$2**
1–12–9	**$14**	**1–12–10**	**$2**
		12–1–6	**$2**
		12–1–9	**$2**

I had covered myself against the possibility that Tent Pole or Speed to Spare might sneak into third place; against the possibility that Pitch Game might run back to his best races of the previous year and beat Band Practice. But I invested most of my money with the aim of getting a big return, and my aggressiveness was rewarded.

NINTH RACE
Hialeah Park
FEBRUARY 20, 1982

6 FURLONGS. (1.08⅗) ALLOWANCE. Purse $20,000. 4-year-olds and upward, which have not won $7,205 twice since August 15 other than Maiden, Claiming or Starter. Weight, 122 lbs. Non-winners of $15,000 since December 1 allowed 3 lbs. $9,600 since November 1 5 lbs. $7,200 twice since July 15 7 lbs. (Maiden, Claiming and Starter races not considered in allowances.)

Value of race $20,000, value to winner $12,000, second $3,600, third $2,000, fourth $800, balance of starters $200 each. Mutuel pool $135,560. Perfecta Pool $100,472. Trifecta Pool $112,921.

Last Raced	Horse	Eqt.A.Wt	PP	St	¼	½	Str	Fin	Jockey	Odds $1
11Feb82 ^{9}Hia^{2}	Band Practice	b 4 117	1	2	$1\frac{1}{2}$	1^{2}	1^{3}	$1^{2\frac{3}{4}}$	Perret C	1.70
30Jan82 ^{7}Hia^{6}	Monetary Gift	b 4 112	6	6	$7^{2\frac{1}{2}}$	7^{3}	$2\frac{1}{2}$	2^{5}	Velez J A Jr^{5}	7.90
23Jan82 ^{7}Hia^{5}	West On Broad	4 115	9	5	2^{hd}	3^{2}	3^{3}	3^{1}	Brumfield D	6.00
24Jun81 ^{8}AP^{8}	Go With the Times	6 115	2	4	6^{2}	6^{hd}	5^{2}	$4\frac{1}{2}$	Fires E	32.60
17Oct81 ^{6}Kee^{8}	Satan's Parade	4 115	3	11	$9^{1\frac{1}{2}}$	9^{4}	$6\frac{1}{2}$	5^{2}	Espinoza J C	59.50
6Mar81 ^{8}GP^{5}	North Course	b 7 115	7	10	8^{hd}	8^{hd}	7^{2}	$6^{2\frac{1}{2}}$	Thornburg B	11.90
19Jan82 ^{8}BM^{1}	Quick Rotation	b 4 110	11	9	11^{hd}	$10\frac{1}{2}$	9^{2}	7^{nk}	Verge M E^{5}	28.50
28Oct81 ^{8}Lrl^{3}	Pitch Game	5 115	12	1	$4\frac{1}{2}$	$5\frac{1}{2}$	$8^{2\frac{1}{2}}$	8^{nk}	Vasquez J	7.20
6Feb82 ^{6}Hia^{2}	Tent Pole	b 5 117	8	3	$3^{1\frac{1}{2}}$	2^{hd}	4^{hd}	9^{1}	Gonzalez B	2.80
6Feb82 ^{6}Hia^{8}	Glare Ice	b 5 115	5	12	12	11^{3}	11^{5}	10^{3}	Soto S B	97.90
11Feb82 ^{9}Hia^{8}	The Payoff	b 4 108	4	8	$5\frac{1}{2}$	4^{1}	10^{hd}	$11^{3\frac{1}{2}}$	Lynch H D^{10}	178.30
23Jan82 ^{7}Hia^{8}	Speed To Spare	5 115	10	7	10^{4}	12	12	12	Saumell L	17.00

OFF AT 5:10. Start good, Won easily. Time, :22⅕, :44⅘, 1:09⅕ Track fast.

$2 Mutuel Prices:			
1–BAND PRACTICE	5.40	3.40	2.80
6–MONETARY GIFT		6.40	4.40
9–WEST ON BROAD			3.60

$2 PERFECTA 1–6 PAID $37.40. $2 TRIFECTA 1–6–9 PAID $181.20.

B. c, by Stop the Music—Fleet Empress, by Young Emperor. Trainer Laurin Roger. Bred by Kercheval R G (Ky).

BAND PRACTICE rushed up along the inside to take command along the backstretch, increased the margin in early stretch and was being eased through the final sixteenth. MONETARY GIFT in hand early, rallied between horses in the stretch run and was best of the others. WEST ON BROAD raced with the winner along the backstretch, could not keep pace on the turn and weakened in early stretch. GO WITH THE TIMES was a factor to the head of the stretch, then faltered. PITCH GAME could not keep pace. TENT POLE pressed the pace to the head of the stretch, then faltered.

Owners— 1, Minttree Stable; 2, Del Rob Farm; 3, Darby Dan Farm; 4, R L Reineman Stable Inc; 5, Ostrow Ruth; 6, Helmore Farm; 7, Due Process Stable; 8, Frances A Genter Stable; 9, Sharp B; 10, Cabrera's Stable; 11, Hooper F W; 12, Ring G.

Trainers— 1, Laurin Roger; 2, Miller Robert M; 3, Rondinello Thomas L; 4, Bollero Joseph M; 5, Draper Manley; 6, Sanborn Charles P; 7, Nobles Reynaldo H; 8, Calvert Melvin; 9, Peoples Charles; 10, Cabrera Efrain L; 11, Newman James L; 12, Garcia Carlos A.

I collected a $181.20 triple payoff, for a return of more than 11 to 1 on my total investment. The one–two finish of Band Practice and Monetary Gift was never in doubt, and West on Broad fortunately had an easy trip to beat out longshot Go with the Times for third place. If he had instead finished fourth, I would have lost everything. But I would not have banged my head against the wall. When I choose to play a race in this fashion, I weigh and accept the possible negative consequences in advance.

This is the undoing of almost every horseplayer in exotic races: One day he will spot a horse he likes, play him in exactas, and go home moaning, "I shoulda bet to win." The next day, chastened, he will play a 2-to-1 shot to win, watch a logical but hidden 20-to-1 shot run second, and go home moaning, "I shoulda bet the exacta." This constant second-guessing wrecks a horseplayer's mental attitude, and I try not to indulge in it. Having adopted the strategy of betting aggressively in exotics instead of betting to win, I know there must be times when horses like Band Practice will win and I won't collect. I am willing to miss 8-to-5 payoffs occasionally in order to collect 11-to-1 returns when I do hit. Once I have decided that the proper way to play a race is in the exotics, I indulge in second-guessing only if I think I failed to make a proper saver bet.

Band Practice earned a big figure when he won this race, and so did the second-place finisher, Monetary Gift. Three weeks later Monetary Gift came back in a similar type of race at Gulfstream Park. He was five lengths superior to his competition. He was as much of a standout as Band Practice and his odds, 9 to 5, were slightly better. Again, I took a hard look at the rest of the field, trying to find opportunities in the exacta. This time, however, I could make a strong case for five other horses as possible second-place finishers, and a marginal case for a couple of others. If I attempted to use all of these horses in an exotic play, I would be spreading myself much too thin. Even though Monetary Gift was an outstanding horse, the race overall did not offer outstanding possibilities. In this case I bet Monetary Gift to win (which he did), but my investment was about half of what it had been in the Band Practice race, because the potential for profit was so much less.

While a handicapper may sometimes love a horse but conclude that the race offers little potential, he will also find races where he cannot identify the probable winner but which look very promising nonetheless. The most creative bets, the ones that members of the win-place-and-show generation have the most trouble envisioning or approving, are the ones that do not revolve around a single horse.

Such circumstances will commonly arise on a biased track. If speed on the rail is prevailing, I like to combine all the horses likely to take advantage of the bias while throwing out all those who won't. (I know one good handicapper at Pimlico who, before doing anything else, automatically boxes post positions 1–2–3 in the exacta, and makes money doing it.) If the public is making a serious mistake and overbetting a horse I think has no chance, I will attempt to capitalize on it, even if I have to make a three- or four-horse box of all the legitimate contenders. A handicapper must recognize that the opportunities offered in such situations are every bit as legitimate as the traditional ones in which he likes a single horse to win a race. The most lucrative single bet of my life came on a daily double where I didn't have a strong opinion about either winner. I wasn't embarrassed to take the money; I was proud of myself for making such a creative wager.

---

⑧ SARATOGA (6 FURLONGS SARATOGA)

6 FURLONGS. (1.08) 66th Running THE ADIRONDACK (Grade III). $50,000 Added. Fillies, 2-year-old, weights, 119 lbs. By subscription of $100 each, which should accompany the nomination; $400 to pass the entry box, with $50,000 added. The added money and all fees to be divided 60% to the winner, 22% to second, 12% to third and 6% to fourth. Winners of two races of $15,000 an additional 2 lbs. Non-winners of a race of $15,000 since June 15, allowed 3 lbs. Of a race other than maiden or claiming since June 1, 5 lbs. Maidens, 7 lbs. Starters to be named at the closing time of entries. Trophies will be presented to the winning owner, trainer and jockey. (Nominations close Wednesday, July 29, 1981.) Closed with 42 nominations.

Trove — 116
Own.—Hickory Tree Stable
B. f. 2, by Key to the Mint—Mazaca, by Pappa Fourway
Br.—Hickory Tree Farm (Va)
Tr.—Stephens Woodford C
1981 3 2 0 1 Amt. $28,464

Aga Pantha — 114
Own.—Kentucky Blue Stable
Dk. b. or br. f. 2, by Cyane—Footloose, by Native Dancer
Br.—Johnson & Proskauer Mrs G G (Pa)
Tr.—Jolley Leroy
1981 3 1 2 0 Amt. $19,984

Mystical Mood — 119
Own.—Hudson E J
B. f. 2, by Roberto—Mystery Mood, by Night Invader
Br.—Carroll Del W
1981 6 2 2 1 Amt. $65,635

Sympathetic Miss — 112
Own.—Epstein J
Dk. b. or br. f. 2, by Proudest Roman—Gaelic Logic, by Bold Reason
Br.—Seltzer E A (Ky)
Tr.—DiAngelo Joseph T
1981 1 M 1 0 Amt. $3,740

Sensitive Penny

Own.—Bronfman M

B. f. 2, by Sensitivo—Fool's Penny, by Fool's Paint
Br.—Briarwood Farm & T C R Breeding (Fla)
Tr.—Papania Robert A

114

	St. 1st 2nd 3rd	Amt.
1981	3 1 0 0	$15,601

25Jly81– 8Mth fst 6f	:22	:45⅖ 1:12⅗	⑤Sorority	10 2 4³ 4³ 6¹¼ 4²¾ Brumfield D **72** 119	22.00	75–20 AplchHony119¹½Dstnctv Moon119noLghngGill119¹ Wide, Drifted In 14
7Jly81– 8Mth fst 5½f	:22⅖	:46 1:05⅗	⑤Colleen	8 2 3¹⅓ 43½ 5⁶ 5³ Gonzalez B **73** 15	11.00	84–20 Sabatoge 115½ Laughing Gull 121² Distinctive Moon 115½ Tired 9
16Jun81– 6Mth fst 5f	:22½	:46⅗ 1:00	⑤Md Sp Wt	5 1 1¹½ 1¹½ 1⁴ 1² Tejeira J 117	5.20	86–19 SensitivePenny117²FrenchRuffls110¾½Pltinum Bll117¹ Drew clear 9

LATEST WORKOUTS   Aug 8 Mth   4f fst :48⅗ b   ●Aug 2 Mth   5f fst 1:00   h   Jly 22 Mth   4f fst :50   b   Jly 16 Mth   6f fst 1:15   b

Fresh Candy

Own.—Jablow Andrea

Dk. b. or br. f. 2, by Diplomat Way—Candy Drops, by Candy Spots
Br.—Farnsworth Farm (Fla)
Tr.—Zito Nicholas P

114

	St. 1st 2nd 3rd	Amt.
1981	3 1 1 0	$13,940

3Jun81– 8Bel my 5½f	:22⅖	:45⅗ 1:04⅘	⑤Rosedale	8 9 9⁹½ 9¹² 8¹³ 8¹³ Fell J **44** 116	3.50	79–13 Betty Money 116½ Raise Me 116² Mystical Mood 116² Outrun 9
20May81– 4Bel fst 5f	:22⅖	:46⅗ :59⅗	⑤Md Sp Wt	1 1 2ʰᵈ 3² 2ʰ 2¹ Fell J **81** 117	*2.10	— — FrshCndy117¹BoldAndJyfl117⁴½BckIndMss117¹¼ Lost whip, clear 8
7May81– 3Bel fst 5f	:22½	:46⅗ :59⅘	⑤Md Sp Wt	1 6 6⁸ 5⁴ 2⁵ 2⁴½ Fell J **66** 118	2.30	— — ShiningTrinket118⁴½FreshCandy118⁵RegalBidder118³ BEst others 7

LATEST WORKOUTS   Aug 8 Sar tr.t 4f fst :48⅗ h   Aug 3 Sar ① 4f fm :49   b   Jly 23 Bel 3f fst :36½ h   Jly 11 Bel 4f fst :53   b

Sparkling Savage

Own.—Flying Zee Stable

Ch. f. 2, by Jungle Savage—Champagne Carol, by Bold Lark
Br.—Taylor E P (Md)
Tr.—Martin Jose

114

	St. 1st 2nd 3rd	Amt.
1981	1 1 0 0	$10,200

25Jly81– 4Bel fst 5½f	:22½	:46⅗ 1:06	⑤Md Sp Wt	2 1 1½ 1¹ 1⁴ 1³½ Martens G **63** 117	5.90	85–14 SprklingSvg117³½SympthticMiss117²◻DHPlyThtTun117 Ridden out 7

LATEST WORKOUTS   Aug 7 Sar 5f fst 1:00½ h   Aug 1 Sar 3f fst :37½ b   Jly 23 Bel tr.t 3f fst :36½ b   Jly 23 Bel 3f fst 1:01¾ hg

Apalachee Honey

Own.—Muckler D

Dk. b. or br. f. 2, by Apalachee—Elisa Honey, by Abe's Hope
Br.—Muckler Stables Inc (Ky)
Tr.—Muckler Tim J

119

	St. 1st 2nd 3rd	Amt.
1981	2 2 0 0	$96,972

25Jly81– 8Mth fst 6f	:22½	:45⅗ 1:12⅗	⑤Sorority	9 9 11¹² 9¹⁰ 3¹ 1¹½ Morgan M R **79** 119	16.40	78–20 AplchHony119¹½DistinctivMoon119no LughingGull119¹ Drew Clear 14
17Jun81– 5AP fst 5f	:22½	:46⅗ :59	⑤Md Sp Wt	5 6 4¹½ 3¹½ 2ʰᵈ 1ʰᵈ Morgan M R 119	13.30	91–20 Apalachee Honey 119ʰᵈ Miss Reneged 119⁸ Maniches 119² 10

LATEST WORKOUTS   Aug 4 Sar 4f fst :49½ h   Jly 21 AP 4f fm :49   b   Jly 15 AP 3f fst :35   b   Jly 8 AP 5f fst :58⅗ h

Fire in the Sky

Own.—O'Boyle Margery K

Ch. f. 2, by Nostrum—Devilish Tom, by Tom Cat
Br.—Marben Farm (Ky)
Tr.—Picou James E

114

	St. 1st 2nd 3rd	Amt.
1981	4 1 0 0	$11,220

25Jly81– 8Sar sly 6f	:21½	:45½ 1:11½	⑤Schulerv'le	7 3 2² 2⁵ 4⁷ 5¹¹ MacBeth D **54** 114	10.20	70–18 Mystical Mood 114⁴ Aga Pantha 114²¾ Trove 116²¾ Tired 7
2Jly81– 4Bel fst 5½f	:22⅖	:46½ 1:05⅗	⑤Md Sp Wt	8 3 1½ 2ʰᵈ 3³ 3⁴ MacBeth D 117	5.30	89–14 Fire in the Sky117⁴RoomDance117⁵½SugarCoated117¾ Ridden out 9
1Jly81– 4Bel fst 5½f	:22½	:46½ 1:06⅗	⑤Md Sp Wt	5 5 43½ 3³ 3⁶ 4¹⁰ MacBeth D 117	2.50e	81–14 Trove 117ʰᵈ Finest Element 117⁶½ Twosome 117⁴½ Weakened 8
8Jun81– 4Bel fst 5f	:22½	:46⅗ 1:06⅘	⑤Md Sp Wt	10 5 3³ 3³ 3⁶ 4⁹ MacBeth D 117	3.70	74–19 Exploding Wind 117⁵ Doblique 117½ Norsan 117¾ Tired 10

LATEST WORKOUTS   Aug 5 Sar 4f sly :48¾ h   ●Jly 28 Sar 3f fst :35 b   Jly 25 Sar 4f fst :49 h   Jly 23 Bel 3f fst :36⅗ b

Doblique

Own.—Keller M

B. f. 2, by Nodouble—T V Day, by T V Lark
Br.—Lasater Farm (Fla)
Tr.—Brice Harold B Jr

114

Turf Record				St. 1st 2nd 3rd	Amt.
1 1 0 0			1981	4 1 1 2	$18,020

24Jly81– 2Bel fm 7f	①:22⅗	:46 1:25	⑤Md Sp Wt	6 3 5⁶ 74¾ 1¹ 1⁵ Attanasio R 117	2.40	79–18 Doblique 117⁵ Tie A Bow 117ʰᵈ Captivating 117½ Ridden out 12
24Jly81– 6Bel fst 5½f	:22⅖	:45⅗ 1:04⅘	⑤Md Sp Wt	10 3 2½ 2¹ 2³ 3⁵½ Attanasio R 117	18.30	86–14 Chilling117¾Toranda117½Doblique 117¾ Weakened 10
8Jun81– 6Bel fst 5f	:22½	:46½ 1:06⅓	⑤Md Sp Wt	8 7 6⁹½ 6⁹ 4⁶ 2⁵ Attanasio R 117	24.80	79–19 ExplodingWind 117⁵ Doblique 117½ Norsan 117¾ Rallied 10
29May81– 6Bel fst 5f	:22½	:46½ :59	⑤Md Sp Wt	10 8 8¹² 8¹¹ 6⁷ 5⁶¾ Attanasio R⁵ 112	25.20	— Bold And Joyful 117⁵¾ Grey Bid 117⁴ Doblique 112³ Rallied 8

LATEST WORKOUTS   Aug 7 Sar 3f fst :35 h   Aug 3 Sar 4f fst :51 h   Jly 22 Bel 4f fst :37⅘ b   Jly 16 Bel ① 5f fm 1:00 h (d)

Thrilld N Delightd

Own.—Pierce Sheila

B. f. 2, by Explodent—Evening Ecstasy, by Night Invader
Br.—Pierce J H Jr (Fla)
Tr.—Pierce Joseph H Jr

114

Turf Record				St. 1st 2nd 3rd	Amt.
			1981	5 1 1 1	$14,010

2Aug81– 6Sar fst 5½f	:22½	:45⅗ 1:11⅘	⑤Md Sp Wt	5 5 6²½ 6¹½ 2¹ 1ⁿᵏ Cordero A J **77** 117	10.50	82–11 Thrilld N Delightd 117ⁿᵏ Noranda 117²¼ ForPleasure117¼½ Driving 9
24Jly81– 8Bel fm 7f	①:22⅘	:46 1:25	⑤Md Sp Wt	2 11 2³ 2² 2¹ 4⁵½ Asmussen C B 117	4.00	73–18 Doblique 117⁵ Tie A Bow 117ʰᵈ Captivating 117½ Weakened 12
15Jly81– 6Mth fst 5f	:23½	:47⅖ 1:07⅗	⑤Md Sp Wt	1 5 5³½ 5¹½ 3³ 2ⁿᵒ Edwards J W **70** 117	3.50	79–24 IndinLightning117noThrilldNDlightd117¼½AmbrBy117³ Angled out 7
6Jly81– 9Mth fst 5f	:22	:45⅘ :58⅗	⑤Md Sp Wt	4 3 4² 4¹½ 4²½ 3¹ Edwards J 117	9.80	92–19 Key To Heaven 117ⁿᵏ AmberBay117¾ThrilldNDelightd117¾ Rallied 9
24Jun81– 5Mth fst 5f	:22½	:46½ :59½	⑤Md Sp Wt	8 4 3¹ 3¹ 4⁸ 8¹³ Perret C 117	3.20e	77–20 Distinctive Moon 117⁷ Intermission 117¾ Miz Mosca 117ⁿᵏ Tired 9

LATEST WORKOUTS   Aug 1 Mth   3f fst :35½ h   Jly 23 Mth 4f fst :49⅔ b   Jly 2 Mth 6f fst 1:14 h   Jun 17 Mth 5f fst 1:01¾ hg

9 SARATOGA

INNER TURF COURSE
1 MILE SARATOGA
START   FINISH

1 MILE. (INNER–TURF). (1.35½) HANDICAP. Purse $37,000. 3-year-olds and upward foaled in New York State and approved by the New York State Bred Registry weights Friday, August 7. Declarations by 10:00 a.m., Saturday, August 8.

Sir Ack

Own.—Goldmills Farm

B. h. 5, by Ack Ack—Somersault, by Never Bend
Br.—Goldmills Farm Inc (NY)
Tr.—Veitch Sylvester

121

Turf Record				St. 1st 2nd 3rd	Amt.
3 0 1 1			1981	3 0 1 1	$80,996
			1980	16 2 6 5	$134,806

20Jly81– 8Bel sly 1	:45⅘ 1:09½ 1:35	3+ ⑤EvanShipman	2 1 2ʰᵈ 1ʰᵈ 2² 2²½ Vasquez J **108** 121	8.60	90–15 Fio Rito 117²½ Sir Ack 121½ Naskra's Breeze 117ⁿᵏ Game Try 7
10Jly81– 8Bel fst 6f	:22½	:45⅘ 1:10	3+ Allowance	4 4 2½ 2½ 5⁴ Foley D⁵ 114	3.70e	88–12 Tax Holiday 112¾½ West On Broad 109¾½ Jiggs Alarm 109ⁿᵏ Tired 8
19Jun81– 8Bel fst 7f	:23½	:46½ 1:23½	3+ Allowance	5 1 1½ 1¹½ 1ʰᵈ 2¹ Foley D⁵ 114	3.90	84–18 Adirondack Holme 114¹ Sir Ack 114ʰᵈ Rosin TheBow119½ Gamely 6
10Jun81– 8Bel fm 1	①:47 1:11 1:42½	3+ ⑤Allowance	2 4 3² 3² 4⁶ 5¹¹ Venezia M 126	12.80	71–19 Adlibber 121¾½ Without Words 119⁴½ Move It Now 121² Tired 5
30May81– 8Bel fm 1¼	①:50 1:14½ 1:42⅘	3+ ⑤Allowance	6 3 3³ 3³ 3² Maple E 121	2.20	81–11 Move It Now 119² Holy Mackrel 117¹ Sir Ack 121² Evenly 7
4May81– 8Aqu fst 6f	:23½	:47½ 1:11½	3+ ⑤Pelham H	2 3 2¹½ 1ʰᵈ 2ʰᵈ 4¹ Maple E 122	6.70	84–31 Prince ShutOut110¾DedicatedRullah123¾Kim'sChance126ʰᵒ Wknd 6
12Mar81– 8Aqu my 6f	①:23	:47½ 1:12½	3+ ⑤Handicap	2 3 2¹½ 2ʰᵈ 2²½ 2²¾ Hernandez R 122	*.30	73–26 Bacon and Eggs 114⁹¾ Sir Ack 122¾ Holy Mackrel112⁶¼ 2nd best 6
4Mar81– 8Aqu fst 1⊘	:47½ 1:13½ 1:42	3+ ⑤Kings P'nt H	5 2 2½ 2¹½ 2ʰᵈ Hernandez R 117	9.20	92–15 Kim's Chance 127ⁿᵏ Sir Ack 122⁵ Oddsmaker 110½ Drifted out 5
21Feb81– 8Aqu sly 1⊘	:48½ 1:13½ 1:43½	3+ ⑤Handicap	6 1 1³ 1⁶ 1¹⁰ 1¹² Hernandez R 122	*1.00	83–27 Sir Ack 122¹² Rosin TheBow112¾½Quintessential117ⁿᵏ Easy score 7
12Feb81– 8Aqu fst 6f	:22½	:46½ 1:11½	3+ ⑤H Hughes H	1 3 2½ 2¹ 2² 2³½ Hernandez R 122	4.00	84–18 Kim's Chance 123¾½ Sir Ack 122½ Table For John 114¾ 2nd best 7

LATEST WORKOUTS   ●Aug 5 Sar 6f sly 1:13½ h   Jly 27 Bel 4f sly :50   b (d)   Jly 16 Bel 5f fst :59¾ h   Jly 6 Bel 4f fst :49   b (d)

My Crew — Dk. b. or br. g. 3, by Final Ruling—George's Maris, by Maris
Br.—Nolan H C (NY)
Own.—Mogavero J A — Tr.—Woodson Richard — 109
St. 1st 2nd 3rd Amt. — 1981 16 1 0 0 $16,560 — 1980 8 M 1 0 $7,820

31Jly81- 3Sar fst 6½f :23⅕ :47 1:18⅘ 3↑Ⓢ Md Sp Wt 1 3 2½ 2½ 1½ 1nk Rydowski 111 5.80 78-15 My Crew 111nk Trieze 116½ Cold Spring 116¹ Driving 8
6Jly81- 9Bel fst 1 :47 1:13⅕ 1:39⅘ 3↑Ⓢ Md Sp Wt 1 3 2½ 21½ 54 612 Migliore R b 116 4.10 57-15 Navidas 1165½ Trieze 116nk Beaverboard 115½ Tired 10
26Jun81- 6Bel fst 6f :22⅘ :46⅗ 1:12 3↑Ⓢ Md Sp Wt 1 1 65½ 43½ 23 22 Corrales J 114 17.60Ⓓ 80-10 FivePoint... 114²MyCrew... Jungl114hd Bore out 9
26Jun81-Disqualified and placed fifth
5Jun81- 1Bel fst 1$\frac{1}{16}$:48⅘ 1:14⅕ 1:46⅘ 3↑Ⓢ Md Sp Wt 2 7 75½ 63¾ 611 718 Arellano J 114 19.80 50-17 Fairest Forest 109nk Go Gabriel 114² Geronimo 114¹¾ No factor 9
25May81- 4Bel fst 1 :48⅗ 1:14⅖ 1:41⅕ 3↑Ⓢ Md Sp Wt 3 5 64½ 53¾ 54½ 68½ Arellano J 113 21.30 53-22 BengalLncer... TheHorn113nk Outrun 8
22May81- 3Bel fst 7f :23⅕ :47 1:26⅕ 3↑ Md 14000 5 2 32½ 54 813 814 Foley D5 b 105 13.50 57-22 Don't Tell Em 109⁶ The Missing Gift 111nkMr.Nicefield114½ Tired 8
11May81- 5Bel gd 7f :23 :47 1:27⅕ 3↑Ⓢ Md Sp Wt 1 6 33½ 43½ 810 815 Adams L b 115 10.90 51-22 Sophie's Pride 113no Bengal Lancer 114nk Cerebella 114⁴ Tired 8
1May81- 2Aqu fst 1 :48⅕ 1:14 1:41⅘ 3↑Ⓢ Md Sp Wt 3 4 64½ 66½ 56½ 46 Quinones F7 108 7.90 51-26 ThePurplChif114½RoundThHorn115¾Whiglt'sPrid119² Brief foot 6
14Apr81- 4Aqu sly 6f :22⅖ :46⅕ 1:13 3↑Ⓢ Md Sp Wt 6 1 68 716 817 815 Montoya D 112 16.50 61-31 Sportmn'sPrinc113⁴½Gronimo1125½NwYorkPrinc1071½ No excuse 14
22Mar81- 6Aqu fst 6f :23 :47⅖ 1:14⅕ 3↑Ⓢ Md Sp Wt 9 2 64½ 86½ 58 511 Montoya D 112 20.40 59-26 Nasholito 1121½ New York Prince 114¾GranpaJake109⁹ No factor 13
LATEST WORKOUTS Jun 16 Aqu 3f gd :37 b (d)

Naskra's Breeze — B. g. 4, by Naskra—Topical Heat, by Tropical Breeze
Br.—Davis C C (NY)
Own.—Broadmoor Stable — Tr.—Johnson Philip G — 116
St. 1st 2nd 3rd Amt. — 1981 3 0 1 1 $12,016 — 1980 12 5 3 1 $112,832

20Jly81- 8Bel sly 1 :45⅗ 1:09⅗ 1:35 3↑Ⓢ EvanShipman 1 5 45½ 44½ 45 33¼ Samyn J L 117 18.70 90-15 Fio Rito 1172½ Sir Ack 121¾ Naskra's Breeze 117nk Mild Rally 7
29Jun81- 7Bel fst 6f :23⅕ :46⅗ 1:11 3↑Ⓢ Clm 75000 2 2 44½ 43½ 43 2½ Samyn J L 122 2.50 86-15 Prosper 109½ Naskra's Breeze 122no Rosin The Bow 122no Wide 5
19Jun81- 5Bel fst 7f :23⅕ :46⅕ 1:23⅖ 3↑Ⓢ Allowance 3 3 52½ 44 53¾ 51¾ Samyn J L 117 10.60 83-18 Adirondack Holme 114¹ SirAck114hdRosinTheBow119½ No factor 6
12Dec80- 8Aqu fst 170 ⊡ :48 1:12⅘ 1:43⅗ 3↑Ⓢ Allowance 5 6 66½ 21 22 1nk Samyn J L 115 *1.20 84-18 Naskra's Breeze115nkTableForJohn1155TheBoyMikey117½ Driving 6
28Nov80- 9Aqu sly 7f :21⅗ :44⅗ 1:22⅘ 3↑Ⓢ Allowance 5 — — — — 37½ Samyn J L 115 2.80 79-17 Josies Anchor 114⁴ Table For John1203½Naskra'sBreeze1151¾ Fog 10
30Oct80- 8Aqu fst 6f :23 :46⅖ 1:11 3↑Ⓢ Allowance 2 6 65½ 45½ 45½ 45½ Samyn J L b 119 4.80 82-24 Kim's Chance 122hd Sir Ack 119³ Furrow 1222½ Outrun 6
17Oct80- 7Aqu fst 1 :46⅘ 1:11 1:36⅕ 3↑Ⓢ Allowance 3 3 21½ 22 22½ 2¾ McCarron C J b 116 1.60 84-20 Sir Ack 115¾ Naskra's Breeze1165¾Can'tDiscount113² Drifted out 6
9Oct80- 7Bel fst 6f :23⅕ :46⅖ 1:11⅗ 3↑Ⓢ Allowance 7 7 75¾ 46 34 1hd McCarron C J b 119 4.60 84-24 Naskr'sBreeze119hdBirthdyWitch1161¾Cn'tDiscount1172½ Driving 7
27Sep80- 2Bel fst 6f :23 :47 1:12⅖ 3↑Ⓢ Allowance 7 8 58 43½ 12 15½ Samyn J L b 113 *.60 80-19 Naskra's Breeze 1135½ PrinceShutOut108hdDarvid118½ Ridden out 8
6Aug80- 8Sar gd 1⅛ :46⅘ 1:12⅖ 1:50⅖ Ⓢ D Clinton 8 8 1021 1023 923 925 Gonzalez M A b 114 4.20 58-12 Quintessential 121nk D.J.'sNitecap114²Screenland1182½ No factor 10
LATEST WORKOUTS Jly 28 Sar tr.t 4f fst :52 b — Jly 16 Bel tr.t 4f fst :50⅗ b — Jly 11 Bel tr.t 3f fst :37⅕ b — Jun 18 Bel tr.t 3f fst :36 b

Kim's Chance — B. g. 5, by Triple Crown—Cert, by Final Ruling
Br.—Lehrman S (NY)
Own.—Bar-Jo Stable — Tr.—Jerkens Steven T — 124
Turf Record St. 1st 2nd 3rd — 1 0 0 1
St. 1st 2nd 3rd Amt. — 1981 7 2 1 2 $86,474 — 1980 13 7 4 2 $202,914

31Jly81- 8Sar fst 6½f :22⅘ :45⅘ 1:16⅕ 3↑Ⓢ Allowance 3 3 1hd 1hd 1½ 22¼ Asmussen C 124 *1.80 89-15 DedictedRullh1192¼Kim'sChnce124¹WimbornCstl1161¾ Weakened 6
20Jly81- 8Bel sly 1 :45⅗ 1:09⅗ 1:35 3↑Ⓢ EvanShipman 5 2 34 34 34½ 43¼ Cordero A Jr 126 6.30 89-15 Fio Rito 1172½ Sir Ack 121¾ Naskra's Breeze 117nk Wide 7
21May81- 8Bel fst 7f :23⅗ :47⅕ 1:24⅖ 3↑Ⓢ Allowance 3 2 1hd 1½ 3nk 33¼ Cordero A Jr 124 *1.40 77-18 Dedicated Rullah 1173 Furrow 117nkKim'sChance1242¾ Weakened 6
4May81- 8Aqu fst 6f :23⅖ :47⅕ 1:11⅕ 3↑Ⓢ Pelham H 6 2 11½ 2hd 1hd 31 Cordero A Jr 128 *1.00 84-31 PrinceShutOut...DedictedRullh123½Kim'sChnc128no Weakened 6
18Apr81- 7Aqu fst 1 :47⅗ 1:12⅖ 1:37 Handicap 6 2 2½ 21½ 31 67¼ Martens G 113 6.60 74-23 Fool's Prayer 1163¼ Dunham's Gift 123¹ Ring of Truth 105¹ Tired 7
4Mar81- 8Aqu fst 170 ⊡ :47⅗ 1:11⅗ 1:42 3↑Ⓢ Kings P'nt H 1 1 1½ 1hd 1hd 1nk Cordero A Jr 127 *.60 92-15 Kim's Chance 127nk Sir Ack 122⁵ Oddsmaker 110½ Driving 6
12Feb81- 8Aqu gd 6f ⊡ :22⅘ :46⅘ 1:11⅗ 3↑Ⓢ H Hughes H 2 2 11½ 11 12 13¼ Cordero A Jr 123 *.50 87-18 Kim's Chance 1233¼ Sir Ack 1203¾ Table ForJohn114¾ Ridden out 5
10Dec80- 8Aqu fst 6f ⊡ :22⅖ :45⅗ 1:10⅕ 3↑Ⓢ Joe Palmer 1 3 1½ 1hd 1hd 2nk Cordero A Jr 122 1.30 93-11 Fio Rito 126nk Kim's Chance 122no Sir Ack 1193¼ Held gamely 5
29Nov80- 2Aqu my 7f :22⅘ :46 1:23⅖ 3↑Ⓢ Handicap 7 2 1½ 1hd 1½ 1½ Cordero A Jr 122 *1.20 84-13 Kim's Chance 122½ Darlin Momma 114² Tiempo 112no Driving 7
30Oct80- 8Aqu fst 6f :23 :46⅖ 1:11 3↑Ⓢ Allowance 4 2 11 1½ 11 1hd Cordero A Jr 122 *.90 88-24 Kim's Chance 122hd Sir Ack 119³ Furrow 1222½ Driving 6
LATEST WORKOUTS Jly 16 Bel 6f fst 1:12 h — Jly 12 Bel 5f fst 1:03 b — Jly 8 Bel tr.t 4f fst :49⅗ b — Jly 1 Bel tr.t 3f fst :37⅗ b

Fearless Leader — B. c. 3, by Mr Leader—Salvaje II, by Hot Dust
Br.—Whitney T P (NY)
Own.—Wolosoff J K — Tr.—Preger Mitchell C — 115
Turf Record St. 1st 2nd 3rd — 3 1 1 0
St. 1st 2nd 3rd Amt. — 1981 12 2 3 1 $63,990 — 1980 3 1 1 0 $20,520

2Jly81- 5Bel gd 1$\frac{1}{16}$ Ⓣ :48⅕ 1:11⅖ 1:44⅕ 3↑Ⓢ Clm 130000 3 2 32 2hd 12 13¾ Vasquez J 113 3.40 80-21 FerlessLedr1133¾HdgdPosition1111½ThPurplChif116no Ridden out 8
19Jun81- 2Bel fst 1⅛ :46⅗ 1:11⅕ 1:49⅘ 3↑Ⓢ Allowance 6 7 828 — — — Fell J b 114 *1.50 — — Eddie's Luck1174¼WingedChief114hdStartop'sAce1064½ Pulled up 8
11Jun81- 7Bel fm 1 Ⓣ :44⅗ 1:09⅗ 1:35 3↑ Allowance 5 9 918 1015 913 78¼ Velasquez J b 111 15.00 82-22 Miswaki 111² Wicked Will 1131½ Mortal Friends 1171¼ Outrun 11
25May81- 9Bel fm 1$\frac{1}{16}$ Ⓣ :45⅖ 1:10 1:41⅗ 3↑Ⓢ Allowance 3 8 77¾ 45 23 25¾ Samyn J L b 108 3.30 83-12 Without Words 1195¾ Fearless Leader 108⁴GranpaJake108½ Wide 12
18May81- 8Bel fst 7f :23⅗ :47⅕ 1:24⅗ Ⓢ Albany H 8 1 2hd 21 43½ 45¾ Fell J b 114 12.40 73-24 WimborneCstle1152¾AdirondckHolm127²Accipitr'sHop117¹ Tired 8
25Apr81- 8Aqu fst 1 :45⅗ 1:11⅗ 1:37⅘ Ⓢ Big Apple H 5 2 23 11 1hd 58¾ Maple E b 118 7.40 68-23 AdrondckHolm1262¾ComptrCrlos123nkWmbrnCstl118nk Gave way 9
11Apr81- 6Aqu fst 1 :45⅘ 1:11⅖ 1:37⅖ 3↑Ⓢ Allowance 5 4 42¼ 31 65½ 26 Migliore R5 b 106 6.40 73-22 ComputerCrlos112⁶FerlessLeder106nkProsper112hd Lacked room 10
25Mar81- 8Aqu fst 6f :23⅕ :47⅖ 1:12⅖ Ⓢ Catskill 7 4 31½ 31 41½ 4¾ Velasquez J b 117 7.30 78-28 Proud Northern 114nk Prosper 120hdKnightlySpiced117½ Bumped 7
18Mar81- 4Aqu fst 6f :22⅗ :47 1:12⅗ 3↑Ⓢ Allowance 5 1 1½ 11½ 13 14½ Fell J b 114 *2.00e 78-31 FerlessLeder1144½MissQuote109nkKoshrCowboy1213½ Ridden out 14
20Feb81- 7Aqu sly 6f ⊡ :23⅕ :46⅗ 1:13⅕ Ⓢ Allowance 2 7 611 614 615 919 Asmussen C B b 119 *1.40 59-24 Hanker Chief 1146¾ Sheer Survival 1241½ Onesuch 1193¾ Outrun 10
LATEST WORKOUTS Jly 31 Sar 1 fst 1:43 b — Jly 23 Bel 6f fst 1:14⅘ h — Jly 15 Bel tr.t 4f fst :49⅘ b — Jun 30 Bel 4f fst :50 b

D. J.'s Nitecap — Dk. b. or br. g. 4, by Favorable Path—Come On Bunny, by Sure Welcome
Br.—Green W R (NY)
Own.—Jacobs D E — Tr.—Jacobs Donald E — 111
St. 1st 2nd 3rd Amt. — 1981 6 1 1 2 $13,140 — 1980 9 3 1 2 $51,505

18Jly81- 8FL fst 6f :23⅕ :47 1:13 3↑Ⓢ Allowance 4 4 75 65½ 41½ 1¾ Reynolds R L b 117 2.10e 84-19 D. J.'s Nitecap 117¾ Roshinka 112nk Mari Juno 105no Driving 8
11Jly81- 7FL fst 170 :47⅘ 1:12⅘ 1:45⅕ 3↑Ⓢ Allowance 4 5 510 55 41½ 51 Reynolds R L 117 3.50 74-19 Captain Pat 117nk Fast Frank 113½ Patomac Star 122hd Hung 6
4Jly81- 9FL fst 170 :47⅕ 1:11 1:40⅗ 3↑Ⓢ Gen.sullivan 1 5 57½ 511 39 311 McKeever R Jr 114 9.60 87-17 Fio Rito 1208½ Sea Bourne 117² D. J.'s Nitecap 114⁴ No factor 5
27Jun81- 8FL fst 170 :48 1:12⅗ 1:42⅖ 3↑Ⓢ Allowance 4 4 48 48 43½ 35 Hulet L 117 *2.20 98-08 Publisher 113¹ Captain Pat 117⁴ D. J.'s Nitecap 1173½ Evenly 5
13Jun81- 8FL fst 170 :47⅖ 1:11 1:40⅕ 3↑Ⓢ Allowance 7 5 47½ 39 38½ 412 Whitley K 114 5.60 102-10 Fio Rito 11811 Holiday Chip 118nk Publisher 110¹ Hung 7
23May81- 8FL fst 1 :47⅖ 1:12⅗ 1:39⅕ 3↑Ⓢ Allowance 4 5 67 45½ 23 22½ Whitley K 117 3.60 86-11 Harlequin Blues 1172½ D. J.'sNitecap117½Publisher113hd Bore out 8
1Sep80- 9FL fst 1$\frac{1}{16}$:47⅗ 1:11⅗ 1:44⅗ 3↑Ⓢ G'neseevly H 9 9 86½ 38 37½ 314 Rincon R b 118 2.40 84-19 Fio Rito 12812 Harlequin Blues 1151½ D. J.'s Nitecap 1181½ Hung 9
6Aug80- 8Sar gd 1⅛ :46⅘ 1:12⅖ 1:50⅖ Ⓢ D Clinton 6 5 514 511 33½ 2nk McHargue D G 114 13.60 83-12 Quintessential 121nk D.J.'sNitecap114²Screenland1182½ Off slowly 10
26Jly80- 8FL fst 170 :48⅖ 1:14⅗ 1:45⅘ 3↑Ⓢ Allowance 4 6 68 65½ 21 1nk Reynolds R 115 *1.30 86-21 D. J.'s Nitecap 115nk Johnel 1173½ Thirst 122no Driving 7
20Jly80- 9FL fst 1$\frac{1}{16}$:47⅘ 1:12⅘ 1:45⅕ Ⓢ New YorkDby 3 10 109¾ 59½ 56½ 37½ Reynolds R 120 11.40 87-16 Quintessential1174½Cassie'sBirthday121³D.J.'sNitecap120¹ Rallied 10
LATEST WORKOUTS Aug 5 FL 6f hy 1:16⅖ b (d)

Johnel — B. g. 6, by Shasta Lane—Well Now, by Milesian
Br.—Spencer-Hill Farm Inc (NY)
Own.—Tantalo N — Tr.—Tantalo Nicholas — 110
St. 1st 2nd 3rd Amt. — 1981 16 3 1 0 $24,864 — 1980 9 1 1 1 $9,453

1Aug81- 8FL fst 6f :23⅗ :46⅘ 1:12⅗ 3↑Ⓢ Clm 27000 6 3 51½ 54½ 54 26 Dosher K 119 8.90 80-21 Dancing Target 106⁶ Johnel 119no Wise Old Mike 117² Rallied 5
19Jly81- 8FL fst 170 :47⅘ 1:13⅖ 1:43⅗ 3↑Ⓢ Clm 30000 2 4 57 64 57¼ 512 Berk B7 115 4.60 71-15 Holiday Chip 122hd Captain Pat 126¹ Lord Winston 116³ Evenly 7
5Jly81- 7FL fst 170 :47⅗ 1:13 1:44⅘ 3↑Ⓢ Clm 25000 2 3 33 32½ 2hd 11½ Berk B10 109 5.90 80-14 Johnel 1091½ Can Move 119¾ Canaille 119¹ Driving 8
7Jun81- 7FL fst 170 :47⅕ 1:12 1:44 Ⓢ Clm 25000 2 6 58 56 54 56¾ Berk B10 109 *2.40 88-08 Holiday Chip1191½PatomacStar119¾PersianPrince1152½ No threat 8
23May81- 8FL fst 1 :47⅖ 1:12⅗ 1:39⅕ 3↑Ⓢ Allowance 5 3 34½ 68 67 43 Berk B10 107 5.10 86-11 Harlequin Blues 1172½ D. J.'s Nitecap117½Publisher113hd Checked 8
17May81- 8FL gd 170 :48⅕ 1:13⅘ 1:45⅕ Ⓢ Clm 25000 4 3 42½ 31 3nk 1½ Berk B10 106 3.70 89-18 Johnel 106½ Royal Falcon 116½ Brooklyn Boss 1151½ Driving 6
10May81- 7FL fst 6f :22⅘ :46 1:11⅘ Ⓢ Clm 16000 9 4 54¼ 45½ 35½ 1½ Berk B10 106 12.80 95-12 Johnel 106½ My Montauk 109⁴ Super B. M. 116hd Driving 9
3May81- 8FL fst 6f :22⅘ :46⅕ 1:12⅘ Ⓢ Clm 16000 1 7 47½ 49 36 42¾ Berk B10 106 9.30 87-12 Thirst 116¹ Irish Jake 1121¾ Super B. M. 116no Even try 7
26Apr81- 7FL fst 1 :48⅕ 1:14 1:41⅕ Ⓢ Clm 25000 6 1 11 2hd 64 69¾ Berk B10 106 13.60 70-14 Dan Dan 112² Thirst 116hd Royal Falcon 116¹ Tired 7
8Apr81- 2Aqu fst 6f :23⅕ :46⅘ 1:12⅘ 3↑Ⓢ Clm 25000 3 6 64 711 711 711 Hernandez R 115 24.30 66-22 John Roche 117½ Hanker Chief 100½ Sea Stark 111⁴ Outrun 7

Sportman's Prince Dk. b. or br. c. 3, by Herrenfriseur—Sly Nancy J, by Crafty Admiral
Br.—Czeck S Jr (NY) 107 St. 1st 2nd 3r Amt.
Own.—Morrell S F Tr.—Bradley John R 1981 8 2 1 1 $37,760 1980 0 M 0 0
S 1Aug81- 2Sar fst 7f :23⅗ :46⅖ 1:24⅖ 3↑ [S]Allowance 2 8 43½ 41½ 56 610 Asmussen C B 57 112 7.20 70–12 Resuscitator 1193 Winged Chief 117¾ [D]Hudson Ruler 109½ Tired 10
1Aug81-Placed fifth through disqualification
8Jly81- 5Bel fst 6f :22⅗ :46⅕ 1:11 3↑ [S]Allowance 6 6 55½ 43½ 44 56½ Asmussen C B 114 5.40 81–11 Knightly Spiced 1111¾ GranpaJake1121¾Resuscitator1222¾ Evenly 7
19Jun81- 2Bel fst 1⅛ :46⅗ 1:11⅕ 1:49⅘ 3↑ [S]Allowance 1 3 43½ 43½ 47½ 48¾ Asmussen C B 111 5.00 69–18 Eddie's Luck 1174½ Winged Chief 114hd Startop's Ace 1064½ 8
5Jun81- 5Bel fst 6f :23 :46⅘ 1:11⅗ 3↑ [S]Allowance 6 7 65½ 44 11½ 13¾ Asmussen C B 112 3.70 84–17 Sportmn'sPrince1123¾WingedChif1142Rsuscitor117no Drew clear 9
22May81- 9Bel fst 7f :23 :46⅖ 1:26 3↑ [S]Allowance 10 1 1hd 1hd 31 66 Asmussen C B 112 5.10 66–22 North Country Blue119¾Resuscitator1194AdmiralByrd108hd Tired 10
29Apr81- 9Aqu gd 7f :22⅘ :46 1:25⅕ 3↑ [S]Allowance 8 4 41 44 22½ 37 Hernandez R 113 *2.00 68–24 Strtop'sAce1065½Dmscus'Rp1091¾Sportmn'sPrinc1132¾ Weakened 10
14Apr81- 4Aqu sly 6f :22⅘ :46⅕ 1:13 3↑ [S]Md Sp Wt 2 4 11 15 16 14½ Hernandez R 113 *2.10 76–31 Sportmn'sPrinc1134½Gronimo1125½NwYorkPrinc1071½ Ridden out 14
28Jan81- 4Aqu fst 6f [•]:23⅗ :48⅖ 1:13⅗ [S]Md Sp Wt 7 8 84¾ 73½ 2hd 2¾ Hernandez R 124 4.20e 75–20 Sheer Survival 124¾ Sportsman's Prince1242Fielding124¾ Gamely 14
LATEST WORKOUTS Jly 30 Sar Ⓣ 4f fm :48⅖ h Jly 23 Bel 4f fst :48 h Jly 6 Bel 4f fst :48⅗ h (d) Jun 17 Bel tr.t 4f fst :49 b

North Country Blue Gr. g. 4, by Turn to Mars—Paula Jean, by Turn-to
Br.—Loch Winnock Bloodstock Ltd (NY) 106 Turf Record St. 1st 2nd 3rd 2 0 0 1 St. 1st 2nd 3rd Amt.
Own.—Garren M M Tr.—Puentes Gilbert 1981 18 3 3 0 $50,920 1980 7 1 2 3 $32,200
27Jly81- 5Bel fst 7f :23 :46⅖ 1:23 3↑ [S]Clm 32500 6 5 52½ 32½ 24 26½ Fell J 87 b 115 3.60 80–14 BconndEggs1126½NorthContryBl1153BrooklynBoss1154½ 2nd best 8
20Jly81- 1Bel my 1$\frac{1}{16}$:47⅗ 1:12 1:43⅘ 3↑ [S]Clm 25000 2 2 2hd 2hd 1½ 11½ Fell J b 117 3.20 83–15 NorthCountryBl1171½OrngShrbt1125¾GoodTmLd1152¼ Drew clear 7
6Jly81- 3Bel fst 1⅛ :47 1:11⅕ 1:48⅕ 3↑ [S]Clm 32500 7 4 43½ 34½ 212 215 Cordero A Jr b 115 8.00 71–15 Strtop'sAce11415NorthCountryBlue115½RreJoel1146 Second best 7
19Jun81- 2Bel fst 1⅛ :46⅗ 1:11⅕ 1:49⅘ 3↑ [S]Allowance 7 6 614 512 514 513 Samyn J L b 117 14.40 65–18 Eddie'sLuck1174½WingedChief114hdStrtop'sAc1064½ Carried wide 8
10Jun81- 8Bel fm 1$\frac{1}{16}$ Ⓣ:47 1:11 1:42⅘ 3↑ [S]Kingston 3 8 810 88 612 612 Samyn J L b 117 39.90 70–19 Adiibber 1213½ Without Words 1194¾ Move It Now 1212 Outrun 9
4Jun81- 3Bel my 7f :23 :46⅗ 1:24⅕ 3↑ [S]Clm 45000 1 7 57 66¼ 68 66¾ Fell J b 115 20.70 74–19 Slip 1171¼ Roman Chef 112hd Eddie's Luck 108¾ Never a factor 9
22May81- 9Bel fst 7f :23 :46⅖ 1:26 3↑ [S]Allowance 4 2 83½ 74 2½ 1¾ Cordero A Jr b 119 6.70 72–22 NorthCountryBlue119¾Resuscitator1194AdmirlByrd108hd Drawing 10
14May81- 1Bel fst 1 :46⅕ 1:11⅗ 1:38⅗ 3↑ [S]Clm 45000 1 5 57½ 68 511 57½ McCarron G b 115 11.30 67–24 Slip 119½ Roman Chef 1143 All Guns 1151½ No factor 6
7May81- 5Bel fst 6f :23⅖ :47 1:11⅘ 3↑ [S]Allowance 3 6 75¼ 77½ 45 27½ McCarron G b 119 12.70 75–21 HdgdPoston1067½NorthCountryBl119¾WhtTrgt1102 Gained place 7
29Apr81- 9Aqu gd 7f :22⅘ :46 1:25⅕ 3↑ [S]Allowance 7 1 65½ 67½ 49½ 49¾ MacBeth D b 121 15.00 65–24 Strtop'sAce1065½Dmscus'Rp1091¾Sportmn'sPrinc1132¾ No factor 10
LATEST WORKOUTS ●Jly 15 Bel tr.t 3f fst :35⅕ h Jly 3 Bel tr.t 5f sly 1:02⅘ b Jun 27 Bel tr.t 4f fst :48⅘ h Jun 17 Bel tr.t 3f fst :36 h

Navidas Ch. c. 3, by Sir Wimborne—Bethlehem, by Princequillo
Br.—Tilly Foster Stock Farm (NY) 105 St. 1st 2nd 3rd Amt.
Own.—Kinderhill Farm Tr.—Schoenborn Everett F 1981 7 1 1 1 $21,740 1980 3 M 0 0
24Jly81- 3Bel fst 1 :46⅖ 1:12 1:38⅖ 3↑ [S]Allowance 2 4 59 55 35½ 33 Garramone A 67 116 4.10 73–15 Need A Penny 1112¾ Little Irving 106nk Navidas 1165 Raced wide 6
6Jly81- 9Bel fst 1 :47 1:13⅕ 1:39⅘ 3↑ [S]Md Sp Wt 7 9 95¾ 65½ 12 15½ Garramone A b 116 5.10 69–15 Navidas 1165½ Trieze 116nk Beaverboard 1115¼ Ridden out 10
18Jun81- 9Bel fst 1 :46⅕ 1:11⅖ 1:38⅖ 3↑ [S]Md Sp Wt 3 9 711 510 36½ 28¾ Garramone A b 114 28.60 67–17 Falcon Ed 1148½ Navidas 1141¾ Geronimo 114nk Angled out 12
11Jun81- 1Bel fst 6f :23⅗ :47⅕ 1:12⅗ 3↑ [S]Md Sp Wt 1 6 118¾109¼ 97 76¼ Garramone A b 114 *2.20e 73–15 HappySkipper1141¼NtiveTruth106¾RoughN'Boldly1141¼ Stumbled 13
25May81- 4Bel fst 1 :48⅗ 1:14⅖ 1:41⅕ 3↑ [S]Md Sp Wt 6 7 77¼ 811 710 79¾ Garramone A 113 48.00 52–22 BengalLncer1132½Whiglet'sPride1192RoundTheHorn113nk Outrun 8
10May81- 2Bel fst 6f :23⅗ :48 1:13⅕ 3↑ [S]Md Sp Wt 10 9 77¼ 89¾ 911 613 Garramone A 114 42.60 63–21 Zoom Googus 1137 Go Gabriel 1131½NewYorkPrince1061½ Outrun 10
21Apr81- 3Aqu fst 6f :24⅖ :49⅘ 1:16⅖ 3↑ [S]Md Sp Wt 5 3 53 713 713 610 Garramone A 114 27.20 49–30 Noble Run 114¾ Facilitator 124nk Bengal Lancer 1142 Tired 7
30Oct80- 4Aqu fst 6f :23⅗ :48⅕ 1:13⅘ [S]Md Sp Wt 2 10 1417 1418 1321 1320 Garramone A 118 9.80f 54–24 Star Reporter 118¾ Bodacious 1182½ Spry Chi 1082½ Outrun 14
23Oct80- 4Aqu fst 1 :48⅘ 1:14⅗ 1:41⅕ [S]Md Sp Wt 1 6 98½ 1017 921 1019 Garramone A 118 28.30e 41–27 Admiral Byrd 1186 Need A Penny 118nk Slick Reason118¾ Outrun 11
26Sep80- 6Bel fst 7f :24⅕ :48⅖ 1:27⅗ [S]Md Sp Wt 2 10 811 915 818 516 Garramone A 122 35.60 48–22 WimborneCastle12211HankerChief1172OrngeSherbet1222 Outrun 10
LATEST WORKOUTS Aug 3 Sar Ⓣ 5f fm 1:04 b Jly 19 Bel 5f fst 1:03 b Jly 15 Bel 5f fst 1:02⅖ b Jun 28 Bel 4f fst :50 b

When I analyzed the late daily double at Saratoga on August 10, 1981, I had but one conviction. Only three horses — Sir Ack, Naskra's Breeze, and Kim's Chance — could conceivably win the ninth race. All of them had run well in a stake against Fio Rito, who had subsequently won the Whitney Stakes and beaten some of the best horses in the country. Even though they were not established grass runners, they possessed a great edge in class over their competition, which consisted mostly of low-grade allowance horses. This was hardly a unique perception; Sir Ack, Naskra's Breeze, and Kim's Chance were the three favorites in the race.

The eighth race was a bit more complicated. I preferred Trove. She had earned a superior figure in her next-to-last start, and last time, on a track with an inside-speed bias, she had been racing in the 5-path around the turn. I saw a couple of other possibilities in horses who had also run against a bias. Doblique had run well from post 10 on a rail-biased track, and then had come back to win impressively on the grass. Thrilld N Delightd had been the only horse to rally and win on the speed-biased track of August 2.

Some of my strongest opinions on this race were of a negative variety. I hated Mystical Mood, who had benefited from a perfect trip in her last start and had not even earned a big figure. Against a field full of speed horses, she had let the leaders knock each other out by running a quarter in :21⅘, then shot up the rail to beat them. (My notes read, "Rail T, 2S, lone closer.") Apalachee Honey had won the prestigious Sorority Stakes at Monmouth, but her figure was dismal. Fire in the Sky's victory had come with the aid of a strong track bias. I intended to take advantage of my dislike of Mystical Mood and Apalachee Honey, whom I expected to be the favorites, and use Trove as my key horse in the daily double. But when the betting began, I was shocked. Trove was the overwhelming favorite, at 6 to 5. The crowd was betting Mystical Mood and Apalachee Honey a bit, but was totally ignoring the other horses I thought were contenders: Doblique was 24 to 1, Thrilld N Delightd 36 to 1. In the daily double these were the probable payoffs:

Trove–Sir Ack	$14
Trove–Naskra's Breeze	$25
Trove–Kim's Chance	$22
Doblique–Sir Ack	$136
Doblique–Naskra's Breeze	$305
Doblique–Kim's Chance	$348
Thrilld N Delightd–Sir Ack	$350
Thrilld N Delightd–Naskra's Breeze	$410
Thrilld N Delightd–Kim's Chance	$423

This was one of the many cases where a gambler must let the odds dictate his course of action. I liked Trove, yes, but those daily-double prices were ridiculous. I hardly considered Doblique or Thrilld N Delightd standouts, but their prices were ridiculous in the opposite direction. So I decided to change my emphasis and go for a killing with these longshots, while using Trove only as a saver. I was willing to lose a few dollars if the short-priced Trove–Sir Ack double won. I was less willing to risk having Thrilld N Delightd win at 36 to 1 and miss hitting the double. So for each $100 that I invested, I bet $10 to win on Thrilld N Delightd and $10 on each of the daily-double combinations, coupling my three horses in the eighth race with my three horses in the ninth.

EIGHTH RACE
Saratoga
AUGUST 10, 1981

6 FURLONGS. (1.08) 66th Running THE ADIRONDACK (Grade III). $50,000 Added. Fillies, 2-year-old, weights, 119 lbs. By subscription of $100 each, which should accompany the nomination; $400 to pass the entry box, with $50,000 added. The added money and all fees to be divided 60% to the winner, 22% to second, 12% to third and 6% to fourth. Winners of two races of $15,000 an additional 2 lbs. Non-winners of a race of $15,000 since June 15, allowed 3 lbs. Of a race other than maiden or claiming since June 1, 5 lbs. Maidens, 7 lbs. Starters to be named at the closing time of entries. Trophies will be presented to the winning owner, trainer and jockey. (Nominations close Wednesday, July 29, 1981.) Closed with 42 nominations.
Value of race $58,600, value to winner $35,160, second $12,892, third $7,032, fourth $3,516. Mutuel pool $162,711, OTB pool $171,165.

Last Raced	Horse	Eqt.A.Wt	PP	St	¼	½	Str	Fin	Jockey	Odds $1
2Aug81 ^{6}Sar^1	Thrilld N Delightd	2 114	9	1	9	$7^{\frac{1}{2}}$	5^{hd}	$1^{1\frac{1}{4}}$	Velasquez J	36.40
25Jly81 ^{8}Mth^1	Apalachee Honey	2 119	7	3	$7^{\frac{1}{2}}$	8^{8}	8^{14}	$2^{\frac{3}{4}}$	Morgan M R	4.60
29Jly81 ^{8}Sar^3	Trove	b 2 116	1	6	2^{2}	1^{1}	1^{2}	3no	Maple E	1.30
29Jly81 ^{8}Sar^1	Mystical Mood	2 119	3	9	6^{2}	5^{hd}	6^{1}	4^{hd}	Vasquez J	3.70
24Jly81 ^{2}Bel^1	Doblique	2 114	8	2	8^{1}	6^{1}	4^{hd}	$5^{1\frac{3}{4}}$	Asmussen C B	24.10
25Jly81 ^{4}Bel^2	Sympathetic Miss	2 112	4	5	$4^{1\frac{1}{2}}$	$4^{\frac{1}{2}}$	$7^{1\frac{1}{2}}$	$6^{3\frac{3}{4}}$	Santiago A	35.80
25Jly81 ^{8}Mth^4	Sensitive Penny	2 114	5	7	$4^{1\frac{1}{2}}$	3^{3}	3^{hd}	$7^{2\frac{3}{4}}$	Brumfield D	19.30
29Jly81 ^{8}Sar^2	Aga Pantha	2 114	2	4	$1^{\frac{1}{2}}$	$2^{1\frac{1}{2}}$	$2^{1\frac{1}{2}}$	8^{13}	Fell J	6.30
25Jly81 ^{4}Bel^1	Sparkling Savage	2 114	6	8	5^{1}	9	9	9	Cordero A Jr	11.00

OFF AT 5:21 EDT. Start good Won driving Time, :21⅘, :45, 1:10⅘ Track fast.

$2 Mutuel Prices:			
11-(K)-THRILLD N DELIGHTD	74.80	24.60	7.80
8-(H)-APALACHEE HONEY		6.40	4.40
1-(A)-TROVE			3.00

B. f, by Explodent—Evening Ecstasy, by Night Invader. Trainer Pierce Joseph H Jr. Bred by Pierce J H Jr (Fla).

THRILLD N DELIGHTD, Outrun early, came out between horses leaving the turn, caught TROVE with a rush leaving the furlong grounds and proved clearly best. APALACHEE HONEY, outrun into the strtch while racing very wide, finished strongly. TROVE, moved though along the inside to take over on the turn, settled into the stretch with a clear lead but weakened under pressure. MYSTICAL MOOD rallied along the inside after entering the stretch and continued on with good energy while coming out between horses approaching the finish. DOBLIQUE rallied between horses approaching midstretch but wadn't good enough while lugging in and bothering SENSITIVE PENNY and AGA PANTHA. SYMPATHETIC MISS had no apparent excuse. SENSITIVE PENNY, a factor into the stretch, lacked room between horses while weakening. AGA PANTHA showed good early, remained a factor into the stretch and lacked room while tiring. SPARKLING SAVAGE bore out badly around the turn.

Owners— 1, Pierce Sheila; 2, Muckler D; 3, Hickory Tree Stable; 4, Hudson E J; 5, Keller M; 6, Epstein J; 7, Bronfman M; 8, Kentucky Blue Stable; 9, Flying Zee Stable.

Trainers— 1, Pierce Joseph H Jr; 2, Muckler Tim J; 3, Stephens Woodford C; 4, Carroll Del W; 5, Brice Harold B Jr; 6, DiAngelo Joseph T; 7, Papania Robert A; 8, Jolley Leroy; 9, Martin Jose.

Scratched—Fresh Candy (3Jun81 ^{8}Bel^8); Fire in the Sky (29Jly81 ^{8}Sar^5).

When the longest shot in the field rallied to win the eighth race, I was both thrilled and delighted. I thought I was almost certain to hit the daily double, but I did not want to tempt fate and so deferred what would be a noisy celebration. Novice horseplayers should learn that there is a strict rule of etiquette governing such circumstances, a rule I formulated one day at Gulfstream Park. I was watching a $1000 bet go down the drain while standing next to a youthful bettor who was exhorting his horse in the tone one would normally employ when pleading with the Mau-Mau to spare one's children. It turned out that he had bet $2 on an exacta paying $27. This experience gave rise to the Beyer Rule of Rooting: While discreet cheering is always permissible, wildly emotional displays are allowed only when the potential winnings equal at least 10 percent of the bettor's annual income.

NINTH RACE
Saratoga
AUGUST 10, 1981

1 MILE.(inner–turf). (1.35⅕) HANDICAP. Purse $37,000. 3–year–olds and upward foaled in New York State apd approved by the New York State Bred Registry weights Friday, August 7. Declarations by 10:00 a.m., Saturday, Augus 8.

Value of race $37,000, value to winner $22,200, second $8,140, third $4,440, fourth $2,220. Mutuel pool $119,987, OTB pool $201,283. Track Triple Pool $175,181. OTB Triple Pool $319,876.

Last Raced	Horse	Eqt.	A.Wt	PP	St	¼	½	¾	Str	Fin	Jockey	Odds $1
20Jly81 ^{8}Bel^{3}	Naskra's Breeze		4 116	3	4	6^{2}	6^{1}	5^{2}	2^{2}	$1\frac{1}{2}$	Samyn J L	3.00
20Jly81 ^{8}Bel^{2}	Sir Ack		5 121	1	1	2^{1}	$2^{1\frac{1}{2}}$	$1^{1\frac{1}{2}}$	$1\frac{1}{2}$	$2^{3\frac{3}{4}}$	Vasquez J	2.40
27Jly81 ^{5}Bel^{2}	North Country Blue	b	4 106	9	6	9^{4}	$8\frac{1}{2}$	7^{1}	5^{5}	$3^{1\frac{1}{2}}$	Migliore R	14.00
31Jly81 ^{8}Sar^{2}	Kim's Chance		5 124	4	3	$3\frac{1}{2}$	$4\frac{1}{2}$	2^{hd}	$3\frac{1}{2}$	4^{hd}	Cordero A Jr	3.70
2Jly81 ^{5}Bel^{1}	Fearless Leader	b	3 115	5	5	5^{5}	5^{4}	4^{1}	4^{2}	5^{11}	MacBeth D	4.20
18Jly81 ^{8}FL^{1}	D. J.'s Nitecap	b	4 111	6	10	$7\frac{1}{2}$	7^{2}	8^{2}	$6\frac{1}{2}$	6no	Reynolds R L	17.10
31Jly81 ^{3}Sar^{1}	My Crew	b	3 109	2	7	8^{2}	9^{6}	9^{6}	$8\frac{1}{2}$	$7^{2\frac{1}{2}}$	Rydowski S R	30.00
1Aug81 ^{8}FL^{2}	Johnel		6 110	7	2	1^{1}	$1\frac{1}{2}$	$3\frac{1}{2}$	$7^{1\frac{1}{2}}$	$8^{4\frac{1}{2}}$	Dosher K	40.10
1Aug81 ^{2}Sar^{5}	Sportman's Prince	b	3 107	8	8	$4^{1\frac{1}{2}}$	3^{1}	$6\frac{1}{2}$	9^{5}	9^{2}	Montoya D	28.90
24Jly81 ^{3}Bel^{3}	Navidas	b	3 105	10	9	10	10	10	10	10	Foley D	33.20

OFF AT 5:49 EDT. Start good, Won driving. Time, :24, :47⅗, 1:12⅕, 1:37 Course firm.

$2 Mutuel Prices:			
3–NASKRA'S BREEZE	8.00	4.40	3.40
1–SIR ACK		4.40	3.20
9–NORTH COUNTRY BLUE			4.40

$2 TRIPLE 3–1–9 PAID $371.00.

B. g, by Naskra—Topical Heat, by Tropical Breeze. Trainer Johnson Philip G. Bred by Davis C C (NY).

NASKRA'S BREEZE, reserved early, rallied along the inside leaving the far turn and led gamely to wear down SIR ACK. The latter opened a clear lead while saving ground approaching the stretch and held on well. NORTH COUNTRY BLUE, outrun early, came out for room inside the final furlong but failed to seriously menace with a mile late response. KIM'S CHANCE bore out at the first turn bothering FEARLESS LEADER and SPORTSMAN'S PRINCE, made a run between horses leaving the far turn but weakened. JOHNEL showed speed to the far turn and bore out badly while tiring. SPORTMAN'S PRINCE, forced out at the first turn, made a run approaching the end of the backstretch but was finished after doing five furlongs.

Owners— 1, Broadmoor Stable; 2, Goldmills Farm; 3, Garren M M; 4, Bar-Jo Stable; 5, Wolosoff J K; 6, Jacobs S E; 7, Mogavero J A; 8, Tantalo N; 9, Morrell S F; 10, Kinderhill Farm.

Trainers— 1, Johnson Philip G; 2, Veitch Sylvester; 3, Puentes Gilbert; 4, Jerkens Steven T; 5, Preger Mitchell C; 6, Jacobs Daniel C; 7, Woodson Richard; 8, Tantalo Nicholas; 9, Bradley John M; 10, Schoenborn Everett F.

Scratched—Slip (22Jly81 ^{2}Bel^{2}); Newsman (31Jly81 ^{8}Sar^{4}); Dastardly Dick (1Aug81 ^{2}Sar^{4}); Bacon and Eggs (27Jly81 ^{5}Bel^{1}); Tiempo (31Jly81 ^{8}Sar^{5}); Right On Louie (9Mar81 ^{3}Aqu^{4}); Roman Chef (22Jly81 ^{2}Bel^{1}).

$2 DD 11–3 Paid $410.60. DD Pool $177,314. OTB DD Pool $273,988. Attendance 22,458. Total Mutuel Pool 2,482,217. Total OTB Pool $3,367,975.

When Naskra's Breeze won the ninth race and completed a $410.60 daily double, I was permitted by the Beyer Rule to drop to my knees on the floor of the press box and shout, "I'm king of the world!" I had been amply rewarded for betting well on two races where I had no real handicapping opinion.

While it may be possible to generalize about the proper betting strategy that different horseplayers should employ, the actual amount they should bet will obviously depend on their own financial circumstances as well as their temperaments. Most handicapping books recommend that a bettor's total operating capital should be his point of reference, and that he should wager a certain percentage of it on his top selections. In *Picking Winners* I suggested wagering five percent of the bankroll on "prime bets." If a horseplayer started with

$3000, he would be making $150 bets. As his capital increased, his scale of betting would increase. Very logical. I thought it was a sign of considerable character weakness that I couldn't follow my own system.

As an alternative I would like to propose a less rigid betting system and an altogether different point of reference. A horseplayer should begin by answering this question: When he encounters a virtually perfect situation — say, a horse with a superior speed figure who had a tough trip in his last race and whose odds are good — how much is he willing to bet?

The sum is not necessarily related to his financial circumstances. I know bartenders who will bet their last $1000 on a horse and millionaires who might choke at the prospect of losing $200. Every gambler has a level of betting which is comfortable for him, and beyond which his judgment is impaired. When I was attempting to use the system I recommended in *Picking Winners,* I started making $300 prime bets, but as my bankroll increased and I found that I was required to risk $400, I froze. I became overly conservative. The stakes affected my judgment — a phenomenon as old as gambling itself.

When writer Jon Bradshaw was gathering material for a book on gamblers, *Fast Company,* he flew to Nashville to interview Pug Pearson, an astute poker player and all-round hustler. Pearson met Bradshaw at the airport and took him directly to a golf course, where he had a high-stakes match scheduled with three other players. On the way he suggested that Bradshaw make a bet on him. "What do you usually shoot, Pug?" the writer asked.

. "Oh, about a 77, 78," Pearson replied.

"And the others, what do they shoot?"

"Oh," Pearson said, "them old boys'll shoot anywhere between 72 and 75, depending on the day."

Bradshaw inquired how Pearson expected to win. "You've got to take into account the human element," the gambler said. "Hell, I know them old boys; I know 'em real well. And I know their choking points — the point where they begin to cut their own throats."

With some reluctance Bradshaw bet $300 on Pearson, and watched as the gambler managed to take a narrow lead into the 18th hole. On the last fairway, Pearson teed off first. His drive hit the branch of a tree and bounced back nearly fifty yards. Bradshaw blanched. Pearson promptly announced to his opponents that he would like to press all bets.

The other golfers accepted. One of them, who had been driving straight off the tee all day, hooked his shot into six-inch-high grass behind a tree. The next man hit a wild shot into the rough. Pearson won the hole and the match. Amazed and grateful, Bradshaw collected his $300, having learned a lesson that every gambler must confront.

All of us flesh-and-blood horseplayers have choking points, though in racing they may be less visible than in games that require physical skills. All of us have to "take into account the human element" instead of using some rigid, prescribed betting system. By establishing the maximum bet with which he is comfortable, a horseplayer will have a point of reference on which to base all his other wagering decisions.

This point of reference should help the horseplayer adhere to the most important principle of money management. It is obvious and axiomatic, yet it is a precept that most bettors violate regularly. A horseplayer should make his largest wagers on the races in which he holds the strongest convictions, in which he sees the greatest potential for profit. In less promising races, he should bet less — or nothing. Nongamblers might assume that any rational man would behave this way. But in the emotive atmosphere of the track, the size of a horseplayer's wager is often influenced more by his mental state at the time of a race than by a rational calculation of risks and rewards. A bettor who has just doped out the last two winners is more likely to bet heavily on the next race — regardless of his insights into it — because he is feeling temporarily omniscient. A bettor who has just lost two tough photo finishes in a row and has seen his bankroll dwindle may feel gun-shy at the very time he ought to be aggressive. If a horseplayer keeps his maximum bet firmly in mind as a point of reference, he is much less apt to go astray. If that maximum is $100, but he is having a good day and finds himself about to venture $80 on a marginal situation, he is out of line.

Most published money-management systems do not permit any flexibility; they prescribe wagers of a fixed amount on any playable race. Of course, such systems ignore the realities of handicapping at a racetrack, where a horseplayer's enthusiasm for a bet may fall into a hundred different gradations. I will be influenced by my horse's margin of superiority; his odds; the possibilities in exactas; the safety with which I might hedge my bets in gimmicks; and, of course, my own self-confidence. If I have been winning steadily over a period of time, I will feel more confident in my own judgment than I do during a prolonged losing streak. I cannot distill all these considerations into a simple either/or betting decision. I want the flexibility to bet either a lot or a little on a race.

By establishing his maximum bet and keeping his other wagers in some kind of proper proportion, a horseplayer can deal naturally and comfortably with a question that is often the source of anxiety and guilt: How many races a day should he play?

My friend Charlie bets in the manner usually associated with serious professional gamblers. He wants to play only superior horses at excellent odds, and he is willing to sit for days or weeks awaiting the right opportunity. Most horseplayers assume that this is the one and only proper way to play the races, and they are racked by guilt when they have the urge to visit the windows too frequently.

I don't accept the view that such patience is necessarily a virtue. If a bettor's maximum wager is $100, I see no harm in his playing $2 or $4 on a race as an antidote for boredom. Moreover, I believe that a horseplayer should bet in a style with which he feels comfortable rather than accept someone else's dictum about what is proper and improper. I know people who hate to lose even a small bet and prefer to sit and wait for the highest-percentage opportunities. I would be miserable doing this. I love to gamble. My idea of supreme happiness was a day in Miami when I bet all 10 races at Hialeah, went to Hollywood Dog Track and bet eight more, went to Dania Jai-Alai for a couple of more wagers, and then drove to a bar in Pompano that showed the replays of all 10 races at the local harness track.

After hearing more than the usual number of gibes about my inability to pass a race at Saratoga in 1981, I tallied my action for the whole meeting. Of 216 races I bet 195. Of 69 exactas I bet 60. Of 24 triples, I bet 23. (I must not have been feeling good that day.) But while the frequency of my trips to the windows may have suggested a lack of discipline in my betting, it was in fact highly structured. There was a logical proportion in the size of the wagers. I could afford to take a $50 flyer on a longshot exacta combination or spread $300 in bets on an admittedly chancy triple because my maximum bet, reserved for horses who embodied perfection, was $3000.

I glimpsed perfection once that season, although the horse in question had finished seventh in both starts of his two-race career. Irish Waters had last run in a maiden-special-weight race and had dueled head-and-head with a highly regarded Calumet Farm speed-ball for a half mile before he tired. Even while losing by nearly 10 lengths, he had earned a figure of 67. Now he was dropping into a maiden-claiming race, where the principal contenders had figures of 62 and 57, which they had earned with easy trips, and where there was no early speed to press Irish Waters. I didn't bother with exotics; I made my maximum bet and collected an $8.60 payoff.

Not until the next year did I find another horse who merited my maximum wager. The colt had earned a figure of 122, good enough to suggest that he was one of the best in the country, and he had done it while running against a powerful track bias. This was Link-age, coming out of the Preakness into the Belmont Stakes, where he burned up my $3000 by finishing 22 lengths behind Conquistador Cielo.

I doubt that I would be an especially successful horseplayer if my fortunes depended on identifying standouts and betting them to win. This is a tough game, and it is tough to be right a high per-centage of the time. The beauty of exotic wagers is that they permit a horseplayer to be right a modest percentage of the time and still beat the game.

NINE

The Winning Attitude

I N THE LEARNING EXPERIENCE of every horseplayer there are milestones by which he marks his progress. I still remember the afternoon at Randall Park in 1956 when I cashed my first parimutuel ticket and got hooked on the sport. I will never forget the 20-to-1 victory of a horse named Sun in Action in 1971, which convinced me there was a perceptible logic in the game and that one day I was going to understand it. I look on the whole year of 1977 as the final proof that I could, indeed, beat the races. But it was not until a day in February 1979 that I felt I had truly come of age as a gambler.

Before going to Gulfstream Park that winter, I had analyzed the records of the trainers who would be campaigning there. I reviewed previous years' results, maintained a file of index cards on all the trainers, and tried to identify the ones who were especially predictable, especially competent, or especially chicanerous. The most intriguing one of them all was a little-known horseman named Kenneth O. Kemp. Once or twice a season, the mysterious Mr. Kemp would win with a longshot whose credentials were impossibly outlandish. The previous year, I remembered, one of them had been bet from 30–1 to 18–1 on the last flash of the tote board. There had been no clues in the horse's past performances; the betting action was the only tipoff. I was determined to watch the board closely whenever Kemp started a horse at Gulfstream.

When I saw the past performance of Joanne's Choice in the second race one day, I was immediately intrigued. The colt had lost the only two races of his career by margins of 17 and 19 lengths. Now, after an absence of five months from competition, he had come from Detroit to Gulfstream, where Kemp had entered him not against maidens but against winners. I watched the monitor that showed probable daily-double prices, looking for some betting action, but saw not a ripple — until a minute before post time. When most of the prices on combinations involving Joanne's Choice dropped suddenly, I sprinted to the windows and bet a few modest daily doubles. One of my horses won the first race at 6 to 1, and the price for the double with Joanne's Choice was posted at $524.40. With my $40 ticket, I had a chance to win $10,000 on a race for the first time in my life.

Joanne's Choice was 35 to 1 throughout the betting, and I started to think I had probably misread that one flash in the daily-double odds that had suggested this was a betting coup. But as the horses were being loaded into the gate, the tote board flashed for the final time and Joanne's Choice was suddenly 15 to 1. I had a live one! I watched excitedly as the colt stalked the leaders and blew past them on the turn. As he opened a commanding lead, on the way to what would be a 7½-length victory, I screamed, "I win ten thousand!" — happily oblivious to all that had happened on the turn.

The INQUIRY sign was posted almost as soon as Joanne's Choice crossed the finish line. A few minutes later the odds board went blank and the winner's number came down for interfering with the horse who had finished fifth. I watched the replay, saw that the disqualification was indeed justified, headed straight to the bar for a shot of Jack Daniels', and proceeded to squander a few hundred dollars on the remainder of the card.

The next day friends were still offering their condolences, but I was amazed to realize my own feelings about the misfortune. I felt nothing. The incident was out of my mind. I wasn't pressing my wagers, trying to win the $10,000 back. I was betting as if the disqualification had never happened.

Two years earlier, at the same track, I had been unjustifiably disqualified out of $3000, and was so frustrated and outraged by the injustice that I bashed a large hole through the wall of the press box. (It is still there with a frame around it and a sign that says "Beyer's Hole.") In the wake of that loss I was so upset that my handicapping and betting were adversely affected. I lost thousands of dollars more as a result.

This was part of an all-too-familiar pattern. Throughout my life as a horseplayer I had seen winning streaks turn into losing streaks overnight because a photo finish, disqualification, or some other traumatic experience wrecked my equilibrium and caused me to alter the methods with which I had been achieving my success. It took me years even to perceive the nature of this boom-and-bust pattern, to realize that fretting over a setback is the worst mistake a horseplayer can make, but even after I understood the phenomenon I still could not control these negative emotions. And then, on the day after the disqualification of Joanne's Choice, I discovered that I could. Since that day I have never permitted myself to indulge in anger or self-pity for more than a few hours after a painful loss. When Ruben Hernandez cost me $25,000 by dropping his whip in the stretch at Saratoga, when a longshot named Ta Ho Tom lost a photo finish there that meant $34,000 to me, when I missed by one race hitting a Pick Six at Hialeah that would have been worth $225,000, I regained my composure by the next day.

Tough losses are an inescapable part of the game, and the best way to deal with them is with bemused detachment. In this spirit the New York Racing Association's inimitable Harvey Pack hosted a social event at Saratoga that he christened the Toughest Beat Party. All his guests were invited to step before a microphone and a videotape camera and relate the story of their most heart-rending loss at a racetrack. The blue ribbon for the evening went to Richard Valeriani, the NBC correspondent, who is an avid racing fan.

In 1963, Valeriani related, he was sent to the Dominican Republic to cover the election campaign between Juan Bosch and Viriato Fiallo. Naturally, he tried to enliven the assignment with an occasional trip to the racetrack in Santo Domingo. Valeriani was sitting in the Hotel El Embajador, studying the entries, when he saw one respectable pedigree among all these rock-bottom animals. An entrant in the second race had been sired by the good American stallion Ambiorix. "All the bellhops and the busboys and the waiters at the hotel were horseplayers," Valeriani recalled, "and when I asked them about the horse, they all said he was a dog who couldn't possibly win."

Valeriani was undeterred. When he got to the track, he played the horse in a gimmick resembling the modern Pick Six, the objective of which was to pick every winner on the card. After one of his choices captured the first race, he watched the despised son of Ambiorix win the second race at odds of 99 to 1. Not many other patrons shared Valeriani's euphoria. "People jumped over the fence and blocked the track, yelling that the race had been fixed," the correspondent said. "They set fire to trash cans. Then an announcement was made that if the rioting didn't end, the rest of the races would be canceled and the Pick Six pool would go to anybody who picked the winners of the first two races. Now there was more booing and the crowd started stoning the stewards' box. I felt terrific."

After the cancellation of the races, Valeriani's friends at the hotel told him that evening that there was probably $15,000 or so in the Pick Six pool. But one of the locals also informed him that the Jockey Club was going to hold a special meeting to approve the steward's decision.

The meeting was held on the day before the presidential election. Valeriani had to go with a camera crew to the public square in Santo Domingo, and there he knew he would be able to learn the results of the stewards' meeting at a nearby off-track betting shop. When he arrived, Valeriani found he wasn't the only excited person in the vicinity. Bosch forces were assembled on one side of the square, Fiallo forces on the other. Suddenly bullets started flying in all directions; Valeriani and his NBC colleagues hit the ground and lay there motionless. They did, at least, until Valeriani excused himself and crawled in the direction of the OTB shop. When he got the news, he felt like inciting a riot. "They told me that the Jockey Club had reversed the decision of the stewards," he said. "There would be no payout on the Pick Six. Instead, the whole card would be rerun the following week. I was wiped out."

That is a genuinely tough beat, and any horseplayer who lets himself be traumatized by a routine disqualification or photo finish ought to be ashamed. We all have to accept the fact that such setbacks are an inescapable part of the game, and to believe that over the long run the good luck and bad luck will even out. What is crucial is the way a gambler deals with the good luck and the bad luck.

During prolonged periods of ill fortune, a horseplayer must attempt to remain unruffled, but he should take a dispassionate look at his performance to judge whether he is losing because of his own mistakes. In better times, he should resist the tendency to grow over-confident and work even harder so he can capitalize fully on his good fortune. Not only that, but he should savor the experience, because it is much healthier for a gambler to dwell on his good luck and his winning streaks than on the "tough beats."

Ernest Havemann, the author of a textbook on psychology, espouses this philosophy, though his views were formed by one day's experience at Caliente Race Track rather than any academic study. Havemann had been mildly obsessed by the desire to hit Caliente's "five–ten pool," a gimmick requiring the bettor to pick the winners of six consecutive races. One weekend he took a break from a free-lance writing assignment in Florida, flew to San Diego, drove to the Mexican track, and invested $96 in the five–ten. He picked one longshot after another, and after hitting his sixth straight winner he stared at the tote board with awe and disbelief. He had just won $61,908.80.

Havemann wrote a now-classic magazine story about his triumph, which I read enviously in my youthful days as a horseplayer. Years later I had the occasion to talk to him and ask him how it had affected the rest of his life.

"I've done some important things," Havemann said. "I've written a textbook that two million kids have studied from. But my tombstone will say, 'Here lies a man who won $61,908.80 one day.' And I know that after it's been up for two days, somebody will chip underneath the epitaph, 'It was luck.' "

Havemann has been hearing that for 20 years, but he doesn't mind. "Winning does something for the psyche," he said, "and I think that win did some good things for me. I've never felt since then that anything would go wrong or stay wrong for a long time. I think of myself as a lucky guy. And I am lucky. A few years ago I bought a mare who went hopelessly lame and so I found myself in the breeding business. I bred her to a stallion who was standing for no stud fee and got a filly named Nubile. She won $111,000 and I sold her for $51,000.

"I think a lot of people are losers at the track and in life because they've got a loser's disposition. They dwell on all the bad things that happen to them. But when you've won $61,000 in a day there's a tendency to think about your pleasant memories."

Even for those of us who have never won $61,908.80 in an afternoon, this is a useful philosophy. While I try to put bad experiences out of my mind immediately, I relish my good fortune, crow about the occasions when I have cashed a bet that I didn't deserve, foster the notion that the heavens smile on me. When Pete Axthelm wrote an article about me in *Inside Sports,* he declared, "I am now prepared to reveal the true secret ingredient of the Beyer legend. For lack of a more precise term, call it luck."

Good luck, bad luck, and the emotions accompanying them are just some of the aspects of life at the track that make the experience of playing the horses so much different from the theory. Just as a bettor must cope with the internal pressures that arise from gambling, he must deal too with external influences and distractions.

Traditionally, aspiring handicappers have been counseled to shut out all distractions. "Successful horse playing is a solitary existence," Ainslie wrote. "The less solitary it gets, the less successful it gets. If you make the error of getting into social relations with the . . . angle shooters, alleged insiders, and crack-brained theorists who clutter up the track, you can't concentrate on your work because of the din. So you keep to yourself." Ainslie's philosophy coincides with the popular image of successful gamblers as self-reliant loners. But a horseplayer who chooses to operate in this fashion may be denying himself one of the most valuable resources in the game: the help of other good handicappers.

My friend and mentor Steve Davidowitz taught me about track biases and trainer patterns. My classmate Sheldon Kovitz showed me how to make speed figures. My racetrack colleagues showed me the importance of trip handicapping and taught me these new techniques. I still rely heavily on the support of other people in my small circle of racetrack friends. I like to be able to ask Clem Florio for his assessment of horses' appearance in the post parade, because I lack the skill to make those judgments. I like to be able to ask Paul Cornman what happened to a particular horse during the course of a race, because he is an extraordinarily perceptive race-watcher. I like to be able to share some of the workload in making figures with Mark Hopkins, because he calculates his figures with the same methodology and competence that I do.

Unfortunately, racetrack friendships tend to be very fragile. Horseplayers are naturally competitive, and when they associate together their egos often clash. They develop rivalries and become more intent on one-upping each other than in maximizing their own profits. A serious player has to conquer these instincts and avoid people who can't overcome them. Clem Florio has a good rule: "Never hang around at the track with people who don't want to see you win."

Not only do conflicts of egos create problems, but resentments frequently arise when one horseplayer hits a winner that a friend doesn't. I lost one friendship for years after such a situation. One day at Saratoga a young protégé of mine, known as the Kid, did a brilliant piece of research on a colt named Red Sam, who was entered in a maiden race. In the fine print of the *Racing Form*'s "Official Rulings" column he found an item that said jockey Steve Miller had waived his right to counsel and accepted a suspension from the Keystone Race Track stewards for "failure to put forth a reasonable effort with his mount in the fourth race on July 21." The name of the mount was not mentioned, but the Kid knew it was Red Sam, and it was easy to conclude that he had come to Saratoga for the purpose of a betting coup. "Don't tell anybody about this," the Kid requested.

The next day, before the first race, I ran into Pete Axthelm, who asked me if I liked anything on the day's card. I mentioned a horse in the stakes race on whom I had an opinion; I didn't mention Red Sam. Or, at least, I didn't mention him until after the race was official and Red Sam had paid $27.40. Then I showed Axthelm the clipping from the *Racing Form* about the jockey's suspension and mentioned how many thousands of dollars I had just won.

Not surprisingly, Axthelm didn't speak to me for the next three years. And when he related the story to another horseplayer, the neutral party exclaimed, "Only three years? I would have killed him." The moral, perhaps, is that a horseplayer should establish a firm policy that either he does or does not share his opinions with his racetrack friends. And if he ever deviates, he had better do it discreetly.

I suspect that purists may be appalled by the notion that I am willing to make bets on the basis of other people's knowledge or opinions. The first time I cashed a significant bet on the basis of a tip, I felt uneasy and even guilty about it, as if I had cheated on an exam. But then I came to my senses. A horseplayer has to evaluate hundreds of factors in every race, and one of these factors may be somebody else's opinion or a tip from an insider. Most often a horse-player will disregard these opinions, but if he occasionally decides to base a wager on them that is a legitimate handicapping decision. So instead of dismissing all "inside information," I employ a few guidelines to evaluate it:

1. A tip from an insider should be accompanied by (a) a story or (b) a conspiratorial tone of voice. If a trainer merely tells me that he likes his horse, he may be indulging in wishful thinking. But if he calls me into the men's room to whisper that he had just found a new miracle drug that cured his horse's chronic knee problems, I may find that story irresistible.
2. A tip is useful only if it pertains to an unknown quantity. If an insider wants to tell me about a first-time starter, I will always listen attentively. If he tells me about a horse who won a race last week, I will not be interested; my handicapping judgment is probably better than his.
3. For this rule I am indebted to Harvey Pack: "If you hear a tip on the same horse from three different sources, forget him," Harvey advises. "And if you get a tip on a horse from so much as one person who sells refreshments or tickets, throw him out." A tip is virtually worthless once it becomes common currency.
4. Never listen to tips from owners or jockey agents. Every owner thinks his horse is the next Secretariat. Every agent thinks his rider can make any horse run like Secretariat.

I appreciated the importance of acquiring and evaluating outside information when Florida tracks started offering the Pick Six, with its promise of gigantic payoffs to anyone who selected the winners of the third through eighth races. My friends and I regularly pooled our money and our opinions in an effort to hit it. Because every handicapping decision was potentially so important, we would scrutinize the record of every horse and often argue heatedly about his merits. If a member of our syndicate happened to be friendly with the trainer of a pivotal horse he would be assigned to ferret out whatever information he could. One day, as we looked over a maiden race in the Pick Six, Mark Hopkins pointed out a first-time starter trained by Leon Blusiewicz, a Marylander whom I had recently interviewed for a newspaper column. "Could you find out about the horse?" Mark asked.

"Sure," I said. "But why bother?" I looked at the dismal workouts of No More Blues — a half mile in 51 seconds and the like — and concluded that the filly probably had no ability. "Let's just go with our figure horse," I suggested.

Our group invested $1000 in the Pick Six and hit the first three winners, bringing us to the maiden race. Our choice, Intrepid Heroine, was the favorite, but No More Blues was getting surprising support in the wagering. I saw Blusiewicz as he left the paddock after saddling the filly and asked, "What's with this horse?"

He took me aside and said, quietly, "She's a cinch."

"But what about those workouts?" I asked.

"If I let the clockers see what this filly could do, she'd be 3 to 5," the trainer said.

I blanched. "I wish I'd known this before the Pick Six," I told Blusiewicz.

"Why didn't you ask me?" he said.

I watched the race with a sense of doom, and as soon as No More Blues crossed the wire an easy winner my fellow Pick Six investors were reminding me that I had shirked my duty. An hour later we learned what an expensive shirk it had been. Our horses won the last two events in the Pick Six, and nobody at the track had a perfect ticket. If we had used No More Blues, we would have collected $91,000. True to my philosophy, I promptly shrugged off this near-miss. My friends were not quite so forgiving.

TEN

The Winning Player

TERRY BRENNAN was looking down the barrel of a .45 auto-matic when he set straight the priorities in his life. While he was working as a security guard in a Baltimore nursing home, four masked men broke into the building and tied him up. Three of them searched for drugs while the other pointed a gun at the young guard's head. "If that fellow had pulled the trigger," Brennan said, "I would have left the world with one real regret: that I hadn't fulfilled myself as a horseplayer."

Brennan was only a $2 bettor, but he loved to handicap the horses and he had always wondered what he could accomplish if he directed all of his energy and intelligence to the game. Was he good enough to beat the races? He never expected to put that question to a defini-tive test, but in the flash of insight that accompanied the robbery he began to think that he was short-changing himself. "I'd had nine jobs," he said, "and I really hadn't felt satisfied in any of them. What I really wanted to do was play the horses for a living."

After the gunmen had left him unharmed, Brennan decided to pursue his dream. He studied back issues of the *Racing Form,* pre-paring for the start of the season at Timonium Race Track. He lived a spartan existence so he could amass about $2000 for his betting capital. A few days before the Timonium meeting began, he quit his job at the nursing home to undertake his new career as a professional gambler.

Most racing fans have entertained a similar vision at one time or another, though few have been quite so dramatically motivated to approach the game with a sense of commitment and professionalism. Yet this is the only way to beat the races, and the only way for a horseplayer to measure his own ability. Doc, for example, had been achieving only mixed results as a part-time player, but during one month of all-out effort at Saratoga he learned that he possessed both the skill and the temperament to earn his living at the track. Brennan hoped to make the same discovery.

When Timonium opened, he waited several days before placing his first wager. He finally found what he considered an optimal betting situation and plunged on a horse named Noble Pilot, who led for every step but the final one and lost by a nose. Brennan was immediately shaken. "The financial pressure started to paralyze me," he said. "All of a sudden I saw that if I lost my whole bankroll I'd be out on the street." A few days later he made his second wager — and lost a second photo finish. "When I came home after that," he said, "I collapsed in a heap. I was practically becoming a manic-depressive." A week later, after another painful loss, Brennan went home and found a notice in his mail from Essex Community College concerning registration for the fall term. He had some money left and decided to use it for his tuition. Having discovered that he was not temperamentally suited to the life that had once sounded so attractive to him, he became a casual $2 bettor again.

Nobody can beat the races with wishful thinking. Nobody can make an overnight transition from casual betting to successful professional gambling. Not everyone is equipped to beat the races even with an all-out effort. The complexities of the sport make it a tough game, and the mathematics of the parimutuel system makes it the toughest game in the world. Yet as difficult as it is, anyone who loves handicapping ought to make at least one attempt in his life to do it seriously. Although handicapping can be wonderfully entertaining as a casual hobby, there is nothing quite so satisfying for a horseplayer as the knowledge that he can make a profit from the game.

What does it take to become a winning player?

The first step is to appreciate just how demanding the game is. Pittsburgh Phil said in 1908 that "playing the horses appears to be the one business in which men believe they can succeed without special study, special talent, or special exertion," and three quarters of a century later most bettors still harbor the same delusion. They think they can go to the track once a week, picking up the *Racing Form* as they walk in the gate, do their handicapping between races, and expect to win.

It is no accident that many successful modern-day bettors come from an academic background, because they approach handicapping with the knowledge that success at anything requires special study, talent, and exertion. "In the academic world," Joe Cardello said, "you learn to study and you learn to be thorough, and that's how you master a subject. I thought that if I studied the horses long and hard enough I should be able to win." For the better part of a year Joe went to the New York tracks, hung around the paddock, got to know the professional handicappers there, and observed the way they operated. He accumulated a wealth of knowledge before he did any serious betting. I know another astute handicapper, Paul Mellos, who spent a full year at the track without placing a single wager. He observed and made notes on every conceivable aspect of the game — such as the relationship between the slope of a horse's hoof and his mud-running ability — before he started gambling in earnest.

Few people have the opportunity to give themselves such an extensive education, but even those with family and job responsibilities can lay a proper foundation for success at the track. A serious student of the game should buy the *Racing Form* every day and maintain a set of speed figures for his local track. If he goes to the track even twice a week, and watches the replays of races from the previous day, he can compile trip notes on most of the horses. If he lives in an area where each day's races are shown nightly on home television, he has access to even more trip information. He may also wish to maintain index cards noting the methods of operation of the trainers at his track. As a part-time player, he will gain familiarity with all the tools of a professional's trade.

To achieve the best possible results, though, a handicapper needs to be a full-time player. If he has a normal job, he might bet semi-seriously for 11 months of the year and point toward a month's vacation when he will go to the track every day and play the horses with total intensity. If a bettor has more time available, he should understand his own psychology and decide the most effective way for him to play. I have learned that I cannot gamble seriously for more than a few weeks at a stretch, even though my newspaper job requires me to go to the track virtually year-round. I prefer to spend about ten weeks in the winter and six weeks in the summer channeling all of my energy into handicapping until I am mentally and emotionally drained. The rest of the year I play the horses casually or not at all, and attempt to live a semblance of a normal life. Doc holds an opposite philosophy, and plays the game with day-to-day steadiness. "It's my belief," he said, "that you should never miss a day at the track. My philosophy started one Mother's Day. I was going to take the day off and visit my mother, but late in the morning it started pouring. In the daily double I knew there was a horse by Spanish Riddle [whose progeny love the mud] and so I went to the track and — bang! bang! bang! — I won $15,000. If you miss a day you're always taking a gamble that you might not be there for some special situation."

Before making a serious effort to beat the races, a bettor must have an adequate bankroll and be reasonably free from financial pressures, because the old saying that "scared money never wins" is one of the few enduring truths in the gambling world. Terry Brennan's venture was probably foredoomed because he was undercapitalized. One or two losses ate into his funds so deeply that they wrecked his equilibrium. A horseplayer's betting capital should be separated from his living and eating money so he does not feel this kind of pressure. And the bankroll should be large enough that he can withstand at least a couple of bad weeks without panicking.

With this capital, a horseplayer must learn to bet sensibly and — when circumstances dictate it — to bet boldly. He does not need to follow the betting strategy I suggested in this book; it may be unsuitable for many people. But he must formulate some kind of money-management plan and a broad betting philosophy. He should keep an accurate record of all his wagers so he can monitor and review his own performance.

He must also develop the capacity, in the face of tremendous stress, to maintain his emotional balance and especially to prevent bad luck from affecting his judgment. This does not come naturally for anyone, but a gambler must realize that his emotions are his own worst enemy and that they can undermine all his handicapping and betting skills.

If a horseplayer does finally learn to beat the races, achieving a goal that has thwarted millions of people as well as every computer ever built, he has to maintain a measure of humility. For if the racing game seems fiendishly designed to exploit any flaw in a player's makeup, the offense that the game punishes most ruthlessly and relentlessly is the sin of hubris. Pete Axthelm is fond of relating the story of a newcomer to the track who cheered wildly as he won a daily double at Aqueduct and exclaimed, "How long has this been going on? What an easy game!" Harvey Pack happened to be observing this spectacle and called after the newcomer, as he raced to the cashier's window, "Have a good life, kid." From that day on, the kid was known as Good Life, and he was last seen in the remote corners of the Aqueduct grandstand, trying to scrounge the price of a bet, before he disappeared from the track altogether.

"The youth," Axthelm wrote in *Inside Sports,* "had angered the Goddess of Wagering. The Goddess must be appeased, soothed, tithed. She must never be affronted by statements hinting that a gambler has taken fate into his own firm grip. The premature gloater always gets punished. The purveyor of certainty suddenly finds that his rent is in doubt. And the bettor who claims to have everything under control is plunged into chaos."

It may not be the Goddess of Wagering who is responsible, but the very nature of the racing game does punish arrogance and over-confidence. If the most astute of handicappers becomes complacent for a long enough time, he will wake up one day to find that his once-successful methods don't work anymore. So even after a horse-player has struggled for years and finally learned how to beat the races, he had better not pause too long to rest on his laurels. The game will keep slowly changing, and the winning player must keep on observing, adapting his methods, and changing with it.

The Basics

THERE MAY HAVE BEEN an era when a handicapper could beat the races simply by knowing how to read, analyze, and interpret the past performances in the *Daily Racing Form*. If so, those days are gone. Because of the cruel mathematics of the parimutuel system, nobody can hope to beat the game by knowing what everybody else knows. That is the reason more arcane techniques — such as speed handicapping and trip handicapping — have flourished. But before a neophyte can use these sophisticated methods, he must first master the basics of handicapping. They still often hold the key to the outcome of races while more advanced methods prove irrelevant.

Beginners may be slightly intimidated by the fact that there is so much to learn in the game, but they may consider themselves fortunate in one respect. The *Daily Racing Form* gives the modern American racing fan access to more accurate and extensive data than horseplayers in any other time or place have ever had. Its past performances are models of concision:

El Bombay — B. c. 4, by Bombay Duck—Maria L, by Mystic II
Own.—Luca S — Br.—Luca S (Fla) — Tr.—Luca Santo

110^{7}

Lifetime	1982	12 2 0 1	$22,800
24 3 0 1	1981	10 0 0 0	$330
$33,330	Turf	5 0 0 1	$2,400

15Aug82- 9Sar	fst	6f	:21⅕	:44⅕	1:09⅖	3↑Alw 19000	1	3	3^{3}	$8^{7\frac{1}{2}}$	8^{10}	$8^{7\frac{1}{2}}$	Cordero A Jr	117	4.70	85-11	PuritanChief117¾EasternPrince112$^{1\frac{1}{2}}$GuilfordRod112^{no} Brief foot	12
5Aug82- 2Sar	fst	6f	:22⅖	:45⅗	1:10⅕	3↑Clm 45000	3	1	1^{1}	1^{2}	1^{2}	$1^{1\frac{3}{4}}$	Cordero A Jr	113	8.70	89-16	El Bombay 113$^{1\frac{3}{4}}$ Puritan Chief 117$^{1\frac{3}{4}}$ CourtWise119$^{4\frac{1}{2}}$ Drew clear	8
18Jly82- 9Bel	fm	1	Ⓣ:46⅕	1:10⅖	1:35⅗	3↑Alw 20000	1	12	12^{19}	11^{12}	11^{10}	$10^{8\frac{3}{4}}$	Maple E	117	27.60	79-19	Who's For Dinner 112½ Beagle 107$^{1\frac{3}{4}}$ James Boswell 117¾ Outrun	12
9Jly82- 3Bel	fm	7f	Ⓣ:23⅖	:46	1:22	Clm 45000	7	2	$5^{4\frac{1}{2}}$	$7^{8\frac{1}{2}}$	6^{12}	6^{13}	Alvarado R Jr^{10}	107	15.70	81-13	In Deep Water 119^{4} Tony Mack 117^{nk} Royal Jove117$^{2\frac{3}{4}}$ No factor	8
4Jly82- 9Bel	fm	1	Ⓣ:46⅘	1:11⅖	1:36⅗	3↑Alw 20000	8	3	3^{1}	$4^{1\frac{1}{2}}$	10^{13}	10^{13}	Alvarado R Jr^{10}	107	34.10	69-17	Roulette Wheel 112no Who's For Dinner 112^{1} Gengii 117^{nk} Tired	12
29Jun82- 5Bel	fst	6f	:22⅖	:45⅕	1:09⅘	3↑Alw 19000	1	3	$7^{6\frac{3}{4}}$	$7^{7\frac{1}{2}}$	5^{8}	5^{7}	Alvarado R Jr^{10}	107	19.80	86-10	Shifty Sheik 113^{hd} Citius 113$^{4\frac{1}{2}}$ King Naskra 109¾ Outrun	11
12Jun82- 6Bel	fst	6f	:22⅘	:45⅗	1:10⅕	3↑Alw 19000	5	3	5^{4}	7^{9}	7^{12}	7^{15}	Bailey J D	b 117	12.90	76-14	Muskoka Wyck 114^{nk} Roughcast 117$^{1\frac{3}{4}}$ Tory Willow 111$^{4\frac{3}{4}}$ Outrun	7
5Jun82- 2Bel	gd	7f	:22⅘	:45⅖	1:23	3↑Alw 19000	8	1	1^{hd}	2^{hd}	1^{hd}	$5^{2\frac{3}{4}}$	Bailey J D	117	16.00	85-11	Faces Up 113½ Straight Main 110^{hd} Hardy Hawk 110^{nc} Weakened	10
28May82- 5Bel	fm	1	Ⓣ:47⅖	1:12	1:37⅖	3↑Alw 20000	9	1	2½	2½	$6^{3\frac{3}{4}}$	$9^{9\frac{1}{2}}$	Maple E	119	13.80	68-18	Groomed 108^{nk} Hunter Hawk 113^{2} Honed Edge 108$^{1\frac{1}{2}}$ Tired	11
8May82- 1Aqu	fm	1	Ⓣ:47⅖	1:12⅖	1:38⅕	Alw 20000	6	2	$1^{1\frac{1}{2}}$	$1^{1\frac{1}{2}}$	1^{hd}	3^{3}	Santagata J^{10}	109	9.70	84-13	Key Irish 117^{nk} Hivoltage 117$^{2\frac{3}{4}}$ El Bombay 109^{2} Bore out trn	7

LATEST WORKOUTS ●Jly 31 Aqu 5f fst :59⅘ hg ●Jun 24 Aqu 4f fst :47⅖ h

Each horizontal line in El Bombay's past performances summarizes one of his previous races. In little more than an inch of space, the *Form* gives an astonishing amount of information about his life history. A handicapper must learn the meaning and the significance of all of its symbols.

COLOR, AGE, AND SEX

B. c. 4

The first pieces of information in the past performances disclose that El Bombay is a bay colt, four years of age.

The colors of a thoroughbred are bay (b.), brown (br.), black (blk.), chestnut (ch.), gray (gr.), and roan (ro.).

A male thoroughbred is a colt (c.) until he reaches the age of five and becomes a horse (h.). A female is a filly (f.) until she turns five and becomes a mare (m.). A gelding (g.) is a castrated male.

Some horseplayers are reluctant to bet 3-year-olds against their elders, and many more refuse to bet fillies against colts, but these are prejudices rather than sound handicapping guidelines. A bettor has to deal with the relative merits of individual horses instead of relying on such generalizations.

There is, however, one generalization about the relative development of male and female thoroughbreds that seems to have some validity. "When horses are 2-year-olds," trainer Angel Penna says, "they are like young children, and as children girls are often able to beat boys in foot races. But by late summer, the colts have passed the fillies, and they remain stronger until the next fall when the fillies catch up." This theory is supported by an abundance of empirical evidence. The Kentucky Derby is run at a time of year when females are supposedly behind the males in development, and only once in its first 100 runnings did a filly win. But the world's most prestigious race, the Prix de l'Arc de Triomphe, is contested in October, and females won seven of its eleven runnings from 1972 to 1982, demolishing the myth that a good filly can't beat a good colt.

BREEDING

by Bombay Duck—Maria L, by Mystic II

El Bombay's sire was Bombay Duck. His dam was Maria L., who was a daughter of the stallion Mystic II.

After a horse has compiled a racing record, his pedigree is not an important factor in handicapping. Whether El Bombay is a son of Bombay Duck or the great Northern Dancer would not alter the fact that he is a sprinter worth about $50,000. Bloodlines may be relevant when a horse's capabilities are not fully known: when he is starting his career or attempting to go a distance for the first time. But there is one situation in which pedigree is all-important: when a horse is running on the grass for the first time. As more tracks started to offer great numbers of turf races, astute handicappers perceived that certain breeds had a special affinity for the grass. The first bettors to discover this phenomenon were able to collect astonishing prices when offspring of Price John or Stage Door Johnny had run dismally on the dirt and were making their turf debuts. William Quirin analyzed the performance of turf sires for *Winning at the Races: Computer Discoveries in Thoroughbred Handicapping* and found in his sample that the progeny of Stage Door Johnny won more than 40 percent of their starts on the grass.

CONSISTENCY

Lifetime		1982	12	2	0	1	$22,800
24	3 0 1	1981	10	0	0	0	$330
$33,330		Turf	5	0	0	1	$2,400

The upper-right-hand corner of his past performances summarizes El Bombay's lifetime record. In his career he has three victories, no

seconds, and one third in 24 starts, with earnings of $33,330. He is
2-for-12 in 1982; he was 0-for-10 in 1981. If he had been a maiden
— a horse who had never won a race — the letter "M" would appear in the place where the number of victories is shown.

Handicappers learn to be wary of "sucker horses," animals with
a preponderance of second- and third-place finishes that suggest they
lack the will to win. But to reject a horse automatically because he
has a record of 0–3–4 in 14 starts can be a mistake, too. He might
have been doing his best against opposition too tough for him. Only
after one of these perennial bridesmaids has failed in a race that he
clearly should have won will I proclaim him a sucker horse. Then I
will shun him until he changes his ways.

TRAINER

Tr.—Luca Santo

The trainer — his identity, competence, honesty, and *modus oper-
andi* — is one of the crucial factors in handicapping. I devoted a
lengthy chapter in *Picking Winners* to the importance of trainers
and have had no reason to change my views on the subject.

Some computer whizzes have undertaken statistical analyses of
trainers, and they can reveal that one man may win 8.3 percent of
the time in sprint races, 17.2 percent in routes, and 14.9 percent on
the grass. I analyze trainers in a somewhat cruder fashion, on a
stack of index cards. Whenever a trainer does something interesting,
when he wins a race in a way that reflects his skill, I make a note of
it. I am interested if a trainer wins with a first-time starter. With a
horse who has been laid off. With a horse he has recently claimed.
With a significant jockey switch. With a sharp drop in class. With a
horse going a distance for the first time. With a horse who received
unusual betting action. Before going to Santa Anita for the 1983
season, I spent a year compiling trainer data. Part of my index card
for trainer Richard Mandella looked like this:

12–27	Raja's Song	$48.40	8th at TuP 6 wks. ago. OK prior form.
1–16	Maple Tree	$17.60	From N.Y., off 6 wks. Turf to dirt.
1–23	Grass Tumbler	$28.20	First-time starter. Best work 1:13 4/5.

1–29	Tabled Passion	$4.60	First-time starter. 1:11 4/5.
1–31	Sweet Mystery	$5.20	First-time starter. 1:12.
2–11	Regal Falcon	$8.00	First-time starter. 1:26.
2–17	Ah Nah Heed	$7.20	Claimed for $20,000, good dope, up to $25,000.

And so on. Mandella had won with seven first-time starters in the first six months of the year, and so I thought I knew one source of possible betting opportunities that I would find at Santa Anita.

DATE AND TRACK

15Aug82- 9Sar

El Bombay last ran on August 15, 1982, in the ninth race at Saratoga.

Once the recency of a horse's last race was considered a crucial handicapping factor. If he was coming back in a week or less, that was a reliable sign that he was sharp and his trainer meant business. But now that the sport is conducted year-round in most states, horses are so regularly overraced that the back-in-seven-days angle has become virtually meaningless. William Quirin found in a study of more than 2000 races that horses coming back after about a week win 13 percent of the time, while those who have been laid off two or three weeks win 11.5 percent of the time — hardly an earth-shaking difference. Even if a horse has been idle longer than that, a handicapper should not fear to bet him, assuming that he has a competent trainer and that there are no negative signs in his past performances (such as a sharp drop in claiming price) to indicate that this absence was due to a serious physical problem.

TRACK CONDITION

fst

The track was fast for El Bombay's last race. The designations fast (fst), good (gd), sloppy (sly), muddy (my), slow (sl), and heavy (hy) describe tracks with increasing amounts of moisture in them. A frozen track is abbreviated "fr." Turf courses are described as hard (hd), firm (fm), good (gd), soft (sf), and yielding (yl).

It is a well-known phenomenon that some thoroughbreds like running in the mud and others don't. The late handicapper Mannie Kalish believed that this preference was due to the animals' conformation, and on every rainy day he went to the paddock to inspect the shape of the horses' feet, as well as the type of shoes they were wearing. He was a master at betting on off tracks.

Modern-day handicappers don't distinguish so much between mudders and nonmudders. Instead they talk about "wet-track horses." There are many times when a racing surface will be wet, but will still be hard and designated as "fast" in the *Racing Form*. Some horses tend to improve sharply under these conditions, just as they do in mud, and astute handicappers know who they are.

DISTANCE

6f

The abbreviation "6f" indicates that El Bombay's last race was run at six furlongs — a furlong being one eighth of a mile. Route races are shown in terms of miles: "$1\frac{1}{16}$" means a mile and one sixteenth.

Before betting any horse, a handicapper should be sure that the distance of the race is long enough for him. There are few circumstances in which I would bet a slow-starting plodder who has been running in route races and is now entered at six or seven furlongs. The speed-favoring nature of the American racing game makes such horses very unreliable betting propositions.

But when a horse with doubtful stamina is entered at a distance that appears to be too long for him, the issue is much more confusing. A horse's distance-running capabilities are determined by many factors. He may be able to go a long distance if the opposition is weak enough; Bold Forbes wasn't a $1\frac{1}{2}$-mile horse but he was able to stagger to the finish line in front of a weak field in the Belmont Stakes. A horse who can take an uncontested early lead, as Bold Forbes did that day, will be able to go farther than he can under other circumstances. And if a horse is in extremely sharp current form, he may be able to accomplish what would otherwise be impossible for him. Conquistador Cielo was not a $1\frac{1}{2}$-mile horse either, but in the Belmont Stakes, coming off a record-shattering mile race five days earlier, he was able to handle the distance.

FRACTIONS

:21⅕ :44⅕ 1:09⅖

The first quarter of El Bombay's last race was run in 21⅕ seconds, the half mile in :44⅕. The final time for the six-furlong race was 1:09⅖. These are the times for the leader at each stage of the race, not for El Bombay. In most route races, the fractions shown are those for a half mile, three quarters of a mile, and the finish.

CLASS

3 ↑ Alw 19000

El Bombay's most recent race was an allowance event for 3-year-olds and up, offering a total purse of $19,000. The many class designations for thoroughbred races pose one of the greatest sources of confusion for newcomers to the sport.

The most common type of race in America is the claiming race, in which every horse is entered for sale at a specified price. The class of El Bombay's next-to-last start was listed as "Clm 45000," which means that before that race any owner or trainer at the track could have deposited a slip in the "claim box" in the racing secretary's office and bought the colt for $45,000. The purse money for the race would still go to the old owner, but after the race the animal would be led to a new barn. (Had El Bombay been claimed, the past performances would have read "Clm c-45,000.") The claiming system is a highly effective way to insure that the competition in races is fairly equal. A trainer could surely win a $45,000 race by entering a $100,000 horse in it, but he would not do so for fear of losing the horse.

The other broad type of races are allowances, a catchall category in which the eligibility of horses is determined by certain conditions — for example, "3-year-olds and up which have never won three races." These conditions are not printed in the past performances, but the size of the purse gives a rough indication of the relative quality of allowance races.

Maiden-special-weight races are events for horses who have never won. A claiming race for maidens would be indicated "Md 45000." Stakes are the highest class of race and are shown by their names: "Ky Derby," for example. A handicap (Hcp) is a race in which weights are assigned to give every horse a theoretical equal chance.

The letter Ⓕ denotes a race limited to fillies and mares. The symbol 3↑ means the race was open to horses three or more years old.

In bygone days, most handicappers evaluated horses on the basis of class. (The word is actually somewhat misleading. Class isn't some inherent quality, as in "He's a classy guy." A handicapper would attempt to evaluate horses by *classifying* them, by analyzing the strength of different categories of horses and judging who could beat whom.) The approach seems a bit old-fashioned now, though there is one good recent book that espouses class handicapping, James Quinn's *The Handicapper's Condition Book*.

Class handicapping has become somewhat passé because it is a clumsy way of doing what speed handicappers do with precision: measure the ability that horses have shown in their previous races. But there is still one common situation in which every handicapper must deal with class; it arises whenever a horse is making a sharp drop in claiming price.

A trainer will lower a claiming horse in class for one of two reasons. He may be trying to maneuver the animal into a winning spot. Or else the horse may have such dire physical problems that the trainer is trying to lure somebody else into claiming him. For a handicapper, making the distinction is as crucial as it is difficult. As a general rule, the better a horse's form looks, the more negatively a drop in class should be construed. If a horse has lost by a nose for $40,000 and is entered for $25,000, something is probably wrong. If he has lost by 10 lengths for $40,000 and is dropping to $25,000, he may be in just the right spot. If he has lost by four lengths for $40,000 and is now entered for $25,000, however, the move could easily be interpreted as either positive or negative — and only the trainer will know for sure.

POST POSITION AND RUNNING LINE

$$1 \quad 3 \quad 3^3 \quad 8^{7\frac{1}{2}} \quad 8^{10} \quad 8^{7\frac{1}{2}}$$

The first number in this central part of the past performances indicates the horse's post position. El Bombay broke from post No. 1. The rest of the line shows his position at various stages of the race. At the break he was third. After a quarter mile he was third, 3 lengths behind the leader. After a half mile he was eighth, 7½ lengths behind. Turning into the stretch he was eighth, 10 lengths behind. He finished eighth, losing by 7½ lengths.

The post position, stretch call, and finish all appear in the same place in the past performances. But in races from 1 mile to 1⅛ miles, the first call shows his position after a quarter mile instead of at the break. The next two calls show his position after a half mile and three quarters of a mile.

This is obviously very important information, but many horseplayers try to analyze it the way seers look at tea leaves, trying to ferret out mystical clues. In *Picking Winners* I told readers to look for a type of running line I called the Z Pattern, which showed a horse dropping back until the stretch call and then coming on at the finish. (For example: $3^2 \ 4^5 \ 6^8 \ 4^6$.) But such handicapping methods are misguided. The numbers in the running line are only symbols of what happened during the course of a race. Trip handicappers are winners because they analyze what really happened.

JOCKEY

Cordero A Jr

The jockey should never be the crucial factor in the decision to bet a horse — even if he happens to be Angel Cordero Jr., the most accomplished member of his profession in America. The jockey, however, may be a major factor in a decision *not* to bet. A handicapper has to deal with enough risks and uncertainties in the game without inviting more by wagering on riders who are prone to make costly mistakes. Ideally I prefer to bet on a horse ridden by a solid, competent jockey who doesn't attract money from the crowd (e.g., Mike Venezia) rather than one whose reputation is going to hurt the horse's price (e.g., Bill Shoemaker).

WEIGHT

117

El Bombay carried 117 pounds in his previous start. The figure in larger type that appears next to his lifetime record — 110^7 — is his weight assignment for today's race. The exponential seven means that he has an apprentice jockey entitled to a seven-pound weight allowance.

How important is weight? Here is a theoretical situation: Horse A defeats Horse B by a nose, with both of them carrying 114 pounds. Now, a week later they are meeting again, with Horse A scheduled to tote 122 pounds and B to carry 114 again. What does a handicapper do here?

I would bet Horse A and expect to make money in such circumstances over the long run, because the public will overbet B on the basis of the weight shift. Old-time horseplayers and trainers of all eras swear by its importance, but weight is the most overrated of all handicapping factors. The only time I pay more than scant attention to it is in handicap races, where high-class horses are required to carry imposts in the 123-to-130 range. Then a pound or two can be important, but even then weight is less important than speed, condition, stamina, and the other factors that determine the outcome of races.

ODDS

4.70

El Bombay went off at 4.70 to 1 in his last start. An asterisk by this figure would indicate that he had been the favorite. The letter "e" would mean he had been part of a stable entry.

SPEED RATING AND TRACK VARIANT

85-11

The *Daily Racing Form* attempts to aid its readers by computing its own speed ratings and track variants. El Bombay earned a rating of 85 on a track with a variant of 11. Many horseplayers add these numbers together and use the sum as the basis for comparing the prior performances of different horses. But there are so many inaccuracies built into the way the *Form* computes these figures that they are barely better than nothing. Of course I am prejudiced. As the proponent of what I would unabashedly argue is the best speed-handicapping method ever devised, I look on the *Form*'s figures the way Picasso might have viewed paint-by-the-numbers kits.

COMPANY LINE

PuritanChief117¾EasternPrince112¹½GuilfordRod112ⁿᵒ

Puritan Chief was the winner of El Bombay's last race. He carried 117 pounds and finished three quarters of a length in front of Eastern Prince, who in turn was 1½ lengths in front of third-place Guilford Road.

COMMENT AND SIZE OF FIELD

Brief foot 12

There were 12 horses in El Bombay's last race. The *Racing Form*'s comment of "Brief foot" is not particularly edifying, but sometimes the comment will say "Blocked" or "Checked" or give some other indication of serious trouble that occurred during the course of a race. The most valuable comments of all are the ones that say "No factor," when a good trip handicapper has spotted trouble that the *Racing Form*'s chart-caller has overlooked.

WORKOUTS

LATEST WORKOUTS   ● Jly 31 Aqu   5f fst   :59⅘ hg

El Bombay had his most recent workout on July 31 over a fast track at Aqueduct, going five furlongs in 59⅘ seconds. The boldface bullet indicates that this was the best workout for the distance at the track that day. He did it handily ("h"), under moderate urging by his exercise rider, and "g" would signify that he broke from the gate instead of from a running start. The symbol "b" would mean breezing, indicating that he was under somewhat more restraint. The symbol "(d)" would mean that the "dogs" were up — barriers placed on the track to keep horses away from the rail, forcing them to cover more distance on the turns.

All of this would be very valuable information, if only a handicapper could believe it. Unfortunately, members of the clocking profession have a reputation for honesty that ranks slightly below that of used-car salesmen, and the reputation is generally deserved. Clockers everywhere are underpaid, giving them ample incentive to keep the most important workout information for themselves and their clients. No state but California has any kind of system to insure that workouts are reported accurately. So chicanery is part of the business. When a new recruit went to work as a clocker at Hialeah, he spent a few days going through on-the-job training, learning how to wield a stopwatch and identify horses. After he had received this basic education, a cynical veteran of the profession told him, "It's time that you learn clockers' arithmetic now."

"What's that?" the kid wanted to know.

"It means that 46 and 4 equals 50," the veteran said, and everybody within earshot laughed, knowing he meant that if a promising young horse worked in :46⅘ it would appear in the *Racing Form* as 50 seconds flat. Under the circumstances, it is best not to base many serious handicapping decisions on published workout information.

READING CHARTS

NINTH RACE	6 FURLONGS. (1.08) ALLOWANCE. Purse $19,000. 3–year–olds and upward which have never won a race other than Maiden, Claiming or Starter. Weight, 3–year–olds, 117 lbs.
Saratoga	Older, 122 lbs. Non–winners of a race other than claiming since August 1 allowed, 3 lbs.
AUGUST 15, 1982	Of such a race since July 15, 5 lbs.

Value of race $19,000, value to winner $11,400, second $4,180, third $2,280, fourth $1,140. Mutuel pool $1,455,637, OTB pool $158,019. Triple Pool $256,556. OTB Triple Pool $347,966.

Last Raced	Horse	Eqt.A.Wt PP St	¼	½	Str	Fin	Jockey	Odds $1
5Aug82 2Sar2	Puritan Chief	4 117 10 4	71	51½	4½	1¾	MacBeth D	9.80
3Jly82 8Del5	Eastern Prince	b 3 112 9 1	11½	1½	2½	21½	Rogers K L	3.00
2May82 2Aqu6	Guilford Road	b 3 112 6 8	104	7½	65	3no	Velasquez J	13.40
20Jun82 9Bel6	Fast Reason	b 3 113 5 5	41½	33	51	4½	Maple E	8.70
16Jan82 10Hia1	Shining So Bright	3 113 11 2	21½	2hd	11	5hd	Vasquez J	9.20
7Aug82 2Sar3	King Naskra	3 105 4 7	6½	41	3½	63¾	Alvarado R Jr7	3.60
17Jly82 9Bel4	Pams McAllister	b 3 112 8 9	9½	61	71½	71	Hernandez R	15.60
5Aug82 2Sar1	El Bombay	4 117 1 3	3hd	86	86	85	Cordero A Jr	4.70
5Jun82 2Bel10	What A Charger	3 112 3 11	112	12	91½	91½	Venezia M	42.60
8Aug82 10Del10	Brother George	b 3 112 12 10	12	11hd	105	105½	Martinez L A	48.50
30Jly82 9Mth6	The Primate	3 112 7 6	8½	101	114	114¾	Graell A	17.10
6Aug82 8Suf1	Chief's Pride	3 117 2 12	5hd	9½	12	12	Lapensee M	42.20

OFF AT 6:14. Start good, Won driving. Time, :21⅕, :44⅕, 1:09⅖ Track fast.

$2 Mutuel Prices:	10–(J)–PURITAN CHIEF	21.60	9.80	6.20
	9–(I)–EASTERN PRINCE		5.40	4.40
	6–(F)–GUILFORD ROAD			10.00

$2 TRIPLE 10–9–6 PAID $1,560.00.

B. c, by Mr Prospector—Missy T, by Lt Stevens. Trainer Trovato Joseph A. Bred by McMakin N (Ky).

PURITAN CHIEF rallied leaving the turn, worked his way between horses leaving the furlong grounds and outfinished EASTERN PRINCE. The latter showed speed in to the stretch while racing well out in the track and continued on with good courage. GUILFORD ROAD finished with good energy between horses. FAST REASON made a run from the outside leaving the turn but lacked the needed late response. SHINING SO BRIGHT moved through along the inside to take over entering the stretch and leaned over on KING NASKRA while weakening inside the final furlong. KING NASKRA loomed a treat long the inside near midstretch but was caught in close quarters during the late stages. PAMS MCALISTER rallied leaving the turn but lacked a further response. EL BOMBAY was finished early. CHIEF'S PRIDE broke slowly.

Owners— 1, Schwartz B K; 2, Sheikh S M; 3, Phillips J W; 4, Saron Stable; 5, Calumet Farm; 6, Meadowhill; 7, Reynolds D P; 8, Luca S; 9, Anchel E; 10, Davis Betty; 11, Black Sash Stable; 12, Centennial N.

Trainers— 1, Trovato Joseph A; 2, Veitch Sylvester E; 3, Rondinello Thomas L; 4, Drysdale Neil; 5, Veitch John M; 6, Johnson Philip G; 7, Kelly Thomas J; 8, Luca Santo; 9, LaBoccetta Frank; 10, Retamoza Richard C; 11, Pagano Frank X Jr; 12, Vivian David A.

Overweight: Fast Reason 1 pound; Shining So Bright 1.

Scratched—Tarantara (7Aug82 2Sar2); North Coast (5Mar82 9Aqu8); Dave The Dude (17Jly82 9Bel6); Roughcast (17Jly82 9Bel2); Cintula (21Jun82 6Bel1).

$2 Late DD 11–10 Paid $545.00. Late DD Pool $258,512. Late OTB DD Pool $313,113. Attendance 32,464. Total Mutuel Pool $3,424,643. Total OTB Pool $3,573,243.

All the information in the *Daily Racing Form* past performances is derived from the result charts, but the format of the charts is different in one important respect. The running line shows how far a horse was in front of the horse immediately behind him, instead of his distance behind the leader. For El Bombay, the quarter-mile call says 3hd, meaning that he was a head in front of the fourth-place horse. In this chart it can be seen that the leader was 1½ lengths ahead of the second horse, who was another 1½ lengths ahead of the third horse, El Bombay. From this data comes the figure in the past performances — 3^3 — that shows El Bombay was three lengths behind the leader after a quarter mile.

Serious handicappers should clip and maintain a set of charts because they include some important information that the past performances don't. The footnotes on the race are more thorough than the one- or two-word summaries in the past performances. And the charts also give the full conditions of a race, which the past performances don't. In this case, the race in which El Bombay ran was limited to "3-year-olds and upward which have never won a race other than maiden or claiming."

A Notation System
for Trip Handicapping

WHEN A TRIP HANDICAPPER watches a race, he will attempt to observe and note everything of importance that the *Daily Racing Form*'s past performances may not tell him. To do this properly, he must have a good shorthand system. If it is logical and comprehensive, it will help him focus his attention on the most important aspects of a race. It must be concise, because after watching a race a horseplayer will be scribbling frantically to record all the things he has seen before the observations fade from his memory. Most trip handicappers' programs appear virtually indecipherable after a day's races. A typical page of my program — from the fifth race at Hialeah on January 12, 1982 — looked like this:

EXACTA WAGERING ON THIS RACE

	WIN	PLACE	SHOW

1⅛ MILES

CLAIMING PURSE $11,000

FIFTH RACE

FOR FILLIES AND MARES, FOUR YEARS OLD AND UPWARD. 122 lbs. Non-winners of two races at a mile or over since December 12 allowed 2 lbs.; one such race 4 lbs.; a race at any distance since then 6 lbs. Claiming price $25,000; for each $2,500 to $20,000 2 lbs. (Races where entered for $18,000 or less not considered.)

Track Record—HIS MAJESTY (5) 119 lbs. 1:46⅖; January 17, 1973

MAKE SELECTION BY NUMBER

OWNER	TRAINER	Jockey/Morn. Line

1
CAROLINA STABLE — Orange, White Sash — J. SANCHEZ
Rool B GP back and 2nd (handwritten)
GLORY ALLELUIA Ⓕ 116
Gr.f.(1978), On to Glory—Classic Queen
EDDIE ROJAS — 10 — $25,000

2
S. MILLER — Green, Black Bell and Braces, Cerise and Black, Halved Sleeves, Black Cap — J. LENZINI, JR.
Stckt(2s) 4e (handwritten)
DONZAR 116
Ch.m.(1977), Don Poggio—Czardash
JEFFREY FELL — 5 — $25,000

3
J. CARDALLA — Flamingo, Black "HIALEAH" Flamingo Cap — J. M. HARDY
Rul T, smoke, Sp s (handwritten)
SPECIAL APPEAL 116
Ch.f.(1978), Irish Stronghold—Trolly Dolly
EARLIE FIRES — 15 — $25,000

4
PEACEFULRIDGE FARM — Fluorescent Orange, Green Dots, Green Bars on Sleeves, Orange Cap — E. J. YOWELL
Rail hard dvd (handwritten)
ARKANSAS BEV. *113
B.f.(1978), Admiral's Shield—Happy Weaver
JOSE A. VELEZ, JR. — 3 — $25,000

5
J. POPKIN — Blue, Blue "P" in White Circle, Red and White Diamonds on Sleeves, Blue Cap — H. MAZIARZ
WALLAWAY RED Ⓕ 116
Dk.b. or br.f.(1978), Irish Ruler—Hunts Princess
GONZALO PROSPER — 10 — $25,000

6
BEVERLY R. STEINMAN — Green, Pink Sash, Pink Band on Sleeves, Green Cap — D. BUTLER
3t (handwritten)
GREEK ICE Ⓕ 116
Gr.f.(1978), Icecapade—Greek Marine
CARLOS MARQUEZ — 4 — $25,000

7
H. SADKIN & KARON & M. ZACCO — Yellow, Green "Z" and Shamrocks, Yellow Cap — M. ZACCO
REBECCA'S OCEAN Ⓕ 112
Dk.b or br.m.(1974), Ocean Bar—French Smoke
SMITH, JR. ALFREDO — 15 — $20,000

8
GRAJER STABLE — Gold Cap — D. F. IMPRESCIA
LB hardvel easy (handwritten)
Wiggles Not Holme 112
Dk.b. or br.f.(1978), Sir Wiggle—Holme At Once
ROGER DANJEAN — 8 — $20,000

9
P. VanANDEL — Green Cap — R. S. DuBOIS
27 mov mtlead ease (handwritten)
KISSIN' JUDGE 114
Dk.b. or br.f.(1978), Judger—Aerialette
GENE ST. LEON — 10 — $22,500

10
R. A. HALE — Light Blue, Yellow and White Stripes, White Cap — OWNER
MISSI CHOOSY 116
B.f.(1977), Triumphant—Cafe Hostess
BRIAN SWATUK — 8 — $25,000

11
V. C. D. STABLE — Green, White "VCD" and Horseshoe, White Sleeves, White Cap — O. REYES
4 FC 38 (handwritten)
IN ORBIT 112
Dk.b. or br.f.(1978), Yumbel—Hurry Star
FRANK PENNISI — 30 — $20,000

The notation for Glory Alleluia is "Rail B GP behind duel." The scrawl by Donzat's name says, "Steady T (2-3L) 4E." The note for Wiggles Not Holme, "2B hard duel eased," enabled me to cash a $46.40 payoff the next time she ran. No one can hope to make all these observations off the cuff. A handicapper must have a pre-established system for note-taking.

STAGES OF THE RACE

G	The gate; anything that happens at the start of a race.
FT	First turn.
B	Backstretch.
T	Turn.
E	Entering the stretch.
S	Stretch.

THE PACE

Duel	A horse is fighting for the lead.
Stalk	A horse is sitting behind a duel for the lead.
Move	A horse accelerates strongly, in a way that almost makes his rivals look as if they are standing still.
MIHP	Move into hot pace. A horse makes a strong move, but does it at a time when the leaders are accelerating, too.
Inherit	A horse gets the lead by taking over from rivals who have collapsed.

TYPES OF TROUBLE

Slo	A horse breaks from the gate behind the field.
Rush	A horse rushes into contention suddenly after breaking slowly.
Steady	Mild trouble, caused by a lack of running room.
Check	Serious trouble that forces a jockey to stop his horse's momentum.
Alter	A horse is forced to alter his course sharply.
NP	No push; the jockey is not asking his horse to run at some stage of a race.

Stiff	The jockey has not asked his horse to run at any stage of a race.
V	A horse is in heavy track without encountering actual interference. (For "vise.")
GP	The opposite of "V": A horse is in the clear with no rivals inside or outside him.

POSITIONS ON THE TRACK

"Rail" denotes a horse on the innermost part of the track. Each successive horse width from the rail is described as the 2-path, the 3-path, and so on. A notation of "3T" would indicate the 3-path on the turn.

TRACK BIASES

GR	Good rail.
GR+	Very strong good rail.
BR	Bad rail.
BR+	Very strong bad rail.
S	Speed-favoring track.
S+	Very strong speed-favoring track.
C	Track that favors closers.